Steve Hogarth

The *Invisible* Man

diaries 1991–1997

Steve Hogarth: The Invisible Man **- Diaries 1991-1997**

This edition first published June 2014 by Miwk Publishing Ltd.
Miwk Publishing, 12 Marbles Way, Tadworth, Surrey KT20 5LW.

ISBN 978-1-908630-99-5

A CIP catalogue record for this book is available from the British Library.

Cover and book design by Robert Hammond.
Front cover photography courtesy of Benoît Mahé.

Typeset in Utopia and Bembo.

Printed in Great Britain by TJ International, Padstow, Cornwall.

www.miwkpublishing.com
This product was lovingly Miwk made.

contents

introduction

Back in 1992 I went back to Doncaster to visit my mum and dad.

"What have you been up to then, Son?" my dad said

"I've been on top of a mountain on a glacier in Iceland, Dad. I was dropped from a helicopter…"

My dad thought for a minute before replying. "Would you make me a promise?"

"Sure." I said

"Would you begin to keep a diary? What's happening in your life doesn't normally happen to people."

And so I did.

This isn't a "sex, drugs and rock 'n'roll tabloid 'rockstar tells all'" book – this diary is about what it's like to be a 'famous' (whatever that is) touring musician travelling the world. It's also about how it is to go home, do the garden and plumb in the dishwasher before popping into London to rub shoulders with Princess Stephanie of Monaco. It's about having a bath with the kids, and having lunch with Neil Armstrong (although he's actually in volume 2…)

I didn't write the diary every day. Sometimes I was too busy, too bored or in no frame of mind to write anything. Some years are almost ignored, or totally absent – probably because I was holed up on a farm or in a castle writing an album, and didn't have the brain-space to think about anything else. Some days are detailed moment-by-moment chronicles, while others are sketchy. Some start with detail and then remain unfinished, probably because I was called away on some errand or other – a gig or having to get in a car and drive somewhere else. Or sleeping.

Some days, of course, weren't worth remembering, and some are best forgotten.

This diary is simply whatever I managed to write on certain days. It also occasionally reminisces.

I apologise if I repeat myself in these pages. Often I'm recalling the same things from the vantage-point of entirely different years, so it's only natural that a town or a gig will remind me of the same things each time I'm there. Also, there's a tendency for me to switch from the past tense to the present tense from one sentence to another. This is often because I am arriving in the present as I write.

I am in the habit of giving nicknames to the people I love, as well as using their real names, so I must point out that the following people may be referred to by more than one name, as listed below (in approximate order of appearance):

Sue – Dizzy Spell, Dizzy, Diz
Sofi – Fi Fi, Hargreaves
Nial – Nially, Crompton
I also went through a phase of calling my family "the team" for some reason. Lord knows why, but it's who I was.

Mark (Kelly) – Mad Jack, Jack
Pete (Trewavas) – Trousers
Steve (Rothery) – Rothers
Ian (Mosley) – Mosley, The Cat, The Count

Over and above these are the many names of management and crew who vary from tour to tour, but the principal players will be:

John (Arnison) - John A: Manager until 1999
Ann (Lawler): John's Assistant
Chris (Hedge) – Priv, Privet: Sound Engineer
Paul (Lewis): Tour Manager
Smick (Hardgrave): Production Manager
Tim (Bricusse): Tour Manager
Paul and Trish (Devine): Lighting Designer and Wardrobe respectively
Alan (Parker): Lighting Designer
Nick (Belshaw): Tour Manager

acknowledgements

I would like to thank the following:

Arthur Anderson for introducing me to the unwholesome pleasures of a wicked sense of humour.

Elsie Nora Anderson for showing me that it's okay - indeed preferable - to be different.

Elaine Noni Anderson (later Hoggarth) for nurturing me, teaching me spelling and making me feel special while all around me made me feel quite the opposite. A mother cannot give her children more.

Ron Hoggarth for giving me wanderlust, romantic notions and teaching me that, even if I occasionally failed, I should be honourable and 'proper'.

My sisters, Gilly and Sue for endless laughs and taking me on when I get 'up myself'.

Sofi and Nial for giving me something to be truly proud of.

My ex-wife Sue for bringing up two beautiful and 'proper' people – often with little help from me, and for loving and trusting me until she no longer could.

Linette (not mentioned in this volume – yet to be discovered) for love and light, and for taking the piss.

Vibes for being my lovely mate and stopping me working (someone has to!)

The Beatles, The Kinks and The Who for lighting a fire inside me when I was a kid.

Deep Purple for 'flicking the switch'.

Joni Mitchell for truth and the reckless courage to tell it.

Robert (Benneth) Connor for helping me to get started.

The Europeans, Colin Woore, Fergus Harper and Geoff Dugmore for taking me into them and allowing me to become a professional musician. I am sincerely sorry that I had to walk away.

Marillion: Ian Mosley, Mark Kelly, Pete Trewavas and Steve Rothery for taking me into them and allowing me to become someone whose diaries might be of interest somewhere.

Paul Lewis, Nick Belshaw and Dee McLoughlin for getting me in to, and out of, trouble.

Louise Veys and Gaby Weiss from EMI, who always helped more than they were paid to.

Benoît Mahé, Jill Furmanovsky, Niels Van Iperen and Paul Cox for their photographs.

Lucy Jordache for advice and care.

Robert Hammond for wanting to publish this diary and for putting it together.

publisher's note

Minor grammatical amendments have been made to the text of this book. Everything else remains unchanged to preserve h's personal style, and to reflect the circumstances in which the diaries were written.

1991 JULY

Wednesday 17

NEAR MISS STUDIOS
MILLIONAIRE STUDIOS
TERRIBLE ROOM STUDIOS
NO ROOM STUDIOS
THE HISS FACTORY
SOUND PRACTICE
TIGHT BOTTOM
TOY BOX
MIXEMETOSIS
SPECIAL PROJECTS
THE RACKET CLUB

A COLLECTION OF GOLDEN GRATES

1 9 9 1

Tuesday 13 August *Iceland shooting the* Dry Land *promotion video*

Flew to Reykjavik in the evening. During the flight I witnessed a treat. We were just above the cloud, which appeared from my window as a dark-purple feather bed. The sun had set and, above the cloud, the sky was crimson fading to pink. On the cloud-horizon a perfect crescent moon shone silver, but exactly half submerged in the cloud-floor so that it appeared as a shining silver shark-fin emerging from a purple sea into an unworldly sunset sky. For the first of many times during my stay in Iceland I cursed not having brought my camera.

In Reykjavik I was met by a car, and I eventually arrived at the hotel to find Howard Greenhalgh (the director) with a scalded foot. He had wandered into one of the volcanic steam-pools earlier today while looking down a camera lens for interesting shots of the geyser. Producer/assistant Megan was nursing a cold, so they made a pretty miserable pair, and the response to my enthusiastic appearance was somewhat low-key. Left 'em to it and spent the evening in my room. Back to the geyser in the morning to start filming with a helicopter…

Wednesday 14 August *Iceland*

Spent nearly all day in a café with a model (locally-hired Icelandic Norse Goddess, Hrøn – probably aged seventeen and bunking off school) waiting for Howard and a helicopter, which was not to arrive owing to technical fault. Drank fourteen gallons of coffee and made several 'interesting' attempts to order flowers for Sue in England by Icelandic payphone – it's my wedding anniversary on the 16th and, of course, I'll still be in Iceland.

Howard showed up at 5.30 in the afternoon, extremely vexed. Never mind. Stood about looking heroic (it's what he likes me to do) with the 30-foot geyser exploding periodically into violent orgasm behind me, then onto the waterfalls for more of the same. When the light failed, we drove for hours and hours along badly potholed 'roads' to somewhere very remote where we stayed in a kind of hotel/hostel in order to get to the iceberg-lagoon at first light tomorrow. I occasionally encountered other hostel residents, done up in thermal outward-bound gear, Gore-Tex boots, rucksacks etc. It's all anathema to me – I'm not one for the pleasures of a force ten gale, 500 miles from the nearest café. In the unlikely event that anyone could ever even persuade me to go on a skiing holiday I'm sure I'd never leave the bar...

Thursday 15 August *Jökulsárlón Iceberg Lagoon*

Spent most of the day shooting at the iceberg-lagoon. I was surprised how bluey-white the icebergs are. They really seem to shine with a colour all their own – like there's light inside them. I'm told that no one can be sure whether the ice below the water is losing weight or gaining weight and so the entire things may turn upside down at any moment as the ratio changes with thaw and freeze. For this reason it was decided not to film me on top of one. We hired a little boat and sailed around the lagoon. It's unwise to get too close to the icebergs. These are only little ones but they are, nonetheless, as big as houses and, if they capsize, you wouldn't want to witness the splash at close quarters.

I wrote some postcards. We finished shooting and drove for hours to Bik (pronounced Vik) where we were to stay at another sort of hostel/guesthouse thing. Interestingly, my friend Pep (pronounced Pep) lives in the mountains near Barcelona in a village called Vik, pronounced Bik. What are the chances?! Anyway, meanwhile in Bik (pronounced Vik) we ate with the landlady, who gave us haddock which was washed down with Beck's beer and Glenfiddich malt whisky – care of Megan.

Howard wants it noted in my diary that he can't juggle either.

Friday 16 August *Reykjavik – Blue Lagoon*

Woke up to rain and grey skies – not great for moviemakers. It brightened up later amidst much debate as to whether or not I am in possession (as I claim to be) of a weather-angel.

Shot walking on a black beach washed by white foam – like a negative. We then returned by road to Reykjavik and beyond, to the Blue Lagoon – a natural volcanically-heated swimming pool where the Icelanders may bathe warmly out in the open air at any time of year or day. There's a fence around the lagoon and a little ticket office with a turnstile that you have to go through to gain admission, complete with changing rooms like any public swimming pool in England.

Shot a lip-sync playback of me standing on a rock singing *Dry Land* with bathing onlookers just out of shot. I alighted from a small rowing boat in long black coat and sunglasses before trying to look serious and mimed to the playback-tape while middle-aged ladies in swimsuits pointed and giggled. I don't blame 'em! "Howard, I'm not comfortable," I complained, as they continued to chuckle.

Gave up after the light worsened and returned to our hotel in Reykjavik to freshen up for a Friday night out! Socially speaking, Iceland's a small place and you can't turn up there and wander around with movie-making equipment for very long before everyone-who's-anyone knows you're in town.

Howard's office in London had received a fax mysteriously inviting us to the birthday party of Doris Day-and-Night - an Icelandic socialite - at some nightclub in town. When we arrived I was greeted at the door by her - Dora (for short) a sort of middle-aged Icelandic media-catalyst who was throwing a fancy-dress bash, including sit-down meal, for Iceland's colourful and beautiful. I was seated next to a hairdresser who said he'd flown in from Europe for the event. Dora's obviously popular and I can say she was certainly an excellent host.

Met Björk, lead singer of the Sugarcubes, who was pleasant and eccentric: "You have to CARE," were her passionate opening words of our short conversation. Me, of all people.

"I care; I CARE," I said.

I cared enough to buy her a drink and she cared enough to drink it. She didn't care enough to buy me one back though.

It was a good party. I'm sure I would have had a great time if I'd known anyone – half of those present were in fancy dress; someone had come as a television!

I ended up losing Howard and eventually found myself out in the street at around 5.30am, trying to get back to our hotel. Reykjavik at 5.00 in the morning is like Covent Garden at 2.00 in the afternoon – there were people everywhere, it was broad daylight and the cafés, and even some of the shops, were open. There was a thirty-metre queue for taxis, which I joined alone amidst the boisterous, drunk and still uncomfortably Viking crowd. It was cold and I hadn't come out dressed for standing around outdoors. I stood there shivering nervously - an English wimp surrounded by hardy and hard-drinking Icelanders - wondering what the taxi driver would do when he realized I hadn't enough money to cover the cost of the journey. I should know better by now.

Saturday 17 August *Vatnajökull Glacier – Reykjavik – Home*

Up at 8.00 feeling well-tricky after 2 hours sleep. Thermal underwear on along with extra shirts, big black coat and borrowed padded Rucanor jacket. The helicopter had been modified for filming, i.e. one side had been removed. I discovered that, no matter how theoretically cold an open helicopter ride above Iceland might seem, the reality underneath umpteen layers of intimate clothing, was colder. It must have been worse for the cameraman who was holding the freezing metal of the camera with ungloved hands as we rushed through the high altitude air. Rather him than me…

We kept landing at predetermined beauty spots where I was dropped off and told to stand precariously close to torrents of rushing water above sheer drops, which all looks great on film and was actually fun to do, not to mention a welcome relief from the journey between locations in the flying freezer. The helicopter pilot seemed fearless: at one point I watched as the thing flew below me - and towards me - between the two rock-faces of a river valley, while I stood trying to look nonchalant – balanced on a wet rock on yet another precipice. After that particular shot they landed and Howard climbed down: “If that shot dun't make you feel important, I dun't know what will!” he declared, in his broad West Yorkshire accent.

The big one was actually yet to come. Towards the end of the morning I was dropped onto a glacier on top of a mountain. As far as I know, no one had ever been here. You can only be here if you're dropped from the sky. The helicopter pilot slowly throttled back as we landed, waiting to feel if the ice was solid enough beneath us to take our weight. As I climbed down onto the helicopter-skids and extended a careful toe onto the ice surface, the Icelandic pilot broke a rueful grin and said, “Nice knowing you.”

The chopper took off and disappeared into the distance. I heard the engine noise die away to silence and I was suddenly alone, absolutely alone, and irretrievably isolated from the world. Quite a feeling – Neil Armstrong without Aldrin!! (By a strange twist of fate I was to meet Neil Armstrong, nine years after writing this, and he bought me lunch!) After a few nervous, uncertain steps my confidence on the ice-surface increased. I got the hang of walking and tried running; sunglasses on and coat billowing like a black flag. When the helicopter returned after five long minutes I was fairly adjusted to the conditions. They filmed me walking around from above, and as I was investigating the sound of running water far below me at the edge of a crevasse, Howard decided we'd pushed our luck far enough and I was, somewhat demonstratively, beckoned back into the helicopter. We flew back across Iceland to the airport where I was already late for the flight back to England. As we approached Reykjavik airport I noticed we were on a collision course with an incoming passenger jet. Our pilot had been given clearance by air-traffic control to cross above the runway, so I waited until the last minute before tapping him on the shoulder to point out the plane coming towards us. He took evasive action, banking hard to the left to get out of the way. Phew! I assumed he'd seen it, but evidently not. Well, it would have been a glamorous rock n'roll way to go! I thanked everyone and told Howard I'd see him at the edit back in London. I practically ran from the helicopter to board the plane to Heathrow stopping only to check-in my suitcase. When I sat down in my seat I began to boil. I had come straight from the top of a mountain-glacier, and was still wearing thermal-underwear and several layers of shirts and pullovers. I made my way to the toilet. In the limited space of the plane loo I struggled out of my clothes and underwear, then redressed normally, emerging from the toilet carrying an impressive pile of clothes up the centre-aisle past the.other passengers.

Finally arrived at Heathrow in the evening to discover that no one had thought to arrange a car to take me home and, this being Saturday, I couldn't ring the management or the film company. Great. You can't get black cabs to take you to Windsor from Heathrow - they all want to go to London - and there are no trains or buses.

I still don't know how I got home.

Sunday 18 August *Home – Wales – Home*

The car was late but I wanted it later. Still recovering from Dora's 'do' and the glaciers. Driven to Merthyr Tyddfill in a nice new Range Rover (not as comfortable as you might think) with Ian and Jack, to mime on a Radio 1 Roadshow. Surprised by the number of people there... Must be bugger all else to do in MT. Seemed to go okay. Met Mike Read (Radio 1 D.J.) for the first time. He seemed a bit distracted. Also Timmy Mallet's wife – who seemed very nice. Insisted on lying down to sign autographs. Mike Read invited us for drinks later. We didn't go - ever the ambitious pros – ha ha.

Back home by 8.00. Straight to bed, glacially exhausted.

Monday 19 August *Home – London*

Met Paddy Spinks (Hit & Run US Management) in the pub by the Hit & Run office in Chelsea. To look at, he's a perfect cross between Peter Gabriel and my dear departed chum Des O'Connor (school friend, guitar player and co-writer in my first band Harlow – now sadly lost to this world to leukaemia). Two good men - maybe it's a good omen...

Walked down the street chatting to a chap who looked about my age. He had a faint Scouse accent. I thought I'd met him before and was trying to work out why he seemed so familiar. Didn't even twig when John Crawley (Charisma music publishing) introduced us: "Steve, this is Julian... Julian, Steve"

Got to the pub and ordered a beer. Julian ordered a Guinness and as he did so, my brain underwent a small explosion as I realised he was Julian Lennon. Holy shit. He's eerily like John. Different body, same spirit – albeit slightly softer.

Me: "I didn't recognise you."

Julian: "Good."

Beyond that we didn't have much chance to talk. He seemed like a very nice chap. Down to earth – almost unfeasibly so. I was surprised at how old he looked considering he was the son of my all-time hero. Funny how when someone dies, they remain the same age forever so it comes as a shock to see their children looking as old, or older.

Gave my favourite clothes to Sally Higgins (coincidentally Liverpudlian - a seamstress and friend of our tour manager Paul Lewis), who took them to Liverpool to make copies for touring.

Picked Diz and Fi Fi up from Kings Cross, back from Doncaster. Took ages to get home after a lorry had overturned at the Egham turn-off of M25.

There's been a coup in the Soviet Union. Mikhail Gorbachev is detained in the Ukraine and Boris Yeltsin has barricaded himself in the parliament building, Moscow. That's handy then…

Tuesday 20 August *Home – London*

Popped out for an hour at 1.00 to edit *Dry Land*, down at Abbey Road with Steve R. Got finished by about 3.30, but got nobbled for approving artwork at EMI. Wrong photographs etc. Didn't get home 'til half seven. Fed up. This should have been my day off.

Wednesday 21 August *Home – Poland*

Spent most of the day travelling to Gdansk for the Sopot festival, which we are to play tomorrow. Hue & Cry and Deacon Blue were also on the plane from Heathrow. My suitcase fell open as I claimed it from the carousel in Warsaw – underwear everywhere. No one had actually booked the connecting flight from Warsaw to Gdansk, so we had to wait from 3.00 'til 7.30 at a fairly dead offshoot of Warsaw airport. Fortunately we managed to find a bar, and it was during this wait that we heard that the Russian coup had collapsed and that Gorbachev was alive and returning to Moscow.

Finally got to the Marina Hotel at 10.00pm and had dinner. Stroganoff. Surprisingly good. Had a few beers in the strange nightclub in the hotel (a bit like a school disco) and went to bed. Slept well under an odd-shaped Polish duvet in a room with an orange telephone. I repeatedly tried and failed to call England on it. Bollocks.

PS – Poland is a very big surprise. Very open and green. Gdansk has more in common with Torquay than Clydeside. The women don't look like blokes in dresses as the news footage would have us believe. They are, on the whole, very beautiful, as is the surrounding countryside. You begin to wonder if there's been an agenda all these years to portray the Eastern Bloc as worse than it really is. I thought the Beeb was above that sort of thing. How naive of me.

Thursday 22 August *Gdansk*

Rose around 10.00 and went for a walk along the beach. It was a sunny day and the beach was crowded with locals in swimwear, sunbathing. Apparently you shouldn't swim in the Baltic just here (if at all) as it's extremely polluted and (rumour has it) quite radioactive, but many were bathing, especially children. I collected small cockleshells for Fi Fi. Maybe I should boil them before I let her anywhere near them. She'll be delighted if they glow in the dark!

Returned to the hotel for a press conference at 11.00 only to be told not to bother, but to return at 1.00 for the cocktail party. Attended the cocktail party but didn't drink as I wanted to remain lucid for the show. I'm singing live to the Eastern Bloc and Japan – best not fuck up!

The rehearsal in the afternoon was a nightmare. No one checked the tapes and there's no fades on them. Oh well – at least it'll sound real…

Bumped into How We Live drummer and old pal, Arran Ahmun back at the hotel – he's drumming for Alison Moyet.

Lost my rag with an interviewer and went for another walk by the sea.

Set off for the show at 8.00. Nervous wreck. To make matters worse, everyone's singing live and we're on after Hue & Cry and before Alison Moyet. I'm singing live to Poland in between two of the best singers in the UK. No pressure...

It actually went very well after last minute finger-tying*. Saw the show later at the hotel and everyone agreed it was good, including Alison M. Bless her. Even got a pat on the back from aforementioned Hue & Cry-ers. Praise indeed. Chatted to Alison M later whilst terribly sloshed. She took it rather well.

*I used to wear little bandages like ribbons on my fingers. It was a vibe I started with the Europeans. After a while superstition prevented me abandoning them, so I continued the ritual when I joined Marillion. At some point it all became too much trouble and I moved on to finger-ribbonless performing without too much incident. Every now and then, I'm tempted to do another tour with 'em on.

Friday 23 August *Gdansk – Home*

Spent all day travelling home. Another interminable wait at Warsaw airport so went into the city with Louise Veys (EMI International babysitter and, by now, good friend) for a look around and a spot of lunch. It was a beautiful day so we sat out on the street. Spent lunch discussing and lamenting Warsaw's tragic past. Everyone else stayed at the airport. They must be mad.

Finally got home around 7.00. Kissed my girls and went to bed!

Saturday 24 August *Home*

Went to the Egham show. Cows, vintage cars, Geoff Capes, steam engines, Bill Smith's coconut shies, show-jumping, pigs, horticultural tent, etc. Missed it all in favour of the bouncy castle and Punch & Judy show. Never mind. As long as Hargreaves is happy.

Went out to dinner in the evening with Dizzy to local friends, Sue & Graham. Much talk of nursing and skydiving i.e. blood and gore and sudden-death. Broke in a new babysitter Rachel. We'll soon have enough for a hockey-team.

Sunday 25 August *Home*

Borrowed Bessie's ladder and pruned the wisteria.

Monday 26 August *Home*

Painted the front lounge (again). Back to Magnolia after my recent previous attempt rendered the room egg-custard yellow. Started about 12.30 and had the pictures up by 5.00. Diz thinks it looks much better and makes the room look somehow larger. I tend to agree.

We went to Windsor for a teatime noggin at The Dome café being as the pubs weren't open 'til 7.00, it being bank holiday! Walked down to the river and half way up Eton High Street before Diz pegged out (she's expecting…).

Tuesday 27 August *Home*

Another lovely day weather-wise and otherwise. We drove to Richmond. Bought liquid soap at Dickins & Jones and nipped upstairs for a coffee as Diz was feeling a bit tired. Refreshed, we then went for a walk along the river. Fi Fi had a nice time wall-walking.

Bought this diary in order to keep the promise I made to my dad ("I promise I'll keep a diary, Dad…").

Spent the afternoon drilling and banging – running an electricity supply to the dishwasher, which, as yet, doesn't exist.

Diz had another ante-natal. Blood pressure normal – so far she's doing just fine.

Up late getting this diary started.

Wednesday 28 August *Home – Loseley House*

Took Fi Fi and ourselves to Loseley House where they make the ice-cream. Had a walk round the gardens (Fi Fi didn't want to go in the house – me neither). Probably the most 'English' place I've ever been. Wonderful and magical. The ice-cream's pretty damned good too. Fed the cows and hurried home for John who popped in at 5.00 with t-shirts for approval and the tour-programme. T-shirts not bad, programme looks very good. Apparently MTV are playing *No One Can* several times a day and the album's been in the top 30 in Germany for 8 weeks. It's hardly **Dark Side of the Moon**, but I was pleasantly surprised.

Changed the kitchen round a bit. Diz doesn't like bending down to the fridge so it's gone up in the air.

Spoke to Sally Higgins re. multi-coloured silk waistcoat.

Went to bed at 12.00. Got up at 2.00. Couldn't sleep. Watched Rocklife video (Köln) 'til 5.00. Made notes. Went back to bed.

Thursday 29 August

Had my roots done. Put shelves up in the kitchen. Took Fi Fi to the park. Had a bath with her. Went to bed early.

Friday 30 August *Home – Berlin – Köln*

Rose at 6.00. Jason (regular driver) took me to Heathrow. Fairly uneventful flight to Berlin. The TV show was silly. We were on after **Marmalade**... 'nuff said.

Flew to Köln for EMI sales conference. Very nice Italian restaurant/meal. They sat me at a table with Erwin, the MD (married to Tina Turner). Needless to say, everyone ended up (as is customary) at Woody's bar drinking Tequila which did much damage to all and sundry, not least ABC who perhaps aren't as used to it as us. Martin Fry's a nice chap. Also had a bit of a chin wag with Kim Appleby who seemed nice too.

Saturday 31 August *Köln – Home*

Rose at 10.00. Had quick breakfast with Swiss EMI rep, Gabi Weiss then off to the airport with ABC and EMI staff. Got back to UK mid-afternoon and spent the rest of the day in the garden and recuperating indoors.

Sunday 1 September *Home – Malham, Yorkshire*

Up at eight. Finished defrosting the fridge. Planted "pinks" in the borders – a gift from Bessie next door. Mowed the lawn and waited for Priv and Mark to take me to Windsor where we are to photograph Radio 1 and EMI girls. William Chung took the pictures and much fun was had by all. Diz and Fi Fi came and chatted and pottered (respectively). We were a bit short of women (only 12) so I persuaded a few passers-by and the girls from behind the bar at the Windsor Castle pub. Ian brought Michael and they flew a kite, which was retrieved from trees and untied by Mad Jack with a little assistance from Fi Fi.

At 3.45 we'd finished, so the girls went back to London on a coach and the band climbed aboard the horse-box/bus and drove to Malham in Yorkshire (5-hrs) to be greeted by Mike Bell (director) and Ivan (cameraman). Had a couple of pints of Boddingtons and fell out with the management who refused to give us a drink after 10.30. Bastards. What's all this about Northerners being friendly?

Monday 2 September *Malham – Home*

Rose at 9.00. Checked out of the hotel from hell and had breakfast at the café round the corner. Additional film crew arrived at 10.15 and we drove to Malham Cove which was to be location 1. Threw hotel room key over the edge of the cliff and sunbathed in the glorious sunshine in between bits of 'heroics' and lip syncs. Much trudging about and Jim Kerr-ing on rocks. Finished at sundown.

Managed to drag Ivan away to the pub for a quickie around 9.00 and then home in the horse-box via Aylesbury and the shires arriving at 3.30a.m. Thank you and goodnight.

Tuesday 3 September *Home – London*

Had a lie-in. 11.45. Woke to the sound of the phone. John Arnison with awful news. Capitol Records, America have changed their minds. No deal. They lie to you in L.A. Hit & Run should have seen it coming. Maybe they did. Oh well. So much for 'management with clout'. I remember Tony Smith coming out to Stanbridge Farm when we were writing **Holidays in Eden** to talk us into allowing him to "absorb" John into his management company. He promised much in return.

Took my girls with me to London, in the afternoon, for an interview with Midlands TV in Wardour Street. Got back at 7.00 and went to the Bar 163 in Egham for tea.

Bob Harris rang in the afternoon to set up a visit to sit-in on his show on Wednesday 11th. I'm looking forward to it. He's a lovely chap and, by far, my favourite DJ. Heard from Phil Ward-Large that Alan and Jo Jones have lost their baby. As he said, it puts everything else into perspective. I don't know what to do. Leave them alone for a while? Or phone and say how sorry I am?

Wednesday 4 September *Home – London – Home*

Rose at nine. Was collected by Grubby John and Range-Rovered to Nomis (rehearsal studios, Kensington, London) early as I couldn't use the car today. Dizzy had ante-natal at 1.00. Everything okay at bang-on 33 weeks, although she's had some slight bleeding which we'll obviously have to keep an eye on.

Day 1 of the rehearsals seemed to go well. Mad Jack doesn't seem to have quite the programming nightmare on his hands that we suspected. Phew. I'm singing well.

Got home in time for a cuddle with Fi and stayed up late learning side 2 of **Misplaced Childhood**.

Thursday 5 September *Home – London – Home*

Arrived at Nomis to discover John and Keith Drinkwater (merchandising man) with programmes and posters to approve. Much moaning was absorbed by Mr Arnison re. Capitol USA but really it's all spilled milk. Finally started rehearsing around 2pm.

Woman's Own wanted a quote about what makes England special. I said it was the BBC - without which, we all might as well move out. Got home to find long-awaited dishwasher awaiting installation in the kitchen. Major project.

Friday 6 September *Home – London – Home*

Rose early and spent until mid-afternoon drilling, screwing, and sawing at the kitchen cupboards in order to install the new dishwasher.

Went into Nomis, covered in sawdust and plaster dust, for 3.00 and rehearsed until 9.00. Someone phoned about going on **The Clothes Show**. There's talk of Lichfield being on as well. I wonder if I'll get to meet him?

Saturday 7 September *Home – London – Home*

Work. Work. Work. Spent the morning on drains and plumbing once again.

Arrived late at Nomis and was lightly reprimanded. Narrowly escaped being pulled by the police on the way in when I passed a police car at 100mph on the M4. Fortunately they overtook me and did the bloke in the Merc in front of me. I should think so too.

Rehearsals are going well. For once, everyone's panicking except me. *Cover My Eyes* was sounding much better today. I think I've just about got the **Misplaced** side 2 stuff licked.

Sunday 8 September *Home*

Finished off the dishwasher. It works!! The drains dripped a bit but I fixed them with a bit of PTFE tape. Took the girls up to the Green for a pint, a kick of a ball, some swinging and then back along Barley Mow Road picking blackberries. Diz made a crumble and very nice it was too!

Angie Fountain popped round in the evening but I didn't talk much as I was tinkering with persistent dripping drains. Tomorrow, however, I will be a rock star…

Monday 9 September *Home – Amsterdam*

Up at 8.00 and off to Heathrow. Uneventful flight to Amsterdam. Arrived at the American Hotel at 1.30 and had a couple of hours off before the first interview. Had lunch in the hotel café and went for a walk. Saw a nice pair of chisel-toed shoes, which I should have bought. Went and had Irish coffee in the Leidesplein square where people skate in the winter. Took me back to the old Europeans/Paradiso days. We had opened for Dead Can Dance and The Cocteau Twins. I remember the Cocteau's going down a storm and being really jealous, and then really confused to see Liz Fraser crying backstage after the show. Now I kind of understand. You can get upset "going down a storm", and I often have. Maybe she couldn't hear herself. That'd do it.

After interviews and a couple of photo sessions we went off to **Countdown** - the Dutch TOTP - with *Dry Land.* This is in Hilversum – about an hour's drive from Amdam. The lip sync was a bit tricky as they were using the edited version, but they should have it if they edit between both takes. After that we had Cajun food at a restaurant in downtown Amsterdam and then back to bed. An early night! (1.30)

Tuesday 10 September *Amsterdam – London – Home*

Up at 9.00 and time for a quick breakfast before heading off to Schiphol for the 10.30 flight to Heathrow. Uneventful, if not on-time. Took off to *Crazy* by Seal (on the Walkman) which is what I have been taking-off to lately.

Arrived back at Terminal 4 and we were met by a limo to take us straight to Nomis for rehearsals. Seemed to go quite well despite everyone being tired. Princess Stephanie of Monaco was in the room next door. Didn't look too hot in the flesh actually (I'm sure she speaks highly of me…). Nomis is one of those places where you can pop to the cafe and rub shoulders with legends in the queue. I remember sitting next to Van Morrison once and thinking perhaps he was a plumber. Mick Jagger once went past. I saw John McEnroe and Vitas Gerulaitis wandering down the corridors with guitars – they used to jam with Motorhead in the evenings. Also said hello to Ian Dury in these corridors… and Boy George who said about Europeans, "Aren't you that lot that wear the leotards? You'll never get anywhere dressing up!" Strangest of all was a chap in a business suit and little spectacles, who I later realized was Jim Osterberg. When he isn't wearing the suit and specs, he becomes Iggy Pop.

Wednesday 11 September *Home – London*

Up at 8.00 with Fi Fi. Had to go to Nomis for 11.30 to meet Lou Musgrave (EMI rep) who was coming down with a technical bod from TVS. Frantically packed my clothes and half of my record collection for later in the day. After Lou had finished at 1.00 I was supposed to go to lunch with a Brazilian, but it was cancelled (much to my relief – a long day in the offing…).

Rehearsed the set with the boys until, tired and hoarse, I staggered into yet another waiting car which took me through slow, heavy traffic to a studio near Tower Bridge where I was to be shot, i.e. head-shot vocal performance close-up for the *Dry Land* video. I arrived late, exhausted, stressed and jibbering. Told Howard I wanted the performance to be weird rather than 'Englebert' so that's what he did – hair ringing wet, dripping, and eyes glued threateningly to camera. I was trying to get that Charlotte Rampling vibe from Woody Allen's **Stardust Memories**. At 11.45pm I dashed out of there into a cab and straight to Radio 1 where I co-DJ'd with Bob Harris and played my fave records until 2.00am when I bade farewell. Philip Schofield popped in and I mentioned I'd seen him at Sarah Ball's private viewing*. Bob's wife, Trudy, tried to take a snap of me with Bob, but her camera had ran out of film. They're going to try again at Hammersmith. He gave me a copy of his **Best of the Test** CD which he dedicated and autographed. What a lovely chap.

*Sarah Ball is the artist who painted the front cover of Marillion's **Holidays in Eden** album. I discovered her work after seeing it on a Penguin paperback of **Love in the Time of Cholera** by Gabriel Garcia Marquez.

Thursday 12 September *London – Maidstone – London – Home*

Stayed in London overnight in order to get to EMI in the morning to go to Maidstone where I was to address the conference. It took ages. I knew it would. I remembered only too well, from my days in the back of the Euro's transit van, that drive through Lewisham and Blackheath, to play in the corner of The Ship – that little Maidstone pub.

I opened my speech as follows, "I'm thinking of having a vasectomy. Has anyone here had one? Hands up!" No one made a sound. I must never go into comedy.

They took me back to London in the old stretch Merc, which I seem to be spending half my time in. I find riding around in a limo opens me up to all manner of wanker and dickhead hand-gestures from passers-by. Looking anyone in the eye seems to invite hostility. No wonder people have tinted glass. It's like being back in Doncaster when I was seventeen – except that I didn't need a limo, just a bathrobe and yellow clogs.

Didn't start rehearsing 'til 5.30. One run-through and that was it. Thank you gents. Gear down. See you in Liverpool. Went straight from Nomis to Twickenham, via Mark's place by the river in Putney, to see Cry No More at the Turk's Head. Met Diz, who had come down with Englefield Green chums, Sue and Graham. Roy was his usual indomitable and utterly obscene self, relentless and high-spirited, despite the slack audience attendance. Criminal (the slack audience, not Roy). Mark and I decided we'd even share hotel rooms to get them on the second leg of the European tour. We *were* drunk though.

Friday 13 September *Home – London – Home*

Had the morning off. Stayed in bed 'til 12.00. Took Fi Fi to the park then drove into town for an interview with Radio Scotland. Got a bit cross with the interviewer, who was a pillock.

Priv was mixing the Cumbria Rock festival show at BBC Maida Vale so I dropped by to see how he was doing. Slogged round Covent Garden trying to find shoes for the tour. No luck. I'd earlier bought black jeans in Chelsea. The staff in American Classics recognised me and knocked six quid off.

Saturday 14 September *Home:* Day off

Tidied the shed. Mowed the lawn. Did the accounts. Took Fi to the steam-fair on the green. Lovely. A little fair in the Victorian tradition, completely powered by steam engines - all chugging away round the back of the carousels and side shows. Ran into lots of village chums. Saw Darryl Way and his giggly wife, Juliet, with little Lauren who is now walking. Went to The Barley Mow for a half. Fi Fi fell down and did a complete forward roll in the road. Nasty bump on the head and much noise, bless her. She's okay though. Maybe she'll have a lie-in tomorrow. We live in hope.

Sunday 15 September *Home – London – Liverpool*

She didn't. To make matters worse, Diz was up all night with Delhi-belly and feels awful. Oh no. Got up with Fi at half-seven and spent the morning doing my accounts and trying to pack for the tour. At 12.15 I was chauffeured to Soho to Why Not?! Films to have a look at the off-line edit of the *Dry Land* video. Mark and Steve were also there. My performance is weird and intense. EMI will hate it. Had a word or two with Howard and then ran off to Putney to get on the tour bus to go to Liverpool. Half way up the road, I realized I'd left my address book/diary at home which, of course, contains all my guest lists and important numbers. The traffic was lousy on the M6 so we didn't get to Liverpool 'til 10pm.

Checked in and popped round the corner to have a look at the production. The new drapes look great and work really well with the lights. Time for a quick drink and off to bed. My room smells of Harpic.

Monday 16 September *Liverpool, Royal Court Theatre*

Woke up with a cold. Bollocks.

Met Sally and Ally - who had made stage-clothes for us - at the hotel. Everything looks good, but you can tell they're only copies of the designer stuff. Under lights they'll probably look fine. Went out with Trish (wardrobe-girl and wife of Paul Devine, our lighting designer) to Boots to stock up on glycerin, knee supports, cold remedies etc, and then had a walk round Liverpool trying to find stage shoes. Didn't – but found The Beatles shop, so bought a Yellow Submarine badge and a Blue Meanies badge, a t-shirt and a few postcards.

Had lunch in catering at The Royal Court and set Trish off sewing mirrors into my black coat. Paul Lewis, our old TM came down for a chat. Around 3.00 we started running through the set, which went quite well! We ran through the set twice which took until around 10.00pm then I went down to a cocktail bar with Mad Jack for a last drink. While we were in there, they played *No One Can,* which was pure coincidence.

We returned to the hotel bar where John A had arrived bearing news of meetings. EMI hate the wet-hair performance stuff in the *Dry Land* video. Surprise, surprise! Rupert Perry (the CEO) has promised to sort out America by the end of October. I'll believe it when we're in the charts.

Tuesday 17 September *Liverpool, Royal Court Theatre*

Had a bit of a lie-in and went down to the venue to have breakfast in catering.

John brought another off-line of the video, which was safer, so we compared them and decided that the original was far better, although a couple of changes were required to make the performance a bit less out-right-menacing. It is, after all, a love song.

Back to The Royal Court for another run-through. Priv recorded a board-tape which sounded great so we're getting there. Did an interview with someone from a radio station and then back round the corner to the hotel. Signed stuff for the love-scruffs at the stage door. Had a much needed quiet hour and then returned to the venue which, by now was full of people.

The show went well. I sang quite well, but felt I was a bit tentative. After the show, Paul Lewis came back and said he enjoyed my singing. Made my day. At the beginning of each tour, we are all given laminated passes which we are supposed to hang round our necks. These get us past Security, into the gig, backstage etc. for the whole tour. This is the first show and I have already lost it...

Back to the hotel for Snowballs in the bar, which tasted like liquid lemon-meringues, and then went to bed.

Wednesday 18 September *Liverpool – Oxford Apollo*

Checked out of the dodgy St George's Hotel (must be Protestants) at 11.30 and assumed my normal position, spark-out in the back seat of the car. We arrived at the Oxford Hotel at the Pear Tree roundabout which was most reminiscent of an American motel (remember Saratoga?), and after half-an-hour drove into Oxford to the Apollo. Arrived to find Julia Simpson - DJ from GWR radio - waiting for an interview so chatted to her over dinner and then into the soundcheck-from-hell. Everything that could go wrong went wrong, including Privet! The bus had a puncture. John A. took Pete and me to Fox FM out on an industrial estate on the edge of town. Radio's not as glamorous as you might think. Half the time, I don't think there's even anyone in the building – just pre-recorded shows automated to air. Got interviewed and then straight back to the show.

The show went really well until the encores, which were a bit iffy due to disappearing keyboards, but everyone I spoke to didn't even notice.

After the show, backstage was busy. I chatted with Ben, old school friend and drummer in my first band, Harlow. His real name is Robert Connor but he got christened Benneth for some reason at school and it stuck. He had driven up from London, and stunned me by admitting he had both my Marillion albums, saying he thought *Cover My Eyes* was the best single he had heard that year. I was (and still am) very flattered.

Back at the hotel/motel I was interviewed by **Metal Hammer** or something, and then finished the GWR interview at 2.40. Phew! No wonder I get knackered. Only an idiot would contemplate getting up for a haircut after a night like this.

Thursday 19 September *Oxford – Henley – Cambridge Corn Exchange*

Got up for a haircut. At 7.30. Showered and then drove to Henley-on-Thames with Dee to visit Lisa, my hairdresser. I must be deranged, but I decided my hair is badly in need of a tint and a cut. Lisa gave me a trim and Sarah gave Dee likewise. Well, he might as well now he's here. Back to Oxford to pick up the boys and then off to Cambridge.

Checked into a hotel out of town and had an hour's snooze before returning to the city centre. Drove around for ages trying to find the Corn Exchange. Ran into old fans, Inge and Ciska, who press-ganged me into a short interview for Radio Delft. My voice felt hoarse all day and I was mucho tired, so I returned to the hotel after soundcheck and went to bed again for an hour, returning to the show at 8.15. Mark was still programming. He's mad, it's official, and we don't call him Mad Jack for nothing.

The audience was fantastic and it was definitely the most rewarding show of the tour so far.

Paul Elliot from **Kerrang** was backstage afterwards, so I gave him jip for our lousy Cumbria review which was a pack of lies by some journalist called Chris Potter who, I was later told, wasn't actually there for our set!

Back at the hotel, we gathered in Ian's room and toasted the tour with champagne sent up by Louise Veys, bless her. An hour's chin-wagging and tales from the road by Dee and then off to bed zzzz...

Friday 20 September *Cambridge – London TV – Manchester*

Up at 10.30 and off to the station with John A. A moment's panic ensued when someone nicked our cab and we had to wait for another one, but we arrived at Cambridge station on time at 12.00 to catch the train to London. It was, once again, a beautiful day (the past few weeks have been lovely), and watching the countryside roll by evoked dreamy images of steam trains and railway children in my head – probably a flashback to my early childhood, of getting the steam train up to the Lake District to see my Gran. Chatted with John about his old days with the rock-poet, John Cooper-Clarke (John used to manage him) who loves trains and went everywhere on them, including his tours. I've gradually come to know and trust John A more than ever. Everyone gives him shit, night and day. It can't be easy. We really are surrounded by some wonderful characters.

The TV clip was filmed at EMI and went well in an uneventful sort of way. I saw the on-line of *Dry Land,** which the girls in promo said was their favourite of the three so far. Nonetheless, I still went round to Why Not? and changed a couple of things I wasn't happy with. I gave Howard Greenhalgh my crew shirt.

Took the train from Euston up to Manchester. Had dinner on the train (First Class for the second time. Oooh! Get her!) and arrived at the good old Britannia Hotel around 10.00pm. What a lovely hotel. Had a few drinks in the bar. Paul and Annie Lewis were there. I really think he regrets having to leave (Paul used to be our Tour Manager but had to knock it on the head in favour of steady employment). Stayed sober (tomato juices). Went to bed.

*To this day I think *Dry Land* is the best ever of our promo vids - h

Saturday 21 September *Manchester*

Rose around 11.00 and abluted to the Psychedelic Furs on the Walkman speakers. Went out for a walk and muddled my way through to Marks & Sparks. It wasn't raining! Bought yet more underwear as I never seem to have any, and a black cotton turtle-neck shirt. Vibed out in a café for an hour and then muddled back. Saw a lovely pair of red boots for Fi Fi and have since arranged for a pair to be sent home.

Dropped my things off at the hotel and took a bus down to the Apollo (they all seem to go there). Made a wind and voice noise to go on the front of the video for Howard, with much help from Mad Jack. Gave the DAT to Smick to "Red Star" to London. Soundcheck was a bit boomy but otherwise okay. I tried on the finished mirror-coat which Trish had finally finished sewing. Unfortunately it didn't really do what I'd hoped it would when I 'flashed' it under lights, so we elbowed the whole idea (Sorry Trish – think of it as a Zen exercise.)

Back at the hotel we met up with Tony Smith who had popped up in one of his unfeasibly expensive fast cars. He said he felt embarrassed about America. I'm not surprised. He didn't say he was embarrassed about taking his increased management percentage though while nicking OUR manager.

Anyway, the show went really well. My sound was still boomy but the audience was incredible. At the end of *Incommunicado* everyone in the place, right to the back of the balconies, was singing. Best audience yet on this tour.

Sunday 22 September *Manchester – Edinburgh Playhouse*

Up at 10.00. Didn't quite feel ready – I could have managed another hour.

It was raining when we left Manchester. Signed yet more record sleeves for someone who was waiting patiently outside the Britannia. Drove up to Edinburgh in Steve R's Porsche 928, which made the journey a bit less of a hike than the bus, and checked in quickly and then out again to the venue for soundcheck. All went well – my sound on stage was much better than Manchester. Heard that Fish is coming to the show along with his band and half his crew... Yikes. I ought to be past caring, but I'm not.

Back at the hotel I stared out at the trees on the hill which were just starting to turn from the green of summer to the reds and browns of autumn. Crows blew like unanchored black kites over the hill in the wind above the trees, their leaves blown sideways and upwards along the branches like people's hair in open cars. Autumn comes tomorrow here. Down south, in England, perhaps we have a week or two more of summer.

Back to the Playhouse – scene of my previous worst nightmare gig: I was young – it was the eighties. How We Live were on tour, opening for Chris de

Burgh – not an ideal slot, but we shared his management. Colin Woore – my partner in How We Live (which was essentially a two piece act – all the rage in the 80s) had been playing live already for over ten years and, in all that time, his mum and dad had never been to one of his gigs. They were quite posh Glaswegians and he'd never played a venue he felt he could invite them to *until* our gig with Chris at the Edinburgh Playhouse. He had arranged a box for them. It was gonna be a big night for him.

The band was driving, by minibus, to Edinburgh from our previous show-town, Manchester. By the time we got to the Scottish border I was bored stiff. Our sax player, Andrew was skinning-up a joint and passing it round the band. I don't smoke but I felt left out, so I asked him to break off a bit of the dope for me to chew. After half-an-hour, I had felt no change whatsoever, so I asked him for a bit more. Never having eaten marijuana before, I didn't know that it takes much more time to kick in than alcohol.

A couple of hours later we arrived in Edinburgh and, as I stepped down out of the minibus I felt a sudden otherness. Soundcheck progressed without incident but all the time I was feeling stranger and stranger. By the end of the soundcheck, Elvis had left the planet. I had the strangest sensation of time. The past had ceased to exist, and the 'now' was residing on the bridge of my nose and falling away into an abyss with each passing second. I had no immediate past memory (Something we all take for granted until it's gone!) I was trying to explain this to the band: "I can't remember what I have just said to you! And I can't remember telling you that I can't remember. And I can't remember telling you that I can't remember that I can't remember!"

"What about the songs?" said Colin.

"What songs?" I said.

"Oh dear," said Colin.

They tried everything to straighten me out. Walked me round Edinburgh shivering in the cold air. Held me in a cold shower etc. Nothing helped.

We were on stage at 8.00, and at 7.45 - already in my stage clothes - I began to feel nauseous. I ran down the stairs, umpteen floors, and out of the stage-door into the car park to be sick – carefully shuffling backwards with each retch so as to keep it off my outfit. The gig was sold-out. Colin's mum and dad were in pride of place in the box with the champagne and the Terry's All Gold chocolates. At 8.00 I heard the band strike up inside the venue from my position on my hands and knees in the car park.

Somehow, I got to my feet and ran into the building and straight onto the stage. As I approached the centre mic, looking out at a packed Edinburgh Playhouse, I had NO IDEA what I was going to do. Consciously, I didn't recognise the song the band was playing, nor did I know the words or the melodies. This was definitely up there in my top 5 most terrifying moments of being alive (and I've had some crackers!). It was *Dry Land.*

I stood mystified as the first line came, improbably, out of my mouth:

"*In all the time that I've known you...*"

There's a guitar phrase before each line of the verse. During this I was shouting across to our keyboardist, Raine Shine (Real name! She used to be Vangelis's studio-engineer).

"Was that right?"

"Yes!" she nodded.

"Was it the tune?"

"Yes!! Keep going!!!" she shouted.

And so the song, and the show, progressed.

By the end of our set, the adrenaline and terror had straightened me out and I was 'back in the room'.

Well, that was the last time I had played here...

This time, fortunately, I wasn't off my head and the show went very well. Fish must have been, at best, feeling weird and, at worst, feeling sick. After the show John A came to me and said, "He wants to meet you." So off I went down the corridor to find him alone in our dressing room. I said hi and we chatted. He was gracious and pleasant. When Ian turned up, I went to get dressed and left them to it. I said, "Terrified to meet you, relieved to talk to you," by way of a goodnight. Steve R said later that if I ever leave the band he'll kill me. I *think* he meant it as a compliment.

Monday 23 September *Bradford, St Georges Hall*

Left the hotel around 11.00 in the rocket. The journey was rainy and grey back down the M6 and M62 to Bradford. At one point, a white Rover 2000 drove alongside us in the outside lane and Mark said, "Did you see that lot in the car eyeballing us?"

I said, "It's because we're in a sports car – people are bound to stare."

"Well, let's pull up alongside them and stare back – c'mon Steve... get alongside," says Kelly.

Steve caught up to the car which was now in the inside lane and Mark said "One, two, three... NOW!"

I gave the car my hardest-ever sneer which quickly turned to horror as I saw they were all uniformed police. That boy Kelly really is getting madder by the hour. By some miracle we weren't stopped – they must have had something more important to do. Phew!

The show went well. I twisted my ankle early on which was quite painful but I later realised, not serious. My mum and dad came and sat on the balcony over the stage. John Leedale and Steve Major, my oldest boyhood pals from Intake, Doncaster came also. It was John who sat with me all those years ago whacking marbles into the air with tennis-rackets. He said that he and Steve were at Manchester but that this was even better. Great!

During the show I encountered screaming girls for the first time...

Tuesday 24 September *Bradford – Leeds – Nottingham – err…* "Day off"

I awoke from a deep sleep to hear the phone ringing. "Who the hell is calling me in the middle of the night?!" I thought

"Ten o'clock," said the voice of Dee down the phone. "Leave at 10.30."

I went back to sleep and was called again at 10.35. I was bundled into the bus, apologising, and still half-asleep. We drove into Bradford to Pulse FM where we did a quick interview and then onto Leeds to Aire FM where Mark and I were interviewed by a twat whose name escapes me. He kept going on about the band being finished and how the band had vanished since Fish left. I checked to see if I was still there… I seemed to be! Couldn't help losing my cool eventually. You TRY to be nice, but they seem to love the artists who don't.

We arrived in Nottingham and I went for a walk around – first with mad Jack (I took him for a pint in Yates's Wine Lodge) and then alone. This is where I went to college to do my degree in Electrical Engineering. This city is inseparable in my memory from the long hot summer of 1976. Sitting in the old market square on a Wednesday afternoon watching the cool fountains playing in the shimmering heat, and making dinner (cod in butter sauce, Cadbury's Smash – they advertised it with laughing Martian robots) on a 'camping Gaz' stove in the sweltering attic of my digs on Corporation Oaks.

Bought boots and resisted the temptation to buy Fi Fi more shoes, but it was close. Found the original Paul Smith shop and had a mooch round. I may go back tomorrow. Returned to the hotel later for a cheese and wine party in full swing in Trev's room. Sandra Cassali (press officer from EMI) phoned to tell me the Cambridge show received a rave review in **Kerrang** and to ask my inside-leg measurements.

Went to bed for a snooze after phoning my girls. Got up at 8.00 pm and went for a curry with the crew.

Wednesday 25 September *Nottingham, Royal Centre*

Stirred by the phone at 10.30. It was Louise Veys phoning to say hi and ask how it was all going. She says she's coming up to Nottingham tonight and staying with her mum and dad. She's originally from here. Sweet of her to call. Got up, showered and put some film in my camera.

Went out and installed myself in a café with coffee and apple-pie to catch up on this diary. Went back to the venue and took a few snaps of the boys loading-in before embarking upon a nostalgia trip around Trent Uni. I was trying to find the grand pianos I learned to play on. The full concert grand in the Arkwright lecture theatre had gone, along with the lecture theatre! The Bonnington lecture theatre was locked. I found my way around and through the Byron Student Union building and back up the road. I found a second-hand shop where I bought a leather coat for £12.00!

Back at the Royal Theatre a room full of recording equipment had arrived and chaps were frantically connecting it up to record the show. We've bought most of it and borrowed some of it. The show went well although the audience was relatively sedate. I think we thawed 'em out in the end though – I made my first balcony-run of the tour (achieved by climbing the PA speaker-stack and jumping onto the balcony, running right round and climbing down the PA on the opposite side of stage).

Back at the hotel I chatted with John from Radio Trent who reminds me of Michael Palin and has been added to my list of favourite radio broadcasters. It's short.

Thursday 26 September *Cardiff St. David's Hall*

Rose at 9.30 as I was awake before alarm call. Chatted with a chap in the hotel lounge (suit, shirt and tie) who I had passed wearing a Marillion shirt the night before. He said he's a Smith/Kline/Beecham rep (they make 'Resolve') and he's coming to Hammersmith. He's even in one of the photographs of the Borderline show in the *Dry Land* 10" single.

The journey to Cardiff was uneventful. I spent most of it asleep on the back seat of the bus. Checked into the hotel and had 20 minutes in the solarium, then drove into Cardiff which looks like quite a beautiful city. Saw the most intense rainbow I have ever seen - like two rainbows superimposed - and complete from end-to-end on the horizon. We stayed at the show from soundcheck onwards. Dee took me to Red Dragon FM for a short interview and then back to the venue where John had arrived with dates for Europe second-leg. The dates include Florence, Venice and Vienna. Yeah! Makes a change from industrial Germany.

The show at Cardiff went well although, again, the audience was quiet until the end, when they spontaneously suddenly went wild. I had tech trouble with the T1 (Korg keyboard thing) during *The Party* (Jack had made a few 'adjustments' during the soundcheck). After the show he came out of the shower and said, "The Hammond's got to go!"

Before going to bed I had a look at the final edit of the *Dry Land* video. I think it's okay.

Friday 27 September *Aston Villa Leisure Centre*

Left the hotel at 11.30 and drove up the motorway back to Birmingham. We arrived at the Holiday Inn around 2.30 and drove down to the venue at 4.00. Memories of Christmas dinner here came back as I sat in catering. That was Christmas '89!

Sandra Casali from EMI had come down with a journalist from **The Daily Express**, who was to review the show. The soundcheck went well and I finally got the projectors rehearsed for *A Collection*. After the soundcheck we returned to the hotel and I had a walk round the corner to check out the new Hyatt. Very nice. Shame we're not staying.

The show went really well. I was relaxed, the band played well, and the sound, on and offstage, was great. I chatted with the man from the **Express** (Mike) who, according to Sandra, really enjoyed the show. We'll see...

Old school friend Lynda Todd (who used to go out with my best mate Karl Gerich) showed up with husband-to-be. It was nice to see her after so long. She said I haven't changed a bit. Oh dear, I'd hoped I'd improved...

Paul Divine said the slides looked good – you could have knocked me down with a feather.

Saturday 28 September *Birmingham – Home*

Left the hotel at 11.30 and drove down, dropping Steve at home, then Ian, before arriving home. Introduced Dee to Fi Fi whose hair had grown while I was away. She looks more like a little girl and less like a toddler now. Dizzy is fine and it was great to be back. Nothing had exploded or malfunctioned around the house. Diz made me some lunch which Fi Fi shared, including fab blackberry crumble with the second half of the berries we'd picked in the village back on Sunday 8th. Realised I'd left my toilet bag at the Holiday Inn, Birmingham! Phoned them. It's okay, they have it.

It rained all day so we stayed in. Watched a bit of TV and went to bed at 8.00. Big mistake. Woke up at 11.00, couldn't sleep and ended up getting up, watching Dracula and writing this diary until now, which is 2.00am. Adieu.

PS thought I was going back to bed! Met Fi Fi on the landing coming the other way - "I want to come downstairs with you!" Went downstairs for another half an hour and then was emotionally blackmailed into bed with her, "...just until I'm asleep!" One hour later (3.00am) she was still awake and so I put her in our bed with Sue and went back to Fi Fi's bed. Bloody marvellous. Can't sleep with my wife even when I'm home!

Sunday 29 September *Hammersmith Odeon, London*

Mid-tour disorientation, combined with 27 pairs of eyes from the encircling fluffy toys, threw me into terror during the first few waking seconds until I remembered that I was at home in Sofie's bed – she'd swapped with me. It's common during a tour to spend your first 5 or 6 waking seconds trying to remember where you are – which country, which town, which bed you got into and, if you're really together, what day of the week it is and whether you've got a show or a day off. Waking up at home in a toddler's bedroom is, therefore, especially puzzling. I got up and spent the morning drinking coffee and eating toast. Took Fi Fi to the park for a swing - I had to dry the swing with a tea towel, following the heavy rain of yesterday.

At around 2.00 I drove into London and checked into the Gore Hotel in Kensington, just in time for the Spanish Grand Prix, which I enjoyed, relaxing on the bed with the curtains closed. I needed the peace. Mansell won.

Soundcheck at Hammersmith Odeon went well. Had my hair trimmed by

Lisa, my hairdresser from Henley, who had come over specially. She bought me a present of a jar of 'moulding mud' gel which she's currently using in the salon. I used the stuff for the show and would later discover that, when it gets in your eyes, it causes temporary blindness. The show went well despite the projector jamming and the rhythm sequencer not working during *A Collection.* I even ended up telling the joke about the nun and the blind man, while Steve R tuned the twelve-string (This was to be an omen - later that day I would feel the initial effects of blindness which were to worsen and become total by tomorrow night's show).

Backstage after the show, I met Sarah Ball (who painted the **Holidays in Eden** cover art) along with **H.I.E.** producer, Chris Neill and his wife, plus Bob & Caroline from Stanbridge Farm where we had rehearsed. Caroline said, "You'll be there forever!" to me. Wow. I wonder what she meant.

Went back to the Gore hotel bar with EMI-ers and various other chums, wives and colleagues. Took lots of pictures with my little camera. I was seeing fog and rainbows around the lights. Couldn't help wondering if someone had slipped additional substances in my drink – it was the hair gel. Went to the Up All Night Café with Steve, Nigel Luby, Lana Topham and others. Had eggs on toast and chinwags about Yes with Nigel, and about Bowie and the Psychedelic Furs with Lana. Got to bed about 5.00 in the morning having already had breakfast. Drifted off into sleep blind drunk, and woke up just plain blind!

Monday 30 September *Hammersmith Odeon – Home*

I couldn't see properly and my eyes were still stinging. Last night's spiked-drink theory gave way to the realisation/remembrance that it had all started on stage at Hammersmith. I remembered the sweat running into my eyes and how it was stinging more than usual. It must have been the 'moulding mud' hair product! On the side of the tub I could just about make out a warning about keeping it away from the eyes. Whoops. I was yet to make a bigger mistake when, during soundcheck, I bathed my eyes with Optrex. This unexpectedly and immediately made them much more painful.

By the time I was to go on stage for the second Hammersmith Odeon show my eyes were sore and streaming and the audience were no more than blurred figures. Oddly enough, I enjoyed the show more than the previous night – perhaps because of the blindness, which made it easier to get inside what I was singing. The show was fraught with problems for Steve R who had a graphic go down and broke a string during the *Easter* guitar-solo. The audience seemed relatively quiet, although I'm sure 99% of bands out there would have been delighted with the response – we're used to being spoilt.

After the show, EMI big guns Rupert Perry, Clive Swan, Mike Andrews, Steve Davies and John Walsh came back to say hello. I showered and was taken home, still in a lot of pain, by Steve (not the) Gadd, the runner, who was lovely. I couldn't see well enough to drive home myself. I climbed into bed, eyes streaming and hurting and eventually willed myself into sleep.

Tuesday 1 October *Home*

Rabbits, White Rabbits. Woke up biblically – "I can see! I can see!!" My eyes were much better. What a relief! Dizzy marched me off to the docs anyway and he gave me some antibiotic cream.

"Doctor, Doctor - I've got a strawberry growing out of my bottom"

"I'll give you some cream to put on that."

I picked Fi up from school at 12.00 and we went to the Thatched Tavern at Cheapside (near Ascot) for lunch. Got back around 3.00 and I went to bed for an hour whilst the girls went to an ante-natal and then to the park. I got up again around 4.30. A few people phoned to say they had enjoyed the show. Nice. Rondor sent me a basket of fruit, which had an accompanying card saying, 'Not bad, even for a blind man!'

Bathed Fi and put her to bed. The evening was spent watching **Morse** on the telly – an episode I hadn't seen. I find **Morse** very relaxing.

Diz went to bed at 10.30 but I hung around 'til 12.00, scribbling this diary up to date. Went to bed for a couple of hours, couldn't sleep so I got up again for an hour around 2.00. Finally got to sleep at 3.00. Somehow I'm jet lagged but I haven't been away!

Wednesday 2 October *Home*

Up at 10.30. Did my accounts and VAT Return. Picked Fi Fi up from school at 12.00. Went out in the afternoon to Windsor. Took Fi for a swing and then we all went to the Dome for a coffee. Quiet stuff. Came home, mowed the lawn, pruned the roses, had tea, got in the bath with Fi Fi and, after she was in bed, watched the football on the telly. Sue went to bed early as she gets very tired now (only 3 weeks to go). Fortunately, she still seems well.

Not much packing to do as I haven't touched my suitcase since I got back on Monday night. I'll stick a jumper in for Scandinavia.

Dreamt of lying in bed singing loudly and being given electric shocks in the face...

Thursday 3 October *Home – Rotterdam*

Up at nine-ish. At 10.30 a cab arrived and took me over to Terminal 4 (fortunately, we live quite close). Checked in and had coffee in the café with Mark and John. The flight was, of course, late, but uneventful.

Met at Schipol by Reinold (EMI rep) and a man in a minibus. Arrived at the hotel around 2.00 and went shopping for a new battery for the black watch (that's a time-piece, not a Scottish regiment). Came back at 3.00 for a solarium session, past a man with an old wooden barrel organ. Transported back to old childhood thriller-movie **Puppet on a Chain**. Solariummed and showered then we went over to the Ahoy Sports Palace which still (and I suspect always will) sounds like a tube station. Rondor had sent us all baskets of Dutch stuff (cheese, fruit, sweets, etc, which is very generous considering that I'm the only member of the band who's signed to them) and also included advocaat (which all Dutchmen seem to loathe) and lemonade so that I could make myself Snowballs. A sweet thought, bless 'em.

The show went well. High points (apart from the attendance figures) were the crowd singing *Easter, The Space* (which I sang really well – my voice having had two day's rest) and *Incommunicado* when Paul Devine lit the audience. 10½ thousand people all singing!

Afterwards, EMI cracked champagne back stage, then it was back to the hotel to drink blue things and off to bed, conscious of the dreaded early-morning call…

Friday 4 October *Rotterdam – Maidstone*

Up at 7.30 to catch a 9.30 plane (40-seater prop job – these tend to blow about a bit in the wind) to Gatwick.

Picked up in a limo by good old (young) Jason and taken to a hotel outside Maidstone. There were equipment problems at TVS i.e, the chap who had brought our equipment to TVS was there and TVS thought he wasn't etc. TV people tend not to 'interface' very well with rock n'roll people. We had lunch at the hotel and wandered down to TVS studios to rehearse tomorrow's **Motormouth** show. Midi gloves and *Dry Land* playback. Fraught with hassle and nerves, things broken, monitors not right etc. Eventually got finished mid-evening and had an early night.

Saturday 5 October *Maidstone TVS – Paris, Le Zenit*

Up at 7.30, had breakfast and went to TVS for the live TV. Couldn't believe it! – Everything worked and everyone was happy. Gabi Rosslyn, the presenter, told me *No-One Can* was one of her favourite singles – I wonder if she meant it?

With huge sighs of relief we left TVS and flew Dan Air 737 (packed, and it landed like a stone) to Paris where we were met by the European tour bus. Went immediately to bed and decided the bus and I were going to get along just fine.

Soundcheck went well. It usually does at Le Zenit – it's a great sounding stage. On the whole, you can't fuck up a good room, just as no amount of expensive technology can make a bad room sound very good. I was looking forward to getting out there on my own terms to my favourite audience.

I was not disappointed. I never felt such emotion from 4000 people. The show was sold out and they were wonderful. The whole band was in shock afterwards. Sometimes audiences are particularly enthusiastic and loud, but the Paris audience seem to pour out heart and soul as well. Nights like these make everything worthwhile and are unforgettable. One moment from a show such as this compensates for every Ford Transit van repair I struggled with – every agonising knock from steel against bone on snowy-cold days, every shitty gig I hauled my piano in and out of, every humiliation suffered in working men's clubs, EVEN the two years of pain getting my right thumb working again after our nasty little bass player tried to kill our drummer on that cruise ship in the 70s and I got in the way and almost bled to death.

Promised to send Gerard Drouot a yellow submarine. Left about 1.00ish on the bus. Went to bed and woke up in Dusseldorf.

Sunday 6 October *Dusseldorf, Phillipshalle*

Got up (or should I say out) at 10.00. We were in a car park next to the crew bus. Something was missing. Trucks! The load-in was supposed to be 8.00. The trucks arrived around 12.00 with tales of steep hills and bad traffic so we hung around at the gig and watched the show being assembled. "So that's what they all do," I thought. Took photographs of the show under construction – time lapse. Went to bed at 3.00pm. Soundcheck at 5.00.

Soundcheck went well. I was somewhat hassled by fans – they seem more insistent here in Germany. "Give 'em an inch, they take a foot and, before you know it, you haven't got a leg to stand on," as Melchett pronounced in **Black Adder**. The show was going to have to be something special not to seem a step-down from last night. Nonetheless the audience was fantastic and perhaps warmer than usual, the band played really well and the evening was a great success. There was a large record-company contingent so I imagine we did ourselves a lot of good. Peter Rieger, our German promoter, was around and seemed pleased (so the gig was probably making him plenty of dosh).

After the show I was told off for eating crew sandwiches.

Overnight to Munich.

Monday 7 October *Munich, Circuskrone*

We arrived around 10.00am. Checked into a day-room at a hotel in town and walked down to the venue. It really is a circus and although I didn't see any, there are elephants tucked away somewhere (probably in the fridge). The catering crew had set up tables outside as it was a sunny morning and while I was sitting in the courtyard awaiting breakfast, a perfect white horse, completely unaccompanied, wandered past me and into the building. It's a good job I don't take drugs – it was a pinch-yourself moment.

Before soundcheck I had a mooch round the town with Helen - Smick's fiancée - who was still with us having missed an earlier flight back to Stockholm. We had Irish coffee at a street café – very civilized. I went back to the hotel for an hour's sleep and then back to soundcheck, which was cavernous. Trish said she's made me some pockets for my new leather coat (How sweet of her!) so I gave it to her so she could sew 'em in, and dug out the Peruvian job from the wardrobe.

There were hiccups all round in the live show but it was, nonetheless, well up to standard and, from what I heard, no one went home unhappy. Although I have no doubt that the Circus Krone is a great place to see a circus, it's not a great acoustic space for rock music.

Enduring memory of the day was the support-band playing the brass coat-rails in the dressing rooms – being brass players, they had inserted mouthpieces into the coat-rails. They had a room each along the corridor and it was echoing around like a deranged symphony.

After the show I took revenge for last night's ticking off by replacing all the crew sandwich labels (they have their names on them for after the show). I wrote Steve H on all of them. Went down well…

Tuesday 8 October *Berlin, Tempodrom*

Arrived in Berlin around 8.30am and checked into the hotel. Had a bit of a kip and went out for a spot of breakfast in a street café. Later on went to the war memorial in the East German part of the city. This was, of course, a memorial to the Russian war dead. Quite a sight. Like all war memorials, a reminder of the scale of the slaughter, which always seems so pointless, looking back. Trust me to forget to take the camera.

Came back to the hotel around 2.00 and went back to bed. Rose at 4.30. Dee phoned to say that the trucks were stuck behind a car crash on the corridor road and they didn't arrive until early afternoon, so there was chaos at the gig. The Tempodrom is a tent. The design is such that there is no headroom at the back of the stage so we couldn't use drapes, and the lighting rig has been dismantled completely and redesigned. Paul Devine didn't even moan – they all just got on with it. I guess they learned to be flexible a long time ago. Fab crew.

Soundcheck was tedious – Steve R had backline problems and the whole thing felt like a pub-gig, so it was time to just relax and enjoy the show for what it is. I thought the show went well, the audience seemed older than usual and a little sedate for Berlin. The band didn't enjoy it – Steve R had flu and Mark K ripped his leather trousers on a flight case catch. After the show EMI rep, Nada, took us to a cocktail bar full of yuppies. I bolted a White Russian, and bolted!

Wednesday 9 October *Berlin:* Day Off

Had a lie in 'til lunchtime, then went looking for the Reichstag and the Brandenburg Gate. There's no trace of where the wall used to be. Beneath the gate there are East-German street vendors selling Russian paraphernalia – furry hats, badges, uniforms, army surplus watches, binoculars, babushka dolls and the inevitable brightly spray-canned pieces of concrete purporting to be fragments of the Berlin wall (who knows – but I doubt it).

Walked down the long street, which used to be divided, to the magnificent Berliner Dom domed-church and then back for coffee at the Opera café (very splendid and German-urbane, all exotic cakes and chocolates – reminded me of

Vienna). Made my way back to the hotel with babushka in pocket for Fi Fi.

Showered up and went out with the record company to a medieval German restaurant – horns of mead and seven courses of fat.

Thursday 10 October *Hamburg, CCH3*

Left the Berlin hotel at 12.00 and rattled off to Hamburg in the bus, arriving around 4.00. Made our way up through the maze of corridors at the CCH centre and finally found catering which was attended and staffed by a motley array of zombies. The crew had had a night off in Hamburg.

Soundcheck was stressful – we had decided to turn the monitors down after Berlin so everything had to be re-tweaked. After the soundcheck there was a photograph behind the mixing desk and I did 'one of those' interviews, best forgotten. Had half an hour relaxing on the bus.

The hall was different to last time – no seats and more atmosphere. The show was well-received although the band was a bit unsettled by the quiet monitors.

Friday 11 October *Copenhagen, Saga*

Arrived at the Sheraton around 9.00. Checked in and went to bed 'til 12.00. Went for a stroll which, in the end, turned out to be a four-hour walk around the town. Breakfasted at the Hard Rock Café and noticed a poster on the wall for our concert. It was a pleasant afternoon and I walked through the old town and down to the waterfront. Bought a pair of gloves and wrote postcards in a street café. Stopped to listen to a really good rhythm and blues band busking on the street. Danish rhythm and blues!?!

Arrived back at the hotel late for soundcheck and made my own way to the Saga. Soundcheck was fun – the monitors were back loud again. Had a bit of luck during the show – I fell off the stage (not realising there was no extension at the wings) during *Garden Party*. One minute I was on the stage, the next I was flat on my back on the floor looking up! Fortunately I wasn't even bruised. Kept singing, climbed back up and threw myself off the other side of stage for symmetry. It was a good night and, afterwards, Thomas from the record company was foaming at the mouth with enthusiasm. Says he'll get us on a couple festivals next year...

After the show, Pete and I went to a hotel round the corner to shower. Street-life was very seedy. People shooting-up outside video shops advertising rape and child porn. Bloody hell!

Saturday 12 October *Stockholm, Palladium*

Arrived at 8.00 and checked into the hotel. Went for a walk with John A round the old town. Had coffee in a little café and nearly bought a loud shirt for Fi Fi. John went back to the hotel and I carried on window-shopping. In NK, the department store, I fell in love with a glass bowl – it was blue and shot with dream-like Marc Chagall-ish figures floating in the air. A bit out of my price range at £4,000. Nearly bought a Swedish Monopoly but the shop-assistant wouldn't take my credit card without ID.

Bumped into Ulrika, Jenny, Anna and Helen's mum in the street. They'd driven here from Gotebörg for the show. Went back to the hotel for 140 winks. Later taken down to the show by Mike, the promoter, who wasn't even slightly Swedish but very **Eastenders**. Soundcheck went well. Didn't go back to the hotel as we had to hang around for photographs. Catering did chips! There was a shop opposite the gig with illuminated globes. How would you get one home?

The show went really well. Audience was fantastic. After the show we did a runner straight back to the hotel. Showered up, then the record label took us to a nightclub called Café Riche which was the kind of place where smooth, rich middle-aged folk go to get picked up. Not really comfortable here, so legged it to a club called The Frog, which was just closing, and then to the Café Opera 'til they threw us out at 3.00. Walked back through the old town, which was deserted and ghostly. Felt like an old scene from a Bergman movie (Ingmar, not Ingrid!). Other-worldly and quite magical. Someone was delivering newspapers to the houses on Stortorget… must have been getting late.

Sunday 13 October *Stockholm – Ludwigsburg:* Day off

Spent all day AND night on a bus.

Monday 14 October *Ludwigsburg*

Arrived around 11.00am at the venue and went to catering for breakfast. I think I've played here before with Chris de Burgh. Drove down the road to a neighbouring town, where we were to stay, and checked into the hotel. Went out and found a hairdressers and had my roots done. All my underwear is in the dressing room trunk again, so went and bought another pair so I could shower. Got back to the hotel around 2.00 and went to bed.

Woke with a start at 4.15 to discover they'd gone to the gig without me – I'd changed hotel rooms so the tour manager must have been ringing the wrong room. Went to soundcheck by cab and, during soundcheck, suffered stabbing pain in right jaw joint. Went back to the hotel and back to sleep 'til 8.00. Peter Rieger, the promoter, had arranged a doctor to check out my jaw, which was still hurting. He said it was inflamed and injected a painkiller directly under my jaw into the joint. I've never seen the band exit a dressing room so quickly. Trish, on the other hand, said, "I want to see this!" and hung around. Women!

The show went well – the audience was extremely responsive, bless 'em. After show, declined to go for a quick drink with opening act, The Violet Hour (I knew I'd end up sloshed and lost!), and went back to the hotel for another 14 hours sleep.

Tuesday 15 October *Offenbach*

Up at 11.00ish and onto the bus. Sat up front for most of the journey, which was memorable only for bad traffic. Arrived at the gig in the afternoon. There was no hotel, so much hanging about was to be had. Promoter's rep, Heiko's wife, had decided to do back and neck massage for £20, so I had one to loosen up the joints and pass a bit of time.

Did an interview with the German fan club chaps – they played me a selection of music, which I was to listen to and comment on. It was fun. The show went well. To be honest, I can't remember much about it, but it must have hit the spot because one of the Germans said he had been to quite a few shows on the tour and this was the best. After much debate over whether to leave the owl* in the dressing room, Trish decided we should keep him. Mind you, she hadn't seen the letter that came with it!

*This was a sort of tribal wood carving which I was given as a gift at the same venue two years ago. It was wrapped and accompanied by a letter from a strange young lady – definitely a potential serial-killer. We've been carrying the owl around in the dressing-room case ever since trying to find out if it's good or bad voodoo.

Wednesday 16 October *Zurich – Winterthur*

Woke up to discover the bus was on the periphery of Zurich and soon after we bundled out and up the narrow lane to the Hotel Rössli. Pete and I had stayed here earlier in the year during our fateful Swiss promo trip when the EMI rep, who was supposed to handle everything, had a drug-and-mistress-induced meltdown before our eyes and resigned from EMI rather than do the gig. His friend - a barman - ended up arriving and co-ordinating all the interviews in Geneva with amazing efficiency considering he's never done it before.

When Pete and I first arrived at Geneva airport, Customs hauled Pete in for a body-search (he always looks like he's up to something – it's just his natural body-language), no one met us at the airport but by some miracle, Pete had a piece of paper with the hotel address on it. After waiting an hour, there was still no sign of the EMI rep so we changed up some Swiss francs and took a cab to the hotel. They'd never heard of us so we had to find our own hotel. As I said, the EMI rep was in a vortex. He turned up four hours late, telling fibs, and took us to dinner with an Icelandic girl who was nuts, and everyone involved was running to the loo every twenty minutes to take more and more cocaine. I bailed out early and that was the last we saw of him. The barman did the promo, and, in the end, Gaby Weiss travelled to Geneva and rescued us. She bundled us onto a train to Zurich, and here to the Rössli where Pete was to discover he'd lost the air tickets back home (that was in the days when you had to have an air ticket to travel), so new ones had to be bought. It was an interesting couple of days. Anyway, where was I…?

Well, it was nice to be back. Checked in and went to bed, couldn't sleep, went for a walk and bought smellies and went to the gig which is in a town called

Winterthur, which is Swiss for 'Long Johns' (I might be making that up...). When I arrived it was a beautiful day so the crew were mostly outside, some juggling in the afternoon sunshine (juggling has rather caught-on during this tour). The dressing rooms were fallout shelters. The hall acoustics were 'second-to-everything' and the audience was quiet. No wonder – showtime was 7.45 and everyone must have come straight from work. The most memorable moment was towards the end when a large section of the audience shook their hands - palms facing us - whilst making a strange Zulu-like whooping noise. Very spooky. I found it disturbing and intriguing in equal measure. I nearly ran off.

Thursday 17 October *Zurich*

Typical that on the day off the weather should desert us. Grey and rainy! Nonetheless I had a good walk around and came close to buying a £400 watch! ("You should have!" said Dizzy later on the phone – bless her.)

Had lunch in a beautiful café on the Bahnhofstrasse. I had venison which is, I'm told, a very typical Zurich-Swiss thing to eat. Very nice. And Irish coffee. Must go there again if I get the chance.

In the evening I bumped into Queen drummer Roger Taylor in the hotel bar. He was in town with his band, The Cross.

Spent half the day panicking about my address book which I thought I might have lost. I'd left it on the bus.

Friday 18 October *Milan*

Got up early and bumped into Mad Jack in the breakfast room. I planned to go into town to buy the Tag watch which I didn't dare buy yesterday. Mark came with me for a stroll in the rain. Found jewellers and tried on said watch. Didn't like the look of it on my wrist so didn't buy it. Phew. At least I got it out of my system!

Went back and checked out of the hotel. Roger Taylor was in the breakfast room so I wished him luck with the show at the Volkshaus. The drive to Milan was an experience. There's a number of tunnels through various mountains – one of them is 5 km long! As we emerged on the Italian-Swiss side of the Alps, the weather changed completely to warm sunshine. Took a few photographs of mountains and lakes and went for a sleep. Woke up in Milan and went to the Cathedral Square before soundcheck.

The gig was typically Italian – overflowing toilets and no room to move, no security, and nutters wandering in and out. The show was weird. Screaming girls! It was like being in New Kids on the Block.

Afterwards, I had a big row with Ian who lost his rag with me for moaning at John Arnison. Both John and Paul, (the tour manager) had left me on my own amidst a scrum of near-hysterical Italian fans and I was merely pointing out that one of them should have been on hand instead of sitting on the tour bus chilling out. It was my first ding-dong with Ian. But I hope it's the last. It was a face to face confrontation and he nearly hit me.

Saturday 19 October *Lauzanne*

Arrived at the hotel Jan at 7.30 where I de-bunked and checked in. Went straight to bed and didn't wake up until 3.15 in the afternoon.

Soundcheck was at 4.00 so didn't have time for a walk. Damn. After soundcheck I had an interview with Peirre-Michel Meier, the balmy Swiss DJ. I like him, although he seems determined to stitch me up...

The audience was first rate – you could feel the French influence (heart and soul) and we had a terrific evening.

After the show, Daniella and Christian took us out for drinks to this sort-of-cocktail bar with a Latin-American band. Had a couple of beers and chatted to Bruno (a journalist from whence I forget). Then it was adieu and onto the bus and into the sack.

Ian came upstairs and apologised to me for losing his rag in Milan. Bless him.

Sunday 20 October *Brussels:* Day off

Got up around 9.30. I hadn't slept well on the bus so I went downstairs and chatted to Ray who was driving. Belgium is not at its best when viewed from the motorway on a grey day, so it was a boring journey apart from Ray and Tony's good-humoured banter. Ray said he was once driving home for Christmas and had to pull up to avoid hitting a turkey which was walking on the motorway. He opened the door and it got in and sat next to him all the way home. He arranged an appointment with the local butcher but later changed his mind and set the bird free. I wonder how long it lasted?

Arrived at the Sheraton, checked in and ordered lunch. Went for a walk in the rain and later bumped into the Violets (The Violet Hour - our opening act). Had a beer with them and walked them all back to the Sheraton in time for the cocktail party I had instigated at 5 o'clock. Took photographs of the impressive collection of drinks. Got sloshed and went to bed too early to witness Doris fighting with her boyfriend, Martin (Violets guitarist) gaffer-taped to a chair and left out in the street unconscious, and Privet who broke one finger and had eight stitches in another while rolling down the street on a cable-drum. Just a quiet affair really.

We were later billed quite a lot of money by the Sheraton for replacement of a hotel room carpet. Lord knows what they all got up to after I'd gone to bed!

Monday 21 October *Brussels, Ancien Belgique*

Had determined lie-in until 11 o'clock. Woke up not remembering going to bed but feeling, nonetheless, not bad considering the cocktail party last night.

Showered, dressed and went walkies. Bought Fi Fi a jacket and jeans and bought Crompton (my new pet-name for Nial) some shoes. Couldn't help buying chocolates for Diz although she probably won't eat them.

Came back to the hotel around 3.00 then off to soundcheck at the Ancien Belgique. Painless enough. We had to meet a roomful of competition-winners at 6.00 so we stayed at the venue until showtime which was early at 7.45!

Last night of the tour was accompanied by traditional jolly-japes – the crew had replaced some of my *Collection* slides with dodgy porno pics and I was unable to control the projector to stop them. During *Incommunicado* they all filed on like Tiller Girls and did high-kicks. The audience were great and everyone enjoyed themselves – even the band! After the show I showered at the hotel and left all my underwear in the dressing room trunk.

Tuesday 22 October *Brussels – Home*

Got up, packed, checked out, went to the airport, bought socks, flew to Heathrow and arrived home late afternoon. Dished out gifts to my girls. Sue's mum was at our house. Everyone was relieved I'd got home before Sue had the baby, which is due tomorrow. Went to bed early but…

Wednesday 23 October *Home – Chertsey Hospital*

Was woken at 4.30 am. Sue thinks she's going to have the baby!! Drove to St Peter's Chertsey and checked her into the labour-ward. Spent the next six or seven hours waiting and dozing in a chair while poor Dizzy underwent the rigours of the early stages of labour. By around 11.00 she is too far down the line to go home but her contractions have nearly stopped. Wendy, the midwife decides to induce her, but to first break her waters. I go with Diz to a shower after this, while we're in the shower, she starts having painful contractions so we have to hurry back to the labour room. Everything goes okay for a while but then the contractions ease again and they decide to connect a drip to keep things going.

At the advanced stage of labour, the baby's heart rate drops and I sense the staff becoming nervous. The baby is born 10 or 15 minutes later (Well done Dizzy!) but they can't get him breathing… People start appearing and my nerves are shredded. Dizzy hasn't really noticed that there is a problem. They pump him with oxygen and eventually take him from the labour ward to Special-care baby unit (SBCU). When Dizzy is able to move, she's wheel-chaired down with me to an office where a doctor ushers us in. He tells us that the baby didn't breathe for 7 minutes after birth and that there's a possibility that this would cause brain-damage. Unfortunately there's no way of knowing at this stage. I feel my insides turn to water. I've never known distress like it. Diz and I stare into space. I ask the doctor how soon we'll know for sure and he says it might take several months before we can be certain. When we get out of there I try to hug Dizzy but it's difficult – she's physically beaten-up and wheelchair bound. She's also in a state of post-labour exhaustion and I don't think she's really quite 'with it'. I'm not sure she's registering the gravity of what we've just been told. We go back to a ward and the nurses make her 'comfortable'.

I go home and have to tell her mum. I have never been particularly close to Sue's mum so it's particularly painful to cry in front of her, but I can't help myself.

PS (2014) I never wrote down any more for a week or so. I wasn't in a frame-of-mind to do it. It was an awful few days going back and forth to the hospital and to see our little new-born Nial in the SCBU, covered in tubes and monitors and wonder how his life was going to unfold. On the third or fourth day I arrived in SCBU alone to find the chief paediatrician holding him in her arms. This was the first time I had seen him outside of the incubator. I asked how he was doing and she said one of the most wonderful things I've ever heard: "Don't quote me on it, but between you and me, I don't think there's anything wrong with this baby."

I almost fainted with gratitude. We still couldn't be certain, but this was an enormous, albeit guarded, relief. I felt like proposing to her on the spot. As it turns out, at the time of publication, Nial is 22 years old and, apart from a certain (inherited!) mild eccentricity, his brain works perfectly and he's a fine young man. You might have seen him helping me out on stage where he's been known to look after my backline, radio-midi-cricket bat and pass me the occasional guitar and bottle of Beck's. He has a great sense of rhythm and is currently very serious about his drumming.

Saturday 2 November *Home – Lisbon, Pavillion Charles Lopez*

Up at 8.00 and a tearful goodbye from Dizzy. Fi Fi takes it a lot better and I climb into a cab at 9.00 to Heathrow. On the plane Mark's listening to a live tape of Cry No More, which is plainly very funny. Roy seems to be on form. During the flight, Ian passes me a press-cutting from **The Daily Express** which congratulates me on the birth of a "bouncing baby boy, Nial" ('wobbling' would have been nearer the truth).

The hotel in Lisbon is opposite some vast new building, still under construction, which I later discover to be a bank. Must be the biggest bank on God's earth. It looks more like a university. We all have a walk about and coffee. Soundcheck is painless. The hall is cavernous, but the sound out-front seems good to me. The venue is a 200-year old convent and is ornately decorated with columns, statues and, of course, tiles (This IS Portugal – they like a tile.) It looks more like an old bath-house or brothel than a rock-venue. The record company takes us out for an omelette, which takes AGES to arrive and, back at the venue the crowd are in and it looks like a bull-fight! It's like a scaled-down Wembley arena with side-seating terraced upwards.

The show is terrific. The crowd warm and enthusiastic. Considering the band haven't been here for 6 years and that it's my first time, the reaction from the crowd is mind-boggling. I enjoy the show more than I can remember in quite a while (Paris?) despite becoming hoarse half-way through.

Sunday 3 November *Porto Coliseum*

Rose at 9.30. Discovered I'd left my toilet bag in the bar last night. Eventually traced it to Dee's room. 1 day in and I've already lost something! Had breakfast with Pete on the 9th floor overlooking Lisbon which, from our vantage point, looks like it's been thrown there. Unfinished-yet-inhabited grey concrete mish-mash architecture (or lack of it) interspersed with big-money skyscrapers. Rather like Sao Paolo actually (same language).

Checked out of the hotel to discover my phone bill was about a fiver. Nice surprise as Steve R says it's the most expensive country in the world to phone from. I wonder where he was staying when he came to that conclusion?

Flew to Porto, which is further north, greyer and rainier than Lisbon. The venue is a large theatre. It's been raining on the drum kit but the really bad news is low ticket sales. After soundcheck I'm taken to a little restaurant round the corner. Washing is hanging to dry everywhere and the room we eat in looks like a Mexican chapel! Steak and eggs.

By showtime there's only 500 people in, but that relaxes us and we have a great show. My voice is in top form and I can't remember singing *Dry Land* better. I narrowly avoid disaster when I throw the mic-stand up and it goes backwards and nearly takes out the T1 (my keyboard/piano thing).

After the show I shower on the third floor. Hot and hot running water. That's a first. Back at the hotel Jack does owl impressions and nearly falls out the window. 17 floors up.

Monday 4 November *Porto – Madrid:* Day off

Up at 8.30!! Feeling iffy after last night's Brandy Alexanders. Check out and go to Porto airport. On the flight to Madrid, Ian plays me last night's desk-tape which sounds great. They ran a DAT as well which I think we might as well release next time we need live footage.

No one turns up to meet us at Madrid airport so we take two cabs to the hotel which is very pleasant. The Spanish really seem to have their act together these days. Went for a short walk and had lunch with Steve R in the hotel restaurant, which is where I am right now. I think I'll go and have forty winks – I'm knackered! Sleep 'til 7.00. Get up and go out at 7.30 to eat. Dee, Jack and myself go walk about and eventually end up in an area known as Plaza Santana which is lively and full of bars. We eventually find a good seafood restaurant and I have lobster for the second time in my life. The first time was at Virginia Beach USA just after puncturing my face with a jet-ski. We return to the hotel and later, try to find the venue but it's closed, so we go to another club. Ian's stoned, and gives the cab driver £40.00 of Mark's money for a £4.00 fare and tells him to keep the change. Spend the rest of the evening being ripped-off everywhere and eventually get to bed at around 5.00am.

Tuesday 5 November *Madrid:* Day off

Up at 12.30 for lunch with the record label at 1.30. We all assemble in the lobby and at 2.00, Raphael, Kiké and Maité turn up complaining about the traffic. They take us to a beautiful restaurant called Armstrongs and we eat, drink and get merry until around 5.00. We have the use of minibus and driver, Manuel. He has the supernatural knack of appearing like a genie whenever he's required. He does so and takes us back to the hotel.

I go walking the streets for a couple of hours and return and call my girls. Good news! Dizzy's feeling much better and sounds like her old self, or should I say 'new self'. Fi Fi is fine and says she hasn't been crying for me. She's proud of herself, bless her. I go back to bed 'til 9.00 as the indefatigable Raphael is coming at 10.30 to show us the Madrid nightlife. He takes us to 3 bars which are all unique. The first has a carved wooden ceiling like figureheads from an old galleon and old tiled walls with 30's lithographs. The second is ornate Arabic with a great sound-system. The third is art-nouveau-mental with little cubby holes underground joined together by meandering corridors. I chat with Miguel, Laur and the bar-staff, who are friendly and generous with the measures.

We return to the hotel care of Manuel who appears out of thin air with the minibus and I almost make it into the lift... but Mark's famished, so I accompany him and Ian back out into the street and we take a cab to a café which serves us omelette, shish kebab and roast potatoes at ten past three in the morning! We return, stuffed and ashamed and I sleep 'til 11.00.

Wednesday 6 November *Madrid, Canciller*

Yeah – 11.00. Go downstairs to the coffee shop and write all this.

We had made arrangements to meet Raphael at the hotel at 1.00 to go to the record-label but he doesn't turn up, so it's back to the hotel café for a club sandwich and then back to bed for another hour before soundcheck.

The club is small and the on-stage sound very loud and awful. There's a press-conference but I'm sure the journos end up with nothing on their tape-recorders except the screeching of the barriers being dragged into place round the mixing desk. Return to the hotel for more sleep – it's a late show, on at 10.30.

Manage to cope with the sound during the show despite Grubby being off the stage and out of view. Great crowd. Some good moments – *Waiting to Happen* was special. All in all another victory – we seem to be giving them what they want.

Thursday 7 November *Madrid – Barcelona, Zeleste*

Up at 9.00 to check out at 9.30. Into the minibus and off to the airport. Flew to Barcelona and was met at the airport by Martin, a freelance English PR hippy and regular geezer. He accompanied us to the hotel Condor where we checked in and had lunch (steak and chips) care of EMI expenses. Went for a stroll round Barcelona with Jack – there's more evidence of wealth here than Madrid, more shops selling good quality gear etc. Oh yeah, Barcelona airport deserves a mention. Its Terminal building is huge and white, there's a feeling of space, palm-trees inside mirror a line of palms outside, visible through the huge glass wall. My favourite airport so far. Jack and I got a bit lost and arrived back in time for departure to soundcheck.

Chaos ensued from the moment we arrived. First, a press-conference (attended by journalists for whom 1980 had yet to happen); second (and third), two TV crews who weren't sure what they wanted to do, or how. Fourth, apparent apathy from John Arnison in response to Smick's myriad problems, especially the Italian promoter. This resulted in the time between late soundcheck and show being filled with band meetings and tense phone calls. No wonder I missed the beginning of *Splintering Heart.* They were televising it!

Friday 8 November *Barcelona – Nice, Theatre de Verdure*

Woke at 12.00 and checked out of the hotel Condor after frantic consumption of coffee on the first floor. Stole my very last apple-sweet from reception and climbed aboard the minibus to the airport. The flight at 2.00 was delayed 'til 3.00 and we arrived in Nice at 4.00. I had to run back to the plane for my sunglasses which had fallen out of my jacket.

Arrived at the hotel Opera at about 4.30, checked into the smallest room of the tour so far, and took a walk along the sea. Bought postcards and queued for 20 minutes at the bureau-de-poste for stamps.

Nice wins the prize for most radical difference of stage-sound from soundcheck (cavernous) to show (studio-dead!). My voice was not at its best so I had to struggle to stave off frustration/depression during the gig. I was helped no end, however, by what I have come to regard as the typical French audience – enthusiastic, soulful, incredibly loud and touchingly emotional. Gerard Drouot, our promoter, had made the journey from Paris. I listed our promoters around the world and told him, in all honesty, he stood out as the only real gentleman. I hope he doesn't doubt my sincerity. He later invited me to Paris to stay whenever I have free time. What a diamond. Gerard bought the band a drink or two at the Meridien hotel bar after the show and I eventually collapsed into my cabin-sized bed around 3.00. It's nice in Nice.

Saturday 9 November *Nice:* Day off

Woke at 12.00 to realise we were still in Nice. Dee had checked out the trains and the only alternative to the 7.00-in-the-morning to Pisa is the 7.00-in-the-evening! Got up and out, and posted a few cards. Walked along the sea and into town. After much mooching in glorious sunshine and fresh autumn air, I settled down to pizza (the best pizza I can ever remember having, and better than anything I sampled subsequently in Italy) and coffee on the Ave. Felix Faure, beside the fountains and palm trees, and wrote this!

Spent the rest of the day wandering round the town or sitting by the sea. I could definitely live here. We left the hotel at 6.00 accompanied by a stunning sunset topped by a silver crescent-moon. There was some confusion at the station until we realised that the dubious pieces of paper that Dee had been given were, in fact, train tickets to Pisa. The train wasn't until 20.10 so we found a restaurant at the station that sold us curious cartons of stew which gets hot when you pull a tab underneath. We consumed them later on the train and it wasn't bad! When the ticket collector pulled back the sliding door to ask to see tickets, both Mark and I were 'owling' on the luggage racks. He wasn't amused. And after we'd gone to so much trouble!

Arrived at Pisa at 3.00 in the morning! The hotel was no distance from the famous leaning tower so we went for a quick walk before retiring.

Sunday 10 November *Pisa, Theatre Politeama (Cascina)*

Woken around 1.00 by a call from Mark who was going for a walk. Promised I'd be down in fifteen minutes but didn't make it as I needed to shower, and phone my girls.

Later bumped into Mark and Pete in the square. Paid my 5000 lire and had a look round the domed tower. I didn't find it particularly interesting, other than structurally. All amazing stuff when you consider its age (12th century). Everything in the square, including the church, looks like it has suffered from subsidence of the ground beneath it, even during construction. Hence the lack of right angles anywhere. I walked up into the town centre, over the river and along the street markets selling bric-a-brac. I was attracted to some of the glass lampshades but didn't feel inclined to barter in a language and a currency I can't understand. Had lunch in a back street family restaurant. Everyone was having Sunday lunch (pasta, pizza) with their kids and seemed conscious of my alien status. Friendly though.

The venue was a bit like a bus-garage. The audience was good (about 900) although it was a cold place and no one removed their coats. Mad Jack had a few brain seizures during the gig and was a bit depressed afterwards. We drove back to the hotel to a welcoming party outside. Signed a few bits and bobs and went to bed.

Monday 11 November *Pisa – Genoa*

Up at 10.00. It took an age to check out of the Hotel Duomo so I bought a few postcards and wrote them in the morning sunshine. We took cabs to the airport and picked up a couple of estate cars which are to form our transport for the rest of this leg of the tour. The drive to Genoa was uneventful. I bought an Italian Monopoly at a motorway sevices. Genoa seemed worthy of a more thorough inspection than I was capable of. Sandra from EMI press faxed me a **Daily Express** piece from the previous Saturday along with some draft tabloid questions about Christmas. I spent a couple of hours thinking of the answers... although you wouldn't know it.

The venue had been changed at the last minute from the original theatre to a cinema-ish theatre round the corner. At the venue the crew were shaking their heads in dismay on account of the theatre manager who was nervous about the presence of a rock-band in his beloved Gaumont. Needless to say, he thought the soundcheck was too loud and he was expecting a riot as we later discovered during the second song of the set when a line of uniformed armed police positioned themselves along the front of the stage – backs to us, facing the audience. Terrific. After that, both band and audience lost their sparkle.

I returned to the hotel after the show to be treated with disdain by the night staff. Had a row. Complained to the management in the morning. I left Genoa thinking I'd be in no hurry to return.

Tuesday 12 November *Genoa – Rome, Palladium*

Spent all day driving to Rome. Arrived at the American Palace Hotel ('Armenian Poultice' would have flattered it) at 6.00 and left immediately for the show. Once again, the Italian promoter (either by reasons of no choice or otherwise) had 'done it' to us. There had never been a rock show held here before. What started out as a 9 o'clock show became a 9.15 show and then a 9.30 show. Apparently the audience weren't in the auditorium because of flooding in the foyer following a leak (we never found out whose). This was to be one of the most disappointing shows I've done with Marillion. The audience was a long way from the band and, as a result of the hall-shape and follow-spot positions, I couldn't see the crowd at all. I assume it was the same for the whole band. I could have been facing a black wall. If there was any crowd noise, we couldn't hear it from the stage. Before *Sunset Town* I downed a beer in an attempt to sort out my attitude but it didn't help and I came off stage pretty depressed. Went back to the Armenian Poultice and went to bed.

Apparently the crew ended up showering in John Arnison's room having got him out of bed at 2.30.

Wednesday 13 November *Rome – Venice:* Day off

Up at 9.30 to check out at 10.00 with Steve R and John A for the drive to Venice.

The weather was lousy and the drive uneventful.

Finally arrived at the hotel Michelangelo around 3.30 and discovered, to my surprise, that the staff were friendly and the rooms were very pleasant. Flowers had been placed in my room for Sue who was arriving imminently from England. Went out looking for a bottle of Jack Daniels for Trevor by way of a present for services rendered fixing my midi gloves. Couldn't find any so returned around 4.30 wondering what had happened to Dizzy. When I got to my room the phone rang and there she was, calling me from Venice. Her bus from the airport went through Mestre, where the hotel is situated, but she'd not expected me to have arrived yet and, not wishing to spend a few hours in a hotel alone, she'd stayed on the bus and gone to Venice. Quite understandable, but it was frustrating to have her so close and have to wait even longer to be with her. I was reluctant to go out and get a bus to Venice now so she said she'd return to Mestre once she'd had a cup of coffee.

Someone told me where I could get hold of a bottle of JD so I went back out and bought one for Trevor. When I got back Diz still hadn't arrived, so I had a couple of beers in the bar. Sue finally arrived at 6.30 so we had a couple of drinks and later went down to eat at the hotel restaurant.

PS This was typical of the kind of a day. These days, now we all have mobile phones, this just wouldn't have happened. Sue and I would have organised our day by text message while I was travelling from Rome. Back then, you had to wait. Mobiles and the internet have made it so much easier to tour the world and remain close to those we love. Easy to take it all for granted now, but I remember how alienated Sue and I quickly became when I was away. It was tough.

Thursday 14 November *Dolo, Venice Theatre Excelsior*

Had a bit of trouble getting up, owing to slight hangover. We managed to get out about 12.00 to catch the bus into Venice for my first visit to the city. Sue, of course, had been yesterday. We disembarked at the Plaza Roma and, armed with Dizzy's previous experience, made our way to the water-bus quay and caught the barge to St. Mark's Square. There's no describing Venice – you have to go or you have to watch **Don't Look Now**. There's a unique atmosphere to the place - an undercurrent of drowning gothic history which unsettles me somehow despite the beauty of the place. Today was foggy and chilly, and mist sat upon the surface of the jade green water. I'm glad I saw Venice like this rather than in the bright sunshine of later visits.

We had coffee and toast in St Mark's Square – not bad for £10.00! Walked through to the Grand Canal and got lost among the tangly maze of back streets and back canals. Took quite a lot of photographs. Resisted the temptation to buy Venetian glass or clothes from the myriad clothes shops. After a couple of hours we made our way back to the quayside for the water-bus back to Plaza Roma where the buses leave across the long bridge which is the only link across the lagoon to mainland Italy. Had more coffee in a café by Plaza Roma and photographed the biggest sausage I've ever seen.

Back to the hotel for the departure to soundcheck. Crew complaining about the size of the towels in Italy etc. Once again, the gig was strange. Lots of men in ties and women in expensive clothes. Where does the promoter find them?!

After the show, went back to the Michelangelo to receive a bottle of Champagne care of the hotel staff. Went straight to bed. Dizzy has an early start tomorrow.

Friday 15 November *Venice – Locarno*

Dizzy's alarm went off at 8.00 and she rose, showered and kissed me bye-bye at 8.30 to catch a flight home to Heathrow. I went back to sleep and rose later to check out of the Michelangelo around 10.30. Said fond farewells to the friendly and helpful staff and climbed into the car with John and Steve to drive north for Locarno.

The weather was rainy and grey. I slept in the back seat for much of the journey. We arrived in Locarno mid-afternoon and checked into Grand Hotel Locarno – decayed splendour! Lovely (I like decayed splendour). My room was as big as a flat – one double, one single bed, sofa, chest of drawers and two French windows onto a balcony overlooking the town.

Went out for a mooch about and bumped into Steve R so we had lunch. Mozzarella and tomato. Bought moccasins for Nial and returned to the hotel for a power-sleep (Jack's latest concept) in order to be ready for 8.00 when we're being taken out by Mark Lambelet's wife, Janna. Sweet of her to bother. Mark has sent apologies but he's promoting a Ray Charles gig tonight elsewhere. Brother Ray… a shame we can't get to that.

Went down to the bar where Louise Veys has arrived (no-one's really sure why – there's no promo to do. God knows how she gets her expenses past Neil Cox back at EMI!). We somehow lose Dee (or he loses us!) on the way out of the hotel, and go down the road to an Italian, where I have salmon and leave my sweatshirt (I get it back the next day). We then go to a club (Pirate) which is empty but the owner is gracious and stands me a free beer or two. Just as well, 'cause he's charging £7.00 for 'em. Walk home. Get lost. Eventually find a cab. Cabs are very hard to find here…

Saturday 16 November *Locarno, Palazzo Fevi*

Had a lie-in and rose at 1.00, opening my curtains to stunning views of the Swiss mountains and Lake Locarno. Wow. Ran into Jack down in reception who announced he was about to drive up the mountain and have a look. Dee came too and drove while Mark and I enthused until half-way up when Dee's fear of heights overtook him and he stopped the car and got out! Charitably we abandoned him and carried on up – Mark driving – until we were in snow with

Locarno far below. After 20 minutes the road ended, where the snow-ploughman had decided it must, with a 4ft wall of snow in which Jack took great pleasure burying the front end of the car. We jumped out, jumped about and took photographs before returning down the mountain, picking Dee up (none the worse for exposure) on the road down.

Back at the hotel, presents were arriving in my room courtesy of the Swiss record label, EMI Suisse. The word was out that I had recently become a dad again and Daniela, bless her, had done the honours.

The venue was big (5000 capacity) and empty (500 people) but the band were relaxed and I was singing well, so for us, the show was a success. Mark, the promoter, however, took a bit of a hammering financially (I heard he lost 15 grand) but took it well and came out to dinner with us after the show. What a gent. We went on to a club called Alcatraz which wasn't bad. Didn't stay long.

Sunday 17 November *Locarno – Vienna:* Day off

Up at 10.00 for a 10.30 departure from the Grand Hotel Locarno and the LONG drive to Vienna. The road over and under the Swiss Alps was long and winding, but the views were breath-stopping. Up to 18 inches of snow at the side of the road, log cabins, mountain peaks. There were little volcano-shaped cones of snow which peppered the fields. I later realised that they were fir trees. It was a pity we couldn't have stopped the car to take in the view at a more leisurely pace but we had a 10-hour journey ahead.

We stopped briefly in Lichtenstein and I ran up the road to find the border office so we could get Lichtenstein stamps on our passports. It's one of the world's smallest countries (sixth smallest apparently after the Vatican, Monaco, Nauru, Tuvalu and San Marino). After dark the journey really seemed interminable through snow, sleet and rain and we eventually arrived somewhat weary and frazzled at the SAS Palais Hotel, Vienna at 9.00pm to a warm welcome from the friendliest hotel staff ever (thank you Dorena, thank you Wolfgang) and given a double-magnum of Champagne care of EMI. John Arnison bought us dinner at the hotel (thank you Hit & Run) and the monster bottle of Champagne was offered around the handful of people in the bar to, amongst others, Diedre (a ballerina) and her partner Harris (PR director of the Vienna State Opera). I got talking to them via Bela, the bar piano-player. After a while, Harris invited me to be his guest at the next performance of the Opera on Wednesday. Can't go of course – we'll be home in England. By way of consolation Diedre invited Mark and myself to sit-in on the rehearsal of *The Nutcracker* ballet the following morning at the State Opera House. Bloody hell - what a privilege.

Monday 18 November *Vienna, Ca Zelt*

Woken by Jack at 11.15.

Showered and walked across Vienna to the Opera Haus. Diedre was as good as her word and had left a pass, along with instructions, at the stage-door. We took the lift up 4 floors and walked to the end of the long corridor. I was a little unsettled to discover that this was a rehearsal in a white rehearsal room full of ballerinas and there was nowhere to hide. Mark and I stuck out like, well, two blokes in jeans in a room full of tutus. We were ushered into the room and seated next to the piano player who, apart from the old genius directing the girls, was the only other man in the room. We sat transfixed and silent as the ballerinas were shuffled into their starting, and finishing positions, and then witnessed the endearing and rare spectacle of some of the world's best ballet dancers 'getting it wrong'. In order to avoid the 11 separate signatures necessary to officially allow us into the rehearsal Diedre had told the director we were her brothers! Amazing.

The rest of the day was spent (after a quick, but respectful, mooch round St. Stephen) being interviewed being interviewed at the hotel and then off to soundcheck and an early show at 7.30! Initial fears of slack attendance were dispelled by stage time whereupon a respectably large crowd had gathered. They were initially cool in a curious sort of way, but the band was on form and, for me, this was one of the most rewarding shows of the tour so far. By the end of the show, the place was jumping. After the trials and tribulations of Italy, this was a long-awaited reward. Went to dinner with Hans, the MD of EMI here. He'd financed the gig!

Tuesday 19 November *Vienna – Home*

Woken by someone knocking on my door in the middle of the night. It turned out to be 9.00 in the morning so I got up, had breakfast and wrote some postcards. Constantly interrupted by various members of the hotel staff thanking me for last night's show and generally being sweet. Given cake. Signed guestbook. Cost me a fortune to check out, but never mind.

Had a funny turn on the aeroplane home. Broke a sweat and turned green. Arrived in Heathrow clutching sick-bag, but escaped unscathed (and unsoiled). Phew. Got home, went to bed, and came back down an hour later feeling much better and went to the chip shop.

Up half the night with insomnia and awake the other half with children. Woof.

Wednesday 20 November *Home*

Staggered out of bed at 8.45 to take Fi Fi to school. When she finished at 12.00 we went to Windsor to 'Old Macdonald's' for a burger and a bit of shopping. Hung about 'til around 4.00 – coffee at The Dome etc.

Thursday 21 November

Caught up with a bit of paperwork and took the CD Walkman to the Sony service centre in Staines. Diz and team were at Donna's for a couple of hours.

Friday 22 November

Spent all morning waiting for the rug in the back room to be returned from the cleaners. Went to Kingston with the team to get the answering machine repaired and the phone swapped. Had coffee in the café at Next and drove home.

Saturday 23 November

Up at 7.30 with Hargreaves and Crompton. Fed little Nial and changed him. He peed on the sofa and then threw up all over himself while I was attending to the aforementioned. Didn't seem to bother him much. Dizzy got up at 8.30 and took Fi to ballet along with her friend Julie from round the corner.

Spent most of the day feeling a bit strange and depressed. I think I'm going down with something…

Went to the launderette in Egham to dry some clothes (our washer isn't tumble-drying).

Went to bed in the afternoon from 2.00 'til 4.00. Took Fi to the park on the green at around 4.30… it was already dark. Had tea, watched telly. Went to bed. Videoed Woody Allen's **Bananas**.

Sunday 24 November

Up at 8.00 with Hargreaves. Drank coffee and watched TV until 10.00-ish. When Diz got up I went back to bed 'til around 12.00. Got up and went to the pub with the team. Had steak & kidney pie and chips, and a tonic water. Came home. Sofie went to Bessie (next door) for a couple of hours and I went to bed again.

Got up at 4.30 and festered around. All I seem to do is sleep at the moment. At one point during the early afternoon I started work on a list of possible names for our studio-to-be *(shown here on page 12).*

Monday 25 November

Up at 8.00 with Hargreaves. Got us both dressed and took her to school. Came home, had a bath, drank coffee and made a compilation tape for the car to replace the ones I lost in Brussels. Drove to Aylesbury to meet band, crew and John A at what looks set to become The Racket Club, i.e. our storage, rehearsal and recording facility. At the moment it's a large room made of breeze blocks on a small industrial estate in a field. The metamorphosis to some kind of useful sound facility begins in earnest during December. I seem to be the only member of the band who's less than enthusiastic. I feel I may well end up alienated by the distance between it and home, which is about 50 miles.

Got home around 4.15 to discover the washer fixed! Hoorah! Watched telly, cuddled Crompton, serviced the vacuum cleaner etc. Went to bed.

Tuesday 26 November

Up around 9.00. Fi Fi and Dizzy were out during the morning at playschool and pottery, respectively. I spent ALL morning trying to iron my white silk shirt. Nial kept going berserk – he's not happy unless he's being cuddled… just like his dad really.

When the girls got back I still hadn't finished my ironing and eventually abandoned the project. In the afternoon I went to the local hairdressers to get blackened, and then drove to Rondor to have a pint or two with Stuart Hornall and John Arnison. Much hot air and cold beer until around 10.00.

Wednesday 27 November *Home – Munich*

Got up with Hargreaves at 7.30. Packed a bag. Dizzy got up with Nial at 8.00 and a car came for me at 8.30. Off to Terminal 2 for a day in Munich.

Fog at Heathrow meant we were delayed and still on the tarmac at 12.15. Arrived in Munich and went straight to the TV studio for 1st rehearsal at 3.00. The day was spent sitting about (unable to go to the hotel which was too far away) killing time between rehearsals, which were two hours apart and there were three of them. I sent Chris, our driver, off in search of a German Monopoly and drank hundreds of cups of coffee.

Met Bonnie Tyler who was also on the bill. She seems like a nice girl and hasn't aged noticeably since… when was it?… 1980? Finally got the show out of the way (I don't like TV playbacks) and drove back to the Hilton to check in.

Bernd from EMI took us to a viby Mexican restaurant nearby where I got talking to Willi Bogner and his Brazilian wife, Sonja. Willi is a big star in Germany – he's a stunt-skier and did all the James Bond movies. He's got his own fashion label – sort of stylish sportswear – simply called Bognor. Hilarious of course, if you're British, but I didn't tell him. They were lovely people and I talked to them for so long that when I got back to the table I'd missed the meal. Wasn't really hungry anyway. Sonja used to go out with Micky Finn – the other half of T Rex who is now no more (drugs). I was surprised to hear of his death. It didn't seem very long since I was talking to him on the set of the TV show **The Tube** back in 1984. He seemed fit and healthy then. Went back to the hotel for a quick drink in the bar, and off to bed.

Thursday 28 November

Up at 9.00 with something in my eye. Couldn't find it. Went back to bed and rose at 10.00 to check out at 10.30.

Had coffee in the Hilton lobby and was mini-bussed to Munich airport to fly home. Fog at Heathrow left us delayed on the tarmac in Munich until the time of writing… which is ten past one.

Finally got clearance to leave Munich. Arrived at Heathrow to no fog and was given immediate clearance to land!

Saw Ringo Starr come through Arrivals trailing a small bag on wheels and looking fed-up. I think he may be smaller than me!

Friday 29 November

Up at half seven with Nial and Hargreaves. Diz got up around 9.00 and took Fi to "workshop" while I looked after Nial, who was unsettled and irritable. When he finally quietened down, I watched the first 20 minutes of **Apocalypse Now** until the girls returned.

In the afternoon I had an hour in bed. Still feeling ropey. Rearranged the back room (again). After Hargreaves went to bed, I hired **Room with a View** from the video shop. Very **Brideshead** and fairly dull. I'm finding it hard to relax.

Saturday 30 November

Up at half seven, again, with Sofie. Around 9.30 a man came to value the house. The news wasn't good. It's now worth the same as we paid for it, despite all the work we've done and the small detail of a new roof! We buggered about for 2 hours trying to get out of the house (as only people with babies can understand) then drove for an hour to Oxfordshire to check out the Housing market. We're going to have to move out there to be nearer to Marillion's new studio. Neither of us want to. We like living in Englefield Green. We ended up (after stopping for late pub-lunch at The Fox, Farthinghoe) in Brackley – a small town in Northamptonshire. Saw some interesting properties at almost-affordable prices and drove home.

Went to the video shop and hired **Pretty Woman**. Very sweet.

I have arranged to view properties around Banbury and Brackley tomorrow, but I think we'll cancel as it's such a long way and we haven't even put our house on the market yet.

Sunday 1 December

Up at 7.40 with Fi clutching Postman Pat advent calendar. Took Nial downstairs so Diz could have a lie-in. Chaos until 11.00 when she appeared. I promptly went back to bed until 1.30. I think my cold is worsening.

Got up, had a bath and long debate about moving house. Dizzy doesn't want to move away, but I need somewhere to write. It looks like a conservatory is the solution – I'll get onto it tomorrow. Didn't go out apart from a bit of leaf-sweeping around the paths. Went to bed with Lemsips.

Monday 2 December

Got up with Hargreaves at 7.30. Had breakfast and phoned a man about conservatories. He's coming to have a look on Wednesday.

When everyone was up we all piled into the car and drove to London for lunch at the Hard Rock Café followed by a visit to Santa on the third floor at Selfridges. For once the traffic was below the pain-threshold and we found somewhere to park without being clamped. The Hard Rock is decorated for Christmas and a Christmas tree of unfeasibly large proportions stands outside once again. Drove home.

Darryl Way popped round to meet Nial for the first time, and we had an hour in The Beehive.

Tuesday 3 December

Up at 8.00. Took Sofi to school and Diz to Staines where she was potting.

Drove to London with small passenger to pick up Sarah Ball's original painting for the **Holidays in Eden** album cover. The band had graciously given me first refusal on it so I have arranged for her to frame it for me. Got stuck in the horrendous traffic in the city. I was supposed to pick up Hargreaves at 12.00 but I was still at St. Pauls at 11.40. The traffic eased once I got to the Embankment and I managed to get back to Egham for just after 12.10. Picked Sofi up and dropped the painting home, went back to Staines and we joined Dizzy for Xmas potters buffet. Chatted to Sue Bradley about her daughter who won't sleep! She is willing to try anything and has been taking her to a cranial osteopath for head-massages.

In the afternoon Bessie had Sofi for a couple of hours while we wrestled with Nial and watched **Prime Suspect** which we had videoed last night. Hargreaves returned and pulled the breadboard off the kitchen work-surface onto her head amid much noise.

Wednesday 4 December

Dizzy took Fi to school while I looked after Nial. She then went to the supermarket and hurried back for 10.00 to be there to meet the conservatory man, Louis. We waited in all morning and he never turned up. He eventually called at 1.00, apologising profusely – he thought we'd arranged Thursday. Fraying tempers gave way to controlled excitement as he measured up and showed us what was possible. If he's as good as his word (and if we can afford it) it will look lovely.

Dizzy went for a lie-down around 3.30 and didn't stir all afternoon. I woke her with tea at 5.30. Stayed in for the rest of the evening. Didn't quite manage to go to bed early.

Thursday 5 December *Home – Utrecht, Freidenburg Muziekcentrum*

And so to Utrecht. The doorbell rang at 9.50. It was my cab. I thought I'd better pack! Packed at speed and kissed my family goodbye for 10 days (that's both hands, Fi Fi).

The flight to Schipol was painless, we arrived ten minutes early and were driven to the hotel Smits, opposite the Muziekcentrum. Dropped my bags and went to say hello to the crew who were wrestling with a mains-hum which was to remain with us for the show. It transpires that today is St Nicolas day in the Netherlands and is a big celebration here.

We had restructured the set completely for the next leg of the tour and, unrehearsed, we were a bit uncertain of what we were doing. Bolstered by the feeling that we can get away with murder in Utrecht, we went on and made it up as it happened. This resulted in the show having a spontaneity and humour which was inspirational and electric. From my point of view, this was one of the all-time highs in on-stage experiences. If it could be like this every night, I'd do it for free! Wait a minute… I do!

After the show I put myself to bed with hot lemon as my cold is still plaguing me. Early night. 1.00am.

Friday 6 December *Utrecht, Freidenburg Muziekcentrum*

Put all my efforts into a long lie-in. Didn't get up 'til 1.00. Went for a walk and a pleasant lunch in the town. Back to the theatre – we had arranged to rehearse in the afternoon at 3.00. At 5.30 we left the stage to give the Violets (openers, The Violet Hour) a decent crack at a soundcheck and I rehearsed up *Merry Christmas, War Is Over* with Steve R and Pete T in the dressing room.

Back at the hotel I answered a Dutch fan letter enquiring as to the significance of *The Rake's Progress*, which had been meticulously studied by the enquirer. They want it all explained…

Back at the gig, Inge from Delft showed me a book she'd made from Europeans (my first pro band) newsletters and fan-mail. I asked her if she would make a copy for me.

It turns out that *tonight* is fan-club night. We all thought that was yesterday! What will they be like tonight?! I didn't have to wait long. The audience was totally unbelievable. It's hard to take in and appreciate what is coming at you at shows like these. I get frustrated by my own inability to be blown away by the passion of such reactions. But you simply can't. It's incredible, but it's so unnatural to be presented with it that you simply can't do it justice with a response. It's a good job, really, because if my reactions were proportionate I wouldn't be able to sing. Breathing would be a struggle, let alone anything else.

We changed the set again. The band played brilliantly. I had to be retrieved from the audience by production-manager, Smick, during the encores. I have no reason to be scared of these people. They handled me like a lamb. Or a bomb. I guess I'm both…

Saturday 7 December *Utrecht:* Day off

Woke at 10.00 and couldn't really sleep so I showered, dressed and went out for a walk. There's a street market outside the hotel on Saturdays so I had a wander round. Lots of fish stalls: sea-fish still gasping their last moments of life. How do they get them here so quickly – they were too big to have come out of the canals. Went to a shop to buy a clock and nearly bought a lamp. Came to a café for breakfast and here I am, scribbling. I'm going to go back and buy those lamps if they take plastic.

I went back and decided against it. £400 and what if Dizzy hates them?! She'll think I'm nuts.

Went back to the hotel and spent the afternoon snoozing. In the evening we all went out for an Indonesian (Of course! This is Holland) which was lovely – if not a little hot at both ends...

Sunday 8 December *Utrecht – Dortmund*

Had a bit of a lie-in and got up at 11.00 to check out of the hotel Smits at 11.45. Packed the Walkman speakers away – I've been listening to homemade compilations of Talk Talk, Thomas Dolby, Kate Bush, Power Station, Grace Jones, Crowded House and Bowie, along with the odd Furs track and Peter G's piano and voice rendition of *Here Comes the Flood* which is exquisite.

Waited around in the reception watching my Mexican jumping-bean (from Stockholm, naturally) twitching about until the tour bus arrived to take us to Dortmund. Once again, the hotel was walking distance from the gig which makes the day a lot easier for everyone, and an hour-or-so usefully longer. Soundcheck went well so I returned to the hotel and went to bed. It was dark so I left the curtains open to a view of the communications tower and moving headlights on the distant rush-hour highways (a reminder of the alternative lifestyle it has been my destiny and luck to enjoy).

The show was well-attended but after the euphoria of Utrecht I could only feel something missing. I keep saying it, but most bands would kill for a reaction like this so it feels churlish not to enthuse about tonight. The Dortmund crowd was great – it's just that the bar is so high (in other words, we're so damned spoilt!) Anyway, I feel I could have done more.

After the show, I was cajoled, by a Polish ice-skate,r into swapping my tour shirt for his. He said it was for a friend who had toured the world with him, never coming out of his hotel room and listening constantly to Marillion. Sounds like a drummer I know.

Monday 9 December *Dortmund – Hannover, Capital*

It was one of those non-stop days. Drove to Hannover to check into a hotel which looked like a sleeper-carriage from the inside with staff who didn't want to know. Saving grace was the health-centre which was luxurious but deserted.

Not for long. I had half an hour in the solarium and a dip in the pool which made me late to depart for Radio Hanover (that might not be the name).

After an interminable taxi ride with chain-smoking cabby, I had a quick interview with Tom the DJ followed by one song live ("It's all we have time for, sorry"). I squeaked through *Waiting to Happen* realising for the first time how hard it is to sing so high so early in the day.

Back to the hotel through slow-moving dense traffic (I swapped cabs!) and off to the show – a sort of club/disco. The stage was small but I immediately had a good feeling about it. Fish had phoned in the morning to say he'd heard we were skint and proposed a grand reunion festival. He's being very chummy, speaking to Priv and wants us to come to his show on our day off. The band phoned John and diplomatically declined all offers. "He really does believe he's Peter Gabriel," said Rothers. I stayed out of it.

The show was great, the club packed. After the show, we had a drink with Anna B and Louise V from EMI. There were enough loose screws round the table to make a Meccano set – including mine.

Tuesday 10 December *Hannover – Köln – Augsburg*

Up at 6.30!! On the bus for the four and a half hour drive to Köln.

Dozed until 10.45 and de-bunked in the hope of being half-alive for the live radio performance on WDR at 11.45, which is when we arrived after having walked across town with 2 acoustic guitars and a Roland D50 which Jack was carrying over his shoulder. It turns out that the radio show ends at 12.00 so there was no time to do anything except sing and play un-tuneable freezing cold guitars. Croaked my way through *Waiting to Happen* without a vocal mic, said thanks to Hans, the producer, and went for a coffee at the café opposite the magnificent twin spired Dom cathedral with Christina from EMI.

Back on the bus for another six and a half hours down to Augsburg and arrived at 8.30. Showered up and went walkabout with Jack into the cold night. Later learnt that the temperature was -15C. It certainly felt bloody cold! Found Priv, Trevor and Alan P (sound, keyboards and lights) in the little bar we'd discovered on the previous visit (name escapes me) and was welcomed warmly by Karin, Brigitta and Ali (who looks like a villain from a Bond movie). Ali made us fab pizza and chillies while the girls served beer and schnapps.

Strolled briskly back to the hotel, noting a unicycle in a toyshop window which must be purchased for the good of all tomorrow.

Wednesday 11 December *Augsburg, Schwabenlandehalle*

Dreamt my toilet had overflowed all over the room when I flushed it. What can it all mean, Sigmund?

Woke up around 10.30 and went to the solarium for 20 minutes. Wrapped up warm and went walkies through the Christkindlemarkt in the square. This consisted of a great many stalls selling Christmas tree decorations along with wooden toys, candles, coloured lights, cakes, pastries and interspersed, more than liberally, with refreshment stalls selling Glühwein and, of course, sausages. I returned to a music shop I'd spotted and bought sleighbells for the Lennon song.

Saw nice boots for Fi but didn't know her size. What *is* size 8 in Europe?

Back to the Hotel August (nice curtains) and off to Radio Fantasy for another chaotic acoustic recital. DJ didn't seem to know me from Adam but, by all accounts, got very excited afterwards.

Felt duff at the soundcheck and went back to the bus to sleep. Never really recovered and apologised to the band afterwards for an uninspired and unbothered performance. The audience figure was a much-improved-but-paltry 800 after initial sales of only 400. Maybe the radio-broadcast helped...

After the show I was photographed by some chap (can't remember) for his state diploma. He seemed very good. I can usually tell. Got back on the bus. Went to bed and my bed went to Bonn.

Thursday 12 December *Bonn, Biskuithalle*

Up at 6.00 to check into day-rooms at The President Hotel, Bonn (okay). Had breakfast with Ian and went to bed.

Woken by John A at 12.00 phoning from London. The lighting truck has broken down and was repaired too late to reach Bonn. It's gone straight to Mulhouse and we're hiring lights locally.

Chaos at the gig. Typically the crew had it all sorted in time for a 5.30 soundcheck. Alan Parker programmed the entire show between soundcheck and showtime, despite losing two hour's work when the desk computer crashed at 5.00. It never rains. If there's any justice, fate will shine on that boy. As for me, I walked round Bonn all day looking for furry boots for Fi Fi, and ended up buying nutcrackers. I know...

I felt duff again before the show. There was a presentation of gold and platinum discs to the rest of the band for back-catalogue sales. They wanted me in the photo, so they gave me an engraved plastic thing which said "To.... From your friends at EMI Germany". I was touched that they used the word 'friends'.

I headed for the stage trying to fight off shadows of futility. I'm killing myself here and the punters are buying **Misplaced Childhood** in ever greater quantities. These thoughts were quickly dispelled by the best-audience-ever in Germany – among contenders for the best audience ever! Amazing. I got carried away and pulled every muscle in my body (except one).

Went out for a beer with Peter Rieger, then onto the bus for Mulhouse.

Friday 13 December *Mulhouse, Phoenix*

Climbed off the bus, badly beaten at 8.00am but was revitalised spiritually by the sight of French soil. I do love this country. The Park Hotel is lovely and after coffee with the chaps, I checked into a beautiful corner-room. Had a bath in the hope of deadening considerable muscular pain, and climbed into the cricket-pitch-sized bed.

Couldn't really settle and got up again at 12.00 to go walkies round Mulhouse which turned out to be closed until 2.00. Spent the time in a café drinking miniscule café crèmes and writing up this diary. When the shops opened at 2.00, I bought Fi Fi boots in the shop next door.

By this time I was lost, but it turns out that I was outside The Phoenix so I went down to catering and had scrambled eggs on toast, then the runner took me back to the hotel. Went back to bed again, and didn't sleep again, until soundcheck. My voice felt strained. Recorded a number for Julia Simpson at GWR (radio station, Bristol) on DAT. Back to Hotel du Parc and finally managed an hour's sleep.

The show was okay. The audience seemed pretty stiff – which came as a surprise as they seemed a lot looser last time. After the show, I had a quick drink at the hotel with Gerard, Jean, and Michael. Gave Gerard the Yellow Submarine badge he'd admired back in Nice. The hotel staff were lovely – most of them had been at the show and receptionist, Valerie, said it was the best show she'd ever seen.

Saturday 14 December *Mulhouse – Home*

Up far too early at 8.30. Breakfast in bed care of room-service and checked out at 9.00.

We flew from Mulhouse to Paris CdeG where we learnt that connecting flights were non-existent due to fog at Heathrow. Oh no! It's always when you're going home. Ray managed to get us onto a Boeing 767 which can auto-land in fog (category 3 equipment, apparently) which, although due out at 2.30, left around 3.30.

Back at Terminal 4 the fog was thick and no one saw the ground until we touched down.

At the baggage carousel the bad news became evident as we watched and waited. It took another hour to be certain our bags were still in France.

Called a cab, and stopped on the way home for a Christmas tree, but didn't like 'em. Arrived home at 5.30. Fi Fi didn't like the boots. **Dr Jekyll and Mr Hyde** was on the telly.

Sunday 15 December *Home – Bristol, Civic Hall*

Got up and dug up last year's Christmas tree from the rockery. The cheese plant had to go. I felt like I was murdering an old and faithful friend as I chopped it up and threw it in the bin... Aforementioned Christmas-tree was put in the pot and brought inside with the minimum of fuss i.e. lots. Fi Fi, Diz and I dressed the tree with decorations from the loft and it was nearly time for me to go.

Nipped round the corner to look at a house for £180,000 and got back to discover Ray (tour manager on this leg) and Ian, waiting. Unloaded prodigal suitcase and discovered German electric Advent candles still worked! Back into the hot-dog-van and off to Bristol, still feeling iffy.

The Bristol Civic Hall show went well. The audience was terrific and there was a real sense of occasion, thanks, no doubt, to Julia Simpson's endless plugging on GWR. I donated yet another stage-shirt to charity. I wasn't singing particularly well but I felt a little better after the show. Managed to shake hands, sign Christmas cards (250!) and still get to bed for 11.30, feeling dodgy.

Bill Price's remix of *Cover my Eyes* was circulating at the show. I didn't have time to listen to it. It's since been rejected by our American label I.R.S. I probably won't hear it this side of 1992.

PS Not sure if I EVER heard it!

Monday 16 December *Bristol – Aylesbury, Civic Hall*

Left the unfabulous Bristol Hilton at 12.30. Steve R, Mark K and Pete T had left in cars with their nearest and dearests, so it was Ian and me who departed for Aylesbury in the hot-dog van with Ray driving. Snoozed a lot until Aylesbury, and then checked into the Bell Hotel on the market square, next door to the gig.

Considering we're supposed to be an Aylesbury band, I've hardly spent any time here so I thought I'd better have a look. Went for a mooch round the town and wasn't terribly impressed by the shops. Came back and ran a much-needed bath to discover the water was black and full of gritty deposits in the bottom. "We've had a new boiler," the management informed me. After a while, the landlady came up to clean the bath, but by then it was time to go.

At soundcheck my voice was still gravelly and strained and I felt fairly ill. Came back to the Bell and went to bed until showtime.

For me, the Aylesbury show was attrition. I sang like a dog and half-way through my flu seemed to temporarily take over. I started shaking and shivering and, according to a few witnesses, turned as white as a sheet. I must have looked bloody rough because even John Arnison was considering cancelling tomorrow and Wednesday (and he's not usually known for putting compassion ahead of an earner). Fiona Trewavas (who's a nurse) came to my rescue once again and arranged a doctor to pop by after the show. Typically, I felt much better by the time he arrived so he did nothing but recommend paracaetemol (7 years at college…).

Had a quick nightcap at The Bell with Tom Bradley (ex of Rondor Music Publishing, and a lovely chap) before retiring upstairs. Finally managed a bath. Still fairly gritty…

Tuesday 17 December *Aylesbury – Glasgow*

The endurance test continues. Up at 8.45 for breakfast at The Bell and the LONG drive to Glasgow. I spent most of it in my usual position, horizontal on the back seat.

Arrived in darkness and woke up stuck in what appeared to be a back-alley. We were in a queue of traffic trying to turn left. Perhaps it was my state of health/mind but I couldn't help finding Glasgow depressing. We finally arrived at the Barrowlands and made our way down narrow backstairs into the hall which was, like last time, freezing cold. Fortunately, they had since invested in wall-heaters for the dressing room area. Glasgow and Liverpool are, like it or not, sister cities insomuch as I couldn't help wondering if the new heaters in the dressing room were nicked from somewhere else – they looked a bit second-hand. I know this sounds prejudiced, but I reckon you could swap one end of Argyll Street for one end of Lime Street without anyone noticing. The same was true of the hotel which had the same 'business as usual in terminal decay' attitude as I have only experienced here and in Liverpool.

The show, although poorly attended (recession?) was notable for the atmosphere from the crowd who, although in diminished numbers, were every bit as vocal and welcoming as last time and impossible to compare with the more conservative Edinburgh crowd, earlier in the tour. For some reason of Marillion history/culture (and probably something to do with Fish), the crowd occasionally chant, "Gi-us a bun, Gi-us a bun Gi-us a bun," and throw bread-buns at me (infinitely preferable to cans of urine which used to happen at pop festivals in the 70s… or being spat at, which was a sign of approval during the punk-era. I used to go on stage in a plastic mac…)

My voice was finally returning to form so, spiritually, I was much improved when I came off stage. Thanks loves. Beats paracetamol!

PS Sorry Glasgow. Sorry Liverpool. It WAS 1991. And I WAS fucked at the time. I have since come to love both cities dearly and always look forward to coming. I usually play Christmas solo shows in both cities. And they're magical. Right… have I crawled enough?

Wednesday 18 December *Glasgow – Middlesborough, Civic Hall*

Rose mid-morning and walked along Argyll St looking for Christmas cards/gifts. It rained hard until I bought a brolly for £3.99 at which point it stopped.

Glasgow seems very run-down. Many of the shops lie empty and disused even on this, one of its main streets. I returned to the hotel trying to square what I'd seen with all the talk about Glasgow being a vibrant cultural centre these days. Perhaps they can 'talk it up' 'til it happens.

The drive to Middlesborough was, again, seemingly endless. Sleep didn't really help. Whenever I woke up, outside looked much the same as when I'd gone to sleep. The high-point of the journey was a layby snack trailer run by a sprightly woman who made us 16 bacon & egg rolls and nearly as many cups of coffee. She must be brave to stand there on her own in the middle of nowhere, all day, freezing to death. These are the people whose hard work and joyful spirit make the world a better place.

Middlesborough Civic Hall is quite an interesting place… a bit Bavarian somehow. I took a shine to the red dragons in the rafters. The show went well, although the audience was somewhat sedate. We realised after the show that this was our first time here, so perhaps the reaction was to be expected. They were sussing us out.

Afterwards at the hotel, we bought the crew a drink by way of thanks for the tour – we thought we might not get a chance after London when people tend to scatter.

One of Pete T's relatives here is a hairdresser. I made an appointment for 9.30 tomorrow to get my roots done.

Thursday 19 December *Middlesborough – London*

Up at 9.00, bluffing heavily and staggered down to the hairdressers where Diane (I think) coloured my hair black for a change, ha ha. I consumed several coffees during the process, and persuaded the junior to go out in search of toast.

Got back to the hotel in time to check out at 11.00 for the obligatory interminable journey, this time, to London. Arrived at 4.00 and checked into the Holiday Inn, Swiss Cottage, and left immediately for EMI to meet Bill Smith to approve artwork for America. It was all in black and white so I'm none the wiser.

Had heated discussion about the forthcoming anniversary album. I feel there shouldn't be more 'old Marillion' songs on there than 'new Marillion' in case the album looks like some sort of epitaph. Steve R and Mark K disagreed, but Mark K later changed his mind and Steve R went quiet. Hmm… Pete T agrees with me and Ian seems indifferent. We're going to need another meeting.

Left EMI and went to Willie Robertson's place in Fulham Road for Christmas-drinks with Rondor. Saw Annabel Lamb again who was complaining about Julia Fordham's vegan, non-smoking, no fun touring regime. Also chatted to Mark Shaw (singer, Then Jericho) who is currently without a deal (that's show-business).

Later on Willie showed up and introduced me to his lovely wife, Angie, and chums. It was an emotional reunion – he's as soft and melodramatic as I am. Chatted to Kurt Smith about Colin Woore. Said hi to Chris Kimsey and went down to The Goat In Boots for a half with Jack and the crew before returning to Swiss Cottage for sleep.

Friday 20 December *London, Town & Country Club*

Happy Birthday, our Sue! Up at 11.00 to leave at 11.30. I was delayed firstly by my bath refusing to empty, and, secondly, by the realisation that my luggage had still not arrived from the porters who have had it since yesterday afternoon. Waited 10 minutes for my suitcase to arrive so that I could put on clean underwear. I was, therefore, only wearing a towel when I let 'maintenance' in to empty my bath water. It must be hard being a girl…

Arrived at the T&C at 12.00 and met up with Benedetta from Superchannel for the one-and-a-half hour VJ slot which Mark and I were doing. This actually seemed to take all day. We had a lot of fun on camera (I announced my forthcoming marriage to Madonna etc – it seemed funny at the time...) and in the end Benedetta stayed for Christmas dinner and I invited her onto the stage for soundcheck. She asked me if I'd be interested in doing some VJ-ing in the New Year. I said sure. I bet they don't call though. (*they didn't)

Back to Swiss Cottage to meet a nurse who arrived to babysit Nial. Diz arrived just as I was leaving for the show, saying she'd parked the car up the Finchley Road and got a cab. She always gets lost in London. She's improved a little since the 80s when she used to go EVERYWHERE via St Pauls Cathedral. Not good if you're coming from Windsor.

So this is the stuff which always accompanies London shows – guest-list hassles, parking fines and tow-aways, interviews, domestic chaos and, of course, extra nervous-tension for the show itself which cranks up the stress of all the above and, in turn, stresses everyone else out too. Ian has said he wouldn't care if he never played another Aylesbury or London show again, and I kinda know what he means.

The show, however, went really well. The crowd was in great form and I sang not too badly. Afterwards we reserved the bar upstairs for aftershow drinks. Doris from the Violets announced her departure from the band after their set, so I suppose that's the end of them!? I guess we broke 'em. Shame. Said hello to Steve Tannant from IRS who was complimentary and seemed very vibed up about next year. He said I should have lunch with Miles (Copeland, owner of IRS, and legendary manager of The Police and Sting). I also said hi to Chris Neil (producer **Holidays in Eden** and a list of stars), Nick Eede (lead singer Cutting Crew), Alison from EMI press and John Helmer (our occasional co-lyricist and wordsmith – John Helper, I call him...)

Left the T&C around 1.00 clutching a black bin-liner full of washing and trying to hold onto several coat-hangers full of clothes. An embarrassing 15 minutes was spent waiting outside the venue for a minicab: "Ain't that the lead singer of Marillion there?" snigger...

Finally got a cab and began looking for our car.

"Please take us to Finchley Road."

"What number mate? It's 2 miles long."

"Err... Just drive up and down please."

Somehow, (bear in mind I'd sung for well over two hours and stood in a bar being hustled for a further two. Not digging coal n'all, but try it...) exhaustion remained at bay for long enough to find the car, drive to the Holiday Inn, pay the babysitter, check out, donate my room to displaced German girls (Sandra and Britta), load the car, (I couldn't get my suitcase to fit), drive home to Windsor, drive the other babysitter home, and drive home again. But only just.

Saturday 21 December *Home*

No entries here. I must've been recovering.

Sunday 22 December *Home*

Dave Crawshaw, my oldest friend, from Doncaster (he used to live opposite my mum and dad's house in Wheatley Hills) came yesterday. He had been visiting his brother in Oxford and so he popped over. We spent the morning chatting, catching up with our respective lives etc. Sadly, I don't see Dave often enough but when I do, it's like no time has passed. We had lunch down the street in The Beehive (our local pub). He drove back in the afternoon.

Monday 23 December

Had planned to take Fi Fi to the Watercress Railway again, to Santaland. In the end we didn't go as there was still shopping to do, so we went to Windsor. Fi said she'd rather go to 'Old McDonald's' anyway.

Tuesday 24 December

Last chance to do my Christmas shopping so I went up town in the car and had a blast round Harrods. Bought Diz a purse but decided against a coat in her absence – better to come with her and she can choose.

Drove over to Fulham to Christopher Wrays Lighting Emporium. Diz had made a few noises about a nice bedside lamp. Didn't see anything I liked that I could afford.

Stayed up late wrapping presents.

Wednesday 25 December *Christmas Day*

To our surprise, Sofi didn't appear in our bedroom until 8.30. "Has Father Christmas been?" she enquired. I think it was all a bit unreal to her. I brought her bulging pillow-case back into our room and she opened her presents on our bed. The biggest hit was, of course, the headband and hair-clips. Dizzy Spell bought me a dressing gown (black with white paisley markings) which is really nice, and the new Robbie Robertson CD. We went to The Beehive for a half at 1.00 and then came back and took the turkey out of the oven and had Christmas dinner accompanied by Dave and Su's white wine (Pouilly Fumé '89). The rest of the day was spent adjusting Fi's various hairdressing accessories and attending to Nial. It was strangely pleasant to be on our own on Christmas Day for the first time. I'm glad nobody came calling.

Thursday 26 December

Stayed in bed until 12.00ish. There was chaos in the kitchen – Fi Fi had knocked a jar of black paint water all over the place. Diz was spitting rivets and trying to mop it up while the doorbell was ringing. I thought I'd better get up... It was my sister Sue with husband Mick and young James who had popped over from Merton with our presents from the family in Doncaster. The day was spent eating, drinking and watching telly. Took them out to the Green for a swing just before dark at 3.30.

The Sarah Ball fell off the wall and is now a bit skew-whiff – aided no doubt by James and Fi's bed-bouncing upstairs... Sue and Mick left around 7.00.

Friday 27 December

Went up to town to buy Diz a coat. Parked at EMI Manchester Square in the garage below the building. No one else seemed to be in the building except Ray, the door man (top chap).

Walked over to Selfridges (day 1 of the sale) clutching Nial (we forgot the baby-sling) but they didn't have anything she liked. We gave up and went for a crepe and a milkshake. Diz found a fab red coat by Sydney Smith opposite the restaurant in St Christopher's Place so we bought it.

Saturday 28 December

Stayed in bed 'til 12.00! By the time I was up and about Dizzy was on her way to receive a Christmas massage at the local health studio.

Couldn't get Nial settled so I loaded Hargreaves and him into the car and we went to the chemist in search of drugs to bung up the girls streaming noses – we've all got colds. Nial woke up whenever we stopped, so I drove around Virginia Water, Sunninghill etc. Got back around 1.30 and drove back through the village to maybe catch Diz on her way home. We did bump into her outside Wants (ironmongers) and I took Fi Fi to the sweet shop and bought a paper, then back home.

Nial slept for most of the rest of the day. Fi watched **Mary Poppins** on TV while I wrestled with the car's H.P. agreement, stuck the legs back on a chair, and cleaned behind the oven. Diz went to bed early and I stayed up with Nial who did what he does lately and stayed up 'til 12.00 before nodding off. Chuck Berry and Keith Richards were on the telly. Amnesty International are celebrating 30 years so I watched a bit of the concert on ITV and scribbled this.

Monday 30 December

Stayed in all day. Tried to do my accounts in the afternoon whilst Diz took Fi off to town. Nial couldn't settle so I got nothing done. Mum and Dad were coming in the evening, so I popped into Egham to buy Dad a CD for his birthday tomorrow. Andrew in Musicwise said he'd been listening a lot to **Holidays in Eden** and wanted me to sign a copy. I found a cassette of **Recurring Dreams** in the shop. They must have had it for ages. He gave it me as a present when I told him I'd never had a copy. Bought a Telemann CD for Dad. Spent the evening eating, drinking and gassing with the folks.

Tuesday 31 December

Happy Birthday Dad x

Had a lie-in after a terrible night up with the kids. Got up and sat about in afternoon and finally finished my accounts. Took Dad out at 7.30 for a pint in The Beehive, it being his birthday n'all. Came back at 8.30 and we all went to Ian Mosley's in Gerards Cross for New Year's Eve drinks. All the band were there apart from Steve and Jo, who were probably up north with family in Bolton. Chatted with tour-manager/bus-driver Ray about fishing, and we arranged for him to take me fishing on Thursday for carp and chub, with luncheon meat! I'm really looking forward to it. Had illuminating drunken discussions with Angus (who designed Air studios) about what carp might do and think during their long lives. The world according to carp. We reasoned that, as they can live for hundreds of years, maybe everything happens at double-speed, just as perhaps the opposite happens with Mayflies who might experience a long lifetime as time is slowed down to a crawl during that one day for which they are alive.

Fi Fi lasted very well and was going strong until around 1.30 when she fell over, banged her head and promptly went spare. Lisa said she'd heard DJ's on Capital and GLR saying good things about the band, so perhaps we're getting the message across. Anyway, I have rarely been in a house full of people having a good time and been able to say that every single one of them was a diamond character. It was a great evening. Unfortunately I was driving and couldn't get sloshed. Had a beer when I got in and went to bed.

1992 APRIL

Friday 10

TNT

1 9 9 2

Wednesday 1 January

So here we are in 1992! I wonder what will happen this year. Maybe I'll get famous… or maybe we'll split up. Or neither. Or both.

Had a lie-in. Got up, had breakfast, put a shirt on and we left Nial at home with my mum and dad while we drove to Richmond with Hargreaves to go to *Cinderella* at Richmond theatre. Fi Fi enjoyed it but, Diz and I weren't terribly impressed. Too many badly delivered corny songs. I liked the ugly sisters' dresses. As long as Fi enjoyed it, I'm glad that we went, and she did, so I am.

Drove back and went straight to Windsor for tea at the Dome café. The Dome's really gone to the dogs – they didn't have half the items on the menu, and the menu's not a patch on what it was. The waitress said she'd just found out they haven't got a restaurant licence, so they couldn't give us alcohol on a bank holiday in the afternoon. We had a coffee and decided we'd go home and get an Indian take-away. Went to 'Old McDonald's' and bought Fi Fi a cheeseburger and chips to take home. After dinner we watched **Imagine** on the box – I'd videoed it on Christmas Eve.

Went to bed at midnight (well, ten-past) as I'm fishing tomorrow!

Thursday 2 January

Up at 9.30 to let an estate agent in to value the house. He reckoned around £95k so we hired him. Here we go again.

Ray arrived at 10.30, so I borrowed a pair of Diz's tights and, wearing several shirts and a sweater, set off to Wraysbury on the Thames to do some fishing for the first time ever. Paul Owen - the Europeans sound-man/tour manager - used to talk about taking me fishing, and it turns out that Ray's been fishing with him on days off from Metallica tours. I bet they looked forward to those... Within five minutes of sitting down and casting, Ray caught a good-sized chub, much to my delight. We both had a go at holding it but, sadly, neither of us had thought to bring a camera. We put it back in the river where, I suspect, it had a word with the boys ("Don't touch the luncheon meat, lads!") 'cause we never had another bite all day.

Got home around 3.30 with numb toes and helped myself to a Laphroaig for medicinal purposes. Mum and Dad left around 7.00 and later called to say they'd arrived home okay. Diz went to bed around 10.00 and I stayed up with Nial and watched U2's **Rattle and Hum** which, I think, is filmed to capture the band's performance, and does so really well. I admire U2 for their uncompromising honesty and their inherent cool. Bono's a great rock singer. He does get a bit much sometimes with the "God" thing and the "God's gift" thing though.

Saturday 4 January

Hung about to show someone the house at 1.00. Went to Windsor in the afternoon. Bought teaspoons and a clock at Caleys (the department store on the High Street).

Sunday 5 January

Stuart and Gill (my sister) arrived at 11.30 with Holly and Amy. Stuart has made us a pine headboard for the bed and they've come down the M1 with it on the roof-rack. We had a pleasant day talking and later went out to the river to feed the ducks, which turned out to be geese and swans – all nearly as big as the girls! We got our shoes and the pram-wheels muddy and then went for tea in 'Old MacDonald's'... again.

They stayed 'til around 9.00. Afterwards, we put Hargreaves to bed and took the Xmas decorations down.

Monday 6 January

Spent the day looking around Oxfordshire again. Had a look at The Clock House in Brackley and drove to Upper Heyford, Middle Barton, Mixbury, Bicester etc. Had lunch in The Crown Hotel, Brackley.

Came home at teatime clutching a sheaf of property details. I now seem to have caught a head-cold which is steadily worsening.

Tuesday 7 January

Woke up feeling victim to my cold. Blocked nose, ears and general strangeness.

Had a bath and went to Chelsea for a meeting with John A to discuss this year ahead. The compilation album is going ahead and it looks like we're going to call it **Six of One and Half-a-Dozen of the Other**. The studio won't be up and running 'til the 20th. Mark and I are going to the USA to meet IRS and also maybe Canada and Mexico. That's happening fairly soon.

Had lunch with Tony Smith and John Crawley at an Italian round the corner. Opened quite a lot of Christmas mail. Nice card from EMI Denmark and from Sylvia at Virgin, Hamburg. We seem to be getting lots of mail. Three letters from Russia in this week's pile. One from Australia, a good one from someone in the States – he enclosed an s.a.e. and a note which simply said, "I'm <u>obsessed</u>. Please HELP!"

Came home at teatime. Took too many tablets and felt weird all evening. Went to bed early. Dizzy stayed up with Nial. Thank you, my sweetheart.

Friday 10 January

Took the car in for a service. Spent the afternoon working upstairs. I'm trying to find keys and key changes for *Sympathy* which we're hoping to record later in the month. Spoke to John Arnison, who says he's earmarked the first week of February for the trip to Mexico and US. Looks like it's just me and Mark.

Sue had friends and friends' children over in the afternoon, so I barricaded myself in (unsuccessfully) upstairs.

Saturday 11 January

Quiet day. Took Hargreaves with me to buy new tyres for the car. "They put a <u>jack</u> under the car, mummy". She only needs telling anything once.

Came back and showed a couple round the house. They seemed very interested but we've heard nothing.

I later went into Windsor for a mooch about on my own. Didn't really see anything/anyone of interest. Bought a couple of U2 CDs – **Rattle and Hum** and **Achtung Baby**. Diz doesn't like U2 so I'll have to play them when she's out.

Sunday 12 January

Angie Fountain popped over from Eton with friend Linda who might buy our house. She says Malc Foster (bass player Pretenders) sends his regards and it looks like he might be doing the Elton John tour.

Had lunch with the family at the Beehive.

Came back and watched the footie. Sue's friend Julie had a baby around 4.00. Her husband Gary (who's just designed the new Genesis sleeve) phoned to let us know.

Watched telly. Got bored. Stayed up past midnight with Nial. He's currently up 'til late, but too young to know where the party is.

Tuesday 14 January

Darryl and Juliet came over in the evening for dinner. They brought Lauren, who is now toddling and has become a right character. I thought she was a sweetie. A pleasant evening was had by all.

Stayed up 'til 1.00 with Nial… Sigh.

Wednesday 15 January

Up at 8.45 with Hargreaves who's a little tired after staying up late last night. Popped out mid-morning for French bread and taramasalata.

Ian phoned, so invited him around to hear my *Sympathy* efforts. Hilda came for lunch with sons Max and Jake, who looks like a Buddhist priest. Ian thought the *Sympathy* idea sounded promising, so I called Mark who came round at 6.00 to take a DAT copy to listen to. Phoned Rothers and maybe we'll meet up tomorrow.

Gill phoned at 8.00 to say thanks for Amy's birthday present and told me it's Pete's birthday! Apparently Simon Bates played *Incommunicado* and mentioned it on the birthday file. I thought I'd better phone Pete and check that he knew (that it was his birthday, I mean) and he said he did, although he hadn't heard about the radio mention.

Monday 10 February

Day 1 at Metropolis with Chris Kimsey. Spent most of the day setting up and we managed to get a good take of *Sympathy,* before bedtime. The drums sound great. I'm enjoying working with Chris.

Tuesday 11 February

Overdubbing on *Sympathy.* Dined out in the evening in St Martin's Lane.

Wednesday 12 February

Started the day with a lead vocal on *Sympathy.* Did a few takes and made a comp for CK to live with. Put it to bed and started work on *Walk on Water.* Slow going. Didn't finish 'til 2.00. Drove home knackered.

Thursday 13 February

Chris says he likes the *Sympathy* vocal. Fabbydoo. Spent more time arranging

WoW. All night recording but managed a good take before dinner. Overdubbed bass and my keyboards. Chris says my lyrics are "cool". That's not bad from a man who's worked with the Furs and the Stones. Cheered me up no end. Stayed over in the Chiswick Hotel.

Friday 14 February

Went to EMI and then to The Float Centre in St John's Wood, near Abbey Road. It's a place where you can climb into a pod and float in/on a solution of heavily saline water. Supposed to be a relaxing trip. Someone had had the bright idea of interviewing people inside there, and I was invited. I chatted to journalist Matthew Wright who chickened out of climbing in with me and talked to me from outside. It might have been an 'experience' if not for the photographer generally getting in the way and holding things up. Dunno about the float-tank thing – I felt peculiar for the rest of the day.

Sunday 16 February

Went to Richmond for lunch with small people. Nial's crabby 'cause he's got a cold.

Thursday 20 February

Dizzy brought me into town and then went to Yorkshire with Nial and Sofi. Had a meeting with IFA Merv and pushed the button on the mortgage for the new house. Phew!

Finished the lead vocal for *I Will Walk on Water*. Stayed up 'til 3.00 listening to the mix. Kimsey's working well.

Friday 21 February

Up and over to Metropolis for breakfast. Borrowed Ian's car and went home in the afternoon to pack and get the cot down from the loft. Back to London to hear the mix. Sounds great!

Trevor brought me home so that I could have an early(er) night. Left CK and Spence doing a 12-inch mix. Went home. Tidied up a bit. Went to bed 11.00ish.

Saturday 22 February *Home – New York*

Got up around 10.00. Had a bath and dithered about 'til 11.00 when the doorbell rang. It was old chum/driver, Jason who took me to Terminal 3. Met up with John and Mark and said hi to Beverly Lillywhite, who was working on United Airlines check-in. Flew to America. Oh yeah.

I bought a camera at Duty Free, having forgotten mine. The journey took eight hours. Arrived at the Mayflower Hotel NYC around 7.00 – too late to phone Dizzy who'd be sleeping back home by midnight. Showered up and had dinner with John and Mad Jack. Tony Visconti was having dinner at a large table with what looked like a band. Made eye-contact with him a couple of times, but I don't think he remembered me. He'd produced a song called *American People* for The Europeans. The process was memorable, for him leaving much of the session to his studio-engineer, Kit Woolvern, whilst showing us pictures of him and Bowie ski-ing and, most bizarrely, half way through the afternoon, proudly announcing: "I'm going to make you guys a salad!", whereupon he went out for an hour down Old Compton Street and returned with carrier bags bulging with French bread and green salad vegetables. It WAS a good salad, but a bit pricey at his not-inconsiderable producer's fee. He also introduced us to his ex-wife Mary Hopkin who popped into the studio Good Earth (great name) on Dean St, in Soho. She was very nice. Tony was lovely too, but his mind, for whatever reason, didn't seem to be on our record.

Anyway… I lasted well and went to bed around 11.00.

Sunday 23 February *NYC*

Woken by Jack at 7.30 wondering if I fancied breakfast at 8.00. Yes I did… I'd been awake since about 2.00.

Had breakfast with Jack and John and saw David Bowie go by outside on the sidewalk (America is like this), before going to the Museum of Modern Art with Jack. It didn't open 'til 11.00 and we got there at 10.30. It was a lovely day in Manhattan, blue sky and not really cold.

After the museum we went to Greenwich and I almost bought a fountain for $1200. We'd have had some fun getting that home. Had dinner and returned to the Mayflower and got sloshed for hours.

Monday 24 February *Promotion, NYC*

Had breakfast around 8.00 with Jack and John, then took a cab across town to Soho where the IRS offices are. Did a couple of phoners and then left for Philadelphia with Steve Karas and Meredith Hayes, the radio promo girl. It was a bit weird walking into the offices of the tip-sheets. I felt superfluous and awkward at the first one – FMQB (Friday Morning Quarterback).

The second visit, to Bill Hard (good name!) at The Hard Report was more relaxed. His offices are in a log-cabin. Bill struck me as a nice chap. He wanted to show us his new premises (they're in the process of moving) so we all jumped into the minibus. When I enquired as to a beer he said we could call in at his home and pick a couple up… and what a home! It's a large house made entirely of logs, next to a lake. It was beautifully decorated inside. Downstairs in the basement was like a youth-club with bar and pool table, drum kit, PA etc. He had Bowers & Wilkins loudspeakers in his lounge, which were the size of wardrobes.

After visiting Bill, we drove back to New York (2 hours) for a college press-conference, then dinner with IRS heavyweight, Barbara Bolan (tough but charming) and on to the White Horse Tavern (famous for where Dylan Thomas staggered outside and died) for a meet 'n'greet with record store and distribution people. Phew. IRS really know how to run a promo operation. The vibe was very positive for the album.

At one point during the drive to and from Philly, Meredith (whose driving was… characterful, to say the least), spawned this verse to the tune of *No Particular Place to Go* by Chuck Berry.

"Driving along with Meredith Hayes,
Been on the road a couple a days.
Hit the kerb at 95,
Really lucky to be alive.
Drivin' n' playin' the radio,
With no particular place to go."

Tuesday 25 February *NYC – Montreal*

Still can't get to grips with the time-zone. Got up around 7.30 having been awake for hours.

Had breakfast with the chaps and then did interviews, (phoners and face-to-face) until 12.30. Packed in a hurry and checked out of the Mayflower. I took four Malaria tablets on my way out of the door. Big mistake. Almost immediately felt odd. Got into a car to drive to the airport, feeling distinctly ill. To make matters worse, there was a smell in the cab which was like some very stale secretion of someone who had worn the same pants for a straight month after a slight accident below-stairs. I think it was the driver.

To make matters *even* worse, I was sitting next to him.

To make matters **EVEN** worse, when I finally arrived at the airport, feeling REALLY ill, I discovered I'd left my passport at the hotel and had to make the one-hour round trip in (thankfully) another cab, only marginally more savoury. We caught the plane with minutes to spare.

In Montreal there was thick snow but it wasn't too cold. Checked into the hotel and went out with the record company for dinner with a few record store people. I picked the wrong place to sit and suffered an ear-bending from a well-meaning but over-enthusiastic wannabee for most of the evening.

Came back around 11.00 and went to bed for what turned out to be another 4 hours sleep. Jet lag. Tomorrow, LA and another 3 hours to cope with!

Wednesday 26 February *Montreal – Chicago – Los Angeles*

Woke up early and went out for a trudge through the snow. I was trying to find some shops to buy some boots, as the old stout walking shoes had developed a hole. Eventually found a mall which seemed to be full of shoe shops. All closed.

Wound my way back to the hotel and ordered breakfast. Richard arrived from EMI and the rest of the day was spent doing interviews. Highlight of the day was Musique Plus – the kinda Canadian MTV. Sonia, the VJ, was totally into the album (**Holidays in Eden**) and full of praise.

At 5.00 we left for the airport and flew to Los Angeles via Chicago. We arrived in LA to be met at the airport by David Millman, head of publicity for IRS, and we climbed into the longest limo I have ever seen… like an Inter-City 125 with wheels at each end. I took to David immediately – intelligent, witty and slightly eccentric; the perfect combination. The car deposited us at Le Réve Hotel ('The Dream') and I alighted, swooning at the scent of the blossoms which saturated the warm and fresh evening air (rare for LA but it had rained earlier).

Went for a quick walk up the hill to Santa Monica Boulevard with Jack before retiring to my room which was warm and homely. The Réve is a much less corporate-feeling atmosphere than the LA hotels I've previously inhabited. IRS sensitivity and taste is apparent in all areas. They're art-ier than EMI.

Thursday 27 February *LA*

Here we go again! Woke at 5.00 but snoozed 'til around 7.30.

Got up, showered and went walkies - east on Sunset - to find a children's clothes shop called Bloomers. It didn't open til 10.00, so I had breakfast at one of the cafés, sitting out on the street, watching the endless expensive traffic which traverses Sunset Boulevard. The waitress took my picture. Back to Le Réve for interviews on the roof. Paddy Spinks (Hit & Run's American rep) came over and said hi. He left with John A, and Mark and I were picked up by Nancy Shamess, who was bouncy and hyper.

Went to Tower Records on Sunset, who didn't seem bothered. I guess with M Jackson and B Springsteen swinging by regularly, they weren't likely to wet their pants over me and Jack! We had lunch over the road with people from CEMA distribution.

After lunch we went to IRS to meet the company. I was particularly taken by Huw, who is their creative marketing chap – talented, hip and pleasant. More interviews, then a meet 'n' greet beer-tasting where I met Michael Scurlock who struck me as experienced and corporate, but relieved to be no longer working for a corporate company. He said he was excited about the songs.

We returned to the hotel to shower, then off to Barneys Beanery for more socialising with journos. Barbara Bolan came over looking knackered. I told her to go home and go to bed, but she was having none of it. Millman played excellent host. We later went to a club to watch new signing, Dada. I enjoyed them very much and thought they shouldn't spend too much time 'producing' the album. Just capture what they're already doing.

Friday 28 February *LA – Buenos Aires*

Up at 8.00 to do a phoner to Grand Rapids, Michigan. Nancy arrived and drove us all over the place all day, apart from a visit to Album Network tip-sheet with Michael.

Panic over errors made in our air-route (whoops – not going to be cheap) to Buenos Aires, were averted by the purchase of new tickets.

In the evening Stevo Glendenning took us to dinner and Paddy S tagged along. A pleasant evening was had, and we left for the airport around 10.00. The vibe from within IRS seems incomparable with Capitol. I like the people and would spend time with them just for fun – especially David M who is a gentleman and a wit. After an initial delay of one hour, we took off in a 747, the size of my street, at 1.00am bound non-stop for Buenos Aires. I have flown many times on Jumbo Jets but, this time, I found myself gobsmacked-afresh by the concept of something as long as my village and as wide as my house floating in the sky at 600 mph! Magic. Bugger the science, that's GOT to be magic.

Saturday 29 February *Buenos Aires*

The flight (11 hrs) from LA to BA proved less boring than anticipated. I managed to sleep until 6.00 and the rest of the day seemed to pass quite quickly. The in-flight movie was good and the staff friendly and helpful.

Arrived in Buenos Aires at 5.30pm and hung around for 2 hours (!) waiting to be met. It never happened, so we got a cab to the Sheraton. I was very surprised by BA – much greener, more European, and not as poverty-stricken as I had naively imagined. The people have the Latin-American warmth and vitality, and I feel much more at home here than in America.

In the evening I went down to the bar to meet up with the rest of the band, who seemed in good spirits despite a long flight via Paris. Silvina, from the record company took us out to dinner and then on to a club where we were given Champagne – compliments of the management. The jet-lag was now working the other way round and so Jack and I didn't feel tired until 5.00am.

Sunday 1 March *Buenos Aires*

Had a lie-in until 2.00 and wound my way down to the poolside to try and write a bit more of this diary. Constantly distracted by loud American women; I gave up and returned to my room.

Did an interview at 3.00 and then left for the TV show, for soundcheck at 4.00. There was a permanent encampment of kids outside the hotel waiting for a local Spanish act who are, needless to say, very popular. At the TV station, the street was full of teenage girls – Vanilla Ice was also doing the show. Soundcheck was uneventful. I couldn't understand why they were checking the tom-tom mics – we were miming! (Perhaps Mosley had insisted, just to see if they'd do it…).

Back at the hotel I had a bath, and then we returned to do the TV show.

Backstage all was chaos. People everywhere – camera crews, interpreters, dancers, Vanilla Ice's entourage, record-company people, etc. When we eventually hit the stage the TV audience were all vibed up. There were more of our fans in the audience than we had imagined, waving banners and whatnot. The spot went well and the show's host gave me a leather-jacket! Afterwards we showered and went out to dinner with the record company girl, Silvina, and the promotion company girl, Nora. Mad Jack told them Roy Hill's E.S.P joke (which, by definition, isn't fit for publication here). Tried to find a club but they were all closed.

Monday 2 March *Buenos Aires – Mexico City*

Had a lie in! Up at 12.00 to get ready to leave by 2.00. I popped to the shop in the hotel to buy souvenir t-shirts then checked out and we left for the airport. Ian, Pete and Steve went separately to leave for London while John, Mark and I were to fly to Mexico City via Rio de Janeiro. Had a banana milkshake and a beer and wished goodbye to Silvina, Nora and Ernie. The general feeling seems to be that we'll come back in the autumn to play live.

It was strange to be landing in Rio after so much time. I wish we hadn't gone via Rio because when we got into the terminal, I realised I'd left a poster (Norman Parkinson's **Hat Fashions,** which I'd bought at the Museum of Modern Art in NY) on the plane. VARIG wouldn't let me back to the plane to get it and maintained that they'd searched the plane and it wasn't there. But it was.

Rio airport seems to be under reconstruction and looks like a garage. We found a kiosk which was selling Caipirinhas in plastic cups. It brought all the good times back. Groan… After 3 long hours we boarded the plane to Mexico City and, still stinging with frustration at the theft of my poster, I drifted off to sleep to dream of murdering VARIG aircrew… When I woke, I could see an enormous expanse of streetlight coming up through mist. It wasn't mist. It was pollution. This is Mexico City.

Tuesday 3 March *Mexico City*

Arrived at Mexico City and managed to get off the plane without leaving anything on board. We were met at the baggage carousel by Michelle, from EMI Mexico, who had already 'arranged' our hassle-free passage through the airport. Here in Mexico, EMI seems to be able to facilitate a stress-free journey through immigration and Customs. I bet the airport manager has an impressive CD collection.

Drove through the busy streets to The Holiday Inn, checked in and went to bed. Up at 12.00 and was driven half-mad by the hotel operator as I tried in vain to call home to England. I eventually discovered that she thought England was in America – hence the problems with long-distance dialling. Had lunch with John and Jack feeling jet-lagged once again.

At 2.00 Michelle returned and we drove to visit a couple of radio stations. The vibe at both radio stations was one of awe – they treated us as if we were legends. In the evening we went out for dinner to Carlos and Charlie's Restaurant and Clothesline – a sort of Mexican version of the Hard Rock Café, but with its own take on food, good taste and its own sense of humour. I bought a denim jacket for Stuart (brother-in-law) as a thank you for his efforts in creating our headboard back home. I also bought myself a white shirt which had words emblazoned across the back - "I DON'T SPEAK ENGLISH BUT I PROMISE NOT TO LAUGH AT YOUR SPANISH". It was a pleasant evening.

Returned to the hotel and slept for not too long, once again waking in the early hours to watch the insides of my eyelids.

Wednesday 4 March *Mexico City*

Up at 8.00 and out at 9.00 along with Jack, John, Michelle and journalist /photographer to visit the Pyramids of the Sun and Moon at Teotihuacan. Chatted with Robert, a young journalist, who gave us background information on the history of Mexico City as we drove out through the shanties. Water-supply is the biggest problem here, he says, because there is no water locally and it must be piped from the sea 200km away. (Nick Belshaw was later to add that, "...it's 8000ft up in the fucking air as well!"). Corruption within the government doesn't help the lot of the poor people who live without decent water, electricity, housing or sewage systems.

When we arrived we climbed the Pyramid of the Sun, which only took a few minutes. Posed for loads of photographs and bought gifts from the traders who wander around pestering the tourists with silver and obsidian artefacts. I bought a few, and I'm glad I did. There is much talk of these pyramids being a magical place but I didn't feel anything myself – too many tourists I suppose. We then watched the flying men of Papanlta who swing upside down on ropes from a massive Maypole-like post. When they reach the bottom, they run off and return to sell bottles of vanilla extract for cooking (!).

The rest of the day was spent interviewing. In the evening we had dinner (Italian), then went to a small outdoor gig. I got up and sang with a local band. We were all nursing sunburn, especially Jack who had burned his neck, quite badly, at the pyramids.

Thursday 5 March *Mexico City*

Up at 8.30 to leave at 9.00 for a press conference at EMI MC. The news is good – we have a promoter wanting to do a show at the 10,000 seater and confident of a sell-out. The EMI building is in the old Spanish style. High ceilinged, light and airy with wooden floors. We did the conference in a room which felt like a recording studio, but converted for our purposes with a large conference table. The walls were decorated with framed Beatles' album covers. I think they had all of them. It was strange to be surrounded by such significant ghosts. The conference went well, I thought. I managed to voice my opinions and feelings positively and, for once, concisely. The rest of the day was spent doing phoners and then TV interviews at the hotel.

In the evening we made a return visit to Carlos and Charlie's. Ate, and drank frozen strawberry margaritas, risking Montezuma's wrath... Afterwards went to Rockstock club which was like a first-floor garage packed solid with kids who seemed to have breathed all the available air before we arrived. Didn't stay long.

Friday 6 March *Mexico City*

This was a day off, at last. I can hardly believe I slept 'til 9.15. Showered and had Rice Krispies and coffee with John in the restaurant.

Michelle came around 10.00 and, after signing a guitar for some fans who were hanging around, we set off to one of the big markets. This was a fantastic place packed with the fruits of Mexican handicraft – silver jewellery, glass, fabrics, wooden masks, furniture, carved stone, obsidian and crystal. Bought earrings and necklaces, hair slides, woven wristbands and appalling trousers for Trevor. John, Jack and I posed as the three amigos in outrageous Mexican hats... it should be a good photograph. Came close to buying a stained-glass lampshade for the new house but decided that getting it home would be a nightmare.

Returned to the hotel and had lunch with Michelle. Later, she took us to the downtown area of the city where there are beautiful old buildings – a cathedral, government house, and the ballet. This area was originally built on the site of an old lake and, like Venice, the buildings are very slowly sinking.

Back to the hotel. Tried to tempt little street children to be photographed. They took my money, then ran away. Fair enough. Taken out to dinner (Japanese) then to Rockstock, the sweaty garage, once again. Got sloshed. In bed by 3.30!

Saturday 7 March *Mexico City – Sky*

I had forgotten to close my curtains. I was, consequently, woken by the early morning Mexican sunshine streaming across my tired vision. It was 7 o'clock so I rose, showered and set about trying to pack the many things I'd acquired during the last two weeks. It took until 8.30 which was leaving time.

Michelle took us to the airport where we were greeted by the smiling, affable airport officials who took care of us during check-in. Had a spot of breakfast in the airport café and said our goodbyes to Michelle. I felt a bit iffy during the flight to NYC, especially on landing. I wouldn't recommend combining a hangover with cabin-pressure.

We had two hours to kill before boarding the plane for London. In the departure lounge we bumped into none other than Dwane Welch – the chap who made the phone call to my house to ask if I'd be interested in meeting Marillion for the first time, back in '89. He used to work for John A but now works for BMG music in Hong Kong, and was travelling to London on the same flight. He came back to where we were sitting for a chat. The flight has been okay up to the time of writing… only six and a half hours to go. Jack's sitting next to an F1-11 pilot with a compass on his watch strap.

Sunday 8 March *Sky – Home*

Sailed through customs. Phew. I felt like I was carrying half of Mexico's national treasures. There was a driver waiting with a large Mercedes so I jumped in the back and gave him instructions to chez Hogarth. The way it works is that, when we're travelling to do promotional work for EMI, we get the limos and the Business Class air-tickets. When we're touring, the expenses are down to us, so it's cabs, kebab vans and 'Economy' all the way.

The girls were still in bed but got up bleary-eyed when I rang the doorbell at 8.00am. Opened the suitcase and distributed presents. Fi Fi seemed pleased with all of them – pumps from LA, and ring, headband, hair slide and crystal from Mexico. I'd bought Dizzy some earrings which she thought were lovely and often wore after that. Nial's grown a lot in my absence.

We all went to Angus and Renie McPherson's (friends of Ian M) for lunch. Ian and Wanda were there, also Malcolm (who manages Air Studios) and Lisa, his wife, and loads of children. I was tottering about dazed and exhausted, but I got better later. I enticed Angus into describing his theoretical invention – a craft which travels from London to Sydney in 20 minutes on a gallon of petrol. He's either the next Einstein, or he's mental.

Monday 9 March *Home*

Spent nearly all afternoon (having got up at 12.00) on the phone trying to power my mortgage through. Managed to arrange a survey on Brisbane House for tomorrow. Brisbane House is a detached 3 bedroomed Cotswold-stone cottage in a little village called Charlton, near Banbury. We've finally decided we'll have to live within commuting distance of Marillion's new studio. We didn't fancy living IN Aylesbury, so we drew a circle and this has been the first house within it that we both like. Dizzy's not really too happy about it. She's got a circle of good friends in and around Englefield Green and, inevitably they will all be lost and new friends will have to be made. Never easy.

When we went to bed, I couldn't sleep. Got up at 1.30 and hung about 'til 3.00. Went back to bed and got up again with Hargreaves, at 7.45.

Tuesday 10 March

The survey went okay, apparently. Drove to Fleet in Hampshire with a cheque for

£16.73 so that some dead-head called Helen could fax my references to the Norwich & Peterborough Building Society, who have been most helpful. Arranged to meet a solicitor on Friday at 2.15.

Had a Korg T3 delivered. Later found it doesn't work – they're sending another in the morning.

Went to bed at 9.00.

Sunday 15 March *Home – NYC – Philadelphia*

Woke up at ten past eight. Thought I'd better pack. Had a bath first. Cab arrived at 9.00. Kissed my girls bye bye and Nial gave me a farewell vomit.

Someone in the organisation had decided that, to keep costs down, it might be a good idea to let our out-front sound-technician, 'Privet' (Priv) Hedge ALSO tour-manage this leg of the tour. I was to discover that some people just aren't cut out for some jobs...

Arrived at Gatwick South Terminal and eventually found my way to the check-in desk. There was general chaos and long queues – first to be interviewed by American security staff who asked you a load of questions before giving you a sticker and moving you on to the next queue to check in. Being as all the boys had already done this and were nearing the front of the second queue, I joined Priv, Steve R and Pete. Priv was somehow in possession of a spare 'security cleared' sticker and discreetly stuck it on my suitcase. And so began a day of near-catastrophes:

1. I was approached, almost immediately, by a security guard who asked me why I had applied the sticker without speaking to the security staff. He was very serious. I thought I was about to be detained. Fortunately, he only sent me back to the end of the queue. Phew.

2. When we arrived in New York, for reasons I can't understand, Priv picked up my suitcase and took it through customs, leaving me to carry his. I was some way behind him in the queue and he didn't wait around to check the band were okay. When I got to the customs point I was pulled aside and asked to open the case. It had a combination lock on it and, of course, I didn't know the number. "I can't," I said, "it's not mine."

Once again, the fates smiled upon me and, somehow, I wasn't arrested.

3. The connecting flight to Philadelphia was from a departure gate immediately next to an open bar. Pete T and I sat at a table right next to the gate and ordered a beer. There was only a screen between the table where we sat and the departure area, which was full of people. At some point, I craned my head around the screen (for the umpteenth time) to see the lounge completely empty! Everyone had gone. We rushed to the desk to be informed that the doors were closed and the flight had left! Once again our 'tour-manager' was proving himself to be an excellent sound-man. Pete and I stared incredulously at each other. Our bags were on the flight which had just left. We wondered if anyone

would bother to take them to the hotel in Philadelphia, or just leave' em on the carousel. I reckoned they'd just get left. Pete and I had to buy tickets for the next flight to Philly. When we eventually arrived there, we managed to get hold of one of the band at the hotel who told us our bags were in Priv's room. The relief was short-lived. When we called his room he'd gone out on the town for the night with the crew.

Anyone who knows or has worked with Pete and me can only imagine the serenity and calm with which we handled the situation...

Monday 16 March *Philadelphia – Allentown*

Up at 7.00 and down to breakfast. By 8.30 I had the T3 set up in my room and, by 9.00, Pete and Steve had arrived and we were rehearsing. Phoners started happening at 10ish.

At 12.00 we set off with Wally Verson (Hit & Run promo guy) and a minibus packed-solid with luggage, to drive to Allentown P.A. for interviews and a show sponsored by radio WZZO. We stayed at the Hamilton Plaza Hotel, notable for the *papier maché* sculptures of cartoon-old-people in the lobby. Yeah!

The radio appearance was nothing special but the show was to be a pleasant surprise. Soundcheck ceased to exist when it was revealed that we didn't have a 110/240 volt transformer for the backline. They had supplied a shaver adaptor!!! Priv improvised in the end, going across two of the three phases of the power supply which, fortunately, was 3-phase (proving once-again that he was an excellent sound-man!). Unfortunately, the time it took to figure all this out wiped out our much-needed rehearsal time and we ended up soundchecking in front of half the audience.

Back to the hotel and we had just enough time for a hurried dinner with Meredith before returning in style, in the limo provided, feeling nervous and unsure of what lay ahead. When we arrived, the joint was jumping. About 700 people! We tip-toed nervously through the set to rapturous applause. Phew. We're so lucky. Afterwards I must have met everyone in the place. They were all sweethearts and I thoroughly enjoyed meeting them. Club manager, Barry, was generous and helpful.

Tuesday 17 March *Allentown – Scranton – Danbury*

Up at 7.00 and out at 9.30 for the drive to Scranton. As I breakfasted with Wally and Steve, it started to snow. The journey to Scranton was uneventful. I remember Scranton from my young days as an electrical engineer in Doncaster. We exported quite a lot of machinery through Scranton airport to Hanover, P.A. Pete was traveling with Meredith as our bus was full of luggage and flight cases. (He'd not experienced Meredith's driving before so he didn't share the fear...). When we arrived at the radio station we learned that she had crashed the car into the curb and blown two tyres. No one was hurt and they still arrived in time for the radio show, which was a little theatre within the radio station which, in turn, was housed in a lovely old building above the newspaper offices. The show was sparsely attended and I felt like we were giving a lecture.

Afterwards, we had lunch in the slowest restaurant on the planet before driving up to Danbury M.A., arriving at the Holiday Inn at 7.00 amid St. Patrick's Day celebrations. They seem to make more of a fuss about it here than in Ireland! The bar was full of middle-aged dears in their best dresses. Had a beer with Pete and went to bed.

Wednesday 18 March *Danbury – Newhaven – Danbury*

Managed a lie-in. 8.00! Spent the morning filling in insurance documents to be faxed back to England, and typing sleeve notes for the anniversary album, on Steve R's laptop. We left around 11.00 for a pointless visit to a record store in Newhaven. I bought a couple of Yale fraternity shirts at the local college shop called Bula Bula! They also had a Yaleopoly board game which I was unable to purchase because they were out of stock. Damn. There's always next time…

Had lunch and then off to a radio interview at God-knows-what FM with DJ Mike. Nice chap – we taught him about "roger-ing".

Back to Danbury for soundcheck at Tuxedo Junction… Hey! Again, the show was well-attended and enthusiastically received. We played a lot better. Unfortunately, at a lot of these clubs you can't get in until you're 21 and I hear quite a lot of people were turned away. There must be something we can do about that.

Thursday 19 March *Danbury – Vermont*

Left Danbury at 11.00 for the long drive up to Vermont. Some of the countryside was very pretty. At the side of the freeway there are walls of icicles, occasionally solid blocks of ice, which shine turquoise like icebergs.

Arrived at The Fairfield Motel and checked in before driving to Burlington for soundcheck. It was a dark little nightclub (K.D. Churchills) and reminded me of a youth club. At soundcheck there was the usual gaggle of kids shivering outside. Some had been there all afternoon. When we got back in the evening for the show, the club was busy and the audience very noisy. I suddenly realised we must be up near Canada, where the audience whoop and holler ceaselessly. Consequently, we couldn't hear much of what we were doing during the show. "No wonder the Beatles stopped touring!" said Pete.

After the show we signed loads of autographs and I got somewhat sloshed on the free drink. Regretted it almost immediately but especially in the morning. Went to bed at 3.00 after speaking to Dizzy in Pretoria. Fi Fi didn't want to speak to me. Sent her a postcard instead.

Friday 20 March *Vermont – Quebec*

Up at 8.30 to pack and leave at 9.30. Had breakfast in Libby's Diner, which was like being in a movie, and set off on the long drive to Quebec, snoozing and reading. Passed landscapes of frozen lakes just before the border. Saw men sitting out on the ice, fishing through holes in the ice. I have never seen this before, first-hand.

Arrived around 4.00 and bumped into Ian in the lobby. Went for a walk down to the local mall and bumped into Pete T. Ate pizza and had a beer then wandered back to the hotel. Bumped into Alan Parker, Ray Holsgrove (the one who took me fishing at home in Wraysbury) and Priv and bought them each a drink. Over to the rehearsal studio to discover that the intro DAT of *Splintering Heart* is lost. Oh dear...

Came back to the Hotel des Gouverneurs and had a quiet night in. Watched **Cape Fear**. Robert de Niro was excellent, as usual, in his portrayal of a violent nut-job, but I wouldn't say I enjoyed the movie much – there's something about Nick Nolte that rubs me up the wrong way. Went to bed at 11.00.

Saturday 21 March *Quebec*

Happy Birthday, Gran!

Determinedly stayed in bed until 11.00. Had breakfast and hung about until 2.00 when we left for rehearsal. More hanging about at the rehearsal studio for monitor checking. I made a new DAT from Priv's safety cassette while I was waiting, with the help of Alain in the recording studio adjacent to the rehearsal place. First rehearsal went well, especially *Cover my Eyes* which sounded solid and more honest than the master! *No One Can* was dodgy but improved on repetition.

Returned to the hotel in the evening and listened to the *Cry No More, Brown Paper-Bag* cassette which had arrived via Jack from England, and then went out to a rock club down the road. There was a good cover band on stage. Got bored and came back about 12.00. Read a bit more of **The Secret Pilgrim** by John le Carre, and went bye-byes.

Sunday 22 March *Quebec*

Bumped into Mad Jack in the corridor. He was still drunk! Had breakfast with him along with Ray and Grubby (John McAllis – monitor engineer). The toast is lovely – nice thick white bread, done to perfection as if over a fire. Mmm...

Second day's rehearsal went well. I'm still not hoarse. A TV crew popped in and filmed a couple of songs.

In the evening we went out to a Thai restaurant called Apsara which was in the old part of Quebec. The old town is much more European and, predictably, has a French flavour to it. Managed to get to bed at 12.00. Show tomorrow...

Monday 23 March *Quebec, Theatre Albert Rousseau*

Self-enforced lie-in. Didn't get up until 12.00. Had breakfast with John A who had arrived late last night.

At 2.00 I was picked up by Louis, along with Mark, for interviews. We arrived at the theatre Albert Rousseau around 4.30 for soundcheck which was okay. Back to the hotel for a couple of hours with George Smiley. The show went well, despite Steve's guitar strap disintegrating before *Holidays in Eden.* The hole this made in the set, after only one song, seemed to increase adrenalin somewhat. Memorable moment was the crowd singing a heavily-French-accented, "Pain and Heaven" on *Cover my Eyes* – "Paaiinnn... Evvernnnn".

Tuesday 24 March *Quebec – Montreal*

Left the hotel around 1.00 and drove in the minibus to Montreal, stopping at a diner for a burger. Arrived at Le Brique around 4.00 to be told soundcheck would not be until 6.00, so I walked down the street for a chat with the staff at Musique Plus – the local music-video station. Treated well by MP, who gave me coffee and biscuits, and beckoned me onto camera to say, "Hi."

Went shopping for ankle-supports, with Alan Parker (lighting designer) who I'd bumped into on the street. I like Alan. He's a very nice chap – good at his art, and a positive good-humoured influence. He's got a bit of the drama-queen about him, which I resonate with for some reason...

Back at soundcheck things were sounding good and tonight's audience was already queuing down the street. The show's sold out. Ray took me back to the good old Manoir le Moyne hotel for an hour's sleep and a spot of dinner. I checked in at 8.00, and out at 10.00.

The audience at the show was incredible – one of the best ever, and I enjoyed myself immensely. We had monitor problems during the show, but it's hardly worth mentioning in the context of the overall vibe of the club. After show we did a bit of a meet 'n'greet and then it was back on the bus, to bed, and Toronto.

Wednesday 25 March *Toronto, Phoenix*

Arrived and checked into the Ibis Hotel around 9.00. Had breakfast with the crew and went to bed. Got up at 1.00. There were phone-interviews at 1.30 and then Jack and I were collected to do, what turned out to be, 6 hours of interviews! The interview at Much Music (video TV) with Ziggy was fun. She introduced our *Dry Land* video as "Dried Up", much to our amusement.

We finally arrived at soundcheck at 7.30, after a fifteen-mile drive, to talk to someone at a radio station who really wasn't worth the effort. It was the last straw and we arrived at the gig feeling frazzled and irked. By stage-time I'd managed another 90 minutes' sleep and was feeling much better.

The show went well although the Toronto crowd-reaction rarely lives up to the warmth and mania of Montreal. After the show we chatted to Dean

Cameron, the MD of Capitol records here. He seemed enthused and was a likeable chap. Macho, but not self-consciously so. He looked like he'd have a go at wrestling a bear if pushed to do so. He gave me a black sweatshirt with an embroidered badge on it, of a moose riding a snow-mobile.

Thursday 26 March *Toronto – Syracuse*

I rose around 11.00 and went out in search of breakfast with John A and Ray. Easier said than done, unless you want burgers. By the time we found a café capable of, and prepared to give us breakfast, Ray had gone back to the hotel to start the check out. John and I had breakfast and chatted, returning to the Ibis for check out at 1.00. It was a long old drive and I spent much of it asleep or enduring other people playing video games.

When we arrived at Carrier Circle, Syracuse, I thought we'd arrived at the end of the world. It was raining hard and The Inn-on-the-Circle was indistinguishable from a prisoner-of-war camp. In order to minimise the time spent there, we dropped our bags and trudged through the downpour to the only-slightly-better-but-at-least-they've-got-a-bar Holiday Inn across the road. At 9.00 we couldn't stand it anymore, so we left to check out tomorrow's venue where, it turned out, the worst band in the world was playing. Spun around on our heels and went next door for a beer then gave up and went back to Stalag 13, to sleep. Had another bath with George Smiley and went comatose.

Friday 27 March *Syracuse, Lost Horizon*

Up at 9.15 to drive to Utica where we were scheduled to perform an acoustic set at lunchtime, so piled into the minibus with Pete, Steve, John and Priv. Arrived and got lost, then got found and turned up at Lily Langtry's around 12.00. It's a sort of bar/café with a little stage (Lily [US spelling] Langtry was an actress in the late 19th century, and notable as a close friend of Oscar Wilde and as the mistress of 'Bertie' – Prince of Wales, soon to become King Edward VII. She also took up with a millionaire or two in the US and became an American citizen before her death).

By 1.00 it was packed and there was a murmur of excitement for a small show, the perpetrators of which had no idea what they were doing. Nonetheless, everyone seemed happy and the radio station said it sounded great on the air. Signed hundreds of autographs and returned to Stalag 13 for a couple of hours sleep.

Soundcheck at the Lost Horizon seemed to take forever. A couple of Jewish fans turned up and gave me a Hebrew Monopoly from Israel. Very nice of 'em.

The sound out-front was surprisingly good, but the sound on stage was unsurprisingly awful both at soundcheck and during the show. Dips in the mains voltage put paid to Rothery's backline for most of the gig... must remember to turn the lights on at soundcheck and see what happens...

The crowd seemed cool, but then the band weren't cooking so who can blame 'em. Oh dear. Never mind. Karen from IRS nonetheless seemed pleased. I dunno.

Saturday 28 March *NYC, The Ritz*

Arrived around 9.00. Checked into the Milburn Hotel on W 76th and Broadway and went bye-byes for a couple of hours. Phoned my girls. Spoke to Fi Fi. They both sounded fine. Diz says it's very hot in South Africa.

Thought I'd pop out for a spot of breakfast. When I hit the street it was very damp and chilling, so I jumped a cab and went to Macy's in search of Halston Z-14 underarm stick, which is getting harder to find all the time. Located three and bought them all. Had coffee and croissant at the café in the basement and browsed round the Italian crockery. Returned to The Museum of Modern Art to replace my Norman Parkinson **Hat Fashions** poster, previously nicked by VARIG airlines in Rio. Bought sewing tools to repair my 'Workers for Freedom' favourite shirt whose buttons had been flattened by some steam-roller ironing process at The Holiday Inn Mexico City, and returned to the hotel to sew.

At the soundcheck, which sounded good, I took a phone call from Vojo Milosevic, (who used to play guitar in my first band, Harlow) asking for a ticket to the gig. Also learned that Colin Woore (the other-half of How We Live) and his NY wife, Marie were coming over. Wow. Better be good then...

The show went well. The audience seemed cool again, especially after Canada, but afterwards the vibe was unanimously positive. Chatted with Vojo who didn't know of Steve Ross's tragic death (Harlow's bass player had taken his own life back in the early eighties), and to Colin and Marie who didn't know of Nial's birth! Silvina and JP from Buenos Aires and Michelle from Mexico City had all called in en route to London. Amazing. Showered, and took the bus to Washington.

Sunday 29 March *Washington DC, Bayou*

Arrived at the hotel at 9.00, checked in and had a spot of breakfast with Ian. He mentioned that he would call the Secret Service agent he'd met at the Syracuse gig with regard to a tour of the White House! It all sounds dubious to me... He'd given Ian a card with his name and a Secret Service logo on it... Only in America could they give calling cards to the Secret Service! "Hello there, George Smiley. Spy. Lovely to meet you. Here's my card. G Smiley Esq. MI5 Cambridge Circus, London W1. Open Mon – Sat."

Found my room and went to bed. I was only marginally successful at sleeping, but I struggled through a couple of hours before getting up and walking from Chinatown (where the hotel is situated) uptown, in search of a good spot to drink coffee and write this diary. Eventually stumbled upon the restaurant within the Stouffer Mayflower Hotel which was most pleasant. There were chandeliers twinkling, a large ice sculpture of a swan as a centrepiece on a large ornate dining table and a trio of two violins and flute playing away in the corner. Very civilised, if a little twee. Obviously a 'must' hub for the 'bob and pearls' Washington set. Ordered Earl Grey tea and a spot of lunch and, goodness, I felt a million miles and a million years away from Intake, Doncaster...

Soundcheck was problematical and doors were open before we left the stage! Took a cab back to the hotel care of Zelma, a fifty-year-old black 'country girl' who was friendly and impressed by the queue of people outside the club.

The vibe at the show was the best so far since Montreal i.e. exceptional! What is it about Washington?! Can't wait to do it again.

Monday 30 March *Washington – Philadelphia, Chestnut Cabaret*

Woke up in Washington. Had breakfast and wrote a few postcards. Mooched through Chinatown trying to find stamps. We all piled back into the minibus and spent most of the day traveling to Philadelphia.

When we arrived at the club I realised I'd been here once before, on a night off, although I don't think I had stayed long. It's a shame we weren't going to have more time here. I like Philadelphia – there's something about the place.

At the beginning of the show, the intro loop begins for *Splintering Heart.* This intro builds slowly in intensity until a double kick-drum joins it - "du-dup... dup dup". I have to count 8 of these and be at the centre mic ready to sing the first line. I stood in the wings all ready to go, listening to the loop building, and, as the kick-drums arrived, some guy from the fan-club suddenly appeared next to me and said: "Hello Steve! I'd like to present you with this cake!" He was proudly holding a large chocolate cake before me.

"Err... Thanks – it's not really a good time right now..." I said, trying desperately to keep count of the kick drums.

"Oh... gee... I guess I'll give it to you later then..."

"Yes – that would be good. Err... that's very kind"

By this time I had lost count. Needless to say I missed the cue and sang the whole of verse 1 in the wrong place while the band nervously looked on. Since that night, every time we play or rehearse *Splintering Heart,* as the kick drums arrive in the loop, I can't help but think, "Cake." And smile to myself.

My voice was on the edge too. Steve R broke a string during the solo so, all things considered, we got off to a bad start. Fortunately it all got better – my voice opened up during the set and we all seemed 'into it'. Steve R found a sense of humour and communication with the crowd, which from my perspective, is a new and welcome development.

Afterwards, I went out into the audience and signed things for people. I also cut the above-mentioned chocolate-cake from the US fanclub. This show was the fourth in-a-row and exhaustion had set in. Boarded the bus and had to wait for the crew to finish up before finding the Ramada Hotel and a shower. Party-mood ensued on the bus in anticipation of the day-off ahead. I hadn't the strength. Lay in my bunk and drifted off to sleep with a grin, listening to the happy sound of a drunken chorus downstairs, singing *Girlfriend Is Better* by The Talking Heads downstairs. Well done, Alex.

Tuesday 31 March *Columbus:* Day off

Woke up in a garage. The bus had blown a tyre and was awaiting a wheel change. Everyone else was sleeping so I went over to the truck stop and phoned England to discover that my house-buyer has finally been cleared for a mortgage so maybe we can exchange soon…

Drove the rest of the way to Columbus, Ohio and checked into The Holiday Inn.

Went out walkies and bought flowers for my room. Spent the rest of the day writing up this diary and waiting for something to happen.

Columbus Holiday Inn was on the campus of O.S.U (Ohio State University), so the environment was like a scene from the Graduate.

In the evening I went out to an Italian restaurant but it was closed.

Wednesday 1 April *Columbus, Newport Theatre*

Rabbits. Up around 12.00. Picked up at 12.30 by Greg from IRS, to go to a live radio interview with Jack. It went very well… We talked about Scotland ("My son does the sound for Ted Nugent") and "Rogering".

Soundcheck went well and I decided to come back to the show early to check out Wes, our guitar tech and opening act, so I told Ray I'd see everyone at the gig. Unfortunately, a hot bath rendered me unconscious and I slept until stage time 9.15!! Freaked, and arrived at the show, still waking up, at 9.30.

The show went well although attendance was a bit slack.

After-show reaction seemed enthusiastic.

Didn't sleep well.

Thursday 2 April *Cleveland, Empire*

Early check-in at the Holiday Inn W150th St. Slept a bit and then had lunch with Steve R, Jack and Ray.

Left the hotel at 2.00 to drive across town to a record store Sam's Jams for a signing. Good fun. Straight on to soundcheck which took about two hours. That's longer than the show! (something of a Marillion tradition). Privet was having trouble stopping Ian's tom-toms ringing.

Sound on stage at the show was iffy and the reaction from the crowd was disappointing compared to last time and therefore, my expectations. Afterwards however, everyone I spoke to seemed blown-away!?

I later learned that Midge Ure played here last night and only 50 people showed up! We sold out at around 700. Puts it into perspective I guess…

Friday 3 April *Detroit, The Ritz*

Arrived at the hotel around 11.00am and checked in. Showered and went down to the breakfast room. After a quick breakfast, Pete, Steve, Mark, Ray and I set off to find The Magic Bag theatre in downtown Detroit (it could have been uptown – I don't know how to tell the difference). This was to be a live acoustic thing without keyboards. When we finally arrived after getting lost, we discovered that there were two other bands on as well. Quickly soundchecked in front of thirty people who were the audience. Chaos on stage – monitors muted for the first half of the first song etc. Someone said it sounded good on air though.

We were then taken to a shop to sign stuff. All a bit of a waste of time really. The shop didn't have any of our CDs in stock! Came back to the hotel and went to bed.

Gig soundcheck was a pleasant surprise but, by showtime, my spirits plunged as my sound had become inexplicably thin and dry. Previous vows never to play this place again were remembered and reavowed as the power went off *twice* during the show. I only just kept my temper and the audience, bless 'em, were supportive and happy with the show.

Afterwards, we learned that the truck had been broken into while we were on stage and all the carnets and documents stolen. I later learned someone had been shot in the car park the night before. Good grief. Get me out of here!

Saturday 4 April *Chicago, Park West*

Arrived around 11.00 and checked into the Allerton Hotel. Went to bed. Got up around 1.30 and went shopping for shirts.

Got back to leave at 3.00 for a signing at the Music Warehouse. Good fun. Straight to soundcheck at the Park West where a tired and emotional Priv was wrestling with a mains hum on one side of the PA.

Sound on stage was 'different' but good. This was to be an early show - 8.30 - so I had time for a quick bath before returning to catch John Wesley's set at 7.30. He was good!

We hit the stage at 8.40 to a sell-out enthusiastic crowd. I really enjoyed the show. I was singing well, despite this being the fourth show in a row, once again. The encores were a bit fast, which was a shame. Ian gets a bit carried away when he's enjoying himself and the tempos inevitably slide up into an area where I can no longer fit the words in (try singing *Incommunicado* at double-speed… "I don't wanna be the back-page interview, I don't want launderette anonymity…" Murder.).

Afterwards Priv declared that "the PA sucked – literally." Maybe it was out of phase.

Fortunately we came good on a crucial evening – there were quite a lot of influential business folk in the crowd.

Sunday 5 April *Grand Rapids:* Day off

Pulled into Grand Rapids, Michigan around 9.00 and checked into The Holiday Inn opposite the Club Eastbrook – tomorrow's venue.

Went to bed and rose around 11.30 for breakfast and a walk in the Mall opposite. Sunday trading is okay here (unlike England) and all the shops are open. Bought little Reebok trainers for Nial and found a hairdresser's so I had my roots done.

Back at the hotel, Judy from IRS made me a present of Halston Z14 cologne which she said she's had for years and didn't need. Cheers, Judy. We all left the hotel at 2.00 (Pete, Steve, Me, Priv, Leo, Judy) to go to Vinyl Solution record shop to play an acoustic set there. We found 300+ people waiting for us when we arrived. Quite a vibe. The set was broadcast live on air (WLAV FM) and was very well received by the audience. Afterwards the rest of the band and crew showed up and we signed *everybody's* records, t-shirts etc, while the crew drank the free beer and ate the deli tray. We were later given a pick of 3 CDs for free. Cor, thanks. I remember picking up a copy of Sting's **Nothing Like the Sun**, which I have enjoyed for years since. Great album.

In the evening we were invited out to dinner with Aris Hampers, the DJ who has done so much to make us popular in these parts, and afterwards, he invited us all to his house for drinks. He took us into the basement to show off an enormous TV and surround-sound system. It looked and sounded like the Odeon, Leicester Square – I was waiting for the organist to come up out of the floor when I noticed a record and CD collection to rival most record-stores. I guess he gets 'em all given. He really does have everything I could imagine from A-Z. I booked time on our next visit to watch **Apocalypse Now** down here.

Monday 6 April *Grand Rapids, Club Eastbrook*

Had a lie-in and rose around 12.00. At 2.00 we found out that we'd agreed to play a couple of songs live on air for Aris, so there was a slight panic while we ran to the Club Eastbrook for acoustic guitars. Everything went okay though, and Aris seemed happy. As I said, Aris is the DJ single-handedly responsible for our success in this area of Michigan. He's a self-confessed fan of our sound and has crusaded to popularise it. If only there were more DJs out there of a like mind. Still – we can't complain, can we? We're doing alright. After the interview we went over to another record-store to sign yet more records and t-shirts. I thought we'd already signed everything in Grand Rapids yesterday. They must have been shopping overnight...

The band went off to soundcheck while I had a wander round the Mall again, looking for Reeboks for Fi Fi. Couldn't find any, but found Z14 talc in JC Penney's – impossible to get hold of in the UK.

Soundcheck was iffy – I think it's the hall. Back at the hotel I called the IRS rep in Atlanta to say hi and apologise for not putting in a show there. Had a float in the pool, a quick shower and then back to the gig.

We were introduced by Aris and Steve. They were representing rival radio-stations, both sponsoring the show. I dedicated *Easter* to Aris as he'd told me it's a favourite.

The audience were quiet to start with, but riveted. It's amazing what a little airplay does for a band. By the end of the show, the crowd were up out of their seats. Somehow, though, I couldn't quite settle down to it, which is a shame. Thanks to Aris, this feels like the US town where we're currently loved most, and, of course, the feeling's mutual. We played additional encores and this took the show up to 2 hours 15 minutes – twenty minutes longer than usual.

Tuesday 7 April *Bloomington, Indiana Jakes*

Staggered off the bus to warm sunlight and the smell of mown lawns. Wow! That's better. Checked in and panicked as I realised I didn't have my credit cards. Took a cab to the club to see if I'd left them on the bus. I had! Phew, etc.

Walked round the corner to find a florist, after chatting in the sun to Alan Parker and Priv who were kicking a football around the car-park. I ordered flowers for Sofi (it's her birthday on the 13th) from Beata, an "old German Jewess" (her words) who was very sweet. Next door was a vintage watch specialist and I spent half-an-hour coming dangerously close to blowing a large amount of money. Didn't though. Went back to the hotel and snoozed outside on the lawn under a tree.

The club was small, the monitors horrid, and the attendance sparse at around 150. I guess this one's a 'filler' – "Not a big college town etc."

Wednesday 8 April *Cincinnati, Bogarts*

Now that's more like it! Sunshine and a warm welcome at the Vernon Manor Hotel, from the weather at least. Best hotel of the tour so far. According to the guest book the Beatles stayed here! No one seemed to know which room. Maybe I was in it! Spent most of the day in bed with the windows open, snoozing and feeling heavenly as there were no interviews scheduled.

Once again, the monitor sound at the show was not great. Poor old Grubby – he's really got his work cut out with these house monitor-systems which are usually ill-maintained and abused (if not totally knackered). I really enjoyed myself, however, and managed to pull off a great crowd reaction. Climbed the PA for the first time in quite a while.

Ian keeps going on about Yasser Arafat who, apparently, went missing and turned up again in the desert – the sole survivor of a plane crash… no wonder they call him "a cat with seven souls".

Spoke to Andy King (our buyer) who says he'll instruct his solicitor to exchange contracts today. I'll believe it when I see it. It's murder trying to buy a house from the other side of the Atlantic…

It looks like Wes, our guitar tech from Florida, is going to get me a Rickenbacker flown to Boulder, Colorado!

Thursday 9 April *St Louis, Mississippi Nights*

Arrived at the Embassy Suites hotel which, for once, was opposite the club. Nice hotel but the staff were somewhat, er... 'slow'. The bad news started arriving as soon as I did.

House trouble. Charlton says they can't move on the 1st. I don't believe it. More heated long-distance expensive phone calls...

The club was small, but seemed to be 'on the circuit' and not a bad place. The show was fairly sparsely attended, but my on-stage sound was good and the vibe in the room was great. I can't remember enjoying a show quite so much in a long time – maybe since Utrecht. Dee McLoughlin (our TM from the last tour) showed up! His girlfriend lives in St. Louis. Today is Mad Jack's birthday and Ray brought him a cake before the second encore *(Garden Party).*

After the show we nipped to a club called Kennedy's to see a 'Flower' band. Went back to the hotel with a daisy, checked out and boarded the bus for the long journey to Boulder, Colorado.

Friday 10 April *St. Louis – Boulder:* Day Off

The drive to Boulder took most of the day, and we eventually arrived at The Holiday Inn around 5.00 in the afternoon. I was on a mission to buy a guitar, so I took the keys to the car which Ian and Steve R had hired, and set off in search of the town with Wes and Jack. Didn't find much in the way of guitars but discovered Boulder to be probably my favourite town in the USA so far. The town centre is a bit like Covent Garden with mountains! There were flower beds full of tulips alongside the pavements and street cafés with tables outside in the sunshine. Had a spot of tea with Wes and Jack and returned to the hotel.

Regrouped and showered and returned to town to do the bars. Ended up getting separated from the crowd along with Trevor. He and I scoured the town for adventure and visited at least half a dozen bars and clubs. Ended up in the Fox theatre where there was a reggae band playing. Fortunately I hadn't finished any of my drinks 'cause I was stopped by the police driving back to the Holiday Inn at 1.45am after shooting several red-flashing lights (I was under the impression that you can drive through them if they're flashing – this is only half-true... you're supposed to stop, check nothing's coming, and proceed. This is actually a much more sensible system than in England where the lights still turn red in the middle of the night and you must stop and wait until they turn green). Unfortunately, Trevor had finished every single one of his drinks (and probably a few other people's drinks too) because he had passed out in the passenger seat next to me.

Well, from here on, the evening developed like this. First of all, what looked like the Blackpool Illuminations went off in my rear view mirror. American police-cars carry a lot of coloured lights on the roof. I pulled over to the side of the road, got out of the car and began to walk back to the waiting police-car. That didn't go down well for a start! In America you're supposed to wait for them to come to you.

The officer leaned out of the car and shouted, "Get back in the car!" I did so. When he ambled up to my side window I was impressed by the mass of paraphernalia hanging from his belt. Gun, some kind of stick/club thing, big torch, and various other objects I couldn't quite define. He was certainly "tooled up".

Policeman: "Is this your car, Sir?"

Me: "No, it's hired"

Policeman: "Did you know you just drove straight through three red lights?"

Me: "Yes. I thought that was okay."

Policeman: "No it isn't… Can I see your driver's licence?"

Me: "No, I don't have it with me."

Policeman: "Let me see your ID sir"

Me: "Err… I'm English – we don't carry ID."

Policeman: "A passport?"

Me: "I can show it to you, no problem – but I'm afraid it's at The Holiday Inn."

The policeman had a long look at Trevor, head back, sleeping peacefully, mouth open amid a mane of long hair, and, having decided he wasn't dead, sighed and continued: "Could I see the rental papers please sir"

Me: "Err… I'm not sure what happened to them. I didn't rent the car myself."

Policeman: "Have you been drinking sir?"

Me: "Yes."

Policeman: "How much would you say you've had to drink?"

Me: "A couple of beers"

Policeman: "Do you mean 1, 2 or 3 beers?"

Me: "Two beers".

Policeman: "What is your name?"

Me: "Steve Hogarth. Actually, it doesn't say that on my passport…

Policeman: "Get out of the car sir. I can see you've been drinking and I intend to give you the standard drink/driving test. The state of Colorado views drunk driving very seriously. It is a felony. This is a voluntary test, but in the event that you fail any part of it, I will arrest you."

Me: "Okay. Let's do it."

Well, he then had me walk along a line which he drew with chalk on the pavement, touching the end of my nose with my middle finger with my eyes closed, and then standing on one leg with the other outstretched while counting slowly to 20.

Fortunately, I managed all this without any difficulty and he told me I was free to go.

I asked him the way to The Holiday Inn because, at the point in the journey he'd pulled us over, I was quite lost!

He instructed me to follow him and he drove back to The Holiday Inn. Marvellous. What a nice guy. I was surprised he was so civil to me all things considered. That's a glowing review from me for the Colorado Police.

I got back into my room at 3.00 having chaperoned sleepy Trev into the building. Phoned Dizzy to tell her all about it…

Saturday 11 April *Boulder, Colorado Fox Theatre*

Last night I was recommended a restaurant called Nancy's, which is an old house with a fab attitude and THE place to have breakfast in Boulder. Went there with Alan Parker. Very nice – stripped pine and great wallpaper… quite English in a way. Great menu. Got talking to a Russian who was in Boulder on an exchange scheme. He says he's an agricultural economist. Invited him and his girlfriend to the show. He said he'd get his boss to milk the cows…

Dropped Alan P at the gig and went to a guitar shop. Decided I'd like a purple Les Paul. Went back later with Steve R, Jack and Pete and decided, on balance, to leave it 'til L.A.

Soundcheck went okay – my sound was a bit ringy. The centre-mic position was underneath some flown PA cabinets. Yuk.

Back at the hotel, a sorority party was in full swing – lots of conservative young missies with their middle-class moms, having a real nice wholesome time… Acapella singing from Ivy League clean-cut guys had 'em mesmerized. I bubbled around in the hot-tub and looked on, fascinated and a little bit saddened by what looked, once again, like a scene from **The Graduate**. How anyone can live like this, after JFK and Lennon, beats me. Does that make *me* strange?

Back to the show. Totally brilliant audience response. The best since Montreal. I want to come here again! Signed the dressing room ceiling. Returned to the hotel, showered up, checked out, got on the bus for the LONG drive to L.A. via the desert and the Grand Canyon. Mike (our bus driver from Nashville, Tennessee) told me that this drive was heading through some amazing scenery, so I asked him to give me a shout in the morning if I was missing anything.

Sunday 12 April *Colorado Grand Canyon:* Day Off

Was stirred by Mike at 8.00am: "You wanted to see scenery? Well, there's a whole BUNCH of it out there right now!"

I rolled out of bed and went to the lounge to have a look. Outside, through the glass, was the spectacular red landscape of the Colorado Desert. Tall pillars of red sandstone rising from a red eroded lunar surface. It took until around 4.30 in the afternoon, driving through such stunning scenery and taking photographs, until we arrived at The Grand Canyon. Perhaps I'd heard too much hype, perhaps I'd already seen the pictures, but I wasn't as awestruck as I expected/hoped to be. It is BIG, it is impressive and, in its own way, beautiful – but it was somehow less magical and less earthly than I had expected. We hung around in the pleasant afternoon sunlight, but I was thinking mainly of getting back on the bus and sleeping.

The tour was, by now, taking its toll on me and I was fast-becoming a boring bastard. Slept and no doubt missed more spectacular scenery until we stopped at a small town called Flagstaff. I showered at a motel before going out with the chaps for a spot of dinner at a local bar, Bunhuggers. Returned to the motel to phone South Africa and wish Fi Fi a happy birthday. Back onto the bus to sleep our way to L.A.

Monday 13 April *The road – Los Angeles:* Day off

Happy Birthday, my sweetheart. Spent most of the day on the freeway, driving the seemingly-endless straight line to Los Angeles, listening to **Nothing Like the Sun** by Sting and **Out of Time** by R.E.M. I had acquired them at the record store in Grand Rapids.

This part of the journey was memorable for the commotion which suddenly sprung up among the crew in the bus-lounge. I rolled out of my bunk to find out what was going on. Alongside our obviously rock n'roll tour bus (they're all air-brushed here with rock n'roll imagery) was a girl driving in a little red convertible. She had obviously made eye-contact with one of the boys and decided to treat one and all to a show. She was driving along without her top on. Mike, the driver, was whooping and hollering and accelerating to overtake her for another glimpse of her breasts. There she was, grinning away. She later overtook the bus wearing absolutely nothing! Ah… California girls.

Eventually arrived at hotel Le Réve in Hollywood at about 5.00 in the evening. Discovered Steve Karas (IRS records) in the room next door, and he invited me in for a bourbon while he filled me in on who'd been fired at IRS. Apparently Barbara Bolan had wept buckets while wielding the axe. I continue to respect her more and more. Steve invited me out to dinner with a manager-friend whose name escapes me, and we ate Italian on Sunset.

Later in the evening I bumped into Wes, who dragged me kicking and screaming (ha ha) off to a club called Black and Blue (I think), where I leaned against the bar and got chewing gum all over my jacket.

Tuesday 14 April *Los Angeles, Variety Arts Theatre*

Rose around 9.00, showered and went out for breakfast to my usual breakfast café on Sunset Boulevard with Mark, Wes and Andy (drum-tech). After ordering, I popped next door to Bloomers and bought a dress for Sofi.

We all walked back to Le Réve at 11.30 for a meeting with Bill Smith at 12.00. He was on the roof by the pool with Andrew Douglas, cameraman for the forthcoming *Sympathy* video. He had brought Cromalins of the singles collection sleeve and, typically, it looks good. I preferred the single sleeve to the album cover, but never mind. As usual, it's too late to change anything.

Caught a cab with Pete and John A to the IRS office. I must admit I felt a bit uncomfortable at the prospect of lunch with Miles Copeland and Jay Boberg.

I'd met Miles some years ago at the Selsdon Park Hotel (Croydon) and he was uptight and uncommunicative to the point of paranoia. I shouldn't have worried – Jay was friendly and pleasant and seemed like a real gentleman. Miles seemed a little 'on stage', but eased up during lunch and then seemed relaxed. I still can't believe that, after prompting from Stevo Glendenning, I did the 'Gene Oktober' routine right into Miles' face.

Europeans supported Gene's band, Chelsea, many years ago and I remember Gene saying the following to me (Gene had the general demeanour of a pirate, so if you apply an over-the-top pirate delivery to the following, you won't be far off): "Y'see... I owe Miles Copeland, seventy grand! And he says ter me... 'Gene, I want you to tour, see.' And I says to 'im, 'Yeaagh... but I don't want to do it, see,' and then he says to me, 'Yeaagh! But you owe me... seventy grand!' ...So I have to do it, see!'"

To my relief, he seemed most amused. I do believe that Miles, as far as is possible, tries to find ways to help 'displaced talent' and, despite his hard-headed reputation, has motives based more on the well-being of those he represents than on the financial aspect. I have seen first-hand how he has tried to help my friend Darryl Way over the years.

After lunch (which was the best broiled salmon I've ever had) we went back to IRS, where we encountered Nancy Shamess and David Millman packing their things (they were leaving). It was awkward and sad to be saying goodbye so soon after meeting these charming people. They all said they were coming to the show which was touching, considering. Nancy drove me to The Guitar Centre on Sunset where I ogled my way round the walls. Everything seems dearer here than in Boulder Co. I made Nancy a present of some beads I'd been wearing by way of a 'thanks and sorry' present.

Soundcheck went really well. The opening act, Dada, watched from the wings and seemed genuinely impressed. I returned across town to Le Réve and had half-an-hour alone under the stars on the roof in the pool and jacuzzi, before returning to the show. This was, of course, the big one – sold-out and with probably the whole of IRS in attendance.

We gave it all we've got. I fought hard against being spooked by M.C's attendance and tried not to overplay the performance. As luck would have it, the rest had helped my voice and I was singing at my best. I came off stage elated. Miles came back shortly after. He seemed excited too:

"I hear you can act...?" he said

"Yup," I said (who wouldn't!)

"I've got a script I'd like you to have a look at..."

Bloody hell.

I quickly showered and went to the next room where chaos ensued. Once again, security was leaky, and talking to the record label meant wading through over-enthusiastic (but well-meaning) members of the audience who'd come back along with our guests. It all seemed to add to the vibe, though, which was electric. Barbara B seemed thrilled, and stunned me by planting me a big kiss square on the mouth. You could've knocked me over with a feather! I thanked everyone for coming and tried not to bask visibly in the attention and compliments I was receiving. Can shows like this really make a difference long-term? We'll wait and see.

Wednesday 15 April *San José, Cabaret*

Checked into the Howard Johnson around 11.00. Met Joe S in the lobby at 1.00, who took me to the local radio station for an interview. On the way back, I dropped into the local guitar centre and tried a few Les Pauls before spotting a Rickenbacker 12-string. It was all downhill from there… I tried it though an amp, and that was it. Love. Nearly missed the soundcheck trying to get out of the guitar shop.

During the rest of the day I gradually decided I must buy the 12-string, and I made plans to go back in the morning.

Soundcheck was laborious – more monitor problems. There were people sitting outside the venue already (some had been there all day), so I sat outside and chatted in the sun. After the soundcheck I returned to the hotel and went to bed for much-needed sleep.

Once again, the show went really well. I wasn't on the same form vocally as last night, but we still delivered, and left the place jumping.

Back at the hotel I chatted with Priv until 3.00, and then went to bed to dream of 12-strings.

Thursday 16 April *San Francisco, Bimbos*

Woke at 10.00 and spent the morning trying to buy a guitar. They wouldn't accept my Visa because it was over the credit-limit (Dizzy's air-tickets) so, in the end, Jo Rothery put it on her Am Ex. "Thank you, milady!" And what a beauty it is. A 'Tom Petty', solid-body sunburst, finished with checkerboard edging and Rickenbackers distinctive 'shark's tooth' fret markers.

Steve, Pete, Jo, Ray and I drove to the CD warehouse, San José, to perform the last acoustic set to an assembled crowd of about 200. Much signing of stuff followed, and I managed to acquire The Who's **Greatest Hits** and the Rare Bird CD before wandering next door-but-one to order a tuna sandwich, and then back (briefly) to The Phoenix hotel to catch another glimpse of my new guitar on the bed. Rickenbackers come with a birth-certificate which shows the date the guitar was finished in the factory. I found the certificate in a pocket in the case and, to my amazement, discovered it had been 'born' on May 14th – my birthday. What a coincidence! It was meant to be.*

We drove to San Francisco and arrived at the venue around 4.00. Oh dear – it looks like some kind of chintzy jazz club. The crew were depressed and the mains keeps tripping! What a terrible way to finish a tour! Went back to The Phoenix Hotel - 'an urban resort' - which I like a lot. It's like a San Franciscan

Butlins with art and piped birdsong which comes through discrete speakers around a central swimming pool surrounded by motel-like rooms. That's another good thing about being signed to IRS – they have a happy knack of finding groovy hotels.

At the soundcheck at 6.00. Nothing was happening. Dada were opening and waited patiently and dejectedly for hours until we left the stage. I *really* don't like our soundchecks. Their guitar-player, Michael, had his parents coming to the show, so he must have been heartbroken. When we later returned to the gig he told me that their set had gone well, so that eased my conscience a bit. Our set went well, despite the limitations of the venue and equipment.

Afterwards we returned to the Phoenix for a bit of a tipple with John A and the chaps from Dada. Michael said he wished I'd produced their album instead of Ken Scott, and said perhaps I should do their next one… I wouldn't mind. Gave Wes the Ricky so that he could ship it back to the UK with the rest of the backline. I wonder if the Customs men will impound it?

*The Ricky now resides in Swindon with Dave Gregory. I kinda gave it to him after the h tours. It seemed criminal that such a beautiful guitar should be hung round the neck of a crap player like me. Dave's the man (along with Lennon and Jimmy Scott) who gave the Rickenbacker 12 his own English sound. No better home for it!

Friday 17 April *San Francisco – Mexico City*

Got up, packed, drank coffee and checked out.

Boarded the tour bus to take us one last short journey to the airport. Said bye-bye to Mike, the bus-driver from Nashville, who has been brilliant throughout this tour. Ate dodgy Chinese food in S.F. airport and boarded the plane to Mexico.

Saturday 18 April *Mexico:* Sympathy *video shoot*

Woken at 7.05 by Ray's alarm call. Went back to sleep and dreamt that I'd got up, had a shower and I was going up and down in a lift – when the phone rang again and it was Ray to say that it was 8.20 and we should have left at 8.00! Oh dear… Showered at the speed of light and we were underway by 8.45, clutching clothes and shoes.

It was a long drive over bad roads. We arrived at Ometusco station (middle-of-nowhere, Mexico) two minutes too late to do the first shot with the train, which had just been through the station. It was our only chance, and Bill and Andrew were furious. I said sorry. The day was spent moving from location to location, shooting the video for our forthcoming single, *Sympathy*. I got to drive an old Cadillac. Other highlights were spinning around in desert dust, and spending the whole day with no socks and laceless black shoes (ouch). The band was set up out in the open inside a chalk-circle which Bill and Andrew had drawn the day before. There was a family living in the station - loads of urchin kids - and they all assembled to watch the performance, so we filmed them too.

All being well, it should look great. The Mexicans were typically shabby and dusty, typically smiley – especially the children, who sat in the Cadillac, giggling. When the light finally gave out in the evening, we returned bouncing along non-existent roads for the first hot-sweaty-dusty 40 minutes until we joined the freeway, whereupon our arses actually maintained constant contact with the seats, and then back to Mexico City.

We regrouped at 10.00 for dinner at the hotel. I nearly fell asleep into mine. Went to bed at 12.00 and died until 11.00am.

Sunday 19 April *Mexico City:* Day off

Well, it started as a day off! Woke up, much refreshed for a lie-in and desperate for coffee. Was told by room service that today is Easter Sunday, so the restaurant is closed. Mexicans are devout and no one works on Easter Sunday. Down in the lobby of The Holiday Inn I thought they'd dropped the bomb! There wasn't a soul anywhere. Reception was all closed up. Even the escalators down to the street level were switched off. After a while I ran into Pete, and he told me I could get coffee at a fried-chicken-takeaway place across the intersection. I didn't have any pesos, so Pete lent me the equivalent of a few pounds and I set off across the road. Suitably coffeed-up, I returned with my precious cargo when a shoe-shine man persuaded me to come over and have "the best shoe shine in Mexico City! I finish the shoes with special oil, amigo – bery good. Will last looong time. You a musician? Last week I shine the shoes of Veence Clarke from Yazoo. Bery nice man!" He gave me a very nice shoe shine to my black leather tractor-sole slip-ons and, getting the exchange rate wrong by a factor of 10, I paid him the equivalent of £28.00 for it. Turns out Pete hadn't given me £3.00, he'd given me £30.00. I guess the shoe shine man took the rest of the day off to celebrate. Fair enough.

Met up with everyone in the lobby at 1.00. We were to go to the market to shop for trinkets and gifts, but Bill wanted me in the video clothes "just in case". I did a bit of shopping, bought a silver chain and earrings for Dizzy. Vowed to go back and buy carved wooden screens when we're here with a truck. They're quite Balinese-looking but are brightly coloured and decorated in the Aztec style. After a couple of hours we left and drove to another market - The Witches Market - where you can buy anything from soil, herbs, toys, honey, sunflower seeds, to birds, dogs, fish, eels and even snakes. We shot quite a bit more video here and I asked one of the traders if I could hold his boa-constrictor. "Make a wish, hombre!" Although I don't speak the language, I'm able to squeeze a giggle out of most of the traders, their women, and the children. The Mexicans have a lovely spirit about them.

Next we went to a church square which was packed with people walking, sitting at outdoor bar-tables and browsing the jewellery and nick-nacks for sale on the pavement. Bill and Andrew wove their way through the crowd in search of Easter-dancing to capture, whilst Pete and I found a bar and had a couple of beers.

Went out to eat in the evening. Ray entertained all and sundry with his magic tricks. Andrew D was hilariously taken in – he prefers to believe in magic – as do I.

PS. It turns out that Bill and Andrew inadvertently left quite a lot of the movie footage in a church in Mexico. This was discovered when they got back to England (hasta la vista!). The *Sympathy* video was edited together from what remained. It's still not bad!

Monday 20 April *Mexico City – Houston – Home*

Got up and went down to breakfast at 9.00. I'd arranged to meet up to have breakfast together with Bill, Andrew, the band and Lana Topham from EMI's video department PMI (Lana is also Storm Thorgersson's occasional assistant – she's producing this video, and has been terrific throughout) – but no one turned up, so I breakfasted alone. Bumped into Bill looking dreadful in the lobby (he'd been out to a few clubs last night with Andrew… We can all relate…) and Yvonne from EMI, who was to accompany us to the airport. Packed, checked out, and boarded the minibus.

Met at the airport by Francisco, who always seems to appear grinning away, and who gives us an easy passage through the airport. I suspect he and EMI have 'an arrangement'. Had more breakfast in the restaurant with band and Yvonne. Waved bye-bye and boarded the plane to Houston. Snoozed on the flight. Arriving at Houston set me wondering how/where Sandy Stewart was, at exactly the same moment I looked down at a book Mark was reading and saw her name in print on the page! Mighty spooky… Sandy used to contribute occasionally to the songwriting of Fleetwood Mac and Stevie Nicks. I was 'put together' with her at one point to write some songs, but never really got it together. We, along with her guitarist, David Johnson, became mates for a time during the How We Live days. She rented a house in Hampstead to which she gave me the keys so I could go and make music there when she was away in America. She and David made an album under the name Blue Yonder which I sang BV's on. It was produced by John Brand, who produced tracks on **This is the Sea** for The Waterboys. Sandy and David were from Houston. Mark was reading Mick Fleetwood's autobiography.

Bought t-shirts in Houston airport for Fi and Nial, and drank a Pina Colada before getting the flight to London. Didn't sleep, but the eight hours passed quite quickly. Spent most of the time writing this diary.

Tuesday 21 April *Home*

Arrived at Gatwick to be met by a cab driver who couldn't find his car. I was bursting to get home and had to contain my temper. Got home around 11.15. Fi Fi was thrilled to see me. Diz is very tanned from her time in South Africa and looks prettier than ever. Nial is completely changed and is smiley, and as heavy as a sandbag.

Friday 1 May *Englefield Green, Surrey – Charlton, Northamptonshire*

Moved house from 54 Middle Hill, Englefield Green, to Brisbane House, Main Street, Charlton, near Banbury. The tree opposite Brisbane House was in full bloom and its blossoms made the air heady with perfume.

Tuesday 16 June *Home, Charlton*

The carpet fitters cometh… Up at 8.00 and started removing doors.

Friday 3 July

Spoilt to death. Car was arranged for 9.30 to take me to Heathrow Terminal 3. Arrived to encounter Paul Lewis (back tour-managing) generally dazzling about the place and looking after everything, wearing a shirt which defied description. Can't remember much about the flight apart from bumping into Claire Kenny, one of my 'bass from the past' people. She had played bass with How We Live and, more famously, 80's all-girl dub band Amazulu. She was currently playing bass for Shakespears Sister - going to the same place as us.

Eventually arrived at a hotel in a town in Denmark (could I be more specific er… no) to be met by a gaggle of blondies from Sweden. It was Helen, Ulrika and Anna, the au pair girls from Stanbridge Farm (we'd spent months at Stanbridge writing **Holidays in Eden**). They'd driven over to see us! How very sweet (it's not what you think). Chit-chatted with them for a bit and caught up on one another's lives, then went to my room to lie-about being bored and snoozing until around 8.30, when we departed for the festival site.

Joe Cocker was already on stage being Joe Cocker – elbows glued to his sides, hands flailing around. I watched him for a while from the side of stage, then beetled off for a couple of interviews before showtime. We weren't on stage until 11.30, but the evening was warm and pleasant so enjoyed just sitting around talking and trying not to get drunk.

When showtime finally arrived, things got a bit weird monitor-wise. I had no vocal in the wedges for most of *Splintering Heart* and being back on a big stage felt odd… it took a while to settle. The process was helped somewhat by the onset of darkness and the front-section of the audience, who were obviously 'our people'. Record company girl Suzanne watched from the side of stage, and when I walked off during the instrumental section of *This Town* she took me by the arm to tell me how much she was enjoying the show. It was a brave and sensitive gesture and helped me lift myself for the second-half of the set, which went very well.

Afterwards, I showered up and chatted with the boys and Ann Lawler, John Arnison's long-standing/suffering management assistant (our Miss Moneypenny). The stage-manager came back to congratulate Privet, saying it was the best sound out-front that he's heard at a festival. I was pleased – especially for Privet, who deserves the recognition.

I was hoping to hang around and party, but we were bundled back onto a bus to take us the half-hour drive to the 'hotel-in-the-middle-of-nothing-special'. Thankfully the bar was still open, despite the late hour. I later lost my room key under a tree opposite the hotel while talking to the crew who were up it. Fortunately it was still there the following morning, as I discovered when the hotel tried to charge me £30.00 for the loss of the antique key-fob.

Friday 10 July

Woke at first light, 5.15, just before the alarm clock went off. By 6.00 I was up and ready. For once, I had packed the night before.

I made some fresh coffee and walked up the street with it to enjoy the village and the dawn morning air. Ifty, my driver, arrived on time, so I wandered back and loaded hand baggage into the cab. Chatted for most of the long journey to Stansted and arrived at 7.30. I was early - we all were - so we had breakfast while Paul Lewis checked us in. The 9.25 was finally called at 9.30, so we boarded the little train to the Terminal and then took the bus across the tarmac to the Air Estonia charter flight (Tupolev something or other). Stood on the tarmac for ages, talking to the stewardesses, successfully persuading them to give me coffee ("It's only for the air-crew") which came out of a tin that looked like it was dug up after the war. Sat with Alan Parker who had bought me a t-shirt from Paul Hester of Crowded House. Thanks Paul. The delay was, it turned out, due to our equipment being too big to fit in the hold. It took an hour to remove wheels from the flight cases and load bits of backline into the rear of the passenger area before we were ready for take-off. We knew things were close to the bone when two of the chaps at the front were asked to sit at the rear just for take-off, and I could have *sworn* that the pilot almost had second thoughts half way down the runway as our speed seemed to level out for a moment. Anyway, we took off and I'm here to tell the tale, aren't I?

Arrived at the Terminal in Tallin to be accosted by Russian TV who asked, "What was it like to play in Moscow!?"

"I don't know. I've never been."

Tallin reminded me, at first, of Gdansk – greener than I was expecting and the people more colourful too. We were taken to the hotel and given lunch, which consisted of weird soup followed by pork chop. I enjoyed both.

The weather was fine so I went out for a quick walk up to the old town with Pete T and Leah, our Estonian babysitter. Sat in the old town square, which could be best described as medieval Scandinavian/Bavarian, and drank a quick beer before we had to depart for the festival site. A sort of Bavarian-ish brass band played in the sunshine.

At the festival site there wasn't much to do – we'd missed Bonnie Tyler who'd left early to get to Zurich. I went for a walk and made my way, unnoticed and unhindered, to the sea five minutes away. They've made such a mess of the Baltic along here. It smelled of raw sewage which, for the most part, along with heavy industrial pollutants, is what the Baltic Sea has become. Back to the backstage area for an interview with Superchannel and the long wait to stage time.

In the end, I wasn't really sure about the show; I couldn't settle and I was never sure whether I was overdoing it or not. The audience response seemed good, but ever since I saw Bryan Adams at Nurburgring I'm waiting for <u>that</u> kind of audience energy level (nice chap, Bryan Adams – he stood at the side of the stage after our set at Rock-am-Ring, clapping and gesturing for us to go back up for an encore). I think I've always expected too much from myself and everyone else. I climbed the scaffolding at the side of stage during the encore and couldn't find anything to hold on to, so I spent two verses and two choruses clinging to stretched material – stretched by my fingers around a scaffold-pole. It was the closest I have yet come to the short-way-down.

After the show we went back to the hotel, where I showered up and went downstairs to a nightclub in the basement. Saw Bob Geldof sitting in the shadows looking preoccupied. Club was boring, so at around 4.00am (and already daylight) I went for a walk and made my way up to the old-town. The place was deserted, so I was undisturbed and free to take in what seemed like a cross between old Stockholm, old Zurich and medieval England. Nothing, apart from the road signs, suggested Russia to me.

There was no point in going to bed – we had to leave at 5.30, so when I bumped into Alan Parker (lights) and Tony Leighton (drum tech) wandering the streets at 5.00, I was relieved and glad of the company.

Checked out, and at the airport I bumped into Alison Moyet, who was on her way *to* Tallin. I gave her the remainder of my Estonian money.

Took the plane home, snoozing most of the way. Priv actually slept through the landing, unclipped and spread-eagled across a row of seats.

Took the cab home via Tilbury (!) He got lost and went up the M11.

Saturday 18 July *Mexico City, Auditorio Nacional*

Rose at 9.00 and had a spot of breakfast with Steve R, before leaving with driver José and promoter's rep, Ingrid, for the market. She said she knew of a market which sells fine glass-and-lead lampshades and would take me there.

When we arrived I immediately saw the perfect article and, after browsing around, I returned to haggle (it is expected) and have it packed. During the process I met the manager of the stall, who offered me coffee laced with Kahlua. Oh dear, drinking again… I had to be at the show for 12.00 soundcheck, so I was eager to collect said lampshade which had been taken away to be packed. When it returned, it had taken the form of a parcel the size of a dog-kennel! Decided I was going to worry about how to get it home tomorrow, and headed off to the Auditorio Nacional, a beautiful modern theatre of huge proportions and, without doubt, the largest stage on which I have stood. Playground-sized – and here comes playtime! I enjoyed soundcheck immensely – at least half of the stage is in front of the PA, and the acoustics of the place are perfect for electric music, so I had the pleasure of monitoring the sound 'out-front'. I stamped about the place singing my head off all afternoon, and I can't remember ever enjoying a soundcheck so completely. I was concerned, lest the show should be less pleasurable, but I needn't have worried; as in Rio, the warmth streamed from the loud and spirited Mexican audience and gave wings to our emotions. Pete T was particularly animated and played brilliantly. Steve R was having a ball, and I was in seventh heaven with reserves of seemingly unlimited energy, despite the altitude. What an audience! What a theatre!! What a sound! It's hard to describe the ultimate high, especially when it recurs so many times in this book. Without seeming to exaggerate, 'you had to be there', on my shoulder, taking it in. It was fabulous.

After the show we were transported to another club for pizza and celebratory drinkies with record company and promoter. By this time I was physically wasted, so we didn't stop too long.

Sunday 19 July *Mexico City*

Rose at 9.00 and breakfasted alone – no one else seemed to have made it out of bed.

It was a lovely morning, so I went for a walk and had Irish coffee at a café out in the street. Came back to the Stouffer Presidente and checked out, clutching my dog-kennel. We were driven to the airport and, with some apprehension, I watched helplessly as they covered my parcel with 'Fragile' stickers and checked it in. We had an hour to spare, so we installed ourselves in the bar/restaurant, which is my favourite in the world: good music, video and food. Said heartfelt goodbyes to Michelle from EMI, Ingrid from OCESA (promoters) and Francisco, the ever-present airport manager, and, after paying extra cash to be allowed on the plane, (this is Mexico!) flew home.

Monday 20 July *Home*

Ifty, my regular driver had brought his boss, Jenny, to Gatwick to share the driving. Went home via Brackley to drop off my shirts etc. at the dry cleaners. Lost the front bezel from my watch which had been dropping off regularly since May.

Got home around 12.30, just before Dizzy got back from Yorkshire with Crompton and Hargreaves. Dished out pressies and spent the rest of the day having carpets laid (I had to clear the furniture from the music room) and fixing the UNDAMAGED lampshade on the kitchen ceiling. It looks lovely!

Tuesday 21 July *Home – Rome*

Picked up at 2.00 and taken to Heathrow, via Steve Rothery's house near

Aylesbury. The two of us arrived at the Terminal and waited around for Louise Veys who was to nursemaid us through the Italian promotional schedule in her own inimitable fashion. Had a large Baileys in the Club Lounge and chatted to Ms Veys about her performing a similar function recently for Wilson-Phillips. Being the sons and daughters of members of The Mamas and the Papas (and having international hits in their own right) they were doing the promo by private jet!

By the time we arrived in Rome airport it must have been around 8.00 in the evening. We were met by Maria Louisa, who suggested that we go to a restaurant on the beach to have dinner before checking into the Cavalieri Hilton. Had a pleasant dinner in the restaurant called Rio, and later visited the adjoining club and listened to the worst band in the world 'til we couldn't stand it any longer.

Checked into the hotel around midnight and made arrangements with Louisa to do a bit of Rome in the morning, as interviews don't start until 2.00.

"I'll call you when I'm up!" I said.

Wednesday 22 July *Rome: Promotion, Cavalieri Hilton*

The phone was ringing in the middle of the night. It was Louise. "Oh dear. Why can she be calling at this hour?" I thought, until she pointed out that it was in fact 1.00 in the afternoon and interviews will commence in one hour. Phew! The old Italian blackout shutters had done it to me again. Got up and opened them to reveal a hot sunny day in the 'Millionaires playground' below. The phone rang again, and I arranged to have lunch with Maria-Louisa who was downstairs waiting for me in Reception (and probably had been all morning). When I got downstairs I couldn't find ML or Louise anywhere, so drank cappuccinos for England until the interviewers started showing up at 2.00. I'd missed lunch and I wasn't likely to get a break from here on in. By 4.30 I was beginning to wobble, so a Club Sandwich was procured and wrapped up for takeaway, and I ate it in the car to Rome airport. Whoever wrapped up said sandwich took the additional precaution of sitting on it afterwards, so I spent the journey showering bits of crisps all over the place.

Had a beer at the airport and chatted to Louise, who seems to be getting increasingly eccentric, bless her. I approve. Flew to Milan early evening and arrived at the hotel Bonaparte courtesy of Germano, my favourite Italian, only to discover I'd left my address book on the plane. Bollocks.

Went out for dinner in Milan with Pierro, Marco, Germano, Louise and Steve R. Had a drink afterwards in a Heavy Metal pub (!) and, after returning to the hotel, went for a walk around the Duomo Piazza before retiring. In bed by 3.00.

Thursday 23 July *Milan*

Picked up at 11.00 by Germano and taken to the EMI office, which is one of the most beautiful of their offices worldwide, rivalled only by the beautiful one in

Mexico City. Spent the day being interviewed by, among many others, the Italian fan club. Claudio had tracked down my address book (my hero!) and returned it during the interview. Cheers Claudio.

After a day of interviews, Germano took us to Milan centre for a tea-time vibe-out in the late afternoon sun. We also visited his father's clothes shop where I would have bought shoes but they didn't have them in my size. Black lace-up espadrilles... weird and wonderful!

After drinks we had ice-creams and licked our way back to the hotel. I split for a two-hour snooze before going out to dinner (pizza) with the fan club. Claudio had hired a basement room in a club for later. There was mucho dodgy PA and backline, so Rothers and I sang a couple of songs for the small gathering of fans assembled. In the end, I think we played for well over an hour, maybe two. Drank lots. And lots. And went to bed.

Friday 24 July *Milan – Copenhagen – Riga*

Left the friendly Bonaparte Hotel at 8.30, waved goodbye to Germano, to fly to Copenhagen where we were to join the rest of the band in transit to Riga. Milan airport was overcrowded and chaotic by comparison to the easy airiness and massive array of shops at Copenhagen airport. The band had arrived on an earlier flight from London and, I surmised, gone into Copenhagen to kill a few hours, so Steve and I sat down in the restaurant upstairs for what was to be a wonderful (if expensive) lunch. I had lobster (which was excellent) and a high-place from which to fall into Latvia's culinary delights (!)

Eventually spotted the rest of the band, minus Ian, who had stayed home on doctor's orders not to fly with an ear infection. His good pal, Mark Sugden, had come in his place, so I braced myself for big fun with him in Riga. He was in great spirits, if not a little nervous at the thought of the TV show ahead.

Among the entourage of people on the plane also heading to Riga for the 'big TV show' are a handful (pardon the pun) of **Daily Star** Page 3 models, all talking loudly in Essex accents and chaperoned by a big genie-of-the-lamp security man called Andy. It's another world from rock n'roll, and yet somehow loosely bound to it in the 'show-business' sense. There's never been that much separating rock n'roll from the theatre, the circus, actors, strippers, and outright prostitution really. We all have our stories to tell, and none of us can claim moral high-ground over the other.

We're off to Latvia at a strange time. It was only in 1990 that Latvia declared independence from the recently collapsed USSR. Everything there is in a state of flux. The public servants haven't been paid for many months, and yet continue to turn up for work in the hope that a new system will emerge and some kind of economy will start up and begin to compensate them. I wouldn't hold my breath...

When we landed in Riga we were met at the airport, given flowers and taken to the Hotel Riga Bay. But this wasn't just a hotel! It was some kind of recuperation sanitarium too. Apparently the Soviet Union sends its cosmonauts here to recuperate after space flights. If you walk down the corridor from my hotel room and keep going, another corridor stretches off to the left and the line of hotel room doors becomes a line of laboratories! I was to discover a lab containing an iron lung, along with white lab-coated nurses who, not having been told to stop work, still arrive each day awaiting further instructions. I slipped one of the nurses a few US dollars (very popular currently in the absence of any local currency – I think Latvia only began printing its own money yesterday!) and she opened the lid and helped me climb in. Steve R took a photograph (which I think he still has somewhere).

After checking in I showered up, had a snooze and set off for the 10 o'clock party at the festival site. Chatted with 'distinguished veteran correspondent' (his words) Peter Jennings over dinner, and later on at the site. Agreed to play a couple of songs live at the pre-show party, but later abandoned the idea. Utter chaos ensued when we tried to board the bus to go back to the hotel. This bus had been arranged for the band but, by the time we arrived, it was packed solid with locals who refused to get off. After 15 minutes of negotiations security genie Andy 'persuaded' the locals to make space for me to board. When the bus finally groaned into motion I was mystified to witness the locals jump up, as one, and start frantically disembarking. Strange people…

Show day was similarly confusing. Soundcheck was set for 12.15, so we were bundled into a bus to the site at 12.00. By 3 o'clock nothing much had happened, but it was a sunny day so we sat around enjoying the sunshine until 4.00. This was a live TV show, but the cameramen didn't turn up for rehearsal. The general suspicion was that a rehearsal would only serve to confuse them, so it was for the best.

We were later taken to a market where a woman was selling courgettes. All the other stalls were empty, so it was courgettes or nothing. A Polish TV crew had taken us there to drink the local beer and do an interview. The locals who were sitting around seemed to comprise entirely of crusty old alcoholics who muttered at us in Latvian. It was hard to discern whether or not we were being insulted. I wouldn't have blamed them.

I don't remember anything about the TV show. But I do remember a commotion in the middle of the night when I opened my hotel room door to see Jack and Priv edge their way down the corridor, sword-fighting with metal stair-rods they'd removed from one of the staircases:

"Have at you, knave!"

"Bounder! Cad!" they were drunkenly enthusing.

I went back to bed wondering whether they'd end up in hospital, and what, exactly, a Latvian hospital would be like. And I made a mental note to go easy down the stairs in the morning – the stair-carpet probably won't be fastened on…

PS. I also remember Mark Sugden and I sitting in the restaurant of the hotel Riga Bay having an early 'beetrooty' dinner while, at a table near us, two of the Page 3 girls were doing the same with their minder (genie of the lamp) Andy.

"I'm not!" one of the girls was exclaiming, smiling.
"You are," said the genie.
"I'm not!!" she said.
"You are."
"I'm not!"
"You definitely are."
"I'm definitely not!"
"Eurgh, sigh," said the Genie, shaking his head in exasperated disbelief.

She shouted over to Mark and I – "Look, I'm not am I?", hitching up her skirt to reveal a hairy darkness. "I'm not wearing any knickers!"

Mark spat his coffee across the table, laughing.

"It's not always like this…" I said.

But sometimes it is.

Thursday 20 August *Home – Stanbridge Farm, near Brighton*

Up at 7.45 with Crompton and Hargreaves. Dizzy had been up several times in the night with Nial who has become quite unsettled since his ear infection. We are hoping it's just 'teething'.

It was around 2.00 in the afternoon before we managed to get out to Banbury. Bought silicone sealer for the bathroom sink and had a wander around the market. Bought shirt buttons at a market stall and mooched round Laura Ashley looking for curtains. Came home and, after sealing said sink, drove down to Stanbridges around 6.00, arriving at 7.30 to a warm welcome and drinks from Bob & Caroline. Their son Jack, who was new-born when we left, is now two years old. Enjoyed a very pleasant roast dinner and had just a bit too much to drink while listening to Caroline putting the world to rights. Stepped outside for a nostalgic gaze at the lights coming through the hawthorn trees in the mist. Apparently hawthorn wards off evil spirits.(It was while gazing at this light back in 1990, slightly off my head on mushrooms, that I noticed the light dripping from the branches and wrote:

> *"She could smell the soil and the trees and see the succulent light*
> *from the little fires in his eyes pulling shapes out of the night"*

for the song *The Party.*

Once again, it was the smells that brought back the memories clearest of all – the dusty-oak-wood of the old house and the bed linen. Great days. Slept soundly in my old bedroom above the dining room, remembering the little bits of silver foil in the top corners – remnants of Duran Duran guitarist Warren Cucurillo's interior decorating. He'd had the room before me back in '90. He travels with a flight-case containing his decorating kit, and when he checks into hotels he drapes the walls with silver foil, detunes the TV to white noise and applies coloured lighting-gels to the screen, thereby creating a space-aged alternative lamp. Our old tour manager used to tour the Durannies and told me it was hard to keep Warren dressed, and he often wandered around the hotels half-naked. Proper rock n'roll.

Friday 21 August *Stanbridge Farm, near Brighton – Berne Switzerland*

Woken by Bob at 7.00. Showered, got up, drank coffee and ate melon before piling into a minibus to Gatwick airport. We joined Paul Lewis and the crew, checked in, and boarded the plane to Berne, Switzerland.

Tried to update this diary and suffered temporary setback when my pen exploded *(see opposite page)*. Found non-exploding back-up pen and continued. (Except that I didn't!)

Wednesday 2 September *Home – Cologne, E-Werk*

Crack-of-dawn departure from Heathrow to Köln (Cologne, Germany). Living-dead journey. Arrived at Köln airport to be hustled by strange man with stare-y eyes who appeared and got hold of my right arm. "I'm here on behalf of my friend Sabina. It is very important that you contact her."

"Just keep walking," said Paul, who had now hooked his arm around my left arm. And so I walked through Arrivals with a strange man on one arm and a tour manager on the other, until we got to a waiting taxi. Sabina has been sending letters to our management office over a period of months, saying she needs to talk to me as we are in "spiritual contact". Can't say I've noticed anything. Anyway, old stare-y eyes was trying to lead me to a payphone, but Paul was having none of it and I can't see that there's anything to be achieved by calling her, other than intensifying whatever scenario she's dreamt up.

Checked in at the Ascot hotel and went walkies to my favourite café, Café Spätz (I think. I could take you there, but I'm not great with names and labels) for Caprese (mozzarella, tomato, basil, olive oil) lunch. Nearly bought purple Doc Martens in a shop with a name like Anthrax or something. Didn't have money or plastic, which proved to be an obstacle.

Soundcheck was a zoo. It had been agreed to allow the entire German fanclub (which, it seems, numbers around 800 looking at 'em) in to watch. Chaos on stage. I couldn't really get a monitor sound, and any frustration I had was compounded by the whole thing being witnessed by the fans. As though soundchecks aren't unpleasant enough…

Fell down a lot during the show - once really badly. After *Easter* as I moved to climb down from the keyboard-riser to return to centre-stage, something seemed to grip the toes of both my shoes! My forward movement projected me rigid off the riser and onto my face on the stage below. It was the spookiest thing, and although it hurt, I was lucky not to smash my nose or jaw. Managed to turn my head sideways so that my collar-bone took the impact. Lucky not to break that either. Ouch. Fortunately I got away with only bruises. The audience were incredible during the show, but the band were a little rusty and struggling against the monitor sound. At one point we played *This Town – Rakes Progress – 100 Nights.* As *100 Nights* begins I walk out in a white shirt to sing, "A hundred nights of fun and games…" As I did so I noticed something fluttering in and out of the follow-spot beam. As I continued to sing it became a distraction. I realised slowly that it was a butterfly. As the verse progressed, the creature fluttered down the light beam from the high roof of the E-werk, and came to rest on my shoulder. The audience gasped as if to say, "How did he do that?!" They clearly haven't heard of the Doncaster school of advanced butterfly training.

We all came off stage a little subdued (in my case happy to still be able to walk), but cheered up a lot after Priv came backstage and said it sounded great out-front.

We went back to the (obligatory) Woody's bar to say goodbye to Alex, who's leaving Peter Rieger's promotion company.

What a peculiar day.

Thursday 3 September *Cologne – Rotterdam, Ahoy Sportspalace*

Came to in my LOVÉLY room, staring up at the chandelier, feeling slight regret at joining Alex for straight vodkas in the bar last night. Had breakfast next door with Rothers, cadging heavily as I had no money or credit cards. Checked out with the rest of the chaps to take the train to Rotterdam. Spent most of the journey discussing how best to co-ordinate the various fan-clubs around the world, feeling slightly guilty about the Germans who seemed genuinely upset last night that other fan clubs are given access to the band ahead of them. If that's true, we hadn't noticed.

Arrived at Rotterdam and took cabs straight to the Ahoy for 5 o'clock soundcheck. Sound on stage is infinitely better, and Priv says the new PA is 'unfeasibly present' in the hall. Decided to stay at the venue and snoozed on the sofa in the dressing room. We swore we would relax this time at the Ahoy, and we did! The show and audience felt the best yet at this venue, and I came off stage feeling I'd sang really well. Thank you Rotterdam!

Afterwards we were taken to a little bar for a presentation celebrating the band's 10 years with EMI Netherlands. I decided to destroy myself (why????) and did so with Tequila. Thank you and goodnight.

A fantastic thunderstorm ensued after I got into bed.

Friday 4 September *Rotterdam – London:* Day Off

Woke up feeling dreadful after last night's excesses and the bruising from Cologne. Staggered to reception to see if the health centre was open (I needed my health centre-ing...). It wasn't, but the delightful girl on reception said she'd open it SPECIALLY – and despite the fact that I looked like a road accident and was shoeless.

Checked out an hour later and rattled off to Rotterdam airport, where a barman knocked a beer off the bar into Paul Lewis's lap. Phoned Conny, the boss at EMI Netherlands, to thank her for last night's little 'do'.

Flew to Heathrow and took a cab to London to check into the lovely Kensington Gore Hotel on Queensgate. Four-poster bed and antique bathroom.

The Stones used to hang in the bar when Brian was alive and, I'm told, the breakfast room/restaurant is one of Bowie's favourite rooms in London. Mine too. Had lunch there with Rothers, and later went walkies and popped into the office in Chelsea with yet-more passport pics to try to satisfy Ann Lawler's endless visa-lust.

Returned to the hotel and had coffee in the lovely back-room with lovely Ann, before changing and mooching off to the Hard Rock Café with SR, once again. We were accosted after a while by someone who said, "Loved the show in Rotterdam last night!" Oh dear – already knobbled by Dutch fans who had come over for the Wembley show tomorrow. Bought 'em a drink, and later returned to the hotel for a last quick one with Rothers in the bar. Decided against it as the bar was full of moneyed fools.

Saturday 5 September *London, Wembley Arena*

Woke up to a pleasant morning outside my window at the Gore Hotel and mooched down to the restaurant around 11.00 for a spot of breakfast. The Irish waiter couldn't decide whether breakfast was on or off. In the end, it was on.

Went for a walk down Kensington High Street to look at light-fittings. Saw something special: glass fruit and tangled metal stems – LOVELY. £900.00 + VAT. Maybe not then.

Returned, packed, and took a cab to the Wembley Hilton. Fought with the cab-driver who shouldn't have been one. Checked in courtesy of brain-dead receptionist, and my room looked like a council house. I should know, I grew up in one. Came as a shock after the Gore.

Couldn't cope with being there, so walked round to Wembley Arena and Dee McClouglin let me in after some difficulty with 'Security'. Priv was eq-ing the PA, which was sounding great! Well, it all got worse from there. My voice began to deteriorate in the afternoon and, by showtime, I was more than a little hoarse. To make matters worse, the BBC were there recording the show. When I walked on stage, the extent of the damage became apparent. I sang *Holidays in Eden* like a dog with a frog in its throat, and *I Will Walk on Water* was buried forever. Attitude is all, so I did my best to bluff through. During *Incommunicado* I misjudged the stage-depth and ran straight off the front. The stage at Wembley Arena is a good two-metres high, and I remember travelling downwards through the air (still singing), having time to wonder whether I was going to break my ankles or not. I didn't, but the only way back to the stage was a run across the room to the corner of the arena (still singing), through security (thankfully, the security man let me through – they sometimes don't), round to the centre backstage stairs (still singing) and back out front. Thank gawd for radio-mics. Most of the people in Wembley must have seen me disappear for a while and return later, despite the voice remaining in the PA. It's a miracle I wasn't hurt. I think I'd have swapped a broken ankle for a decent voice though.

After the show my depression was appeased a little by folks saying they hadn't noticed. Well done, Priv. I hid for as long as I could before forcing myself into the after-show mayhem. There was a party back in the bar of the Wembley Hilton where, despite well-meaning interruptions, I enjoyed a drink or two with Dizzy who had driven into London for the show. It was good to be going home.

Tuesday 22 September *Home*

Tonight, I leave for Argentina.

Wednesday 23 September *Buenos Aires*

Arrived in Buenos Aires at 7.30am and shuffled our way through immigration and customs. Haphazard, slow, and enough of a waste of time to be pretending to be careful. John A was almost arrested for not having a matching baggage tag and was detained for 40 minutes, trying to prove he owned his own luggage. Met in the Arrivals lounge by promoter's rep Nora, who rode with us to the Buenos Aires Sheraton. Bumped into Roberto who remembered me from February and upgraded the band to suites! Had breakfast in the hotel and went to bed.

Up at 4pm to go to a radio station at 5.00 with Jack. Talked about a planet where people smell of old flowers and the State provides talcum powder etc.

Back to the hotel and out with EMI (Sylvina and JP) to LOVELY restaurant. Much giggling. We lifted Jack onto the table whilst 'owling'. This involves crouching in a squat while someone pulls your shirt over your knees so you look like an owl. You then put your hands on top of your feet and curl your fingers round your toes so they look like little claws.

Off to TV studio for a live interview at midnight – jet-lagged beyond description, and back to the Sheraton. Got to bed at 3.00 – that's 7.00am London-time

Sunday 27 September *Buenos Aires*

Met Nora in reception at 10.00 and was taken to the Flea Market – a kind of antique market full of old Argentinian nick-nacks. There was a little troupe of people in the street – one played bandoneon (like an accordion) while a man and a woman (wearing traditional 30's garb) tangoed. People were sitting outside cafés which served beer and monkey-nuts. I came dangerously close to buying more light fittings, but managed to resist.

Returned to the hotel around 2.30 to leave for soundcheck at the TV station. No one from the TV crew showed up, so we hung around 'til 5.00 and then gave up and returned to the hotel. I'm STILL jet-lagged, so went back to bed to fill the hours 'til 9.30 when we left, once again, for TV Ataca.

The show was similar to last time – playback of *Sympathy, No One Can* and *Kayleigh*, lots of kids bouncing around and then a brief chat with Mario who, I think, knows too little about the people he interviews.

Later, we were taken to dinner at Happenings restaurant which wasn't happening at all. Said thanks and bye to Sylvina and to the excellent JP, who I've come to like a lot.

Monday 28 September *Buenos Aires – Caracas*

Got up and checked out of the Buenos Aires Sheraton. $250.00. It could have been worse…

Waited ages at the airport for the "somewhen between 12.30 and 4.30" flight to Caracas, Venezuela, via Lima, Peru. Tried most of the perfumes in the Duty Free and all of the sunglasses. Decided that Dizzy's Halston is still favourite and that none of the Ray-Bans suited me.

The flight was busy and LONG – something like 9 hours with a refuel in Lima. Hey! I've been to Peru! For ten minutes. Spent most of the flight standing up and invited half the plane to the show.

When we got into the baggage hall there appeared to be a riot going on in the street. It turned out to be 50 or so of our fans, waving banners and being generally celebrational. We were bundled into a pimped-up (purple lighting and thick carpet) minibus with our promoter, Octavio, who took pleasure in much use of walkie-talkies and showing me his Magnum .44 handgun. He dropped it in my lap and I gingerly handed it back, saying, "Thank you – that's very nice."

Checked in (through the back door) of the Tamanaco Hotel which looked mucho luxurious – until we got to the seventh floor, which was 'under renovation'. The rooms on the seventh floor were mucho Howard Johnson. I managed to get my room changed (to a smaller one, somehow) after an hour. There's a lesson. EMI had placed fruit and flowers in my room – it's exactly the same smell as my room that first time in the Rio Palace. I was rocketed back to that heavenly time and place like no time had passed. Mustn't grumble etc.

Slept fitfully and woke up freezing owing to my inability to operate the air-conditioning system.

Tuesday 29 September *Caracas*

There's a press-conference at 1.30… or is it 12.30… everything moves backwards and forwards, only to move backwards again at the last minute. Rose, showered and made my way down to poolside with John. Joined Steve and Mark for a spot of breakfast and then returned to my room to do my laundry in the sink until press-conference time. There weren't many journalists there, and the atmosphere was somewhat strained initially as interpreters tried to make sense of Spanish questions and English answers. I came within a hair's breadth of walking out over a question: "What innovations have you contributed to music?" which sounded like an insult. Apparently, I later answered this question by mistake. Things improved somewhat after a new interpreter joined the proceedings and, in the end, everyone seemed satisfied.

Had the buffet lunch and put banana sauce on my steak by mistake, and so christened it a "misteak". Spent all afternoon getting to (and from) the radio station – the traffic was jammed because of rioting.

In the evening we were taken out to dinner by EMI to The Dog's Bollocks restaurant, and afterwards to a club full of Marillion fans. Signed a million autographs and murdered *This Town* and *Kayleigh.*

Wednesday 30 September *Caracas, Poliedro*

Up around 9.30 for a dip in the pool and a slow breakfast on the terrace. Chatted with a Peruvian businessman (whose wife lives in Barnes!) about his wife's work raising money in England for Peru's poor children. Some evangelical church got involved and 'adopted' her funds for their 'good work'. Some German pastor was telling the children that they were poor because they weren't Christian. She no longer raises money for charity…

Went shopping with Myra (promoter's rep) and Valeriano (security) and bought a bucket of Halston which is cheaper here.

Had lunch in Iguana (a street café) and returned to the hotel to leave for soundcheck. Our crew looked flustered – most of the local crew arrived one and a half DAYS late. Soundcheck wasn't bad; the Poliedro is a bit of a shed, acoustically.

Back to the hotel for a lightning Caprici and twenty minutes in bed. At the show it turned out that the first evening is the slack one – only 3000 in. The show itself went well – the crowd were electric and I sang myself fairly hoarse by the end. Got away with it. Pleased to note that some of the press conference's more cynical journalists came back to say they were blown away – I'm thinking particularly of Margarita from El Nacional. The showers didn't work, so I had to endure walking around in my own salt solution for an hour until I could get back, shower and go to bed. Mucho tired.

Friday 2 October *Caracas – Los Caracas – Day off – Sky to Rio*

Having fallen into bed at around 4.00 feeling elated and tired, it took nothing short of super-human resolve to rise at 8.00, but I was on a mission!! I have never paddled in the Caribbean and was determined to do so.

Had breakfast downstairs and got photographed by giggly waitresses who'd been to the show. After customary Venezuelan dithering, I bundled into the mini bus with Myra, Valeriano and driver for the one-hour drive to Los Caracas beach. Bliss! Walked along the water's edge in my white shirt and shorts feeling like an Englishman abroad, paddling in the warm seawater, asking casually about sharks…

"No hombre, there aren't any sharks."

"Just checking…"

At one point it was just too inviting, so I ventured out into the waves –

forgetting about my wallet in my shorts. Returned to my deck chair on the beach to dry out cash and credit cards... Cast care aside, removed my shirt and went swimming. Lay at the water's edge, sipping beer and exchanging chummy grins with the locals. Octavio, the promoter, mystically turned up with his girlfriend, who he offered to me at one point – "You want the girl?"

I said, "Thank you, but I am married - but I wouldn't mind a bottle of rum." He briefly disappeared and returned with a bottle of the local rum which, between us, we drank during the afternoon. This is probably the most drunk I had been for some years. I was taken, giggling and blithering, to a tropical stream to bathe waist-high in the cool, fresh water, staring up at the hillside of rainforest, like a scene from **The Mission**. My over-familiarity with the locals at the river was beginning to make Valeriano and Myra nervous. If they get the wrong impression you can get shot. Personally, I'm a big believer in people of all races and cultures taking things in the spirit in which they're given. Happy drunks are usually a joy to everyone. Anyway, I was told it was time to go, and I was driven back to Caracas by my minders (occasionally stopping so I could be sick) who all looked worried 'cause we were late and they had a comatose singer on the back seat.

When we returned to the hotel, I rallied somewhat and, still giggling and hammered, joined the band who were out in the late afternoon air by the pool. Mosley has often commented on my arrival, with a grin. The rest of the day is a bit of a blur. Pizza, an architect, airport check-in and bye-bye's to the minders (Myra shares my birthday).

We flew down to Sao Paulo overnight, via Rio de Janeiro. Someone had given Pete a little hand-made-tribal-ukulele thing which he could be heard 'plinky plinking' on somewhere on the plane. We all ended up in a transit lounge in Rio airport at 6.00 in the morning. Everyone in the lounge was half-asleep, lolling on plastic chairs, Pete still occasionally 'plinky-plinking' on the uke. Ian asked if he might have a look at it.

"Sure," said Pete handing it over.

Ian cut through each of the strings with his Swiss-army-knife-scissors - 'tink-tink-tink-tink' - and gave it him back. A ripple of applause broke out in the lounge.

Saturday 3 October *Sao Paulo:* Day off

Staggered into the Hotel Della Volpé Garden around 10.00 and went to bed until 2.00. Taken out to lunch by J.P. from the record-company. Only John, Pete and I managed to get up for lunch. Spent the rest of the day on the roof of the hotel listening to Led Zeppelin and cleaning my razor, which I had dropped in the sand at Los Caracas.

In the evening we went to a club called The Limelight which bore a remarkable resemblance to The Limelight on Shaftesbury Avenue, London. Had a couple of mineral waters, feeling somewhat delicate after yesterday's excesses.

Didn't like The Limelight much – not my scene, etc. Went back to the hotel and went to bye-byes.

Sunday 4 October *Sao Paulo*

Went to visit my old friend, the Morumbi Stadium, where we'd played in 1990, to see a football match – Sao Paulo v Corinthians. Sunny afternoon. Atmosphere totally electric in the stadium, and the football was of a class never experienced in England – balletic in terms of grace and skill. Corinthians were somewhat outclassed by Sao Paulo who, to our delight, won 3-0. The tall, athletic No.4 was awarded 'man of the match'.

Afterwards we were taken out by Agnes from EMI to a Churrascaria restaurant (a typical Brazilian thing) where we were almost *forced* to consume hideous quantities of the best meat I have ever tasted. Phew! Pete T pointed out the obscenity and decadence of it all in a city where such a large percentage of the population live in abject poverty. Went to bed feeling stuffed and guilty.

Monday 5 October *Sao Paulo, Olympia*

Woke up feeling weary, for a press conference at 10.00. Usual drill but, for once, no one mentioned the poisson. Not nearly as explosive as Caracas. All over by 12.00, so I went walkies and nearly bought jelly-shoes and sunglasses. Had lovely salad in Tatou restaurant which Camillo had pointed out yesterday.

Got back at 3.00 to be told that soundcheck was sliding back. Surprise, surprise. Sewed a few more buttons on (I had found some really cool blue-pearl and amber shirt buttons in a little shop in Buenos Aires, so I was replacing my shirt buttons) and eventually left for the show at 4.30. To our delight, Sao Paulo No.4 football player Ronaldo (who we'd watched yesterday) popped in to say he was a fan and would be coming to the show tonight. He made me a present of the shirt he had worn for the match! Bloody hell!

Tuesday 6 October *Sao Paulo, Olympia*

Roused at 11.00. Snoozed a bit more and left the Della Volpé Garden at 12.00 for lunch with MTV. All very nice, but I wasn't hungry. Did a couple of TV interviews and decided to take the V.J. up on her offer to make me up like Robert Smith... thought it would give the crew a giggle. It never happened. You can't trust these media-folk...

Drove to Olympia to soundcheck. Security was TIGHT – they wouldn't let *us* in. After much shouting we eventually gained entry, and tweaked the on-stage sound which seemed a marked improvement on yesterday. Returned to the hotel early for sleep and dinner alone in the restaurant, feeling reflective and melancholy. Cheered up considerably by the show which was twice last night in all respects, especially the crowd who were in fine spirits.

The backstage shower deserves a mention. It's electric and it's connected to the mains by various exposed wires which stick out at the top of the unit. All metal parts, including the shower hose and head, are LIVE and shock you if you touch them. The hose, taps and head are covered in insulating tape to reduce the chance of killing yourself to 50:50. I gave it a mention when I signed the guest book. In the 'Comments' section I wrote: "Fix the fucking shower! Someone's going to die!"*

Arranged to meet promoter, Muniz, in the morning for an earlier flight to Rio.

* When I returned to this venue some years later, I noticed the shower was exactly the same!

Wednesday 7 October *Sao Paulo – Rio de Janeiro*

Up at 7.45, packed and checked out courtesy of Katya and desk staff, who were all at last-night's show and seemed speechless with enthusiasm. Had breakfast with Nick B and waited for Muniz who, of course, failed to turn up. Gave up waiting and flew to Rio with Camillo (our lovely and permanently-smiling security man from Rio. I first met him when we played the "Hollywood Rocks festival in 1990. I was out in a street market mooching around in Sao Paulo when I noticed him across the street and I thought I'd seen him in the hotel.

"Haven't I seen you somewhere before?" I said

He grinned and nodded.

"Weren't you by the pool at the Hilton hotel?"

He nodded and grinned.

"I'm Steve H from Marillion. Are you involved in the festival at all?"

He nodded and grinned.

"What do you?" I enquired

"I'm looking after you!" he said.

The weather here today is humid and almost rainy but, nonetheless, the atmosphere (imbued, somehow, with a billion ghosts who've been here, played, partied, danced, fallen in love, and written music about it) still knocks you sideways, even as you get off the plane.

Had a light lunch and a beer, then mooched off down Copacabana along the water's edge to the Rio Palace Hotel at the far-southern end where Copacabana meets Ipanema. We're not staying here, and I was almost prevented from going upstairs by Security, who relented upon hearing my English mutterings. Went up to the terrace restaurant, which was deserted, and gazed out at the sea from the same spot we'd all had Champagne breakfast on my first anniversary with the band. Poolside was dead. We're out of season. Took the lift up to room 401 to stare at the door and check the dreams were all real. I'd had such a fabulous week here two long years ago: I'd placed a huge map of South America above my bed, the room was full of fruit and flowers, the waves were crashing outside my open window, the air was warm and, riding on it, was the sound of samba drums. I was on the front page of the national newspaper and, for a week, I felt like I had the keys to Rio! And I felt like, finally, after 30 years, I'd found the place where I belonged.

Walked back to the Othon Palace and failed to find a beach-whistle that I could wear around my neck tonight.

Left for soundcheck at 4.30 – all the usual problems with house-systems. Never mind. The word is that the show is sold out, so we should just relax and enjoy it.

Returned to the hotel to sleep, but the phone kept ringing. Lovely Jean Job (the mother of our interpreter Geraldine, who offered the band and crew a barbecue at their home in 1990 and became a good friend) called my room to wish me luck with the show. How thoughtful. People have a happy knack here of finding out where I am! South Americans have an ESP for these things. Spoke to Deborah Cohen (old chum from A&M records) who's quit the music business and is setting up a B&B on a tropical island. Asked her to reserve me a room…

As it turned out, the show was more than sold-out. Packed solid in a way that would have been illegal in the UK, but this is Rio. The crowd were completely amazing: exuberant to unfeasible proportions, vocal, passionate… basically Latin! On-stage sound was predictably difficult to work with. I don't think I sang one note in tune all night – I couldn't hear myself against the band and the 3500-strong choir. There was a 'Zenith-Paris' moment when I could only watch in disbelief as they screamed on and on and we had to wait for it to die down so that we could continue. Someone at the front caught my hand and wouldn't let go. The process of shaking free left my right wrist sore and bruised. It's a good thing they didn't get hold of the rest of me!

Backstage, after the show, we congratulated ourselves on having survived Brazil (although you never truly do). When the tour was first suggested, it looked on paper like it could all be pretty nightmarish for crew and band. Full marks to Alan Parker for being positive and cheerful when lesser men would have despaired at the working conditions.

We returned to the hotel to change so that we could go out with the delightful Agnes from EMI but, when we got back, no one had the stamina to carry on, so we thanked her for the offer and went to bed to sleep the few hours before departure to the airport. I slept with the curtains and the windows open so I could once again listen to the sea and the heartbeat of the most wonderful city on earth.

Thursday 8 October *Rio de Janeiro – Sao Paulo – London – NYC – Boston*

Packed and checked out of the Othon Palace Hotel (it sounds simple, doesn't it? It wasn't). After much Brazilian prevarication, I was in a cab to the airport with Priv and Pete, contemplating the INSANE but irrevocable prospect of the flight from Rio to Boston via London! This may sound nuts, but had been brought about by the fact that Muniz had bought our return flights to London as part of the tour proposal. Separate return flights from the UK to America had been similarly purchased via the American agent. To cancel these existing tickets and fly due north from Rio to Boston, although a few thousand miles shorter, would cost the band tens of thousands of pounds.

It was hard to believe as I sat in the front seat that the cab driver hadn't been paid to murder us all – Ayrton Senna would have been nervous. Signed an autograph for the driver and entered the airport for the LONG check in. Realised I'd left all my money and credit cards in the front of the cab!! Aaaagh! By some miracle the cab was still waiting outside in the hope of a fare back into town, and John A rushed out and returned with my wallet. I guess this is not a common outcome in Rio de Janeiro…

The flight to Boston via Sao Paulo, London and BOTH New York airports is too boring to recount. It took 35 hours from leaving the Othon Palace to arriving at The Guest Quarters during which:

1. We were delayed for two hours at Sao Paulo due to a computer failure (we weren't allowed off the plane).

2. Changing planes at Heathrow meant changing Terminals. This took several hours during which I bought a new watch – a comfort present to stave off the depressing thought that my home and family were a five-minute drive away. (Bob Geldof and Paula Yates were in the departure lounge).

3. We flew to JFK, New York, cattle-class (Bob and Paula didn't – they were up front), and then drove from JFK to La Guardia where check-in took hours and the flight was delayed.

4. Upon (finally!!!) boarding the plane to Boston, a man was sitting in my seat. When I asked him why, he produced a boarding pass with my name on it! He had somehow been issued with this even though I also had one with my name on it. I asked him if, bearing in mind he wasn't Mr Hogarth, he might move… He moved and the plane pulled back from the stand, at which point there was a huge bang like we'd hit a wall. The captain announced that there was nothing to worry about and it was just a tow-bolt shearing off. We did, however, need to return to the stand for a further hour while the maintenance engineers checked there'd been no damage to the suspension of the nose-wheel.

Arrived, at last, in Boston, feeling beyond exhausted and hell-bent on rewarding ourselves somehow, so we took cabs across town in search of the excellent New England seafood found here. Band and crew found Legals seafood restaurant on the quay-side, and I ate the best clam chowder on earth, followed by ultimate lobster. Thoroughly recommended.

(The lobster, I mean, not the journey.)

1993 FEBRUARY

Wednesday 10

Marillouatte

1 9 9 3

Wednesday 10 February - Thursday 8 April *Chateau Marouatte, France*

Being here some months before (for a look around) did nothing to diminish the sense of awe upon returning to make a record. The position of the place - literally a castle on a high hill - evokes memories of **Hammer** vampire and Frankenstein movies when looking up the road. The Chateau itself, once you're through the huge oak doors, across the outer gardens, over the moat, under the arched gateway and into the main building (11th Century) mirrors its exterior internally. It's packed with every kind of pre-Renaissance art: tapestries, wood carvings, paintings, antique furniture, and what seems to be half the world's ransacked churches.

Well, that was before our truck arrived! I didn't quite realise how much gear we had. As the first couple of sunny days passed, teams of French chaps transported heavy hardware, like ants, up the spiral stone staircases of various towers. Most of it ended up in two rooms. The band is set up in the main hall, amid gothic wood-panelling, stained glass, carved stone walls and log fire. Producer Dave Meegan and engineer Priv Hedge occupy the more-Regency splendour of the master bedroom, complete with two mixing desks (noise gates, compressors, digital and analogue effects, DAT machines, patch bays, blah blah). Out in the courtyard, if you look up, there's the incongruous sight of multicores draped like washing lines between arrow slits in wings of the chateau. These connect the five of us to the control room via our backline, which is dotted around the place – bass gear in the chapel, guitar amps in the wine cellar… I'm not sure where the keyboards come up, but I can always hear Hammond organ in the kitchen… maybe that's ghosts!

The overall effect of Marillion and Marouatte colliding (I suppose it would be called Marillouatte) looks a lot like a Space Shuttle crashed into a Cathedral… or Camelot. Quite a sight. I still discretely pinch myself every morning as I arrive, bleary-eyed, from my tower across the garden in search of coffee, entering what was once the Queen Mum's room (she stayed here) to find Dave at the helm of a do-it-yourself Starship Enterprise, in what must be the all-time ultimate bedroom recording set-up.

No one here knows for sure whether Dave or Priv actually sleep at all. Neither of them look as though they do. We usually work from 11am until midnight, but Dave and Priv are often working by 9.00a.m and are still at it at 1.00.

To make matters better, the work we've done so far on the music is going extremely well. I can already hear the environment having its own effect on the music. We've written quite a bit more while we've been here, jamming in the evenings over a bottle or two of the excellent local Bordeaux.

Nobody has recorded here before, so I think the album will have a unique sound and feel. I'm predicting ('cause I don't know for sure, even now) a much more raw and natural sounding album – angrier in a lot of ways than **Holidays in Eden**. It's almost a continuous piece of music, just over an hour long! The songs occur like beads on a necklace. The atmospheres are darker, rawer, and more intense than before.

The album is a story – a work of fiction that takes its starting point from a radio broadcast I heard some years ago while working in Bath. The police had found a girl wandering along the M4 motorway at the huge suspension bridge over the Severn Estuary between Bristol and South Wales. She was unable (or simply refused) to speak to them in answer to their questions. In despair, the police decided to issue an appeal to the general public through the media. It was this appeal for information, an attempt to identify her, which I overheard. For some time I have wanted to address the erosion of faith and of truth which continues to pervade our culture. I concocted a collection of thoughts around these themes, and these are told from the perspective of the girl on the bridge. Perhaps I include myself among the pollutants which have poisoned her.

This is a concept album, folks! There's no denying it. Pop, it ain't. Prog, it may be… depending on how you define it. Brave, it certainly is… some might say impetuous. Energetic, most definitely. True? A lot of it. Passionate? Don't be silly – of course. In many ways, it's a lonely album. We've certainly been lonely recording it… that's the trouble with a castle in the sky. I've got the locals working on a beanstalk that we can climb down!

As I write this I am sitting in the control room (actually Miles Copeland's bedroom - he owns Marouatte), listening to Pete T putting the finishing touches of bass on *Living with the Big Lie*. From where I'm sitting I would describe what I am hearing as 'God's own bass guitar sound'. The process of working with Dave Meegan for the first time has been entirely enjoyable so far. He seems dedicated and focussed on capturing our most inspired moments – he records EVERYTHING and collects and catalogues our 'happy accidents' with the fervour of some eccentric butterfly collector let loose up the Amazon for the first time. Our only problem has been keeping him supplied with Lockets (for our non-British readers – a kind of cough sweet), which he consumes at the rate at which most people breathe oxygen. He learned his craft at the Sarm studios in London, working alongside the likes of Trevor Horn and Steve Lipson on a spectrum of projects, from Yes to Grace Jones, and, more recently, touring with and recording U2 for the **Rattle and Hum** soundtrack, along with production work for The Milltown Brothers and, in my opinion, some fine moments for the House of Love. He privately admits he's a hippy at heart, and occasionally sends me out in search of joss sticks.

Someone told me in a bar last night that the Dalai Lama came to the Dordoigne and said there was good magic coming from the ground here. He'd been drinking… but I know what he means.

Tuesday 27 April

Went to Rondor to have lunch with Stuart Hornall and John. Went to the same Italian restaurant that Stuart's taken me to before. He was his usual bluff self, and said if I give him another album on the deal, he'll give me 50 grand now! I said I'd have to think about it – for about 10 seconds…

I was due across town to see Bill Smith, our graphic designer. Stuart offered his drivers and car – a black Merc. Hey, I'm a pop star again! The artwork's pretty cosmic. John said Virgin want me to sing at their radio station launch bash, and the band include Paul Carrack and Andy Fairweather-Low. We rehearse on Thursday at Eezee-Hire.

In the evening I returned to Parson's Green for my car to discover Jo Rawson and Binda Patel (who used to work at Rondor) sat on the wall outside the pub. They say neither of them have been there for a couple of years and, of course, neither have I. Went into the pub to buy a Pimms, and discovered old friends Sally and Felix inside! We've been trying to locate Sally for a couple of years. She is now living on a houseboat on the Seinne in Paris with her boyfriend Dominic. Felix is just back from Australia. They haven't been to Parsons Green for years either!

Thursday 29 April

Turned up at Eezee-Hire (still the same) to find Mike Rutherford and Paul Young running through *Revolution* by the Beatles with the band. Said hello and I listened through until they'd finished, and I was called up to the mic. I was introduced to the band: Pete Thomas on drums, Keith from Squeeze on bass, and Tim Renwick on guitar (whose attitude I like a lot), Paul Carrack on keyboards, Andy Fairweather-Low on guitar, and a horn section. I sang through

I Saw Her Standing There once and everyone seemed happy, so that was that. Chatted more to Mike R and Paul afterwards in the bar, and asked if I might sing a BV on *Revolution.* They said, "Sure".

Drove into the West End and bought a video machine, got a parking ticket, and called in at Gloucester Place to see how the international crowd are getting on. Had a couple of drinks with Louise Veys and went home. Stayed up 'til 1.30 connecting up the video machine.

Friday 30 April

Drove to Hit & Run, arriving around 4.00. Everyone's okay, and Ann's looking slim. Nick Belshaw was in, advancing the Charles and Eddie tour. Nice to see him. A Japanese Brazilian had sent me a shirt in the post. Nice.

Went with John to the Piccadilly Theatre, and bumped into Ken Campbell who used to play with How We Live. He is working with World Party who were opening the show. I went and watched from out-front.

Before I knew it I was on stage, "taking a break from the mega-domes", as Paul put it (thanks a lot, Paul – but unfortunately not quite true!). The song was fun, and I especially enjoyed singing *Revolution* with Paul (one of the best male vocalists I've ever heard) and Mike Rutherford. Dizzy Spell turned up too late to catch me sing, unfortunately. Paul later said he wished I could've got back up for another. When I got out into the theatre (the late, great) Kirsty MacColl got up to sing – just as John Arnison introduced me to Steve Lillywhite, her husband (and renowned record producer). Naturally he was distracted, but politely said hi. I used to see Steve occasionally in The Beehive in Middle Hill, Englefield Green – he's originally an Egham boy. I'd never previously had the nerve to bother him.

Said hello to Gaby Roslin and Chris Evans from the **Big Breakfast**. She's still talking about the midi gloves after I demo'd them to her at TVS! She asked me if we'll do the show. I wonder if she meant it? Stole miniature shot glasses from the dressing room. Stole Nick Lowe's as well, to make a set of six. He'd already left anyway. Afterwards, across the road at the Dome, Jeff Beck was sat at the next table. Didn't have the nerve to bother him either!

Wished Richard Skinner luck with the station. A most enjoyable day.

Saturday 1 May

Drove to Bath with Dizzy, Sofi and Nial. Had a mooch around the shops and a pleasant sit in the sunshine in the public gardens.

Monday 3 May

Mark K came over to drop the hire car off. Took him back home, and when I got back we went to Blenheim Palace to check out the craft fair. It didn't seem up to much, so we just went to the café. Took Nial through the Butterfly house. He only seemed to notice the goldfish in the pond. The kids played in the play area.

Came home, bathed the kids, and drove up to Liverpool, arriving at 10:30. Dropped my things and went to the pub with Priv. There don't seem to be any licensing laws in Liverpool.

Thursday 6 May

Went down to the Albert Dock for lunch at the Bali with Paul and Annie. Afterwards I wandered around the Hockney exhibition at the Tate, and then walked back and up through the town. Bumped into a busker playing uilleann pipes in a doorway on the street. Asked him to come over and meet Dave tomorrow. Thank you and love, Tony Halligan.

In the evening I sang *Mad* and popped over to the Pelé gig at the Adelphi. They seem quite good. The sound wasn't quite right, but the energy level was good.

Came back, went to bed.

1994 MARCH

Tuesday 15

DAY off !!!

1994

Sunday 2 January *Home – Racket Club*

Went for a haircut – it was the only time they could do it. I'm going away for five days so it had to be today. Got home at 1.00 to domestic chaos. Sue, Sophie and Nial had taken the Christmas tree down, the vacuum cleaner had jammed, and Nial was screaming. I had furniture to rearrange, the hi-fi to reconnect, the tree to dispose of, the decorations to pack away in to the loft, and have lunch amid children - one screaming and one making jewellery on the kitchen table - before leaving for the Racket Club to rehearse acoustic versions of four songs from the **Brave** album.

Arrived at the studio and wished Happy New Year to Steve, Mark and Pete. *Runaway* works well, *Made Again* is good but hard to sing, probably because it's the song I have sung least during the album proper. *Lap of Lux* was a struggle but it's getting better, and *The Hollow Man* will be fine – if I remember the piano part.

Got home in time to bath the kids, made myself a curry, and watched a bit of TV before starting to pack for the journey tomorrow. I'm being picked up at 8.30 so I could do with a good night's sleep. No such luck. Sofie appears at 3.00: "There's something making scary noises in my room!" and then Nial wakes at 6.30!

Monday 3 January *Home – Paris*

The alarm went off at 7.45. I had been awake at 7.30, but was sound asleep again at 7.45. Got up, went downstairs and finished packing. Everyone else got up too, so I said my goodbyes and promised Hargreaves a present.

The ride to Heathrow was uneventful (the traffic was good as it was a Bank Holiday), and I chatted to the driver, Chris, who had managed to persuade his girlfriend not to go to Canada. Met up with John and Mark at Terminal 4, checked in, and spent an hour in the Club lounge before boarding BA308 to Paris. The captain's preliminary welcome was the wittiest I've ever heard. I could see him grinning over his shoulder as he spoke. What a shame they're not all like him. These days, these machines fly themselves anyway*, so the least they could do is spread a little jollity about the place. The plane wasn't full so it was a pleasant, relaxed and short flight. I spent most of it writing this diary.

We were met by Laurence from EMI France, who accompanied us to the Hotel California. In the bar I sampled a 1933 Glen Grant single malt whisky with Mark which was £50.00 a shot! EMI were paying so we thought, "What the hell – we're never likely to taste something like this otherwise," and shared one. It was noticeably smoother than the usual stuff… but I'll not get into the habit.

Did a couple of cable-TV interviews, and later went to the museum of ancient artefacts overlooking the Seine at the Eiffel Tower, where EMI had played the album to their salesforce. There are four other playbacks planned in the regions of France – they seem to be making an effort!

Later on, Mark and I went to Les Bains Douche with Olivier, Holly, and Alex (from Rondor, my song publisher). It was nice to have a wander around. Europeans played Les Bains Douche on Geoff's birthday back in '82. Happy memories, even if I did get into a bit of a scrap with a cab driver afterwards – he drove me round Paris to run up the meter. I spotted it and refused to pay so he took my bag, so I thumped him, then he threatened me with a lead cosh which he produced from under the seat… so I paid up!

Had a couple of Caipirinhas and a couple of beers and I stayed up much too late. John A left to go to L.A only 30 minutes after we went to bed!

* Joke currently circulating the airlines: The ideal flight crew of a modern airliner consists of a captain and a dog. The captain's there to talk to the passengers, and the dog's there to growl at him if he tries to touch any of the controls.

Tuesday 4 January *Paris – Amsterdam*

Woke up at 9.30 with a hangover. Oh dear. I'd lost my room key by now, but first things first. Struggled through the first interview with Isabelle, who had brought me a copy of **Les Occidentaux** which was produced by Calum Malcolm. He produces my favourite band, The Blue Nile, and I've been trying to get a copy for a while. After the first interview I began to feel human again, although Jack was definitely suffering for the whole day. Holly took us to lunch at Val d'Isere, where I had grilled sole.

More promo and photographs with Tania, Ann-Sofie Prevot and Laurence, and more trouble with room keys, then off to the airport to fly to Amsterdam.

Met at Schipol by Rondor's Yvonne Ellenbas who, once again, had forsaken her free time to look after us. Checked in at the American Hotel and Yvonne took us out for dinner. We weren't at our best after the heavy night out in Paris, so we had an early night.

Wednesday 5 January *Amsterdam – Hilversum*

We were picked up by Derek (or Dirk) around 11.00 and driven to the airport to pick up Steve R and Pete T (who both seemed well), and then we travelled to Hilversum to the radio station, where we recorded acoustic tracks for Holland. It seemed to go okay. We recorded *Runaway*, *Made Again* and *The Hollow Man*. After further persuasion we remembered Easter, and I did a solo rendition of *Cover My Eyes* on piano and vox. I did a couple of interviews there during the afternoon, and we returned to the American Hotel in Amsterdam around 6.30. One more interview and photo and then, after an impromptu video message for the Web Holland, we went out to dinner with EMI. Mexican.

Thursday 6 January *Amsterdam – Brussels*

I was roused at 9.30 by Brenda from EMI to start interviews at 10.00. Today turned out to be non-stop. There were journalists literally queuing up to speak to us, and they all seemed insistent on speaking to me. Consequently, I didn't even stop for lunch. I managed to grab something in the restaurant, on the condition that I carry on an interview with Mark as I ate. By now I'd got it down to an art and I feel that, at last, I was talking a lot of sense, and justifying the album to the good people of the press in no uncertain terms. I had come a long way since the first uneasy and unfocussed thoughts in the hotel bar in Paris. The reaction to the album seems excited and exciting, from both the record company and most of the journalists.

My last interview of the day ended at 5.00, so I packed and checked out, leaving by limo to drive to Brussels with Jack at around 5.15. During the journey we chatted about the performance aspects of the forthcoming **Brave** shows, and hatched the idea of the use of wigs to change my persona/sex during the show.

We arrived around 7.15 at the Brussels Sheraton, where we were greeted by Sylvie, who checked us in and then took us out to dinner. Japanese. We went on to a spooky little bar and Jack made wax models from the candles while I listened to *Jesus' Blood*, Robert Fripp and Handl.

Friday 7 January *Brussels – Home*

The alarm call came at 10.30 – it was Sylvie back at the hotel to take us to the EMI office, where we were to meet and greet the staff. There was a little playback to the salesforce (all men), and I made a short speech to try and explain what we were trying to achieve artistically. They took photographs with us, and then Sylvie took us back to the Sheraton for the day's promotion. We had a brief lunch with EMI's Mark and Irwin (Head of Marketing), then more interviews, a trip out to the radio station, and back to the Sheraton (room 2606) to pack, moan about MTV ('More Tedious Viewing') and have a farewell drink, before Sylvie took us to Brussels airport for the trip home. Wandered aimlessly around the airport, admired Tin-Tin paperweights in the Duty Free and flew home. The air stewardesses were going on about Richard Gere opening the Harrods Sale and Al Fayed saying he asked to see the hamsters in the pet department. It was in the **Evening Standard**. Cindy Crawford pulled out of the trip at the last minute, so maybe he was just winding her up.

Got home around 10.00. Everyone's fine.

Monday 21 February *Liverpool – Bristol*

Left Liverpool at 10.00 for the long drive down the M6 to the Severn Bridge. Arrived late at the services. Picked up Dennis O'Regan and his assistant, Sarah, en route to the strip of land beneath the structure I have laid claim to. We were to have our photograph taken with the Severn Bridge sprawling across the sky above us. Dennis was his usual pleasant and easy self, and all seemed to go okay. He ruined a pair of black suede shoes in the river mud. We were then taken to the waterside at Bristol for interviews at some American diner, and on to Cardiff, arriving early evening. It was the International Hotel. International means that the clock also tells you the time in Paris, but you still can't get a Club sandwich after 10.00 at night. I went to bed hungry, but I knew what time it was in Paris.

Tuesday 22 February *Cardiff, St David's Hall*

Woke up too late for breakfast. Decided against trying to communicate with the hotel staff (on the basis of last night's experience) and went to St. David's Hall at the end of the street. The weather was cold and raining - really cold actually - and I couldn't find a way into the venue. Eventually gained entry, had a bite to eat in catering, consumed several coffees, and opened a pink letter which had arrived in the production office, addressed to me care of St David's Hall. It seemed to have been written by someone slightly more disturbed than Charles Manson. There were a number of references to 'your whore Queen' and 'goose-stepping nits marching across your infested scalp' etc. It was most definitely the real thing. It was postmarked Bath and remains, without doubt, the most peculiar letter I have ever read. I was going to save it and keep it as a souvenir, but it went missing during the day.

Soundcheck was hell. The keyboard computer was crashing every two minutes. The record company are all coming out in force tonight to see the show. WHY don't they wait until we know what we're doing?! I was too wired to talk to anyone before the show. I mentioned to Tim Bricusse, our production manager, that, bearing in mind the pink letter, I'd like a particularly close eye kept on me tonight...

To our great relief, it all went well. The sold out audience were quiet for most of the show - I remember they did this last time - but went spare towards the end. Kathy, Sandra and Amanda said they enjoyed it immensely, especially Sandra who seemed almost overwhelmed. JFC (the M.D) was not so complimentary and seemed distant. Maybe he's preparing himself for a tough decision.

Went back to the hotel, had a drink, and jumped on the crew bus overnight to Norwich.

Wednesday 23 February *Norwich Universtity*

Arrived in Norwich overnight. Climbed out of the bus and into a van with the runner, who took me to the hotel via the whole of Norwich, several times. Checked into the Hotel Norwich which didn't look like much from the outside (or the inside) but more than compensated by having sun-beds, sauna, jacuzzi and swimming pool, all staffed by friendly chaps and gals. Did all that and snoozed for the rest of the day. Touring is rigorous, but I do get chance to really relax and spoil myself on days like these.

Arrived at soundcheck which took ages – more keyboard hell! The show went much as expected. This was a university crowd, so a good 50% probably weren't fans. The whole of the **Brave** stuff was met with quiet astonishment. It was another 'storage heater' audience. They all came to life in the encores and, by the end of the evening, we had them with us. We feel a much greater sense of achievement when this happens.

Showered up at the show. Someone handed in my eye-pencil afterwards – they must have had an attack of guilt. Sweet.

Ate my load-out cheese and pickle sandwich and went to bunk.

Thursday 24 February *Leeds, Town & Country Club*

Arrived in Leeds overnight with the crew. Climbed out of the bus at 9.30 and had breakfast in catering. Chatted to Simon Lake (our truck driver) about Dave Ridgway, (my old lighting man who worked with the Europeans and How We Live, and when his entire lighting rig wouldn't have filled a transit van – he now runs Neg Earth, one of the biggest lighting companies in the UK), Peter Gabriel (David Rhodes, Peter's guitarist, likes to cut people's hair), and Claudia Schiffer. He also mentioned a German contortionist, but I'll have to remain vague on that one...

I took a cab to the Leeds Hilton and got stuck in the lift! Got out and got upset with the manager who upgraded me to a suite. Hooray! Had a shower and read Jung Chang's **Wild Swans** for a while, before going out to buy dubbin, lip salve,

Vaseline and hair conditioner. Drank a double cappuccino and wrote this diary.

Asked for directions to the venue and a chap at the neighbouring table said he was coming to the show and showed me the way. Had a snooze in the crew bus before soundcheck, which went well. Still not sure about the monitors though.

Went back to the hotel, and mum and dad arrived almost immediately – half an hour early. Abandoned plans for another snooze and went down to meet them. We left the Hilton at 8.00 for the show which, despite keyboard disc problems, was incredible! I can't remember a more enthusiastic audience. Chatted after the show and went back to the iffy Hilton.

Monday February 28 *Wolverhampton, Civic Hall*

Staggered out of bed around 11.00, just in time for Diz to put the lunch on. It was pork, and if we didn't have it today it will go off. Served up with asparagus at 12.00, we all had early lunch. Sofie was home from school. I reflected, once again, how lucky I am to have such a lovely family, despite my constant absences.

Drove to Birmingham for an interview with BRMB radio at 2.00 then on, through all the red lights and roadworks in the world, to Wolverhampton. Soundcheck was difficult as it's not a great room empty. Had a bit of a snooze on the crew bus before the show.

The show and, particularly the crowd, was incredible. The general feeling in the band afterwards was that it was an even better audience than Leeds. I'm not so sure, but then, up at these levels of mania, it's hard to *be* sure.

After the show, backstage was a bit of a zoo. I had already made plans to drive home, so I got changed and tried to find my way out of the building without getting mobbed. In the end Nick (Belshaw, tour manager) and I came out of the front door and circled the building to get to my car. They all spotted me getting in and I declined autographs, just this once. Drove home, post-gig-wired, without crashing.

Tuesday 1 March *Aylesbury, Civic Hall*

Had a bit of a lie-in. Diz had taken the car to the garage and was back home before I made it out of bed. I got up and attended to the bills and accounts. Dizzy's full of cold and says she probably won't come to the show tonight. She fancies Toulouse, so I booked her a flight on the air miles. John A and Nick B arrived around 2.00 and took me to Aylesbury.

The show was slightly disappointing after the ecstatic reception last night. Mark K was having yet more keyboard hell and sounds kept vanishing. The crowd seemed a bit dead by usual standards – which are dizzyingly high. We've become spoiled, I think.

Monday 14 March *Home – Bremen, Bremen Aladin*

Up at 8.00. Took Sofie to school, and spent the morning playing in and out of the garden with Nial. Picked Sofie up for lunch and helped make tuna sandwiches. Took her back to school at 1.30. She seems to be pretty well-adjusted to my prolonged absences. It's not so easy to tell with Dizzy; she puts on a brave face, but it must be so hard bringing up the kids single-handedly for half the year. She makes it look easier than it is – her way of supporting me, as well as the kids. Nial, of course, is too young to know, although he protested when he saw me packing my suitcase, shaking his head and saying, "No." There's a part of me that I hate at times like these. It's the part of me that wants to go.

A car came at 2.15 and took me to Heathrow. Chatted to the driver about Kashmir and arranged marriages. Met up with the chaps at Terminal 1 and flew to Bremen. The hotel was opposite the Beck's brewery. No problem. Nick B's luggage never left Heathrow. It was with the other 4000 pieces which became misplaced during the day after yesterday's IRA mortar attacks.

Showered up and went for a walk in the 'old town'. Judging by the newness of the 'old town', Bremen must have been fairly well flattened in the war. The half-dozen old buildings which were spared are truly stunning, heavily decorated Renaissance beauties. What a jewel this place must have been. Madness.

The soundcheck was prolonged. Mark has, once again, redesigned the keyboard rig. It was good to be back with the crew; even a week off feels like a long time, and there's a sense of a return to old friends. The venue looks like it was designed by Walt Disney – a bit wild west saloon meets Mickey Mouse. It was a long ride back to the hotel, so we stayed at the venue and I went to bed on the bus. Didn't actually sleep, but at least it stops me talking to people and wearing my voice out. Up at 8.00 for the show, which went really well. The audience were noisy – too noisy during the **Brave** set, which was slightly off-putting, though they made up for it with warmth. The reaction towards the end was ecstatic. I had a touching moment watching a Japanese girl singing the whole of *Easter*. After that I was in a great frame of mind. The crowd went bonkers, and were still screaming for a third encore long after I was in the shower. Truly a terrific reaction and an idyllic start to this European leg of the tour.

Tuesday 15 March *Bremen:* Day off

Woke up to Rothery's Mozart coming through the wall, so I got up and went off in search of a hairdressers. I didn't have to look far, there was one next door. Spent an hour-or-so having my roots done, and then another 15 minutes on the solarium.

Wednesday 16 March *Munich, Huxley's*

Rose around 10.00, and went next door for another solarium session. Showered and packed, checking out of the friendly Westfalia hotel at 11.30 for the flight to Berlin. Small prop plane. A bit shaky. Chatted to Nick B during the short flight.

Drove through a hailstorm to the Metropole Hotel in the eastern sector, and wrote this. Left for soundcheck at 4.30, and arrived to Polish fans wanting 'Autograms'. Ate Chinese and soundchecked.

Ian and I entered the venue for soundcheck at the back of the hall. As we walked forward towards the stage, I heard the doors flap open and close again behind us and footsteps approaching. Without looking, I said to Ian, "This is her." I have no idea how I knew. I know she was from Berlin. I have called her Sabine Schmidt. She tapped me on the shoulder, introduced herself and said she knew me in a former life and that it was terribly important that she speak to me! I told her I hadn't got time, but she was most insistent. In the end I told her if she can get to the hotel in the morning by 8.30 I'll be having breakfast in the restaurant and she can tell me all she wants to say. She agreed she'd be there. Far out...

Went to bed on the bus but couldn't sleep.

The show was once again plagued by keyboard problems, most notably during *The Great Escape*. I'm finding it's beginning to get to me. Tomorrow is being broadcast live, so I hope, for once, keyboards will work. Unfortunately I can't imagine this to be the case. Priv and Alan seemed despondent afterwards.

Went back to the Metropole to shower. Chatted to Jon and Nada, record company woman. Went to bed.

Thursday 17 March *Munich – Bonn, Biskuithalle*

Rose at 8:30 showered and packed before going down to breakfast. It had lightly snowed. Sabina was sitting in reception. It felt like some kind of supernatural business meeting! Had breakfast i.e. coffee, and let her talk:

"My name is Sabina Schmidt. I work in the Berlin TV studios. I am actually a little famous myself here in Berlin. I now know about Marillion, but I wouldn't call myself a fan of your music particularly. I didn't come to the show last night – I would have found it difficult. When I was a little girl, I realised that I was in touch with 'the other side' after my grandmother came into my bedroom some time after she had passed away. This became normal for me, and I have been having psychic experiences my whole life. When I was quite young I began having a vivid recurring dream about being with a man. I realised I had known this man in a former life, that he lived in a small town by the sea in the north of France." (She told me the name of the town but I can't remember it.) "Then one day, when I was much older - about 2 years ago - I opened a magazine and saw a picture of the man I had been dreaming of all these years. It was you. The discovery that this person *actually* existed in the world was a profound shock – so much so that I became ill, and had to go to hospital. I began trying to contact you. I sent many faxes and calls to your management office in the hope of meeting you and finding out if you KNEW about me! I always know where you are. When you tour the world I can FEEL you move from one place to another."

I tried to take all this in. It was nuts, and yet she didn't appear to be crazy in any way. I'm used to meeting eccentrics and neurotics, and she didn't fit the usual description. On she went:

"You don't like cats do you? Sometimes you have trouble breathing. I know this because it also happens to me at the same time – we are connected you see… You don't wear the colours red or blue, but you MUST. These colours would be very beneficial to you. There's so much more I need to tell you and there's not enough time now. Perhaps you could visit me at my house – stay a while and I can explain all that has happened and continues to happen."

I told her I'm not really in a position to do that. Busy, married with children – my wife certainly wouldn't want that.

"You have immense POWER! Surely you know that?! Immense spiritual power. You should explore it and learn how to use it to do good things. I can show you."

I didn't know what to say to her. We soon ran out of time and I wished her well and bye-bye.

Some years later, I wrote *Genie* about her. I said:

"She says she's got so much to say
But she's not telling it today
She says "Come back when you're alone…"
But I'm not sure I want to know
'Cause maybe her road is a one-way street…"

I returned to my room and packed in something of a haze.

It's St Patrick's Day. This time last year I was at Chateau Marouatte in the Dordogne (living in my own medieval tower and writing Brave), and two years ago, eastern America. Flew over to Cologne chatting to John, and perusing Dennis O'Reagan's live shots of the T&C show. We were met at the airport by Nigel Hutchings who had driven the minibus over. We're driving from here on in.

Checked into the Ascot Hotel. Petra Zeitz had successfully carried out my request for room 104 – it's almost completely filled with a huge chandelier and is my favourite. Took a walk over to Café Spätz (an old haunt), drank cappuccino and wrote this.

Set sail for the Bonn Biskuithalle. Tonight's show is being broadcast live on SWF national radio. Arrived to find Mark proclaiming that he had solved all of last nights software problems. Five minutes later, the Kurzweil K2000 broke down! It was past 6 o'clock and all the shops were closed. In the end we did the show without half the samples. What looked on the face of it like a disaster was saved by the most incredible crowd, who remained euphoric throughout. Priv had given me a much-needed pep talk before the show and assured me he could compensate for what was missing.

Afterwards he said it did sound good. We were all relieved and, once I could get to my feet, we drove back to the Ascot, showered, and were taken out by EMI to a Mexican restaurant down the road. Chatted to Ian, who said he's enjoying this tour more than the last one, and to John Brierly (EMI Marketing) who is in from England and said he loved the show. Didn't get chance to talk much to Kai (our German EMI project manager) – he was at the other end of the table. Shame.

Friday 18 March *Köln:* Day off

Rose late, went out in the afternoon. It was cold and I haven't brought a coat, so I couldn't do much sightseeing. Went up the communications tower and was reminded of my trip up the CN Tower in Toronto. The elevator was made by Schindler (Schindler's lift...). Had hot chocolate and lemon meringue at the Dom Hotel café opposite the Cathedral.

In the evening Steve, Mark K and Nick B accompanied me to a Japanese restaurant, where we had dinner with Petra Zeitz from EMI. Drank industrial amounts of saké and beer and finished the evening at the Blue Shell bar.

Saturday 19 March *Hannover, Capitol*

Woke up not feeling great, and clambered into the minibus (now suffering spurious electrical problems), where we drove, somewhat haphazardly, to Hanover via Bielefeld, where we were staying. At the show we learned that the man who was to deliver the new K2000 from Frankfurt crashed his car on the autobahn and would, therefore, be a little late. Maybe the keyboards are haunted! The said machine eventually turned up and worked perfectly!

The show was almost glitch-free, and the crowd were, once again, ecstatic. After the show I showered and signed autographs before driving back to Bielefeld, where a team of girls were turning hotel reception into a spice market. Drank too much again and went to bed.

Sunday 20 March *Bielefeld, PC69*

It was good to wake up in the show town and know I didn't have to travel today. Had a long lie-in and showered before wandering off to find a solarium. At this rate I'll have a tan by the end of the tour.

Borrowed Nick's coat for the walk around town. Left a note of support to Taif, my old bass player from How We Live, on the Philip Boa tour posters in the PC 69.

Monday 21 March *Hamburg:* Day off

Got up, went to McDonalds, then checked out. It took around four hours to get to Hamburg, and was late afternoon when we arrived. The minibus developed a fault with the automatic gearbox as we entered the city. When we went round to the rear doors to unload the luggage, the back of the vehicle was coated and dripping oil… oh dear – another headache for Nick Belshaw (the tour manager).

We checked into the hotel Hafen – a hotel with a maritime character, overlooking the docks. I have an affinity to all things nautical which, I think, has its roots in the stories my father used to tell me when I was a child. I could see the docks from my hotel room window. It's still a thriving port, and you can't help but feel a sadness when you compare the bustle of ships, barges and tugs here to the emptiness of the Mersey and the Thames.

It was raining outside, so I decided against a walk. Had a couple of beers in the bar with the crew who were enjoying the day off, before getting ready to go to dinner at Hamburg's oldest Thai restaurant – about five years old by the look of it! We were treated to displays of traditional dancing while waiting interminably for the food to arrive. When it eventually did, it was excellent. I was having an evening off the sauce, so I drank tea and virgin cocktails. Arrived back around 1.00 and went to bed.

Tuesday 22 March *Hamburg, Docks (1)*

Got up and had coffee in the hotel restaurant. I wish I hadn't – it was awful. Today is Emma's (our cook) birthday, so I thought I'd take a walk down the Reeperbahn and see if I could find a flower shop. The first thing I stumbled upon was the venue, so I went inside for a snack in catering, and to see how the show was progressing. Mark was already on stage, programming keyboards – a daily routine of identifying and rectifying the previous shows little 'surprises'.

I set out into the street and immediately bumped into Isabelle, a native of Hamburg and one of about four people who still remember me from the old Europeans days. She said there wasn't a flower shop anywhere on the Reeperbahn (they sell mostly sex here, with a sprinkling of kebabs, hi-fi, knives and guns… it's like Blackpool in the time of Mad Max), and that I would have to take the Metro. She offered to come with me and I gratefully accepted. We eventually found a good florist, and returned clutching a handsome bouquet. I promised (for the third time) to put Isabelle on the guest list, and she went off home while I returned to the venue for soundcheck. Wished the cook a very happy birthday and promised to buy her a drink later; this was a promise I was to break. Soundcheck lasted for hours while Mark, Pete and I went through the whole show debugging keyboards. It was a late show (9.30), so there was still time to return to the hotel for an hour.

The first Hamburg show was to turn out to be my first really bad gig of the tour (PS and, arguably, the worst gig of my life to date – h 2014). The audience contained an unusually high element of hecklers who made noise during all the quiet moments… also the first wide-boys to shout, "Fish" during this tour. Normally I can handle that stuff but, for whatever reason, it all started to rattle me. I hit myself in the teeth with the mic during the mugging in *Hard as Love*, and I could feel that something was damaged. Later in the show my voice suddenly quit, and I lost quite a lot of the high end of my range. That did it – my spirit was broken, and I started to feel hostile towards the whole crowd. This is unforgivable. It's also stupid, because in doing so I damage my own reputation and that of the band, I cheat the audience and I waste a day of the crews' hard work. I knew all this, of course, but sometimes, and in certain situations, you just can't get beyond your own emotions. Shame and anger. Not very smart.

After the show I went straight back to the hotel, depressed and exhausted. In tears, I chatted to Dizzy on the phone – it seems I run to her when I'm feeling sorry for myself. She said all the right things and I went to sleep feeling a bit better, determined to make amends the following night.

Wednesday 23 March *Hamburg, Docks (2)*

Woke around 11.00, showered, and went downstairs for coffee. Tried in vain to get hold of Nick, who was out and about trying to buy a pineapple and get the minibus fixed. Walked down the steps to the waterfront buildings, and perused the nautical shop. It was full of maritime paraphernalia: figureheads, compasses, Captain's plates, lights, brassware – all replica stuff. I was hoping to find a history of the port in English to take home for my dad, but there wasn't anything suitable. Settled for a couple of postcards, and walked through an arch to the waterside. It was a chilly, grey day and I didn't last long in just a jacket (I left my coat in England!), so I jumped aboard one of those floating cafés, ordered hot chocolate and brockwurst, and wrote my postcards. Shortly before my food arrived, a man asked me for 15 marks and told me the boat was about to leave!! I didn't realise that it actually sailed somewhere so I picked up my things, cancelled my order and jumped ship. Phew! Bought souvenir pens at another dockside shop and contemplated a sailor suit for little Nial. Decided against it as I don't know his size, and returned to the Hafen.

Nick had acquired pineapple, honey and a large bowl so we went to my room to prepare the potion. Perhaps I should explain. Having lost my voice last night, monitor engineer Geoff Hooper advised me to eat fresh pineapple soaked in honey – something he had observed while working with Sting, who tends to experience vocal problems on tour. Apparently 'Stingo' swears by the remedy. I was willing to try anything. Chomped through half a pineapple (with all the usual misgivings as to how my lower intestines might be affected) and decided I'd have the other half later…

I tried to keep the singing to a minimum during the soundcheck, which passed without incident. The tambourine I threw at the audience last night had been handed back! You can never lose the things you try to get rid of, only the things you desperately need.

After soundcheck I was driven off in search of a sun studio on the Reeperbahn by promoter's rep, René, and we were pulled over by the traffic police for a random inspection which passed without incident. He later told me he'd been driving without a licence for ten years and had passed his driving test five days ago – tonight was his first ever brush with the law! After 20 minutes in the solarium I returned on foot to the hotel Hafen, and only moments later there was a knock on my door. I opened it to find a black-haired German girl, who said, "You are Steve Hogarth! I am a big fan of you. Can I come in and talk?" I told her no, she could not come in and talk as I was resting, so she asked me if I might put her name on the guest list. I had to admire her cheek, so I agreed. She went away, leaving me no choice but to change rooms – I didn't want to be visited in the small hours by all of her friends.* I was moved to a room with a bath (luxury) so I had one, before climbing into bed for the pre-gig snooze.

The second Hamburg show was infinitely better. I went on stage with my attitude suitably adjusted, arriving a bit late due to there being no buttons on my stage shirt (another victim of yesterday's tense state of mind). The crowd was great by comparison to last night, but Hamburg's not exactly a Marillion stronghold. The potion seemed to have helped – my voice held up unbelievably well. Cheers, Mssrs Sumner and Hooper.

After the show I signed a few things at the stage door (two of the kids had come all the way from Liverpool), and went back for a quick drink in the 'tower bar', which was only a short stagger from my new room. Unfortunately an even shorter stagger away was the hotel extension building site, which commenced at 7.05 the following morning. Nice…

*You can't be too careful. At some point in 1989 (I think) we'd been on tour somewhere in Canada and were playing in a club with no dressing rooms, so I hadn't changed my jeans to go on stage. At some point during the show I decided to hang upside down from the lighting truss over the audience. During this, my hotel room key fell out of the pocket into a sea of grasping hands. Unfortunately, the key had the name of the hotel and the room number on it. When I got back, I had to ask for another key at reception to access my room. Went to bed, forgot all about it – and was woken from a deep sleep around 3pm by the light in my room, which was now on. At the foot of my bed stood half a dozen Canadian men who had been watching me sleeping. Startled and scared shitless, I screamed abuse at them and they loped out of my room like zombies. They were all pissed or stoned, and it had probably taken this long to pluck up the courage to go and enter the hotel room of the key they had so proudly stolen. Even more strangely, they then let themselves back into my room a further two times during the night. It's a good job I didn't have a gun…

Thursday 24 March *Groningen, Evenementenhal*

Checked out of the Hafen and sent my best regards to the builders…

It took about five hours to drive to Groningen in the north of the Netherlands, during which I lost at chess with Ian. I lulled him into a sense of security early on by giving my Queen away – an old ploy which has never worked in the past either!

The hotel was next door to the venue, so I had a wander around there before checking in to the Mercure, which was basic but pleasant. Personally, I don't much mind what level of luxury a hotel boasts, as long as the staff are friendly and helpful.

The soundcheck passed without incident. Geoff and I tweaked the vocal sound, and it's improving all the time. Hit the hotel solarium and snoozed for 20 minutes.

The show was sold out. It all went well – the crowd were a little cooler than usual, although I have to remember that we are playing new areas of the Netherlands and, hopefully, reaching a few new people.

Friday 25 March *Amsterdam:* Day off

Left the hotel Mercure at 12.00 and drove to Amsterdam. Checked into the American Hotel for what must be the fourth or fifth time in as many months, and showered up before meeting up with the record company for dinner. Japanese. Got back around midnight and went to bed.

Saturday 26 March *Geleen, Hanehof*

Dreamt I was in a limo which got lost in Fulham. Ended up in some burnt-out building like a factory. There was a gang of young boys with electric drills and coping saws who were trying to cut downwards through the still-burning joists so that I could get through to Fulham Road. Then Mark K was there. I helped to cut up towels to dampen down the embers. One of the small boys had a gun, and I was nervous he might commit suicide. I persuaded him to let me borrow it, but then he was pointing an electric drill at his head. It was around then that I woke. Got up and wrote it down. This is especially unusual as I very rarely dream while sleeping and, when I do, it's often about gravel (really!) or something utterly without interest. Perhaps my waking life is enough of a dream, so I don't feel the need to dream at night.

Went down for breakfast and bumped into Nick B, who told me he'd just received a fax informing him that **The Daily Star** would be arriving tomorrow! Ughh… there goes my day off. Said hi to Sandra (Press EMI), who travelled with us on the long drive down to Geleen, and didn't try hard enough to conceal my irritation.

We finally arrived around 4.30 and, as I climbed out of the bus, I noticed that my damaged front tooth had broken! However, I was in luck. The gig promoter knows a good dentist, and took me over to see him. He rebuilt said tooth using white filler. It took about ten minutes and I couldn't tell it had ever been broken! He would accept no payment other than his daughter on the guest list and a free t-shirt.

The show went well, again. My voice was holding, although not 100%. Afterwards I showered backstage, which was… interesting. The showers only had hot taps, so once turned on you've got about 20 seconds before your skin peels! In order to rinse the shampoo out of my hair I had to move from dressing room to dressing room, using the first precious seconds of luke-warm water in each shower before I was scalded!

After the show we drove back to Amsterdam, playing word games with Sandra to pass the time. Got back around 1.30 and hit the bed running. Heaven.

Sunday 27 March *Amsterdam:* Day off

Spent most of the day in bed. Got up in the afternoon, showered and went down to the bar where I was to be interviewed by Julia Cutler from **The Daily Star**. It went OK but, of course, God knows what they'll write.

In the evening I went out for a quiet drink with Nick B. Had a couple of beers and put the world to rights.

Monday 28 March *Amsterdam, Paradiso (1)*

Today was to be the first of the two Paradiso shows. I was here back in '82 with The Europeans, supporting The Cocteau Twins and Dead Can Dance. I was surprised when walking back into the building at just how much smaller it is than I remembered. The stage is one of the smaller of the tour so everything was a bit of a squeeze. Soundcheck was OK ; a bit too cavernous for definition, but such conditions dry up with people in the room. Everyone seemed happy so I walked back to the American hotel, which is only a stone's throw away.

I thought the show went well, but I must have become a bit complacent as when I spoke to people afterwards, they said it was the best show ever in Netherlands so it must have worked particularly well. We threw in a full band version of *Sugar Mice* in the encore. **The Daily Mirror** was at this one. I wonder what *they'll* say... Yvonne from Rondor said the lights were particularly beautiful. Well done Alan!

Tuesday 29 March *Amsterdam, Paradiso (2)*

Got up around 10.30, and opened the curtains of my room to discover a bright, sunny day at last! I had been hearing about fine weather in England from home over the last two weeks, but in this part of Europe it's been consistently grey or raining – until today.

Went for a walk and enjoyed the morning mooching along the canals, and eventually discovering the café on the sixth floor of the new Metz department store. Six floors is high for Amsterdam, and I sat at a window table overlooking the city and watching the people, the trams, and the sunlight reflecting on the canal below. Bliss. Had a spot of lunch and worked my way down through the store. It's like a sort of Dutch design centre and concentrates on high-class home interiors with an emphasis on functional minimalism. Not generally to my taste – I like things a bit more crusty. Nice shop though, with helpful staff.

Wandered back to the American Hotel to drop off Easter hares which I'd bought for Sofie and Nial, before walking over to the Paradiso for soundcheck. I was made a present of a couple of books of selected poetry and flowers as I entered the building. Thank you Anna.

Everything seemed to sound better at the soundcheck. I think Geoff must have done a bit more work on the monitors, which are sounding superb. Geoff Hooper is one of the finest sound engineers I have worked with.

Walked back to the American Hotel for an hour relaxing before the show.

Once again, the keyboards worked perfectly. I can feel the attitude of the whole band becoming more confident now we are able to rely on all the sounds and effects. Paradiso 2 was, for me, better than last night – although I don't think there was much in it, and general opinion was divided.

Returned to the hotel and showered in my room, before going down to the bar for a half with the record company. I didn't hang around long – we have another two shows in a row to do.

Went to bed and read through a dozen-or-so fan letters from around the world. The general reaction to **Brave** can only be described as euphoric. Why does media and radio despise us? I guess you either love or loathe Marillion. Conversion is a long and quantum jump. Our music seems to be behind a locked door. It's fun in the room if you find the key!

Wednesday 30 March *Eindhoven, Muziekcentrum Frits Philips*

Got up around 11.00, had coffee with John A and checked out of the American Hotel. It wasn't cheap – we had been there for about five days. There was a moment of panic when Nick locked the keys in the bus, but they were retrieved shortly after by Jack who found an open window. Drove for a couple of hours down to Eindhoven, arriving around 2.00 on what had turned out to be a beautiful day. Checked in to the hotel and wandered across the street to have coffee and carry on writing up this diary.

Went to the venue and ate chicken and beef satay in catering. Priv was running a little late, so I went out with John and Steve R for a walk and had a beer in the late afternoon sunshine at a street café. Had a mooch around a shop full of ethnic and oriental artefacts and nearly bought something. I had spent all my money checking out of the hotel in Amsterdam, so I restrained myself.

Returned to the Musiekcentrum (which reminds me of the Royal Festival Hall) and soundchecked before returning to the Hotel for a snooze. Again, the show went well and was ecstatically received by the capacity crowd. Priv said the sound was superb out front and seemed unusually pleased with himself. Alan said the shows were all looking great. The manager of the venue had arranged for our photographs to be taken after the show (for an exhibition of artists who have played here), and he thanked us warmly. I got the impression he was knocked out by what he had seen; this venue is normally used for classical concerts. Our audience reaction must have come as quite a shock...

After it was over, we walked across town and had a beer or two in a street bar before returning to the hotel.

Thursday 31 March *Utrecht, Muziekcentrum Vredenburg*

Checked out of the hotel in Eindhoven at 12.00 and drove the relatively short journey to Utrecht, which was to be the last show in Europe before returning home for the Easter three-day break. Our hotel this evening was to be the Ibis at Schipol so there was nowhere for us to go but the venue – our old friend, Vredenberg Musiekcentrum. Had a bite to eat in catering and went out shopping for finger bandages. Utrecht is, for me, the bandage capital of the world, and I always go off in search of a certain pharmacy. Bought their entire stock of one-inch elastic bandage and set off for the Holiday Inn to see if they'd let me use the solarium. They wouldn't. I'm not staying there again. Called in at the hotel Smits, opposite the gig and, by contrast, was greeted warmly by the girl on reception who remembered us from our last visit. I offered free tickets to anyone from the hotel who might want to come tonight – they were more than helpful when we stayed before and I thought it might be a nice way of saying we haven't forgotten.

Bought Dizzy a sweatshirt (which I thought was a little unusual) from the shop next door and returned to the Musiekcentrum. We couldn't really see the point of a soundcheck, so we just checked our individual inputs and monitors and left it at that. I retired to my bunk on the bus for my pre-show snooze but never actually managed one. It's a useful ritual nonetheless, because the total solitude stops me from talking and gives my vocal chords a rest.

Returned to the dressing rooms around 8.00 and showered in the hope of perking up a little. I was standing in a bathrobe, cleaning my teeth, when Tony Smith appeared with John A. Phil Collins is down the road (at a slightly bigger venue...), running through a production rehearsal of his imminent tour and Tony had managed to slip out for half an hour to say hello. He seemed relaxed and happy. Unfortunately he couldn't stay to see the show, which was a pity because we were really on form, especially the **Brave** set which, I think, would have given him an insight into what we're capable of these days. Paul Devine (our previous lighting designer who's working on the PC tour) also swung by to watch the show. The audience, who are legendary at this location, lived up to expectations and sang all the encores and a good deal of the new album. If you're reading this and you've never been to a Marillion gig (I know that's highly unlikely), you should imagine a Brazilian football crowd who just learned their favourite song, in English – it would sound and feel quite similar to many of our shows. In the light of such a reaction it's natural to play more than one encore and so our show, which started out as two hours, has gradually crept up to around two hours 20mins. We saved *The Space* for the third encore, pushing my voice to the limit of its endurance – it was on the edge of cracking at the end of the song but I just about got away with it. This is the last show for a few days, so what the hell!

It took longer than usual for me to 'climb down from the tree' after the show. In this state of mind I'm not terribly pleasant company, and I tend to lose things. Left the sweatshirt that I had bought for Dizzy somewhere in the dressing room and drove to the Schipol Ibis hotel. Realised too late to contact the crew, so I won't know if they picked it up until I get to Frankfurt next Tuesday. Bugger! Had a beer in the bar with Nick B, Steve R and John A, and got to bed at 3.30. I had to be up at 8.00. It was going to be ugly.

Tuesday 5 April *Home – Neu-Isenburg, Hugenottenhalle*

Got up around 8.00 with Nial and Sofie, and coaxed them downstairs in an attempt to give Diz an extra half hour in bed. Put **The Wrong Trousers** on the video and showered before packing my suitcase. The car was due at 9.30 but arrived at 9.00, so I sent the driver to Brackley for a morning paper while we had breakfast. Left at 9.30 for the airport – the kids were watching **Carry on Screaming** when I left for Terminal 1.

The cab ride was uneventful (all the best ones are), and I arrived at Heathrow on time and in good spirits, but with some trepidation at the thought of being away for so long. Said hello to Mark K who had bought a new suitcase after his old one finally broke for good last week. Had coffee in the Terminal and chatted with Pete before boarding the flight to Frankfurt. Couldn't help sparing a moment to remember the victims of the plane crash at Schipol yesterday. When the luggage appeared on the carousel at Frankfurt, Mark's new case arrived minus the handle and covered in scratches... baggage handlers are always willing to rise to a challenge.

Drove to the Hotel Imperial (which sounds posh but wasn't) and, shortly after, left for the venue in Neu-Isenberg. The crew seemed happy and in control of the situation. Everything was working OK, but no-one had found the sweatshirt (a present for Dizzy) that I had left backstage in Utrecht. Oh well, I'm bound to find something else for her. Soundchecked and went to bed on the crew bus.

The show went well, once again. The break had helped me and I felt fresh with the **Brave** songs. I really enjoyed the main part of the show. The audience was the quietest and most attentive of the tour so far, and it helped me to get under the skin of the songs – particularly *Brave*, which Priv later agreed was one of the best it's been.

After the show John A told me that Peter Rieger had called from New York. He said he wants me to take the lead role in his production of **Tommy** here in Germany next year, and that he will fly me to New York in June to have a look at the current Broadway production. Hmm...

Drove back to the hotel in Frankfurt and went to bed.

Wednesday 6 April *Furth – Hessen, Stadthalle*

Got up around 11.00 and went off in search of shampoo and a cup of coffee. Sat in a café for half an hour writing up this diary, bought shampoo and wandered back to the hotel via a peculiar mystic shop where I bought an ornate cast crucifix and a couple of postcards.

Checked out of the Imperial (where receptionist Celine let me off my minibar extras), and drove down to Bavaria for a show in a town called Furth, near Nurnburg. The venue looked a bit like a polytechnic – the hall was hexagonal and modern-looking. A bit of a BBC vibe somehow. Soundchecked and went to bed on the bus.

Just before the show, a breakdown unit arrived to have a look at the band minibus which, despite a new gearbox, seems not quite right. This proved to have repercussions –Nick B wasn't around for the start of the show, so my *Runaway* flowers were forgotten and, even more disastrous, I went on stage without hair ties, which completely threw me for *Hard as Love*. The audience was a little cool and only 700 people attended – our smallest crowd so far on this tour. We are in Bavaria, of course, where the band is not so popular. Mark K experienced more keyboard trouble during the encores – this time it was the S1000 going awol. I was determined not to let any of this get to me (a lesson learned after Hamburg) and, by the end of the show, I think we had given our best under the circumstances. Nonetheless, this one was down there with Hamburg and Berlin. File under 'nights to forget'.

We got a bit lost on our way back to the hotel which was situated in nearby Nurnburg and ended up hiring a cab, which we followed. Found Pete in the hotel corridor, naked except for a towel wrapped around him, trying to borrow a power adaptor from Mark K…

Thursday 7 April *Ludwigsburg, Forum*

Woke up around 10.30 feeling absolutely dreadful – everything was hurting from my toes to the top of my head. It's all muscular, combined with a liberal sprinkling of bruising and headache. Experience has taught me to expect this two shows after a break, so I knew it wasn't serious. Staggered out of bed and into the shower, which helped a little. Phoned home to see how my dearest are holding up. Sue says she's had a lie-in! Sofie has taken to getting up and going downstairs on her own to watch videos on TV. What a brave girl. Nial has finally discovered that sleeping at night can be a good thing so, at long last, Dizzy is being given the chance to sleep normally. Bless her.

Went out to the mall round the corner to get a birthday card for Hargreaves and managed to find a nice handmade one with a big heart on it. She'll like that.

Returned to the Arvena Park hotel and had a spot of breakfast with Ian and Steve R. The hotel staff were unusually helpful, supplying us with orange juice, coffee and rolls on the house long after breakfast is normally finished. We thanked them by giving them a CD and signed pics. Nice people.

Set off down the autobahn once again for Stuttgart, and spent the journey writing this diary and reading the epic **Wild Swans** by Jung Chang. Checked into the hotel and grabbed 20-mins on the solarium before returning to the lobby for the drive to Ludwigsburg. John Crawley from Charisma had flown in and came with us in the band bus. I remember the venue from a number of previous visits; last time we were here I was having nerve problems with my jaw and a doctor injected novocaine into it before the show. In future I will associate this venue with the *ultimate* profiteroles which Emma served for dessert.

Soundcheck was uneventful. Like flights and cab rides, uneventful is good. Mark had been at the venue for most of the day repairing a troublesome Leslie motor, but he seemed happy with the keyboards (a Leslie is a spinning loudspeaker which helps the distinctive sound of a Hammond organ). It was a pleasant evening, so I went out for a wander around Ludwigsburg trying to find the hotel we stayed at last time (memorable for the most comfortable pillows I have experienced), but it was to elude me.

Came back through the town and climbed aboard the crew bus for pre-gig snooze. The show proved to be another keyboard-hell evening. A programming oversight at the soundcheck had disabled the midi volume pedal, so Mark was struggling to get through the show without it. He did so valiantly and, despite some obvious problems during *Runaway*, nothing much was missing. For my own part, I was determined not to let another one slip, and worked hard at an initially cool audience. I particularly enjoyed this one – I was singing well and beginning to feel fit again after a day of aches and pains.

After the show Jack had a bit of a black cloud over him and stayed out of the way. I chatted to John Crawley who said he thoroughly enjoyed the set and couldn't see what all the fuss was about. I had earlier decided to go overnight with the crew, so I showered up and got on the bus. Managed to find a cheese & pickle roll with no-one's name on it and watched a side-splitting Tommy Cooper video before retiring to my bunk.

Friday 8 April *Waldkirch, Stadthalle*

Staggered into the bright light of the Black Forest in a place called Waldkirch (literally 'forest church') and a curious cocktail of conflicting images. The hall is situated in a suburb in a small residential street, adjacent to a row of houses. People were staring out of their windows at the furious activity outside as crew hurried in and out of the building unloading the truck; well over fifty feet long, silver and magnified to huge proportions when compared to its immediate surroundings. Beyond the little street with its delicate gardens of edelweiss and light-green spring foliage was the forest of tight pines and the mountains on the horizon. And down in the road, a black-haired, bleary-eyed figure falling out of a bronze, mirrored tour bus, loving everything he sets his eyes upon, although none of it goes together. He headed into the hall, across the stage, and into catering, homing instinctively on the coffee urn.

Everyone seemed in excellent spirits. A driver had been arranged to take me to the hotel in neighbouring Freiburg but I was in no hurry to leave, hanging around chatting to truck driver, Simon, and Mike Hunter who has become a permanent addition to our mad little family. He got drunk at Easter and dyed his hair blond, so he's being pilloried by the crew who address him as Jimmy Savile, General Custer or Bette Lynch, depending on how the light catches him. I could eventually drink no more coffee, so I left for the journey to Freiburg, enjoying the new greens of spring in the fields and the trees beneath the distant snow-peaked mountains.

Checked in to the hotel and went into town looking for a place to get my hair snipped. It's a pretty little town. We're close to France and Switzerland here, and you can immediately feel the difference in atmosphere. Yeah! By the time my hair was sorted it was approaching 3.00, so I bought a couple of things and returned to the hotel to discover that the rest of the band had arrived. Reported to Nick B who had brought my suitcase up from Stuttgart.

At 3.45 we all set off back to Waldkirch for soundcheck. I had tuna pie for dinner which, I later found out, had not been made by our cook Emma, but by lighting designer Alan Parker. It wasn't bad either. Is there no end to this crew's talent? Smick gathered everyone together to present Priv with surprise air tickets to London tomorrow so that he can watch his beloved Chelsea in the FA Cup semi-final at Wembley. He was overjoyed. Crew and band had each contributed to the plane fare.

Soundcheck seemed fine, so I went to the bus and slept, returning backstage earlier than usual to shower before the show. As it turned out, I got talking and never got round to it.

The audience were a little quiet to start with. I prefer it this way, it's good to know they're listening. But after the rapturous receptions in Northern Germany and England, there's a comparative illusion of apathy which probably isn't the case. **Brave** just isn't the kind of album that you can party to. From my point of view, there's a greater sense of achievement in working some enthusiasm into an audience than merely basking in euphoria from the beginning – although, of course, it's a pretty good feeling to start off with a wild crowd! As is usually the case, the audience came to life for the encores – there's a point in the show just before *Made Again* where the 'art' stops and the fun begins. This show is like two separate events - like a visit to the art gallery followed by a visit to the circus - and it involves me changing not only from one persona to another, but from one performer to another. I worry a little in case this comes across as insincere… but then I worry about that anyway; the desire to entertain always potentially conflicts with honesty… and I'm such a ham! Who does one ask? I suppose I should ask a few people…

We encored with *Waiting to Happen*, *Hooks in You* and *The Space*, which, for the fourth show in a row, was pushing my luck, and I paid the price when the last couple of lines of *The Space* cracked and squeaked. Shame.

After the show I showered and signed a few things outside before getting on the crew bus again. I'd decided to go overnight again to Munich. Wished Jack (who was also going overnight) a happy birthday and watched him playing poker with Cod (the merchandising man), gambling chocolate bars instead of chips, before retiring to the precious curtained cubby hole which has become my second home.

Saturday 9 April *Munich:* Day off

Dreamt I was being hounded by an old homosexual who, out of desperation, I had thrown off a boat into the sea (Sigmund… I don't want to know!), when I was dragged out of sleep by Mike Hunter's snoring. Looked at my watch to discover it was 8.30, so I got up and checked into the Munich Park Hilton. Had coffee and a light breakfast and wrote up this diary. Returned to room 431 and called home – everyone's fine, although Sofie's woken up with a cold. Went to bed and slept until around 2.00.

Showered and went downstairs for a coffee with Wes (John Wesley, opening act) talking bollocks for America while I talked bollocks for England. He says I've got to read Hemingways' **For Whom the Bell Tolls**, **The Movable Feast** and **A Call to Arms**. Mike Hunter went by and told us that Kurt Cobain from Nirvana has shot himself dead. Blimey. How unhappy you can be in the face of critical acclaim and commercial success?

Nick B arrived with my bag around 4.30, so I emptied my suitcase and finally found my tour pass and bus key, not to mention the credit cards I thought I might have lost AGAIN! Had 20-mins on the solarium (Ian said it's now been proved that they're bad for you... "Cause of death – vanity!") and returned to my room to kill time before meeting in the bar for dinner.

Went to a Mexican with the band, Susi K and Petra from EMI, and ate overpriced chicken stuff. Got a bit tired and left before Jacks' birthday cake was served. Had a last drink in the bar at the Hilton with Tim B and Nick B and went to bed.

Sunday 10 April *Munich, Terminal 1*

Can't quite remember when I got up... must have been 12.00ish. Showered and wandered down to reception to drink coffee and read for a while, before once again bumping into Wes, who is proving to be the most pleasant American I have met. Chatted to him (this time about computer programs) before going upstairs to go through my 'overnighters' with Nick B, so that he can arrange my hotels accordingly.

At 1.45 I hit the death-ray machine again, and at 2.15 I had arranged a massage in an attempt to remove this javelin from my neck and upper arm. I was given a fairly thorough (but gentle) going over by Ute, who told me I should really have two massages a week for three weeks if I am to completely recover. Some hope. Returned to my room covered in oil, and showered before leaving with the chaps for soundcheck.

Terminal Eins (1), tonight's venue, is literally the Terminal building of Munich's historic International Airport. If I'm not mistaken, it was here that Chamberlain boarded the plane that was to carry him back to England for the famous "piece of paper... peace for our time" speech (paper lies, Adolf). It was also here that, tragically, many of the 1958 Manchester United team were to lose their lives after their aeroplane crashed attempting to take-off in snow. A new airport is now operating for Munich, so this one was disused last year and is currently being demolished. Standing out on the runway amongst the rubble, I could see the snow peaked Alps on the horizon and, behind me, the bullet-scarred stone fascia of the airport Terminal – a sad sight and, as a rock n'roll gig, such an ignoble, albeit joyous, end… (maybe the Opera Haus in Vienna will be a MacDonald's when we get there).

Chomped through another one of Emma's excellent roast dinners and gave the German fan club an interview before we soundchecked. It wasn't too far back to the Hilton, so we returned and I went to bed.

Left for the show at 7.45. From the outside there still didn't seem to be anyone there - this place is, like most airports, miles from anywhere - but inside a respectable crowd had gathered. The show went well, although I was experiencing some problems with my voice… finding it difficult to pitch. These days pitching is something that looks after itself, but tonight I was having to concentrate (I have since have discovered that the placing of sub-bass speakers beneath the stage tends to mess with my ability to pitch, so I wouldn't be surprised if this was the cause). The audience reaction was the best we've had for a while so the band were in good spirits. Backstage was a bit grim, so I had to wait for a shower until I got back to the Hilton. Found out that the Terminal 1 was the last place Nirvana played before Cobain's overdose at the Cavalieri Hilton in Rome (which I know so well), and suicide, this week in America. It therefore follows that I was the next lead vocalist to walk onto that stage. Poor Kurt.

Monday 11 April *Linz, Posthof*

Got up around 10.30 and went down to the café for a spot of breakfast, then paid my extras… Ouch! Everything costs a fortune in this place – I must have had thirty quids worth of coffees! Packed and staggered down to reception with my bags and bits and bobs – I seem to be accumulating extra odds and sods. Petra Zeitz has given me a big bag of cassettes to listen to for some magazine so I'm carrying all these, and Walkman, and headphones, and computer, and books, and suitcase, and bits keep dropping off…

Drove to Linz in Austria through snow and rain for four hours, and popped into the hotel Spitz to drop my bags before leaving for the Posthof, our venue for tonight. Apparently, this one's a 'filler' and it's only sold thirty tickets in advance. I was expecting the worst, but to my surprise the hall was fine – like a college hall. Mark K seems to have developed a stomach bug and wasn't up to soundchecking, so we just checked the lines and returned to the hotel.

Had my customary (and vital) half-hour snooze and went back to the gig. Wes was on-stage and I went out there to have a look at the crowd, which had swollen a little from thirty and looked like a hundred or so. Watched from the sound desk (I was fairly confident I wouldn't get mobbed!), before returning to get padded and dressed. In some ways it's quite pleasant to play to a small crowd – there's always a sense of "We might as well enjoy ourselves!" which makes the band more relaxed and easy. I found the **Brave** set felt more natural, although my voice was still not at its best – pitching was easier than last night, but there was a persistent frog getting in the way of certain tones. For a small crowd they made a lot of noise, particularly after the first encore when, from the side of stage, the noise sounded like that of a few hundred people.

After the show I showered and boarded the crew bus for the overnight trip to Vienna. Cod dragged me back into the venue to see an automatic toilet seat cleaning system – an electric 'arm' comes out of the cistern with a disinfecting pad which descends to the seat. The seat itself then turns through 360 degrees, rubbing against the pad as it does so, before the arm retracts back into the cistern, complete with flashing red light… Austria! Had a quick beer in the bar with Cod and Mike H, before boarding the bed which was to take me to Vienna.

Tuesday 12 April *Vienna, Ca Zelt*

Woke around 8.30 to the sound of the rain pounding on the roof of the tour bus. Bugger! I was hoping for a sunny day to accompany lunch in Vienna. Staggered off the bus and into the Club Zelt which, unfortunately, is nowhere near the city centre and consists of a large, cold, barren tent on a building site on the outskirts. Found my way into the place and said good morning to the crew. Consoled Priv who was sitting in the dressing room, looking dejected at the thought of a day's work in this uninviting damp hole. Hard to believe that we're so close to one of the most beautiful cities in the world!

Smick arranged for the runner to take me into town, so I jumped into his jeep and he dropped me at the SAS Palais Hotel where I checked in care of Wolfgang, who remembered me from last time and accompanied me to my room. What a warm welcome! Snoozed, showered and phoned England to arrange flowers for Sofie's birthday tomorrow.

Around 1.00 I went for a walk. The cold weather drove me off the street into a French créperie, where I had a magic lunch in a corner of the wonderful old restaurant before returning to the hotel to meet the band for soundcheck. We left the hotel at 3.30, got a bit lost, and eventually arrived back at the tent thing to soundcheck. It was still cold but it now looked like a gig. Soundchecked and everything seemed to be fine.

Vienna centre was too far away for a return to the hotel to be practical, and the venue was pretty uninviting, so I went walkabout and found the Danube. I'm not sure where I was, but this stretch of water reminded me a lot of the Thames. The sun was setting and there were students out on the water sculling like they do in Putney or Windsor, a few ducks waddling around (I like ducks) and, after a particularly grey day, the sky was clearing to quite a lovely evening. I felt replenished and returned to the Club Zelt looking forward to the show ahead.

Smick informed me that we'd sold 850 tickets prior to the show which was more than last time we were here (think positive), so I hit the stage in good spirits and found, to my delight, that I was singing really well. The audience were neither indifferent nor rowdy, and the whole band seemed to be enjoying themselves. There was a ten o'clock curfew here so we were on stage by eight, which seemed a little strange. The first encore was very well received. I made up some story about Robin Hood for the intro of *Garden Party*… and *Bohemian* Rhapsody, but this left us only five minutes for encore 2, so we whipped through *Hooks in You* and said a reluctant goodnight. The facilities at this venue were somewhat primitive, so I did a runner straight from the stage into a car, and back to Vienna to shower at the hotel.

Had a drink in the bar with EMI. They're all new people again since last time, and the conversation was both illuminating and depressing – 1100 albums sold in total in Austria, no rock radio… only pop stuff gets airplay here. The hills are alive with the sound of 2 Unlimited, no doubt. It doesn't seem to make any sense for us to play shows here really. Shame – it's such a beautiful place.

Wednesday 13 April *Vienna – Padua :* Day off

Happy Birthday Sofie!

Woke around 9.45 and called home to speak to my little girl. She seemed happy and she said she had received my card. The flowers obviously hadn't arrived yet so I didn't mention them. Hopefully she would have them when she got home from school at lunchtime… Spoke to Dizzy who seemed a little low – she says she's missing me. Told her I'd call her from Padua when we get there this evening.

Packed and checked out of the SAS Palais for the long drive through the Alps to Italy. Chatted to Steve and Ian (Mark and Pete had gone overnight with the crew), and marvelled at the scenery – vertical pine-forested snow-covered mountainsides lost in the steam of clouds. Occasionally we spotted a castle or a monastery perched impossibly on a high peak, and cracked all the obvious jokes about James Bond and the Black Magic man (Nick B bears a close resemblance to both). At the centre of the mountain pass we stopped for lunch at a service station café and threw snowballs at each other, before resuming the journey, ears popping as we descended towards Italy.

Nothing is ever simple in Italy. We were pulled at the border by customs who seemed quite certain we had drugs. A sniffer dog was produced, which snapped enthusiastically at Nick's groin much to everyone's amusement and the concern of the border police who were gathering, seemingly, to enjoy the spectacle. Everyone was smiling and asking us where we keep the marijuana and cocaine. We were taken to an office and made to empty our pockets while police rummaged through the bus. Welcome to Italy. After 45 minutes or so they decided to give up and asked us for CD's which we were then obliged to sign! The phrase "get stuffed" sprung to mind, but there's no point having principles in the company of border police. We signed them and drove off thanking God we hadn't been strip-searched (especially Nick, who later confessed he'd had a little ball of dope in his y-fronts!)

It was still a long way to Padua, and we eventually arrived at the Hotel

Padovanelle around 9.00pm. I heaved a premature sigh of relief, freshened up and joined Nick, Steve and Ian in the restaurant for a late dinner. I had just ordered when Sandra Casali phoned, desperate for me to phone **The Independent** in London – some column called *Going Out* or something wanted to know my favourite restaurants, pubs and clubs around the world. I thought about it for half an hour while I ate my main course, and then returned to my room to call Joseph Galivan at **The I**. He said he was happy with it, so I went back to the restaurant for dessert and a beer with Ian and Nick before bedtime. I wonder what tomorrow has in store for us? This is Italy…

Thursday 14 April *Milan, City Square*

Woke at 10.00 by room service bearing cappuccinos. The sun was shining. It was spring here. Instinctively began sneezing my head off – I'm allergic to spring… I think it's the tree pollen…

Cleaned my teeth while wandering out through my French doors into the garden. I have a tendency to walk about while I'm cleaning my teeth (Dizzy Spell tells me off…), especially on sunny mornings. A spring morning in an Italian garden takes some beating. Not for the first time, I contemplated my amazing good luck in having a job which offered me moments like this.

Packed and met up with the boys in reception and consumed industrial quantities of cappuccino before departing for Milan. The journey was uneventful for Italy: we weren't threatened at a picket line, we managed to get gas, no-one crashed into us for stopping at a red light, no-one got shot, and when we arrived at the Milan Hilton they were actually expecting us!! Things soon returned to normal when Nick phoned the venue: the crew-bus had been broken into, Smicks' suitcase had been stolen, Wes's case had been stolen, Mickey Dean (bus driver) had been threatened at knifepoint, the catering girls weren't allowed to cook, there were no dressing rooms, no showers, no hot water. In fact, the only private area in the entire building was behind the stage and there was no light back there, so everyone was squinting and staggering around with torches.

There were fans outside when we arrived who pushed me around a lot and told me they love me – and that was just the boys. I know they mean well, but I find it really alarming when people I don't know get a hold of me – I sort of get upset. I wish they would just be pleasant and chat to me and not get so hysterical. Soundcheck went OK. Everything was a little cramped, but there were no major problems. Geoff and Adrian warned me that by showtime the mains voltage would probably have dropped because everyone would be home from work with the kettle and the TV on, so the PA and monitors would sound different – this is Italy, and that is the voice of experience. There was nowhere to relax at the venue and not enough time to return to the hotel, so I went and had a lie-down on the bus. The locks were broken, so a security man had been posted outside to stop me getting hugged or mugged as I lay in my bunk. Had a bit of a snooze and then found my tin of dubbin on a shelf, so I killed time cleaning my boots and watching the people arriving at the club while I waited for Nick.

It was somewhat awkward getting ready for the show backstage in the dark. I ended up shaving sitting on the floor while Mark K held a torch to my face. The reaction of the crowd to the music was euphoric and took me back to Bonn Biskuithalle. They're a passionate breed of people, these Milanese. The sound on stage did seem somewhat different, although it's hard to say whether this was due to the packed and noisy crowd or the collective kettle-boiling of Milan's townsfolk. My voice was somewhat scratchy – a worry, considering that this was to be the first of five consecutive shows. As I came backstage to change for *Brave*, I found Nick B sitting in a chair with one naked leg stretched out in front of him and the embarrassed smile that usually accompanies a brave face undergoing considerable pain. He had slipped in the process of confiscating a tape recorder which was being blatantly held aloft by a member of the front row (this is Italy) and dislocated his knee. Fortunately (?) it had happened to him before and he knew how to push it back in. Nonetheless, from the expression on his face, it was obviously pretty serious. Oh dear! We kept the encores short and tried to get him back to the hotel with the minimum fuss. To my amazement, as I ran the gauntlet from the gig to the bus through a crowd of enthusiastic and pushy autograph hunters, he appeared at my side to help. Thank you Nick, you must be mad.

Went back to the hotel. Ian drove following Marco from the record company, who got us lost. Eventually found the Hilton where we were to meet EMI for a drink. No one turned up. Had to go looking for John A who had taken my toilet bag up to his room – thank God he doesn't tour-manage! I felt utterly exhausted. I didn't have the strength to stand up in the shower so I ran a bath, soaked the stale sweat-salt out of my skin and hair, and went to bed.

Friday 15 April *Milan – Genoa, Teatro Verdi*

Rose around 11.00 and went shopping for a pineapple. Ended up in the Milan Central Station, a huge and incredible building like a blueprint for Orwell and Batman (one of Mussolini's big projects). No pineapples of course… someone in a bookshop sent me there when I asked for a supermarket. I probably took a stab at French (supermarché), then Spanish (supermercado) and inadvertently said something which sounded Italian for "railway station". In the end, you give up. So I gave up and headed back to the Hilton. I got lost and ended up down a back street full of Chinese restaurants. We were leaving the hotel at 12.00, and at ten-past I still had no idea where I was. I did, however, find a fruit shop and bought a pineapple. Eventually I stumbled across a small hotel and was given directions to the Hilton, arriving somewhat flustered. I shouldn't have worried – the boys weren't ready either, so Steve R ordered up coffees while I ran upstairs to pack.

Drove to Porto Fino – the legendarily pretty little town on the Italian Riviera, (reminiscent of **Dirty Rotten Scoundrels**): beautiful villas, palm trees, immaculate terraced gardens on steep hillsides overlooking the sea. It took about 3 hours to get here along the winding coast roads. Checked in to the Regina Elena hotel and sat on a small balcony in the sunshine, and wrote a couple of postcards. The news from the venue was not good – the available mains supply wasn't nearly big enough (the promoter will have known this for months), so a generator had to be hired from Milan (which the promoter was steadfastly refusing to pay for). This held up the entire production, so things were running late.

We decided against going to the venue for soundcheck. We'd only have ended up hanging around and, anyway, it was nice here by the sea. Snoozed for a while and left for Genoa at 7.30.

Arrived at the venue to hear Nick B resignedly speaking down a phone: "No. I'm not calling you a liar. I'm just saying that I have a signed contract here and it says there's a 100-amp 3-phase power supply here. And there isn't. We said we require that to power our show, and you have said there is one. And there isn't. Yes, I understand that 'not even your brother calls you a liar' and that you are upset, but I have a signed contract here and it says…" etc.

The show was OK – we didn't play particularly well and, again, my voice was scratchy. The audience reaction was confusing. The first few rows were fanatics going hysterical while, beyond them, the remainder of the crowd seemed to consist mostly of 30+ couples in expensive clothes and posh jewellery – a bit of a Phil Collins audience. We only ever get a crowd like this in the provinces of Italy. I wonder if they're all various off-shoots of the promoter's 'family' (the 'promota nostra').

After the show, 'Italy' (read 'chaos') reigned: Smick and Nick are pulling their hair out as Claudio Trotta, our promoter, is refusing to supply a generator for tomorrow's show in Ferrara. Priv & Alan won't have enough power to run the PA & lights… But that's only the beginning of our problems. The local council have refused to let our truck into the centre of town because it is too heavy (the entire specifications of our production and transport were supplied months ago, with no objections from the promoter whatsoever). The only option available to the crew is to leave our truck outside the town, unload everything into smaller trucks, and ferry the production into (and later, out of) Ferrara in stages. Smick estimates that, working in this way, the load-out wouldn't leave him enough time to have the show in Zurich by Sunday night.

We're going to have to cancel the show.

Talking to the fan-club last night, there were rumours going around that the Ferrara show had never been confirmed anyway. Kids applying for tickets were being told we weren't playing! THIS IS ITALY. In the end you give up. So we gave up. We changed our plans – tomorrow we will drive to Zurich. And it's a shame because there's a lot of people in this country who really care about the band. It took me a good half hour to get from the stage door to the bus last night signing stuff and being hugged. Drove back to Porto Fino and went to bed terribly depressed. It was to be an early start tomorrow.

Saturday 16 April *Porto Fino – Zurich :* Day off

Got up at 8.30, showered and went downstairs for the required kickstart cappuccinos. Packed and checked out of the Regina Elena for the seven hour drive to Zurich. The promoter is going to be angry when he hears we've pulled tonight's show and everyone's joking about having our legs broken at the Italian border. Everyone's joking, but everyone still remembers two of Claudio's chaps turning up in Nice with interesting underarm bulges to 'escort' the trucks into Italy the last time we decided to pull a show. Hopefully this time we'll be out of the country before he has time to persuade us to stay. Nick still has only one kneecap to lose and he's got his right one strapped up, so Ian and Steve R are sharing the driving. We got over the border without incident, and everyone began to relax after we passed our truck parked up in Switzerland. I didn't notice the crew bus, though…

Eventually arrived in Zurich around 5.00 and checked into the hotel Stoller. Had a bath and a snooze and, in the evening, popped over the road with Nick, Steve and Ian for a bite to eat in a Swiss fondue restaurant. Just walking in the smell of cheese was pungent and unpleasant, even to my nose which was in the throes of a bad bout of spring hay fever, so I sneezed my way through pork and chips instead.

Came back to the hotel and managed to prise a drink out of the ignorant, unpleasant and undermanned hotel staff. Think we'll give this place a miss in future. Phoned Dizzy who says everything's OK at home (apart from the garden gate and the kitchen light), and had an early night.

Sunday 17 April *Zurich, Kongress Spirrgarten*

Got up after a good twelve hours sleep, went downstairs and had a couple of coffees. The reception staff had cheered up to the point of mere indifference. Spent an hour or so trying to finish my review thing for **Musiekexpress** (I didn't like any of the music on the cassettes apart from an artist/band called Kent who I have never heard of, before or since, and Nick Cave and the Bad Seeds, which was interesting), and locking myself out of my room.

Checked out and arrived at the gig around 2.00 in the afternoon, hanging around in catering and the dressing room area for hours. We're not in the centre of Zurich here, and it's Sunday, so there's not much point in leaving the venue. The hall is wood-panelled from floor to ceiling and reminds me of a school assembly hall. Priv hates it during soundcheck – the hard acoustic surfaces make it impossible to control the sound out-front. This always improves with people in the hall, so we crossed our fingers and hoped for the best.

Around early evening Gabby Weiss popped in to say hello. She said she's disappointed with the air-play (what's new?). The mood among the band became subdued as, once more, we privately lament the utter indifferent/hostile response our music seems to get from media generally. I know I'm biased, but surely we deserve better. Depressed and frustrated, I think we all went on stage determined to prove ourselves and consequently (and with a little help from a warm and interested Swiss audience) we had a great night. The band seemed relaxed but tight, and I managed to stay inside the words and music. The enforced night-off had rested my body and voice, and I can't remember singing *Brave* better. At the end of the evening Pete came off stage and said, "I think we all needed that!" He was damned right. I was going overnight to Nice along with Pete, so we had a beer in the bar with EMI Suisse and Louise Veys who had flown in from London. Said toodleoos and climbed aboard the bus, soon to be tucked up and dreaming of Nice.

Monday 18 April *Nice, Theatre de Verdure*

Drifted in and out of sleep, imagining being in tunnels under mountains and then across Northern Italy, heading south and then west from the Italian to French Riviera. At 8.30 when I decided I might get up. The bus was still moving, although I guessed from the sporadic motion that we must be in a town. I climbed out of my bunk to discover Brian (lighting tech) at the rear lounge gazing out of a side window at the sea, and I joined him to enjoy the visual feast of the Cote d'Azur on the outskirts of Nice.

Before long we were on the Promenade d'Anglais, the famous sea front in the centre of this romantic and decadent city, outside the Theatre de Verdure ('Theatre in the garden') – a huge circus tent, permanently standing in a little park by the Meridien Hotel. I reached for my sunglasses and climbed down into a sunny morning to be greeted by Jean, an extraordinarily likeable chap who is Gerard Druot's man in Nice, who I remember well from previous shows here. The two previous Nice shows were, I remember, terrific events – there's something about the audiences in France that is soulful and spiritually supportive, as well as enthusiastic. No matter how much of myself I give them, they always seem to give back more. I always get emotional in France. It was great to be back!

Chatted with Jean and Pete, then went inside to find Emma and Helen and get the kettle on. Ate a croissant and drank Helen's tea before going off to the Holiday Inn to check in. Freshened up and went walking down to the old town with Pete T to drink Cappuccinos by the palm tree-lined fountains. I was trying to find the café where I had sat in the sun last time I was here. We eventually found the spot where I had sat, but unfortunately the café was no more so we went to the place next door. Shame. After pizza and coffee we took a walk through the old town, and found a flea market full of second-hand odds & sods. I bought some shells fossilised in sandstone, a pot-warmer and some quartz-agate crystal for Sofie. Pete found a pine cone on a wall and gave it to me for the kids. It was dripping pine sap which ended up all over the lapels of my jacket… Spent half an hour wrestling with washing-up liquid and serviettes until said lapels were semi-restored, then went off in search of a bank. Passed by a troupe of Russian street musicians playing traditional folk tunes on balalaika, bass balalaika, and accordion. They were very accomplished musicians. There was a sign in French saying that they were students of the Moscow Academy, so I invited them to the show. They each viewed me with suspicion, showing little interest. Fair enough.

Came back to the venue and soundchecked. We all know from experience that the sound here will be fine, so we were line checking more than anything else. John A had arrived, so we talked about business. *Alone Again in the Lap of Luxury* is about to be released as a single, so I'm naturally nervous. On the way back from the soundcheck to the hotel I watched the rough cut of the video. The opening shots of me are pretty awful! I'm going to have to spend my day off tomorrow on the phone trying to sort it all out… I hate the whole process of releasing singles; it serves as no more than a reminder of how much we are despised by the media. Never mind. In my view we have all the things that are genuinely worthwhile – I wouldn't swap ten of the people who were to come to our Nice show later today for a hundred, "You guys are great – I heard you on the radio!" types. Come to think of it, I wouldn't swap one of them.

For me this was to be one of the best audiences ever. I was expecting much from this crowd for reasons I've already described, but tonight's reaction was to far exceed my expectations. At times (the right times) the crowd noise was painful. Momentarily, I wished I could have been across the road by the sea just to hear what it sounded like from a distance – I'm sure they could be heard all over Nice! We left the stage feeling as high as kites. Thank you Nice.

After the show I showered and chatted to Ann Lawler, who had flown over for the show. We signed stuff on the way out of the back door to the minibus and I got kissed a lot. Back at the hotel everyone agreed to meet up at a bar in town. I walked over there with Steve R, where the French fan club were waiting. No-one else turned up so Steve and I had a beer and returned to the hotel.

Tuesday 19 April *Nice:* Day off

Woken up by Nick telling me there was a VHS player on its way to my room. I wanted to go through the *Lap of Lux* video, in order to try to improve it before the 'on-line' tomorrow. Phoned EMI in London trying to get hold of someone who could help. John popped in on his way to check out of the hotel to tell me it was unlikely that EMI would allow any further spending on the video, so anything I wanted to change would have to be arranged directly with the editor and done on-line. John returned to London and said he would call me late afternoon with a number for the editor. I called Trudy from video at EMI who had sent the rough cut for approval, and was told she was away for the rest of the week. Great. I walked to the window to take some fresh air and, as I opened the panel, there was a cheer from a small group of fans down in the street. I recognised some of them from last night. They waved for me to come down, so I went downstairs and asked them if they would like a preview of the next video. Took them up to my room to see the VHS, then downstairs to the café and bought them all a coffee. After they had gone I went for a walk through the old town and down the narrow alleys that form the street market. Once again I had arrived too late for the restaurants to give me lunch, so I walked back to the hotel eating a baguette with tuna and mayonnaise. I had hoped for a sunny day off in Nice, but it wasn't to be. At least it wasn't raining. When I arrived back at the hotel, the rest of the band were in reception ready to leave. Nick was having yet more trouble with the minibus - the rear door handle had broken - so they were all waiting while he tried to sort it out. I was going overnight again with the crew, direct to Geneva, whereas the band were driving to Lyon, staying there, and finishing the journey tomorrow.

Went back to my room and spoke to John who was now back home in England. He gave me a number for Howard Myers who was editing the video, and I managed to speak to him later in the afternoon. Howard was friendly and helpful and said he would make the necessary changes. Wes called to ask if I fancied going out for dinner, so we wandered back down into town and ate pepper steak. The crew bus left at 9.00pm from the Holiday Inn, Nice. I felt tired so I went to bed (bunk) around 10.00. Woke up at 1.30am feeling thirsty and went downstairs to raid the fridge. Geoff, Tim and Wes were watching **Prime Suspect 3** on the TV, and I ended up getting embroiled until 3.45. Returned to my bunk feeling stressed – it was quite a disturbing story about child abuse and a police cover-up. I lay awake thinking of Dizzy and the kids until about 6.00. Most of the time I'm OK, but in the early hours of this particular morning, as I lay awake on my way once again under and over the Alps to Geneva, I began to wonder just how long I can go on living like this and how long my family can stand my prolonged absence.

Wednesday 20 April *Geneva, Palladium*

It was around 9.00 when the bus finally ground to a halt. I heard Smick, already out of bed. He runs the production,so he's always first into the venue, having previously arranged load in times by phone. I'd only had about 4 hours sleep, so I wasn't exactly quick to get up.

When I staggered into The Palladium (I had played here before with the Europeans), the first pieces of equipment were appearing in the hall from the truck outside. From an upstairs window I watched ant-like teams of local tattooed crew (these are people who unload and load the truck and work for a straight fee, supplied by the local promoter), wheeling large flight cases into the building while the catering girls were busy setting up the kitchen. Smick arranged for someone to take me to the Movenpick Hotel by the airport – we're flying to Madrid tomorrow, so we're staying there. Checked in and went to my room to call Howard Myers at the on-line edit of *The Lap of Luxury* video. Everything seemed to be OK.

Nick B rang to say that the minibus had broken down again yesterday, and it took the boys nine hours to get to Lyon. He was trying to hire another vehicle, so they were going to be late. Looks like I made the right decision to hang on in Nice.

I went to bed and slept until around 2.00. Got up and took a cab back to the Palladium in Geneva, where Mike Hunter was experiencing problems with the keyboard rig. He needed to borrow my laptop computer but it crashed when we tried to open the required program. 'Crashed' means the process by which a useful and interesting electronic computer becomes an unusual and impractical tea tray. I ate Emma's roast beef and went to the bus to relax. The chaps finally arrived around 5.00 looking somewhat travel weary.

Soundchecked and spent the spare hours before the show watching Mark and Steve trying to revive my laptop (pardon the expression). In doing so they managed to also crash Wes's and then Nick Belshaw's desktop which contains the tour itinerary and all paperwork and information relating to the tour. Handy.

The show went well in so much as nothing went wrong technically and the audience went away happy – but, after Nice, just about anything was going to be an anti-climax by comparison. After the show I felt utterly worn out as usual, so I chatted briefly to a few people who were hanging around and then went back to the hotel with Ian. We were driven back by a girl in a Volkswagen Golf who happened to know the promoter and had offered to help. Nice of her.

Thursday 21 April *Madrid:* Day off

Got up, packed, checked out and, after much dithering around trying to drop off the hired minibus, we arrived in Geneva Airport for the flight to Madrid. Sat around writing my diary – Mark had eventually restored my computer to sanity yesterday by reloading the system discs. Thank you Jack!

Flew to Madrid and checked into the Emperador Hotel. It was a day off, apart from a press conference at 5.00 which went OK. No one asked any outright dumb questions – a bit of an improvement on last time, when I ended up throwing things.

In the evening we were taken out to dinner by Mité from EMI. We had paella for the main course – mine had chicken and snails in it.

Friday 22 April *Madrid, Sala Canciller II*

Spent most of the day snoozing and ordering up room service. The weather was disappointing for Madrid – I had been hoping for a hot sunny day. I had a nice room on the eighth floor with a chandelier, and a balcony overlooking the red tiled roofs of the city. Left with the boys at 4.45. We drove in cabs to the outskirts of Madrid where The Canciller 2 was located – it seemed a long way from the centre. When we got into the place it all looked like it was going to be a struggle: the stage was too small for our backline, the monitor desk was up on the balcony, Alan couldn't get all the lights in, the sound in the hall wasn't great, backstage was cramped, the toilet was blocked… I was beginning to think I was back in Italy.

Soundcheck was academic. I was standing sandwiched between the drum kit and my wedge monitors – aurally between a rock and a hard place. Tonight was to be a late show - on stage at 11.00 - so I retired across the muddy car park, in the rain, to the bus for a snooze, wondering how determined the audience would have to be just to come here!

By showtime (and to my surprise), a good crowd had gathered in the club. It was difficult to assess their mood until we hit the stage, but then it became quickly apparent that despite my own difficulties and misgivings, they were living and breathing every moment and every word. I'm sure the majority of the audience spoke little other than their native Spanish, and yet throughout the show their lips moved in time with mine. Without them I would have had an unpleasant evening – my sound was so chaotic I felt I'd fallen victim to some kind of endurance experiment.

Afterwards (again to my surprise), the general feedback was that the sound on the floor in the club had been the best ever in the venue, although Priv said it wasn't great up on the balcony where he was mixing. What do we know? Security wasn't tight and people kept appearing backstage to say how much they had enjoyed the music – they had come from as far away as the Canary Islands.

Saturday 23 April *Barcelona / Solsona, Sala Xelsa*

Struggled out of bed at 9.30 feeling badly beaten and quickly packed. We were leaving for the airport at 10.00. Managed to get a coffee in hotel reception before leaving. Decaffeinated! What's the point of that?

Flew up to Barcelona chatting to Nick and Mark. Barcelona Airport was built specially for the Olympics a few years ago and is tall, bright and airy with mature palm trees inside. I had remembered from last time that it was my favourite airport;of course, the blue sky and the open sunshine outside help to bias my perception in this respect.

Today is St. George's Day. St. George happens to be the patron Saint of the Catalans, so everyone was out on the streets of Barcelona – good for the vibe here, but not too good for the traffic which was fairly well jammed. The road to the hotel Le Meridien was blocked off, so we climbed out of the minibus at the nearest available place and dragged our suitcases across the cobbles and along the street that was teeming with people in the sunshine. Ian has developed a cold and says he couldn't get to sleep last night, so he was not in the best of spirits and in a hurry to check-in and sleep. I was some distance behind him as he turned right into the hotel street and out of view. An explosion followed, and I knew instinctively that it was probably him. His suitcase had shattered one of the glass doors. Cool as a cucumber-with-a-sore-head (!), he didn't even slow down – just glanced behind him and walked up to reception to check in. I arrived at the hotel lobby to find hotel staff sweeping up crystals of shattered glass. Very rock n'roll.

Went back out for a walk, wandered through the covered market and tried in vain to find a restaurant with tables outside – I was hoping to have lunch in the sunshine. In the end I returned to the hotel and ordered a club sandwich from room service.

Tonight's show was a really late one (11.30), and we were playing a long way away from Barcelona in a place called Solsona. We had decided to soundcheck thirty minutes before the doors were opened at 9.30 in order to maximise our time in Barcelona, so we left the hotel at 7.00 for the 90-minute drive, which turned out to be almost two hours. We drove North out of the city on the motorway and then onto narrower winding rural roads. After an hour we were winding through green fields of spring barley, reminiscent of the English countryside but with peculiar brittle Colorado-like rocks on the horizon – a strange juxtaposition of landscapes, dreamlike and almost unearthly. We began to climb up towards the mountains and, eventually, the Pyrenees came into view – barren and snow-capped in the distance. By now it was hard to imagine more than a shepherd and a couple of mountain goats turning up for the gig; it was hard to imagine a gig!

By the time we arrived in Solsona, perplexity reigned. Solsona appears to be a medieval walled town at the foot of the mountains, populated by farmers and country folk. What are we doing here?! I couldn't imagine anyone making it out here from Barcelona which, by now, seemed like another part of the world. I noticed occasional posters at the roadside and in the village announcing not only *our* show but, at the same venue next week, Iggy Pop! I would like to know what goes through Iggy's mind as his bus winds into this place – a rebel icon from New York City struttin' in a mountain village…

Paradoxically, the venue was great – a good stage size and a practical stage access and auditorium. It could have done with bigger dressing rooms, but there was hot water and there were showers. Bizarre! We soundchecked and my stage sound was bliss. Geoff had re-EQ'd my wedges and all thoughts of Madrid left me.

I went out for a walk through the old town and found a little bar, complete with wood stove, where the locals were watching a football match on the TV. Had a bite to eat and a beer while people asked for autographs and took pictures of me with their children or their girlfriends. Some of the boys were wearing **Seasons End** and **Script** t-shirts which were obviously homemade (or purchased from "The Spanish Mountain Retreat Bootleg Company").

Returned to the venue for the show, which by now was miraculously packed with about a thousand people! They had been arriving on coaches from Barcelona. Everyone rushed to where I was standing backstage, for autographs. In the end I had to refuse to do any more because Wes was going on stage and no-one was looking. Our show went really well. Everyone was singing along again, and in the general euphoria I bit off more than I could chew and couldn't quite manage the end of *The Space.* Never mind. After the show, which wasn't over until 1.30, I signed another fifty or sixty autographs, before showering and climbing onto the crew bus to go overnight to Toulouse. There were still kids hanging around waving when the bus pulled away at 4.00. Nobody seems to sleep in Spain.

Sunday 24 April *Toulouse:* Day off

Woke around 10.00. I had the feeling that the bus was slipping a little and thought we might be in the snow on the mountains, so I got up to have a look. To my surprise I looked out of the window to see the centre of Toulouse – we were already here. Steve R was already up and about as the bus stopped outside the crew hotel.

Mickey Dean, the bus driver, arranged a cab which I took with Steve to the Grand Hotel de L'Opera on the Place du Capitole. We walked down a paved passageway and into reception. Dizzy Spell arrived here yesterday and was probably enjoying a well-deserved lie-in. I freshened up and put some decent clothes on in the toilets downstairs (these are actually built on an old stone spiral staircase. Only the French could contemplate such a conversion and then pull it off with such style). Ordered breakfast and took it up to the room, hoping to fool her into thinking I was room service. When I emerged from the lift at the second floor, I could hear her voice through an open door. She was already up and chatting to Steve and Jo next door. Another romantic notion bites the dust! "Oh! Another breakfast!" she said. Never mind – it's the thought that counts.

Spent the rest of the morning "saying hello" and the afternoon out walking in the sunshine in Toulouse. I have been looking forward to coming here again; it's one of my favourite places in the world, and my first choice in the event that I'm ever given the freedom to live anywhere I choose. I would learn the language and move in. We bumped into Priv, Smick, Alan and Adrian enjoying a glass of wine in the Place Wilson. Priv has finally completed on his new house back in England. As a tribute to the size of the mortgage he says he will call the cottage 'The Millstone'.

Later in the afternoon it came on to rain, and rained for the rest of the evening while we ate at the excellent Indian restaurant in the hotel. Overdid it and went to bed in pain! Got up again and spent an hour writing sleeve notes for the forthcoming release of Mike Hunter's **Brave**-intro-ambient music. Went to bed around 2.30.

Monday 25 April *Toulouse:* Day off

Got up late to discover it was *still* raining! Bugger. I thought we were more or less *guaranteed* some good weather at the end of April in the south of France!

Dizzy was up and about before me and decided to have a mooch round the shops while I got myself together. She took a couple of things to the dry cleaners for me and also made an appointment for me to have my hair done. What a girl! When she returned half an hour later it had stopped raining and I was more or less ready. She showed me the way to the hairdressers and then went off round the town again. At 'lunchtime' (3.30) we had disastrous ham rolls at a brasserie in the Place du Capitole, spent much of the afternoon trying to find a particular shoe shop, and trying to find the dry cleaners where my clothes were. I can't get over the standard of the shops here; the clothes, the shoes, the childrens stuff, the interior design – all of a quality of creativity and taste which, in England, would be rare. No wonder everyone here seems to possess inherent style, it's quite difficult to find duff stuff. We finally found the shoe shop and bought Nial some 'tin-tin' Palladium shoes and Sofie some flowery espadrilles. In the evening we ate at the hotel brasserie and drank nightcap hot chocolates in the hotel bar.

Tuesday 26 April *Toulouse, Salle des Fetes*

Got up around 11.00, showered and had breakfast in the room before going out walking again, mooching around the shops with Dizzy. She was trying to find a little something to take back for Amy and Holly (my nieces). We chanced upon a shop full of buttons of every kind. I love button shops, so we chose some big mother-of-pearl ones to go on Dizzy's mackintosh. Had coffee in a lovely little square around the corner from the hotel, next to a fountain on the cobblestones. I fantasised about having an apartment here over the shops. Diz pointed out that we couldn't bring the children up in an apartment. There's a part of me that regrets never having had a flat in the centre of a town. The old saying isn't true – you *can* miss the things you've never had.

We made our way back to the hotel so that I could pack in time to leave for soundcheck – I'm going to go overnight to Lyon with the crew. Another minibus had been delivered to replace the one that kept breaking down, so we all climbed in and set off for the venue, which was about 25 –minutes drive out of the town. The venue was a modern theatre; a bit like a sports-hall with a stage, and perfect for our needs (this is France again) and all the crew seemed happy – apart from Alan and Tim, who were going down with some plague or other. It was a sunny afternoon, so I sat outside catering while Diz took a walk down to the local shops, still looking for pressies.

After soundcheck we returned to the hotel to relax. When we got back to the show, Nick said that it was probably unwise for me to travel on the crew bus as there seemed to be a risk of catching crew bus plague. Tonight's show was to be the first time Diz attended the **Brave** tour, so I naturally wanted tonight's show to be a special one. I never know what shape my voice is in until I hit the stage, so I had my fingers crossed.

As it turned out, the two days off had done the trick and I sang really well. I dedicated *Waiting to Happen* to Dizzy during the encores. I don't remember dedicating a song to her before, but in the bar last night she was complaining (in jest) that I never sing to her, so I thought I should make amends. The fact is, the song's about her. Afterwards she confessed she cried all the way through it.

Gerard Drouot, our promoter, cracked open a couple of bottles of Champagne before I showered and signed stuff outside. Returned to the hotel and had a beer in the bar with Nick B. He had been here before with Bowie, and was reminiscing about the tour Barbour coats which each member of the crew had been given. Nick had the job of handing them out here, but they were in a box full of oil (Barbours are made from oiled material to make them waterproof). He said there was goo everywhere. Diz was tired and went straight to bed. It had been a good night.

Wednesday 27 April *Lyon, Transbordeur*

Got up and checked out of the hotel L'Opera at considerable cost. Said goodbye to Dizzy; she was flying back to England with Jo Rothery, and driving the return trip to Yorkshire to pick up Sofie and Nial. It's going to take her all day, and I wished I could help. Climbed aboard the new replacement minibus. Unfortunately it's more basic and not capable of going very fast. It took six hours to get to Lyon. I spent most of the journey reading or trying to sleep, and listening to the rest of the band complaining about the transport. We eventually arrived at the venue around 4.00, feeling somewhat travel weary.

Dave Meegan was standing in the hall, sizing up the stage when I walked in. It was great to see him and, once more, be in the presence of the architect of our best work. Priv was behind the desk. I said hello to him and had a moan about the new bus, which would make a better hotdog van than a band minibus. "I shall decorate it accordingly!" he announced, and strode off purposefully clutching a roll of gaffer tape. Chatted to Dave M while we ate dinner in catering. Dave watched the soundcheck, making notes; he's going to be recording our shows in Paris and needs to know the cues. After soundcheck he said he thought I was singing well. Little compliments like these actually make an enormous difference to my state of mind, especially when they come from people whose sincerity is beyond question. We decided to return to the hotel by cab but, by the time we arrived, there wasn't enough time for my ritual pre-show snooze. I called Yorkshire to see if Dizzy had arrived yet, but apparently she had called to say she was delayed in traffic. My mum sounded well and said that Sofie and Nial had behaved wonderfully. Nial had slept through the night every night! It's a miracle.

The show was great until the second encore when we were beset by technical problems (the guitar, followed by the keyboards) which took all the wind out of our sails. Nonetheless, the audience seemed happy. I regret the fact that I just didn't have my usual energy because of having had no chance to really relax today. After the show we went straight back to the hotel, and I had a drink in the bar with Dave M and John A before retiring to my room – which, for some reason, had a jacuzzi in the bathroom. I still hadn't got out of my stage stuff, so

I unstrapped myself (years of abuse on stage have taken their toll on my ankles and knees so I strap them up for the shows) and bubbled about in the bath for a while before going to bed. Couldn't sleep. My neck was hurting; I had strained it again.

Thursday 28 April *Paris, La Cigale*

Checked out of the Royal Hotel and jumped into a cab to the station. After yesterday's long drive in the hot-dog van (now suitably decorated 'Stavros Kebabs', and 'They're runny but yummy!' in Priv's best gaffer-tape font) we had charitably decided that Nick should drive to Paris while we take the TGV – the high speed train. It transported us, almost silently, through hundreds of miles of beautiful French countryside in comfort, while we chatted to John A and Gerard Drouot, our promoter, who had joined us in first class. We were in Paris by 1.15 - quicker than flying - and we jumped into cabs and checked into the Holiday Inn, Place-de-La Republique.

At 2.30 a masseuse had been arranged to massage my neck, so I lay on the bed while she did her best to unknot my upper back, amid endless ringing of the phone. Thank you Catherine. She wasn't cheap.

Left the lobby at 3.30 and drove over to La Cigale, a small theatre in the Montmartre district. The Manor Mobile was parked outside across the street – Dave Meegan's place of work for the forthcoming three days. La Cigale reminds me of an old Music Hall, with balconies which sweep round to the wings... I could imagine Lautrec sketching dancing girls in voluminous skirts and frilly underdresses here (I later found out that he actually did!). Our dressing room was on the third floor, a testing stagger up wooden stairs, especially after a show and two encores. Had salmon for dinner in catering and soundchecked. It took a while as they were also checking tie-lines to the mobile outside. Hung around in the dressing room, trying to relax and chatting to John about the inexplicably low mid-week position of *Alone Again in the Lap of Luxury* – EMI released it this week and so far it's in the chart at 56, which is tragic. We eventually hit the stage to a sold out crowd (all three nights are sold out), trying to forget (but bear in mind) the tape recorders in the street.

It was, for me, a truly special night – we played and sang with a rare combination of precision and spirit, and the audience were incredibly passionate and appreciative. I didn't see Dave M until the following day, when he agreed he'd got a lot of great moments on tape. At midnight tonight it would be Gerard's birthday, so he had booked a room in a high-class restaurant across town. We ate and drank the best of French cuisine while being entertained by Gerard's business partner, the charming, amusing (and often outrageous) raconteur Michael Deeney who, incidentally, is representing the Lloyds "names" in their high court battle to prove fraud in the recent Lloyds collapse. He's a straight and demure looking chap, but very funny and made more so by being possessed of a bad stammer of which he's not the least bit self-conscious ("... I told them to mmm... m, m, mmm... fuck off!"... etc). As a young, rebellious student he once handcuffed himself to the steering wheel of the Springbok Rugby team's tour-bus and then drove the vehicle away in an attempt to kidnap the entire team as a noble anti-apartheid gesture. Needless to say he barely escaped the beating with his life when things understandably turned ugly and 20 or so pissed-off professional rugby players set about him. Tethering himself to the steering wheel had been a "mm, m, m grave error". Tonight he chatted affably about being stranded in a police station in Philadelphia with Paul McGuinness (U2's manager) after their limo driver was arrested, about being thrown out of a nightclub in Nice, about whipping in the Jesuit church, sexual perversion at Eton, his high court Lloyds battle, a certain v. famous rock band's end-of-tour brothel-parties (not U2 btw), and cautionary notes with regard to making love on amyl-nitrate. We sung happy birthday to Gerard, ate birthday cake and went off to bed.

Friday 29 April *Paris, La Cigale*

Rose around 11.00, showered and ordered coffee on room service. It was another beautiful sunny day, so I phoned my old chum Sylvie Hendrick (who used to work at EMI in Brussels but now works at Polygram in Paris) and we met up for lunch. I took a cab to her office and then we walked up to Montmartre and ate salad at one of the street restaurants in the sunshine, chatting about music and Paris. Montmartre is a wonderful place to watch the world go by on a sunny day. Street life is colourful – a rich spectacle of bohemian passers-by, dark mysterious Algerians, modelly girls, street children and the ever-present motley selection of dogs sniffing, scratching and squatting. We walked back down through lawns and flower beds where hose pipes sprayed water against dripping trees, past the famous carousel of circus-colourful prancing horses and cockerels and a park full of preoccupied children, and on to La Cigale where Sylvie left me to return to work while I went inside to soundcheck and get ready for show number two. For some reason this one, for me, didn't quite have the magic of last night, although certain moments were undoubtedly better. I found the audience more boisterous than last night (this one had sold out first) but not quite as soulful – I wasn't as focused singing, and I think the band somehow seemed a little more self-conscious. If this sounds less than enthusiastic, it's only a comparison to last night – normally tonight would have stood out as an amazing evening. Paris usually spoils us.

After the show I showered and joined Steve R at Les Bains Douche, along with Holly from EMI France and Alex from Rondor. Being Saturday night, the club was stacked with Paris's beautiful people, all dressed to kill and trying to out-pose one another. How can that be fun? Holly seemed tired and disinterested – she's probably dragged here several times a month. I ate asparagus and had a couple of obscenely overpriced beers before exhaustion, boredom and the ever-present consciousness of tomorrow night's gig drove me back to the hotel.

Saturday 30 April *Paris, La Cigale*

Woke up to yet another gorgeous sunny morning and opened up my windows to let in the Paris morning air, which seems to be much less polluted than I remember from my last visit. Mooched around and called my Mum and Dad, who were staying at the Holiday Inn at the airport. They were out so I left a message. They've popped over to do a little sightseeing and come to the Paris show, so I will meet up with them later. Went walkabout in Paris and enjoyed a spot of late breakfast in the sunshine. Made my way over to La Cigale around 4.00 in the afternoon to discover mum and dad in catering. They'd been to Versailles in the morning and, on the way back, the coach had passed by La Cigale, so they had got off to come looking for me. Ate Mexican chicken with my mum while the girls made my dad an omelette, and listened to them enthusing about the palace and gardens where they had spent the morning. I've never been to Versailles. I was overcome with tiredness and apprehension at the soundcheck – my voice wasn't sounding too good, so I made my excuses to all and went to the crew bus for an hour's sleep. Woke up feeling much better. Poor Wes (our opening act) had completely lost his voice and couldn't even talk. He'd got record company people who'd flown in especially for tonight's show to see him play. What a nightmare – and how typical! I wished him the best of luck and, from the high altitude dressing rooms, I could hear his set drifting upstairs. It didn't sound too bad and there was much cheering from the crowd. I wondered how *my* voice would hold out…

Well, in the event, it held out but it was a little scratchy. I felt pretty good in myself though, and I was back "inside" most of the songs (Dave later confirmed this). The attitude from the band seemed more spirited than last night, and I much preferred this audience (I should point out that having since spoken to several members of the fan club, their opinion was that number 2 was the best of the three nights – what CAN you do with the punters?!).

Afterwards, I chatted to my mum and dad. Nick had managed to sort out a couple of balcony seats for them and they said they were treated like royalty by the surrounding audience (merci beaucoup, mes amis). My mum confessed to having cried all the way through the show. Said hello to my old friend Sally from Balham, who now lives with a French artist called Dominic on a houseboat on the Seinne. I had called and left a message earlier, so I was pleased that they managed to make it over. Nick ordered a cab to take my folks home and I made them a present of my 'EMI Welcome' bottle of champagne. I showered and signed stuff at the door – there were still about 50 kids hanging around. I gave my beads away to a chap who said his brother was in hospital dying of AIDS. They were a present from Carlotta in Rome. He's probably going to need more than beads, poor chap. Went back to the Holiday Inn and had a beer with the French fan club before going to bed.

Sunday 1 May *Paris / Besancon:* Day off

Rose around 12.30 and ordered coffee on room service. It was another sunny day, so I set off with my laptop to sunbathe in the terrace garden within the quadrangle of the hotel. I was joined by Mark, Ian and Pete. Today is Workers Day, and we could hear what sounded like a riot going on in the Place de la Republique outside. Mark brought a bottle of Champagne from his room and, as he poured out the glasses in the sunshine amid the ornamental gardens, I couldn't help imagining Louis XVI in similar mood just before the peasants came over the wall for his head! I later went outside to have a look but to my surprise it was just a small crowd with a big PA system.

Returned to the hotel for a spot of light lunch. Steve R was in my room watching the fateful Italian Grand Prix at Immola where Ayrton Senna was to crash to his death later in the afternoon.

Checked out of the Holiday Inn and set off for Besancon around 4.30. Unfortunately the workers were marching through the part of Paris we needed to pass through in order to leave, so we were diverted endlessly and couldn't get out of the city until after 6.00. It was 11.15 when we eventually staggered into the hotel Mercure in Besancon to find the crew in the restaurant finishing dinner. Tim Bricusse was looking a little better after a bad bout of tonsillitis in Paris and everyone else seemed fine. The atmosphere was a little subdued on account of Senna's death; it's peculiar how his fame had made us feel for him.

I went for a short walk over the bridge into the town in the mild night air. There was no-one about and cars kept slowing down to check me out – I think they thought I was a girl. It wasn't a very pleasant feeling. What a shame so many men are so predatory – if we all treated women as human beings we wouldn't end up scaring them out of our company. It's only at times like these that I get an insight into what men put women through.

Monday 2 May *Besancon, Le Montjoye*

Woke up to yet another beautiful morning. Threw my windows wide open, ordered a coffee and drank it enjoying the clean air of the provincial south of France.

Gathered my things together and walked down to the river. Bumped into Steve R and we walked down to the town together to find a café in the sunshine. We found a suitable place and a waiter emerged and said, "Good morning Steve, what would you like?" Fame at last!.. He said he'd been at the Cambridge show. Small world. Mark and Wes wandered past and joined us. I left them with Steve and returned to the riverside to write this diary and enjoy the morning. There is a waterfall at this point on the river with public gardens at the bank – a little like the Ham end of Richmond-on-Thames. There was an old man fishing from the fresh water, teeming with little fish – perfectly visible from where I was watching. I sat on the lawns amid climbing roses until a man with a strimmer showered me with grass cuttings and sent me running for a vacant bench. Ian M appeared and we chatted for a while about how lucky we are to live like this, and how it's important not to get too caught up in the "good things that don't happen" at the expense of enjoying the "good things that do". He was going to find a café, so I accompanied him back into the town where we bumped into Pete T who gave us directions to the town square, where we had coffee before returning to the hotel to leave for soundcheck.

The venue was like a garage, I suppose – just very basic and concrete. I sat outside in a children's playground enjoying the sun. After soundcheck we returned to the hotel, and I sat outside under a tree writing my diary in the last hour of direct sunlight.

The show at Besancon was a little frustrating – it was the most restless audience since Hamburg. There were people chattering in all the quiet, tender moments, but I managed to control the extent to which it got to me. Once we were into the encores, things like that weren't really noticeable so it was all OK. It was inevitably a comedown after Paris, just as Geneva had felt after Nice. I met people outside after the show who said this was their favourite show of the ones they'd seen... so, once again, what do I know? Signed stuff. Gave my t-shirt away and got on the bus to go overnight with the crew to Reims.

Tuesday 3 May *Reims, Le Cirque*

Staggered from the bus around 9.00 into yet another lovely morning. I was in some kind of cobbled square next to a round building – reminiscent of a scaled-down Albert Hall or a circus. I went inside to find the crew shaking their heads and scratching their chins. It was small and it wasn't going to be easy... Drank a cup of Adrian's tea and went to the Hotel de la Paix with the runner. Checked in and went for a walk – I was expecting a bit more from Reims than I managed to find. In the end I returned to the hotel, and ordered coffee in reception while I wrote up my diary before going to my room and to bed. Woke up around 2.00 and dithered till 3.00, then wandered over to the venue (it was only a five minute walk) where I ate Caprese salad (my favourite thing). There was still time to kill, so I went outside to discover the fan club girls in the street. I was hoping to have a look around Reims Cathedral, and Isabelle knew the way. Ann-Sofie wanted to take some more pictures, so five of us tramped across town.

Notre Dame, Reims, wasn't quite what I expected – it must have been beautiful once but seems to have fallen into dilapidation. I later found out from Gerard that the Cathedral was fire bombed by the Germans during the First World War. The pitifully few stained-glass windows that remain are very rich and intricate. All the windows must have been like this in the pre-Revolutionary days when the Kings of France were crowned here. For the most part the windows are plain glass now. The stone decorations and statues on the front fascia of the building have also suffered, through bombardment and erosion. Gerard told me the roof was rebuilt completely between the wars. I lit candles for my loved ones and then wandered around the Cathedral, past confessionals and a statue of Jean d'Arc – the local (and national) heroine. Sorry, Jean – nothing to do with me. Ann-Sofie took pics of me against the central aisle.

We wandered back to the venue so that I could soundcheck, eating ice-creams to accompany the warm late afternoon sunshine. The crew had succeeded in cramming our show into the little venue, and the sound on-stage was okay.

Walked back to the hotel with Mark and called home. Dizzy and the little ones are all fine – they had been to Oxford for the day enjoying the spring heatwave. I said hello to Sofie and Nial. Had a quick bath before returning to the gig.

The show went well. The audience were much quieter than Paris, of course, and the average age seemed a lot higher; there seemed to be quite a few people over 35 which is unusual. Perhaps a reflection of the venue – normally used for classical concerts. We eventually stirred them up…

Afterwards I showered and returned to the hotel. Wandered out into the street for a half with Mark, and was spotted by a table of students who invited me to join them. Chatted a while but the air had turned a little chilly so I said bye and went back and to bed.

Wednesday 4 May *Gent, Vooruit*

"I'm going to move to Kent and dig myself a chalk pit" – Mark K.

The phone rang at 10.30. It was Nick to tell me I didn't need to get up until 11.00. At 11.30 we were to meet Gerard and Jean-Louis who, as a parting gesture, had arranged a private tour around the Champagne cellars of the Ruinart* house – the original and oldest of all the Champagne houses. It was quite something. The cellars were originally chalk pits dug underground by the Romans to provide foundations for the city walls around 2 AD. What they left behind were a series of massive bottle-shaped chambers in the white chalk rock about 40 feet under the ground, connected to each other by passageways. The position of the chambers is such that the temperature inside them remains constant at 10 degrees, irrespective of the seasons above. Seventeen hundred and forty years later, Monsieur Ruinart realised these conditions were heaven-sent for maturing Champagne, and moved in. Today there are several million bottles stacked in wooden racks down there, most of which are turned by hand every day. The place has its own wonderful aroma – a combination of wine and the musty, earthy smell of stone. Monastic. And who should be our guide here in the heart of Champagne's original and most distinguished house? Not a crusty, countryside French champagne historian, but an urbane, English middle-aged 'Moneypenny' from Ilkeston near Nottingham, where I spent much of my first year degree. God alone knows how she got here – it's like a coal-miner's daughter ending up selling Old Masters. We joined Gerard and Jean-Luis in a farewell glass of 1986 Dom (I'm by no means a connoisseur of Champagne, but even to my philistine palate it wasn't half bad) before climbing into the hotdog van for the four-hour drive to Gent.

We got lost and drove round the centre of Gent trying to find the venue. Gent centre is very old and almost entirely unspoilt – very Dutch in feel (to an Englishman who doesn't go to Belgium much) with canals flanked by distinctive narrow tall houses. After soundcheck I went for a wander down the cobbled streets and found a café in a square by a fountain, where I drank coffee and wrote this diary (which seems to take all my spare time lately).

There seemed to be much excitement here about us – I was constantly spotted in the street and asked for autographs, and the show was sold-out. It was to be a late show (10.30), so I snoozed on the bus for an hour before getting strapped, wrapped and dressed. John A had flown in and told me that Pete Townshend and Bill Kurbishley (The Who's manager) have seen video footage of me and are interested in the idea of me playing the lead in the stage production of **Tommy** next year in Germany… bloody hell! Pete Townshend knows who I am?! I'll believe it when he calls…

The show was a bit of a strange one – perhaps it was the relative lateness of the hour. I was somewhat phased and I couldn't quite settle down. The crowd was listening hard to the **Brave** music, but somehow I didn't quite feel in touch with them. I noticed that while the front rows almost entirely consisted of boys at the beginning of the show, there were girls filtering in as the show progressed until, by the encores, at least half of the audience immediately in front of me were now women. Someone pressed a silver chain into my hand during *Slainte* – quite a valuable one by the look of it. I'm wearing it right now. Thank you, whoever you are… Everyone seemed happy at the end, and I signed quite a lot of souvenirs in the street afterwards, before climbing onto the crew bus to go overnight to Rastatt in Germany.

*As I re-read this diary in 2014 I'm struck, once again, by the huge change the internet has brought about in daily life. I had forgotten the name of the Champagne cellars we visited. I knew it was a name like Ruinuit. At the time of writing I would have had to phone a Frenchman in the hope he'd heard of it, or go to a wine merchant's. With three clicks of my track-pad on my laptop I had not only discovered the name, but was looking at a short video tour of the place. All without getting out of my chair. If I was so inclined I could have stayed almost motionless, bought air-tickets and onward travel, arranged a tour around the estate, and dropped an email to the owner.

Thursday 5 May *Rastatt, Badenerhalle*

Climbed down out of the bus around 10.00, shortly after we had arrived. The first pieces of equipment were already out of the truck and being set up on the stage. There's an immediately noticeable similarity between this hall and the one in Ludwigsburg – a modern hall with a large stage and a glass wall at the opposite end overlooking gardens. Peter Rieger's rep, Chrissy, took me and Pete to the Hotel Schwert.

Checked in care of the friendly manageress Sigrid, and went for a walk and a coffee in the town. The town is reminiscent of Ludwigsburg; modern, apart from the enormous stunning pink Rathouse which, unfortunately, I didn't have time to explore. Came back to the hotel and climbed into bed to catch up on a little sleep.

Came round around 2.00, showered and drank coffee before the short walk back to the venue. Had a spot of lunch in catering, chatting to John A. Soundcheck was okay… can't remember it anyway – always a very good sign!

Walked back to the hotel and went to John's room to discuss the ins and outs of the **Tommy** thing. It would mean me taking four months out, starting next March, to rehearse. The general feeling within the band is that it would be a good thing to do from the point of view of the profile of the band as well as, obviously, my own personal fame in Germany. We shall see…

Walked back to the venue with Ian and got ready. I really enjoyed the show – it was busy and the reception was really warm. There was a cell of chatterers to my right which was annoying but, in the context of the general audience, wasn't much of a problem.

After the show, I returned to the hotel to shower and pack before boarding the crew bus overnight to Enschede, Netherlands.

Friday 6 May *Enschede, Muziekcentrum*

Got up around 10.30 to discover the weather had turned and it was now pouring with rain. Found my way into the Muziekcentrum via the loading bay, drank coffee and ordered a bacon sandwich for breakfast. Pete T and Nick B had also come overnight and eventually turned up. The runner was busy, so we had to wait a while before being taken to the Dish Hotel. Checked in, still feeling tired, and went to bed. It's good to go overnight on the tour bus, but tour bus sleep isn't ever *proper* sleep so, if (unlike the crew) you have the option of sleeping the next day, you don't have too much trouble nodding off. It was around 3.00 when I surfaced. It was still raining and the view from my window wasn't particularly inviting.

I had nothing else to do, so I ventured out and walked across town in the drizzle to the Muziekcentrum. Had a spot of dinner in the catering area. Priv had been up to his usual tricks, writing sarcastic notes about the band's tendency to invite chums into the catering area for coffee. I responded by posting up a promise not to do it again. This triggered off a further note of reply by Priv, and the whole thing got out of hand when the rest of the band arrived and took offence. After much general outrage and letting off of steam, we had a meeting with Smick and Priv, and everyone calmed down and laughed it off. Storms tend to rage in egg-cups at this point in a tour. Everybody's tired.

The show was sold out and went really well. It was to be my *tenth* show in eleven nights so the voice wasn't at its apex but, nonetheless, I thought it held out quite well. *The Space* was a struggle of course, but I felt I should give it an airing being as we were back in the Netherlands, and, although I had to scratch my way through it, it wasn't too bad.

After the show we had made the mistake of inviting quite a lot of fans backstage for a drink. I wish we hadn't – I wasn't really down from 'out of the tree' when I was put in front of thirty or so people who all seemed to take offence at my inability to remember their names (I can't usually remember my own telephone number at times like these). To make matters slightly more complicated, I had eaten a couple of slices of hash cake (it had appeared backstage before the show) and wasn't quite sure whether or not I was being paranoid... oh, and I'd had a couple of Rothery's tequila sunrises. Everyone seemed to be queuing up to tell me I hadn't sung very well and that they'd preferred such-and-such a show. It's usually our Dutch shows that sell-out first, so there's no doubting the passion for our music in Holland, but they do like to give you the benefit of their criticism here. Perhaps it's a cultural thing and they think they must be honest and do you that "favour". Personally, I can't imagine ever going backstage at someone else's gig and telling them there was this or that wrong with it. Whether honest criticism, whether valid or not, it would simply strike me as rudeness.

I escaped to the street for fear of abusing someone and watched the boys loading the truck, relieved to be out of that room full of mind-games and point-scoring, and reflecting on what a lovely and rare collection of people we have working for us.

I later ended up in a bar with Steve R, Mark K, Nick B and various Dutch 'regulars' (fan club etc), but I still seemed to be having trouble making conversation so I didn't stay very long. Walked back to the hotel, the wrong way round the ring road, with Nick. It took us twenty minutes to complete what I knew was only a five minute walk – I think he was stoned too!

When I got into bed the cakes were properly kicking-in, and I had to keep getting up and putting all the lights on – I was hallucinating whenever I closed my eyes. I have learned from (fairly limited) experience to try not to think about it and relax. I eventually drifted into sleep vowing never to take drugs again.

Saturday 7 May *Home*

Woke up feeling fragile but not dreadful, and checked out of the Dish Hotel, Enschede to drive to Schipol. Flew home to be met at the airport by Dizzy and the kids. I was relieved to receive big hugs and kisses from Nially... I was wondering if he'd remember me – it's been five weeks. Drove home in the rain, thinking what a shame I've missed the good weather.

After we got home I asked the children what they'd like to do. Sofie said she'd like to go to Oxford and have tea at Browns – I said we would. Went to Brackley with Nially to try to buy spares for the kitchen light and to have my tooth looked at following my collision with the mic in Enschede.

Repaired the kitchen light and set off to Oxford for tea. The rain had stopped, and by 7.00 the sky had cleared and it had turned into a nice evening. We sat cuddling like teenagers on a bench next to the little green opposite the restaurant while Sofie and Nial played among the daisies and buttercups. Heaven.

Drove back and read stories to the children on their way to bed. Watched **Have I Got News for You** on the telly and had an early night with my lovely and beautiful wife.

Sunday 8 May *Guildford, Civic Hall*

Woke up around 11.00 by Diz bearing a cup of tea. Thank you, thank you. Wandered about the garden spraying the roses for greenfly and playing with the children. The garden is a picture – it's a walled country garden, not too big but beautifully formed. An enormous clematis hangs along the wall which is in full bloom today. This will only remain for the first few weeks of May. There's a high wall along the left boundary where I planted a 12-foot climbing rose – I bought it already this tall. It was an exhibit at the Chelsea Flower Show, and this year it will flower for the first time since I planted it. It's completely covered in buds so it should look stunning in the summer. To the right there's an apple tree, which is in full pink blossom. Sofie and Nial have swings hanging from its boughs – this is where they spend most of their time. Nial can usually be found digging in the sand pit beneath the apple tree.

We had a spot of lunch before I left in the car to drive to Guildford. I made good time to the M25, so I stopped off at junction 13 and drove up to Middle Hill, our old address, to see if our dear next-door neighbour, Bessie (one of the most beautiful people I ever met, and now well into her seventies) was at home. She was, and invited me in for a cup of tea and we caught up on each other's news. I vowed to return in the near future with Dizzy and the children, and left for the rest of the drive to Guildford.

I arrived to find various members of band, crew and a handful of fans sitting out in the sunshine. It was a lovely afternoon and anyone not actually working was outside on the backstage steps. I sat outside waiting for my turn to soundcheck, enjoying the weather despite the constant comings and goings of people wanting my autograph. I don't generally mind all that stuff – our fans are a bunch of sweeties on the whole, but this afternoon five minutes peace would have been most welcome.

It was nice to see Ann Lawler again. She is John A's assistant, and is demure, calm, and efficient to the nth degree; our very own Miss Moneypenny. I have often said that if you were to call her and ask her to arrange a sabre-toothed tiger on Sydney Bridge this afternoon at 3pm, she would calmly ask, "Which side of Sydney Bridge?"

After soundcheck I jumped on the crew bus for forty-winks before returning across the car park to the show. The show felt very strange after the nightly euphoria in Europe. This is Guildford, Surrey – conservatism rules, and emotional and spiritual expression is laced up pretty tight. I try to immerse myself in the music at times like these, but tonight there was a small cell of well-meaning (bordering on smart-arse) hecklers who prevented me from doing this. I felt I was skating around on it instead of being inside it. Not a good feeling. Again my lesson in Hamburg served to prevent me spiralling down, and I clung on and made the best of it. It was okay… but that's all.

After the show I chatted briefly to Charles Garside from Rondor and Amanda and Kathy from EMI, before driving home and climbing into bed around 2.00. I felt like I'd done a day's work.

Monday 9 May *Sheffield, City Hall*

Spent the morning at home with Dizzy and Nially. Sofie came home for lunch, and I took them both to the park round the corner for a slide and a swing before Hargreaves went back to school.

I threw a few things into the boot of the car and drove up to Sheffield. It was a nice day for a drive and the roads weren't too busy. I arrived in Sheffield around 3.30 and found my way to the City Hall, parking the car alongside the truck. I went into the building through a side door and sat down to a spot of late lunch with Ian and Pete. There was much talk of starting up a catering division of Racket Enterprises as Emma and Helen are looking around for a backer so they can go it alone. I went back out looking for shampoo and conditioner at Boots and The Body Shop – these are the things I have trouble getting hold of in Europe and it was my first chance to re-stock.

I returned to the venue to soundcheck. The hall is quite a design achievement – the balconies swing around in a circular arc below a ceiling of glass panels with an electric cover to let in or block out natural light, depending on the production requirements. This is the venue I was sitting in when I decided to become a rock n'roll star (ha ha) all those years ago. I was gazing in excited disbelief at Deep Purple performing their **Machine Head** album. They were making noises I had never heard before (nobody had!), and the energy and commitment before me left my senses reeling and my brain asking the question, "Surely, everything else is worse than this? Why, given the choice, would you want to do anything else with your life?" I was to return many times in my following school years to see Yes, Genesis, Uriah Heep, Focus, Rory Gallagher and Status Quo. I'm always struck by the sense of the dream having become real when I'm on this particular stage. Of course, I still feel there's much to achieve and the elusive gold album beckons frustratingly, but I know such goals lose much of their meaning once scored. For now, life is surely sweet enough.

Drove my car up the street to the Grosvenor Hotel with Pete, parking in the Hotel car park and checking in with my trusty bowl of pineapple and honey, before climbing into bed for the all-important pre-show shutdown.

Later I returned on foot, walking up the hill to the City Hall (still carrying my fruit bowl) to be met outside the hall by Nick B, who pronounced that I was becoming eccentric. I took it as a compliment.

The show was a little strange – the audience were deathly quiet during the new album and barely any more responsive during the encores. My voice felt in good form, and I thought we played well but we couldn't help remembering the thermonuclear response at Leeds (just down the road) and making comparisons with the silence here at Sheffield. Strange...

After the show I showered and said hello to old school friends and my mum and dad, before returning to the hotel. As I entered my unwelcoming room at around 1.30, I decided I might as well drive home. The roads were clear and I made it back by 3.00.

Tuesday 10 May *Home*

Can't remember much about today. I'm sure I probably got up late again. I spent a couple of hours in the garden mowing the lawn. It was another sunny day and, after Sofie came home from school, we went down to the canal at Clifton for tea and ice creams. Nial fell face-first off the slide into the gravel and cut his lip, bless him. He's almost permanently injured (chip off the old block). Put the kids to bed. Nothing on the telly. Had an early night.

Wednesday 11 May *Oxford, Apollo*

Spent the morning at home again with Dizzy and Nially. Sofie came home for dinner and sat outside in the garden with Nial, eating sandwiches in the sunshine. It was a lovely day. When Sofie finished school for the day, we all climbed into the car and drove to Oxford for soundcheck at the Apollo. This was the first time Sofie and Nial had seen what I do first-hand, so they were both very excited. I took them onto the stage and Nial had a go on the drums. For a two-year old he was remarkably in control of the sticks. When we ran through *Lap of Luxury* they sat in the circle, clapping and blowing kisses... bless 'em. It was lovely. After soundcheck Sue took them home, and was to return for the show with her girl chums from Aynho.

It had become a beautiful afternoon so, after my family went home, I went for a stroll, picking up a few fans as I walked, and went to the pub for a pint of 6X. We stood out in the street in the evening sunshine chatting before I returned to the gig.

In the event, I was quite embarrassed that the neighbours should come to this one, it hadn't sold particularly well. The stalls were sold out but the balcony was empty apart from my guests, who must have felt awfully alone. We gave it our best and I was happy with my performance - I was singing well, after the day off - but the audience was terribly reserved and quiet throughout the show (quite usual for Oxford). Halfway through the first encore they had come to life. I remember saying to them, "Maybe we should start again now..."

After the show I showered, and chatted to the Aynho girls who all seemed to have enjoyed themselves. Annette said it was the best gig she'd ever seen and Elouisa, the Brazilian, said I was "a king" (She had been drinking). On our way from the gig to the car, we chatted to a couple from Philadelphia who had seen "yous guys" at The Chestnut Cabaret on the last tour. I think he was called Jimmy. He was born in Scotland and had decided to return from America – "It's a rat race there, man…"

We wandered back to the car and drove home to relieve Natalie, who had been babysitting. She's learnt to drive and split up with her boyfriend.

Thursday 12 May *Manchester, Apollo*

Got up late around 11.30. Dizzy had let me have a lie-in, bless her. Nial sat on my lap for a while watching **Chitty Chitty Bang Bang** – his current favourite. Since I returned from Europe he has been a little less possessive of his mum and seems happy to be with me. I remember Sofie hitting the same age where she would first come to me and be affectionate. Heaven. Sofie came home from school for lunch and joined us watching the movie while eating pickle sandwiches – her favourite.

Nick, John and Jack arrived at around 1.30 to pick me up, and we drove to Manchester reflecting on the progress of **Brave** and what might and might not have been. John filled us in on the forthcoming schedule in Japan, Central and South America. When we arrived at the Victoria & Albert Hotel, Sandra Cassali (EMI Press) was waiting in reception with a journalist and photographer from **Today** newspaper. They seemed okay.

Checked in to room 404 – all the rooms here are named after various Granada TV productions (Granada is just across the road). Mine was called **A Breakthrough in Reykjavik** and there were photographs on my wall of some play or other which was about Gorbacev and Reagan having a summit meeting.

Went to the Apollo to soundcheck. Our photographer friend was snapping away while the journalist picked our brains. Apparently as a consequence of the 'hysteria' (the extraordinary depth of feeling) following Kurt Cobain's death, the editor had decided to do an investigative piece on rock fanaticism. Well, they chose the right band if they're looking to research the mentality of an obsessively caring audience, as opposed to the kind of juvenile pop hysteria which is perhaps the stereotype. We sat in catering while I introduced the crew and described how the whole show works. They came to the stage for a guided tour of the backline during soundcheck, then went outside to interview the fans while we returned to the hotel.

I went to bed in my Reykjavik room for pre-show recharge before returning to the Apollo for what was to be a well-received show. Paul and Annie Lewis came back to say hello. Paul's looking five years younger than he did last year.

The show went well. We gave a good account of ourselves and the crowd were really vocal – a noticeable and welcome change after the sedate Guildford and Oxford crowds.

After the show I showered up and went downstairs looking for my old chum, Angie Fountain, but she had left. I went outside and signed stuff for people for about twenty minutes before returning to the hotel where we sat in the bar with John A, Jo Rothery, Sandra and the journalists, drinking beer and eating bacon and marmalade sandwiches until around 1.30, before retiring to bed.

Friday 13 May *Newcastle, City Hall*

Checked out of the Victoria and Albert and had a coffee in the bar with Ian, Pete, Lorraine, Sandra, and Mark (the photographer), before we bundled into three cars for the drive to Newcastle. Lorraine went with Steve, Ian and Mark to interview them during the journey. Got a bit lost in the one-way system when we arrived in Newcastle and had to break a few traffic laws before finding the Copthorne Hotel. I was to go overnight to Nottingham tonight, so I wasn't checking in. Mark wanted a photograph of me unpacking my bags in a hotel room, so I borrowed Nick B's room and unpacked his bags instead while Mark snapped away before driving to the Newcastle City Hall for food and soundcheck. The hall was larger than I remembered.

After soundcheck we went outside to do a band photograph with Lorraine and then I went for a snooze on the bus, leaving her in the dressing room with my laptop so she could have a read through my diary. The show went well. I don't remember any particular highs or problems. It was a good night but (obviously) not outstanding. If you're reading this diary, you might by now be wondering how I seem to concentrate on the events of the day rather than the shows themselves. The fact is that the shows tend to erase themselves from my memory as they happen; I think it's the adrenalin. It's a very similar process to dreaming – no matter how intense the dream, all but a very few (and then it's an inexplicably random selection) are remembered. I tend to remember technical problems with a greater clarity than even the most brilliant moments. If I damage myself in some way (falling off the stage, twisting ankles, ricking my neck, breaking teeth, etc) I tend to remember that too…

After the show I chatted to our agent, Ian Huffam, who's just out of hospital from a detached appendix (he nearly died!) and, although claiming to be fully recovered, looked very weak. I told him he should be at home in bed. It's a funny business, rock and roll – if he worked for EMI he'd have probably stayed off work for months. Thank you Ian. I was in no hurry to leave the gig as I was going overnight with the crew, so I hung around in the dressing room with John Wesley and the girls from the French fan club, who wanted to know what I wanted for my birthday tomorrow. I told them socks, fireworks and a can of beans.

Saturday 14 May *Nottingham, Royal Centre*

Staggered, bleary eyed, into the street next to the Royal Centre, Nottingham – just round the corner from the monstrous 'Newton Building' where, twenty years ago, I was locked up studying electrical engineering. It was here at Trent Polytechnic that I first got my hands on a grand piano. I used to skip lectures whenever I could find the Bonnington or the Arkwright lecture theatres empty in order to experiment with my new-found love, banging out crude and uncertain copies of Keith Emerson's piano solos. Nothing's changed much here, and I trundled my suitcase past the Poly (which now calls itself the "City University") towards the Stakis Victoria, thanking my stars that 'all that' was behind me. I had a few good days in Nottingham back then, but painfully few – I didn't fit in.

Checked into the hotel which is a bit of an old shit heap with middle-class pretensions ("fur coat, no drawers"), and went to bed to finish off something that might pass for a good night's sleep, before getting up and going down to Nottingham's favourite rendezvous point – the old market square, where I had arranged to meet Sue and the kids. We used to meet here back then when we were young lovers, and it seemed beautiful that we should meet again, with our children, in the sunshine of my birthday. It was a hot sunny Saturday and, as I sat waiting, I was transported back to 1976 and the freak hot summer I enjoyed in this same spot. Ironically, we got off to a bad start – Nial was tired, hungry and crabby, and I began to wonder if we'd made a mistake in going to all this trouble. Sue had driven up from Banbury (amid all the usual hassle), while I still had a show to do and could have done with relaxing. We eventually got him fed and off to sleep, and he later woke up his usual self – happy and smily. Sofie was fine, and we started to have the day we'd hoped for. Walked over to the Arboretum and lay in the warm sunshine, dribbling ice-creams and orange juices and getting through lots of baby-wipes. Sofie was in her element among the flowers, and enjoying the pleasures to be had balancing and clanking along the park railings. Stopped at the birdhouse so that Nial could enjoy the cockatoos and budgies while I tried to explain to him why we couldn't go inside.

Back at the venue everything had stopped for the FA Cup final, where Priv's beloved Chelsea were to lose to Manchester United. I tried to keep out of his way… We all had a spot of dinner in catering. Sofie has taken a shine to Emma and Helen, and was happily tucking into a roast dinner as Nial caused much amusement trying to blow bubbles with some bubble liquid – my birthday present from the cooks. They sat in at the soundcheck, clapping and blowing kisses, before Dizzy said bye-bye and returned home. I went back to the hotel for a bath and a twenty-minute break before the show.

I hit the stage in festive spirits, and was determined to have a good time. I did! The crowd were better than I remembered here last tour. Bonny from the fan club came on stage with a birthday cake, and the band seemed to be enjoying themselves as much as I was. Afterwards I waited until the truck were loaded and then shared out the cake and had a beer with the crew. Staggered back to my cruddy hotel with carrier bags full of presents, cards and yet another birthday cake. On closer inspection I noticed one card said, "My girlfriend really wants to fuck you!" Blimey. I'm surprised it wasn't a letter bomb…

Sunday 15 May *Bristol:* Day off

Woke up and decided to complain. Had the duty manageress sent up to my room and showed her the rising damp in the bathroom and the generally grubby state of my room, told her there wasn't enough staff on reception, that the lift didn't work and that I wasn't impressed. She said sorry and let me off my extras. Packed, and realised I'd lost my seven silver bangles from Mexico. Tried the theatre and found they had been handed in by the cleaner. Thank you Nottingham. It's almost worth the distress of losing stuff to have human goodness reaffirmed.

Drove to Bristol, arriving at the Bristol Hilton around 2.00 craving a roast dinner. They were doing one in the restaurant, so I took a table for one and had Sunday lunch before phoning home. Snoozed through the Monaco Grand Prix, which Schumacher seemed effortlessly to win once again. Thankfully no-one was hurt during the race, although Wendlinger was in hospital after a serious crash during the qualifying rounds yesterday.

Went out for a walk and found the Arnolfini arts centre where I read the paper and had a coffee. Nick had sorted me out with a suite, which perhaps was part birthday present and part compensation for yesterday. Thank you Mr. B. I had a nice view of the church and sat munching chocolate marzipans (birthday presents) and watching a documentary about these poor chaps in Indonesia who make a meagre living carrying sulphur rocks down from the summit of a volcano, through rainforest, to the factory at the base of the mountain – it's a twelve hour walk undergoing the enormous physical burden. I thanked my stars once again as I reclined in splendour surrounded by tokens of people's affection. Lucky man. In the evening I bumped into Brian, Emma and Helen who invited me along with them to an Italian restaurant. I had Caprese, chicken Kiev and Peroni beer. When we got back we went to the bar, where I was quickly naused off by some friend of the crew bus driver. Life's too short to listen to some people. I made an excuse and went up to bed.

Monday 16 May *Bristol, Colston Hall*

Got up and went off in search of a hairdressers, a dry cleaners and a bank. Found a three-hour cleaners first, and put a couple of shirts and my jacket in. Made my way to the Nat West bank to change up my French leftover PD's. It turned out that one of my 200 Franc notes was a forgery. The girl in the foreign exchange desk had to make a phone call to find out whether or not to have me arrested. Apparently, if it's foreign currency they don't call the police, they just confiscate the forged notes and give you a receipt. Maybe our French promoter Gerard makes his own money – everything's possible in this business! I later discovered that the cash had come to Nick from Cod, our merchandising man – someone had been passing duds in exchange for t-shirts (Sorry Gerard – I wasn't serious.)

Found a hairdressers and got snipped before returning to the hotel. Left soon after for soundcheck. Ian commented that I had been wearing the same shirt for four days, asking had it been washed? I was embarrassed into digging out a purple velvet horror with a big floppy collar, which I wore with pride for the rest of the day.

The Colston Hall is a total cave, empty or full, so my sound was difficult to say the least. Never mind. Returned to the hotel and went to bed. I enjoyed the show, despite the iffy sound, and felt relaxed. I did a psychedelic intro to *Garden Party* so I must have been feeling good (I had vowed no more *Garden Party* intros after coming unstuck in Guildford). I showered at the venue and went down to the hospitality room to chat to Dave Gregory (renowned guitarist of XTC and all round top man) who had come over from Swindon. Dave said the sound was iffy but thought the show went well. Most tactful, I thought!

Tuesday 17 May *Birmingham, Town Hall*

Checked out of the Bristol Hilton (most of the Hiltons are pretty iffy these days, but I would recommend this one) and drove round the corner to Temple Meads Station in order to have passport photographs done for the Japanese visas. Bought coffee at the station kiosk and asked the lady serving what the hours were like (you never know…).

Drove up to Birmingham with Steve R and Ian, and got lost in Birmingham centre. Everyone always does. Arrived at the Midland Hotel feeling decidedly peculiar, checked in, and ordered a Club sandwich. Paul, the porter who arrived with my suitcase, decided my room wasn't up to scratch and offered me four alternatives as I followed him up and down the corridor, somewhat surprised – they usually don't worry unless you complain. I thanked him, but decided against moving. The room seemed okay to me! I was still feeling quite sick at 4.30, so I told the boys I would see them at the town hall at 5.30 and I went to bed.

Woke up an hour later feeling much better and wandered down to the soundcheck. Found the catering girls not in the best of spirits for the first time this tour. Emma said she was depressed at the thought of leaving us. I think the catering company are splitting her up from boyfriend Brian (the cook) and partner-in-crime, Helen, so she's understandably down.

Soundchecked – ouch. It's not a great room acoustically. Said hello to Maurice Jones, our promoter here in the UK. He seemed subdued also. I could tell – he usually hits me if he's in good spirits. Everyone's a little confused about the ticket sales which were much better than expected on the first leg of the UK tour, and are inexplicably low on the second leg; maybe that's what's bothering him.

I wandered back down the paved precinct to the Midland Hotel to pick up my toilet bag and returned to the gig alone in what was turning out to be a very cold evening. I thought I'd take this opportunity to watch the whole of Wes's opening set so I sat behind the PA on stage-right, keeping my head down and listening to the spill from his monitors. My absence caused a stir – Nick B went wandering around Birmingham looking for me as no one had noticed me enter the building. I still had to abandon Wes before the end of his set in order to get tagged, wrapped and strapped for the show. I was feeling somewhat unsettled in the knowledge that a contingent from the village (home) were in the audience. I wondered what they were making of the show nearly all the way through, and found it impossible to focus my thoughts on the lyrics. Silly really.

After the show I chatted with Phil Hendry – an early fan from the days of the Europeans who'd brought his new girlfriend, no doubt to find out what all the fuss was about. It was cold outside and my hair was wet from the shower, so instead of getting caught in the street, I held court just inside the stage door while people filed in and out with things for me to sign – I felt a lot like one of those Santa Clauses in a department store. Walked back to the hotel with Nick and had a drink in the bar before retiring to bed. It was one of those bars where you can get into a fight by looking at someone…

Wednesday 18 May *London, Hammersmith*

Woke up late and set about packing and checking out of the Midland Hotel, Birmingham. I signed a photograph of the band and made a present of it to Paul the porter, who had been so helpful yesterday. Had coffee in the downstairs bar with Ian and Pete. The old dear serving told Ian she couldn't serve him because he was wearing trainers – I could tell we were in the provinces. He offered to remove them and have coffee in his socks, so she acquiesced and told him to hide his feet under the table. Pete arrived in stars and stripes baseball boots so we had to hide his feet too. Good game. Stuff like this always reminds me of all the pettiness that used to go on in Doncaster when I was growing up. There's something quaint about such small mindedness… but, ultimately, it's a little sad. It doesn't seem to happen in London.

We left Birmingham and drove down to London, and I was dropped off at home in Charlton – I was taking my own car into town. There was no one in when I arrived at 1.15. Diz and Nial were out at a tot's party and Sofie was at school. I popped round the corner and gave her a kiss in the playground before she went back inside after lunch. I told her I must go to London and that I would see her tomorrow. When I left she said, "I'll see you next week or something!" Bless her – she's as disorientated as I am. It's funny, but also a little depressing.

I had a coffee and a piece of birthday cake (present from a fan) in the garden and sprayed my precious roses with Tumblebug, before leaving to drive to the lovely Halcyon Hotel in Holland Park (PS it was owned by the actor, Richard Harris, who opened it in order to have "the kind of place I wouldn't get thrown out of". Wonderfully posh, but hell-raiser-friendly. Sadly it died with him in 2002). Checked in feeling a little unwell and decided to have an hour in bed before the soundcheck. Woke up feeling much better and went in the bathroom to freshen up. When I emerged naked from the bathroom, I nearly died of fright – Dizzy Spell was sitting on the bed. I hadn't heard her enter the room and I had no idea she was in London. The sense of shock was, fortunately, reduced by tour-disorientation, which results in a state of mind where the impossible isn't really that unusual. Apparently her arrival had been planned and executed by Debbie Belshaw and the Aynho girls as a treat night off for her and a surprise for me. Yeah! After I stopped screaming we decided Diz would stay for a bath and much-needed peace while I went to soundcheck. I drove over to Hammersmith and ate liver and bacon and mash, courtesy of Emma who must leave us after tonight. Let's hope we work together again.

I enjoyed the soundcheck – my sound was great on stage and I was singing well. A great relief; I had woke up that morning feeling very hoarse. We returned to the Halcyon where Diz was still relaxing after her bath. I went to the bar for a half while she finished getting ready. I decided against a pre-show snooze having slept before soundcheck.

The show went well although I felt a little unsettled, generally. The audience were some distance away and it was difficult to monitor their reaction in terms of crowd noise. I thought I sang quite well until the end of the last encore when I really struggled with *The Space*, which was a shame because I felt it took the edge off the whole show. I was forced to revise my opinion somewhat afterwards in the bar as, time after time, different people said I had sung really well throughout, especially at the end of *The Space*(!?). I ended up wondering what Privet must have done to it!

Chatted in the upstairs bar to Dave Meegan and Gary Stevenson, Chas and Roy, Josie Ayers and numerous others before returning to the Halcyon with Diz to shower. EMI had arranged post-gig drinks in the bar, so we went through and partied until about 3.30. Chatted to Roy about a play he's written which opens at The Garrick in June. It's a musical version of **The Fly**, and he says it's very funny. I can't imagine it being otherwise. He's invited us to the gala opening. Flicked through photographs taken by Mark from the **Today** sessions in Manchester and Newcastle. They were some of the best live shots I've seen of the band. When we played Manchester Apollo he had come on stage during *Paper Lies* and photographed me throughout the song, and these shots were particularly interesting – a side of me I haven't seen in the mirror: manic and disturbed; almost Munch's *The Scream*-like.

Chatted to EMI girls Kathy, Sofie, Louise, Sandra and Amanda who seemed to have enjoyed themselves. Nick Eede was there with girlfriend Nikki. He said he thought the **Brave** show was like a dream and that he loved it. Dizzy seemed to be thoroughly enjoying her night away, chatting with old friends and a few acquaintances that we unfortunately seldom see. Had a last chat with Josie who was totally pissed by this stage and not making a lot of sense. Got to bed late, late. Diz wanted to take the bed home with her.

Saturday 11 June *Lucerne, Eschenback Festival*

Stayed in bed until around 11.00. Nick phoned to warn me that my room must be vacated by 12.00, so I packed and took my case to Nick's room which was being kept on until 4.00. It was still raining which didn't bode well for the open air show tonight. Maybe it'll cheer up later…

Sat around downstairs in the café with Steve, Mark and Pete, and eventually went for a spot of lunch in a crêperie by the lake. We were all just killing time, really, waiting for Paul to return with the tour bus, which would take us out to the festival site. It took about thirty minutes to get there. I was still revising the words to *Warm Wet Circles,* so I hung around on the bus while the other chaps braved the arena, and returned with depressing news of much mud and not much audience. Oh dear. Oh well.

Nick took us a short walk to a nearby Italian restaurant, which had been arranged to provide us with dinner. I sat down with Alan (l.d.), Brian (lighting tech.), Helen (wardrobe and catering) and Rebecca (caterer) to catch up on their news. Everyone seemed in good form, despite having spent ten hours in a cold muddy field. God knows how the crowd must feel. The restaurateur was very friendly (his two little girls asked for autographs) and the food was excellent.

We returned to the festival site and I wandered down to the dressing rooms – a sports clubhouse complete with soccer trophies, which reminded me of the dressing rooms at the Cumbria Rock festival a couple of years ago. By now it was raining torrentially outside and my heart sank to think of the poor sods who'd endured a day's existence in a cold, muddy field. I remember travelling all day once to get to Milton Keynes to see the Genesis/Peter Gabriel reunion show at the bowl, and standing for half an hour in the drizzle before saying, "Bugger this!" and going home again before they even came on stage.

Sunday 12 June *Köln, Tanzbrunnen*

Arrived outside the Hyatt hotel around 9.30 and staggered out of my bunk to see blue sky and sunshine. That's better. Tonight is an open-air show again, so the weather makes a big difference. Checked into the Hyatt and decided to sleep as I hadn't really slept properly on the bus. It wasn't to be. As I was closing the curtains, I noticed a small stage being set up on the bank of the Rhein outside the hotel. Today is the annual party for the employees of the Hyatt (how do we do it?!) and the party started as soon as I got one leg into bed. I lay there for about an hour listening to a Californian cabaret band (who were actually very good if you weren't trying to sleep) before giving up and getting up. John A had arrived and called to say hello, so I met him downstairs for a chat about things in general. He told me that EMI were still very keen to make a solo album at some stage and that I shouldn't worry too much about the future. He senses that I have been a little low lately. We talked for quite a while and then met up with the rest of the band to walk down to the gig for soundcheck.

Had a bite to eat and soundchecked. The sound on-stage was better than yesterday – I suppose the crew had had more time. After soundcheck I said hello to Steve Hackett who was opening for us, and had a chat with Peter Rieger who reaffirmed that Pete Townshend was into the idea of me playing the lead in

Tommy next year. We made a date to go to New York and have a look at the existing Broadway production the weekend after I get home from this little stint.

Returned to the hotel to find a huge present festooned in balloons in my hotel room. It was a late birthday present from Sandra and Britta (probably our most dedicated German fans). I opened the box to find lots of screwed up newspaper intermingled with little presents: beads, toys, puzzles, pictures, sweets, bubble liquid (everyone buys me bubble liquid!) and an album of photographs of the band.

I was called upstairs for an interview which lasted until we left for the show at 7.00. The weather had remained dry and sunny, and we hit the stage to an enthusiastic crowd at eight o'clock for what was to be a most enjoyable gig. There was a high percentage of young kids in the audience, which is always good to see – there seems to be more girls at each successive show. I can't decide whether it's a delayed reaction to the **Holidays in Eden** album, or a consequence of **Brave.** We also seem to have lost the heavy metal denim jacket brigade which I inherited back in '89. Either that or they've had a fashion epiphany.

After the show I showered at the hotel before going out with Pete and Kai and Petra from EMI to a Mexican restaurant round the corner – it always seems to be Mexican in Köln. Kai likes his Tequila. I declined the hard stuff, but managed to put paid to three piña coladas which left me somewhat tiddled. We ate chicken fajitas and the EMI-ers had a bit of a moan about restructuring in the label – they seemed worried and disillusioned. We returned to the Hyatt and I had a last beer with Nick B before going to bed.

Monday 13 June *Köln – Poznan:* Day off

Woke around 11.00, packed and went down to check out of the Hyatt. Had a quick coffee with Ian and Mark before climbing aboard the bus for the long drive to Poznan, Poland. Spent all day on the bus chatting and watched **One Flew over the Cuckoo's Nest** with Pete, who'd never seen it before.

Went to bed around midnight and drifted in and out of sleep until, eventually, the to-ing and fro-ing of the bus told me we were off the beaten track, so I got up and went up front to see that we were deep in the darkness of the Polish countryside – and quite lost. We were in the right village because we kept seeing the signs, but there was no obvious trace of the hotel or the airbase it was rumoured to be a part of. After a number of U-turns, we tried a lane marked 'No Entry' and discovered a checkpoint with a uniformed guard on duty. He gave us directions to the Hotel, which seemed to be a privately run operation in the business of hiring out the officer's quarters to passers-by with the-right-kind-of-money. By now it was 4.00 in the morning.

The promoter, Andy, was in Reception and helped us to check in, which involved handing in our passports (let's hope we see 'em again...). The bus was parked behind a large iron gate in the military compound. I sensed more than just an element of, "Meet the new boss... same as the old boss" in all this. Oh well – I suppose it's the same the world over to some degree or other. At least we were chums with the boss in this instance.

I trundled my suitcase down the path to my accommodation-block and into Room 2, still half-expecting armed partisans to come hammering over the horizon into the compound. My room was like something from a 60's housing estate – fitted black "G-plan" units and decorated cotton tablecloths, thin white curtains and tiled floors with a basic (but functional) bathroom. There was a TV with a remote control which gave the first clue to modernity. I switched it on to discover only one channel coming to a close with some classical orchestral concert, and went to bed.

Tuesday 14 June *Poznan, Arena*

I was woken at 7.00 by the plumbing and never quite managed to get back to sleep, before giving up and getting up at 11.00. Outside in the sunshine, amid the trees and the dormitories, I really felt like I had been magically transported to a prisoner of war movie. After much confusion I persuaded the women in the reception area to make me coffee, which was served in a small vase with an inch of silt in the bottom and accompanied by a tin of condensed milk. I sat gingerly sipping away at it, pouring more and more tinned-milk into it in the hope of making it drinkable, and writing up this diary. Men in uniform turned up and asked me for my autograph – "for my son Pieter". Signed my name for the soldier's sons and for the hotel women, and climbed aboard the bus which took us the half-hour journey to the Arena at Poznan. We drove through endless housing estates of depressing grey Sixties tower blocks, each one bearing a large number in the same graphic typeface that the **Thunderbirds** had (maybe Gerry Anderson designed the whole thing… Da da-da-da… Da-da-da-da da da-da-da-da dah…). Someone quipped that the numbers were there so you could find your way home after a night on the vodka – it's probably true. I found it hard to join in with the jokes. I was quite saddened by the surroundings. I've always harboured a sense of shared guilt for the injustice meted out to the Poles during the carve-up after the war, and a great many of the airmen who laid down their lives in the Battle of Britain had been Polish. We owed them, and we sold 'em out to Stalin. Anyway – the gig…

From the outside the building looked like a huge concrete flying-saucer. There were a dozen or so kids hanging around, looking to say hello and for autographs. We scribbled and went inside where we held a half-hour press conference. After that, Steve and I were taken by the promoter, Andy, to a radio station for a short interview which he conducted himself! I think he seems to have things fairly well sewn up here. We were then taken to a record store to do a signing. About a hundred kids were ushered past us, and some of whom were in a total *state* upon meeting us. One young girl stood quietly weeping as I signed my name. I'm not used to it. You want to cuddle 'em. At the end, we were invited to raid the CD cabinets behind us. I picked up a handful of goodies including the new Pretenders, **Hotel California** by the Eagles, **Nerve Net** by Brian Eno, Ray Charles, Yes, Jimi Hendrix, Spin Doctors, Cure, Tori Amos, R.E.M. ...not bad for free.

Back at the soundcheck everything seemed to be under control; my sound was very dead, oddly enough, for such a large round hall, but otherwise fine. I returned backstage for a short TV interview, and then went to bed for half an hour on the tour bus before getting ready in a sports locker dressing room which possessed the foulest smelling toilet I have ever had the misfortune to pee into.

The show was a good one for me. Amazing again to watch people's mouths move to the words which were once just thoughts in my mind, and in a language totally alien to a great many of them. There was a keyboard crash during *Warm Wet Circles* which was a bit of a shame and, during *The Hollow Man,* Mark went missing. This provided a pause in the middle of the song, which turned out to be quite wonderful. That's the thing about mistakes – every now and then you get an improvement (as Darwin once observed). After the first encore, some clot turned the house lights on and half the audience had left before we were back up for *Garden Party,* which was then a little confused. Perhaps we should have let it be. Shame.

After the show I showered and went outside to meet the hang-arounders, sign sleeves, arms, legs, get photographed, get kissed, be given gifts, hugs and fond regards, before boarding the bus which was to take us overnight to Warsaw. Thank you, you lovely people. I waved bye-bye from the bus and chatted to Richie, Craig and Bob who had come to film the Poland shows and were coming overnight with us. Went to the back lounge to watch **Blackadder** before going to bed.

Wednesday 15 June *Warsaw, Congress Hall*

Staggered out of the bus and into the Forum hotel at 4.00am and went back to sleep to wake around 12.00. I showered and went out looking for a hairbrush – I have recently begun brushing my hair after washing it, something I have not done in twenty years. I eventually found a hairbrush and bought it at a cost of 120 Szloties – about four quid.

When I returned to the hotel, John A was in reception with Pete and Mark. We decided to take a cab over to the old town and have a wander. Mark was on a mission to buy a chess set, and Pete was hoping to find a present for Fiona. I took them back to the shop I found in March, where I bought the decanter and the bangle. It's a designer shop which combines silver and amber art and craft, and it's nothing short of an Aladdin's cave of beautiful things. Not cheap though. Pete bought a bangle for Fiona, and I chickened out of sixty quids worth of amber and silver beads... I already regret not buying them. We sat in the square and had a beer while I was hustled hard by a beggar woman who did the whole hysterical crying routine (no tears) at me. Mark had already given her some money, and I was weakening when she started prodding me and pinching at my leg. I can't cope with that from people I don't know and, as I motioned her away, she spat at me. Nice. To be a successful beggar you need a better grip on human psychology, I think.

Returned by cab to the hotel, bumping into the camera crew in the square on the way to the taxi, and left by minibus to the nearby Palace of Culture and Science – also known, contemptuously, as 'Stalin's Gift' by the locals. From my room on the 24th floor of the hotel I could still look up at this monstrous edifice, which is, perhaps, the bastard son of The Empire State Building and a Pagoda. It was built on the instruction of Joe Stalin in the late forties as a monument to/for the Polish people. The term 'gift' is one of Polish irony, of course – bearing in mind the Russian occupation of the country, the Poles paid for it dearly and the enslaved locals were forced to build the thing. Love it or hate it, however, it's still the most distinctive building in Warsaw and we were to play in the theatre (which juts from the rear at the ground level) following in the footsteps of Bowie, The Doors and McCartney. For me, it was a thrill in contemplation.

The theatre reminded me of the Albert Hall, although newer and cleaner. I was informed during soundcheck that the audience would not be allowed forward to the stage during the show – they were worried about the decor. I told Nick to let them know that, in the event of the security men being violent with any one of the audience, the band would leave the stage. Soundcheck was uneventful. I had plenty of room to run around in front of the monitors. I was getting quite a lot from the P.A.

Returned to the hotel to lie flat before the show.

We got off to a bad start – they wouldn't turn the house lights down until we went on stage, so we couldn't set up the usual atmosphere before we went on. No one told the band, so I was still reeling under the shock when we struck up. Before the fourth song, *Sugar Mice*, someone shouted that they weren't being allowed to come to the stage. "I'll come to you, then!" I found myself saying and, during the guitar solo, I climbed down from the stage and up the centre aisle, tweaking the shoulders of the security men and shaking hands and hugging anyone within reach. It's not something I would normally do - I felt self-consciously Bono-ish - but, although it wasn't planned, it helped the general state of affairs. The security men seemed to relax as they realised there was no prospect of hysteria in the crowd, and I had demonstrated to the audience that I respected and trusted them. Towards the end of the show people were allowed forward to the stage, and we finished the evening on our own terms, feeling comfortable. No one got upset or hurt, and the fabric of the building was undamaged. For me it finished off an unusual and memorable three days in Poland. Afterwards, we were taken to a nightclub for a party in our honour, where I had my photograph taken with pretty girls and hand-shook and paid compliments by men in suits with Lech Walesa moustaches (same as the old boss...). It was now Ian's birthday, and what better setting to celebrate it than this? Typically, he never turned up and went overnight on the crew bus.

Had a couple of beers, loosened up for an hour, tightened up again, and went back to the hotel, falling into bed around 4.00.

Thursday 16 June *Warsaw – Eindhoven*

Happy birthday, misery-guts.

Nick called me at 11.00 to remind me that we would be leaving at 12.00. I packed and checked out of the Forum hotel, picking up free t-shirts which had been left for us by Jack and Kinga at the record company. Drank much-needed coffee before climbing aboard the bus which was to take us to Eindhoven. It was going to take all day and all night. Steve Rothery had flown to Paris to see Californian band, Enchant, whose last album he had produced. Ian Mosley, who celebrates his birthday today (in our absence) had gone overnight last night with the crew, so there was only Mark, Pete, Nick and I on the bus, along with bus driver Paul. We stopped to go to McDonald's for breakfast before leaving Warsaw and I gave the remainder of my Polish money away to the people next to me in the queue. The food was indistinguishable from the stuff I used to get in the McDonald's opposite Windsor Castle – how do they do it?!

Ate my cheeseburger and chips on the bus as we made our way out into the Polish countryside for the long journey west. Watched movies to pass the time. I saw **The Commitments** for the first time – I thought it was okay. I later saw the second half of **Basic Instinct**, which was a bit of a struggle if you've missed the first half – just a lot of death and shagging. I thought the leading man, Michael Douglas, had a bum like a baboon.

When we got to the border, around 7.00p.m, we saw our truck still waiting in the truck line to clear customs – they process the paperwork very slowly. It had taken our (diamond) truck driver, Simon Lake, eight hours to get into Poland, and I was later to learn that getting out took him EIGHTEEN! How the hell do these people expect to conduct trade with the West when they put every truck in and out of the country through this insufferable pantomime? Fortunately for us, buses use a different lane category, so we were only delayed for half an hour or so.

I eventually went to bed somewhere in East Germany. Couldn't get to sleep, so I got up again and went to the back lounge to join Nick and Pete watching Kevin Costner in **Robin Hood** – the movie that Alan Rickman effortlessly stole from under him. I enjoyed it. Went to bed again around 2.30.

Friday 17 June *Eindhoven:* Day off

When I woke up we were arriving at The Holiday Inn, Eindhoven. It was 10.30 in the morning. I arranged to go for a coffee in town with Jack after I'd showered, and, as we were leaving, we bumped into Ian, so the three of us walked into the centre of town past barrel organs and the bustle of Friday shoppers.

Eindhoven is a very modern-looking town, full of people who seem to have both money and time on their hands. In England it's usually one or the other. After a while we found a pleasant street café where Priv, Alan and Brian were already enjoying the first beer of the day off, and joined them for (what was for me) breakfast.

The Holiday Inn is a particularly uninspiring place and I was in no hurry to return, so I spent most of the day in the café writing this diary or wandering around the shops looking for sunglasses for Sofie (a promise). Returned to the hotel around 7.00, and did the solarium and the swimming pool – both deserted. I hadn't brought swimming trunks with me, so I swam a few lengths of the pool naked. No one showed up, so I didn't have any explaining to do. Showered, got dressed and went out again, trying to decide whether or not to eat.

I was recognised in the street and went for a beer with a couple of the locals before returning to my favourite café, where I was given free beer and nachos with melted cheese. It was 11.00 and the kitchen was closed, but one of the cooks was a fan and sorted me out. I invited him to tomorrow's show.

Bumped into Alan and Jack and went to a couple of bars. Ran out of steam around 1.00 and walked back to the hotel to sleep.

Sunday 10 & **Monday 11 July** *Home – Japan*

Got up around 7.30 thinking I was the first up. I wasn't – mum was in the kitchen offering to make me a coffee and dad was in the downstairs bathroom, shaving. I had allowed myself two hours to shower, get ready and pack. It was, for once, almost exactly right. I was ready to leave at 9.30 on the dot when the car arrived. Said goodbyes to Sofie and Nial – Sofie always takes it well, but I'm usually a little nervous as to how Nial will react. Today he was seemingly unbothered. He didn't get up 'till 9.20, and wasn't awake enough to give much thought to my departure. We drove to the Racket Club to pick up Mike Hunter who no longer looks like General Custer but is now clean-shaven, short-haired and not unlike Chris Kimsey in appearance. We were driven to Heathrow Terminal 4 and, as I checked in, I learned from Nick B that Mark Kelly was missing and last seen in Terminal 3. Claimed my boarding pass and went through passport control. Nick had given me Ian's cymbals and, as they came out of the x-ray machine, a man who looked a lot like O.J.Simpson asked me who the band was. He naturally assumed that I was the drummer, and when I said Marillion he asked me what I thought of the new singer. I said, "He's not as good as the old one."

"No – I don't think so either," he said.

I bought some talc in Duty Free and joined Priv, Alan, Ian, and new guitar tech (Phil) in the bar for a Sunday lunchtime drink. The flight wasn't as long as I had feared, but was nonetheless long at eleven and a half hours. Mike Hunter gave me a sleeping pill which did absolutely nothing to me, so I remained awake the whole flight, which I knew was not the best thing to do as we were to arrive in Tokyo at 8.30 am (Japanese time) and so I had the whole day to get through.

The "90-minute" drive from the airport to the hotel was an optimistic estimate – the traffic in Tokyo defies description, and it was to be mid-day by the time our minibus arrived at the Roppongi Prince hotel. My room was surprisingly large (comparable in size to European ones) considering Japan's reputation for tiny hotel rooms. I hit the bed running and would have slept all day if the phone hadn't rang at 2.00 to summon me downstairs. It had been arranged for us to do a video i.d. ("Hello, we're Marillion blah blah" etc...) for Massa Itoh, the DJ who was responsible for our recent success here. After two hours sleep I felt like death on legs, and we were doing it in the searing heat of the street so I wasn't my scintillating best – I hope I don't look *too* disinterested on the telly.

Had a couple of coffees in the hotel café with Steve and started to feel human again. Went out with Steve and Nick for a wander and a spot of lunch. It would have been breakfast in England, but it was teatime in Japan. We wandered along a street dwarfed by a concrete flyover which ran parallel to (and above) us, amid the occasional aromas of drains and sewage, past various shops and noodle houses. There seems to be a prevalence of shops that sell mirrors and light fittings in the Roppongi district. I admired Tiffany lamps, reeling at the price tags of 200,000 yen – well over £1000.

We eventually found a noodle house with pictures outside (when the menus are in Japanese and the locals speak almost no English you need pictures to point at) and I pointed at something someone was eating and said, "One of those!" Even the Japanese seem unable to eat noodles gracefully, so I need hardly describe the embarrassed slurping, dangling and dribbling which ensued – fortunately I was wearing a patterned shirt.

We passed a bar advertising 'Happy Hour', and went inside and downstairs to discover we'd stumbled upon Roppongi's only rock club, Pips – full of snapshots of well-stewed musicians posing with the bar staff. The place was empty (it was 6.00), so we had a beer while enduring a CD of a Led Zeppelin cover band, which eventually drove us back out into the street.

Steve went back to the hotel while Nick and I went off in search of the local Shinto temple. We stumbled upon a graveyard where many people seemed to have been buried in a very small area of ground. I wonder if they bury them standing up? (I was later to discover that people are cremated). Every 'grave' had a little built-in flower vase, some of which were tended, and large wooden tags like giant lollypop sticks carrying calligraphic messages, to wish good fortunes to the dead, no doubt. On the way out of the burial place, we passed a stone Buddha wearing a red beret and scarf. It seemed somewhat bizarre, but I was later to regret being amused – I learned from our local guide, Katsu, that the red accessories represent the bib and cap of a baby, and that this would have been a monument to the death of a baby. The temple shrines all seem to have a bell – like a giant sleigh-bell immediately outside the inner 'altar'. Perhaps its purpose is to draw Buddha's attention to the incoming devotee – a sort of telephone bell for God... or maybe it's a ward off evil spirits.

Nick returned to the hotel while I continued wandering around this hectic, polluted and peculiar place. I found a couple of brass-handled mirrors and bought them for the show – we'd been trying to get hold of one in England without much success. They cost a fortune.

I went and had a beer in a street-side café and watched the Japanese making their way home from work. All the men wear suits and ties, even when they're relaxing… maybe they all simply work late and go out straight from work. Every now and then a woman would go by wearing traditional clothes: silk kimono, the little cushion thing in the small of the back, and all the trimmings – a strange juxtaposition of the beauty of the ancient, and the ugliness, of modern urban-life all around them. I felt grateful to them – it's a lovely sight and I suspect they must go to a lot of time and trouble to dress so immaculately.

I was whacked hard in the face by some enormous flying bug which didn't even slow down after the collision.

Returned to the hotel to unpack and shower. Later went out and drank too much in the hope of being able to sleep. It seemed to work – I got to bed around 1.00 and slept until 7.00.

Tuesday 12 July *Tokyo – Osaka:* Day off

I woke feeling very thirsty. It must be the air conditioning. I decided to go down to the café to get a glass of water, and when I got down there they had breakfast already set out, so I sat down and ate cornflakes in preference to the Japanese items on offer (I didn't feel much like a poached egg floating in brown liquid). Outside the window was the swimming pool area, in the centre of which stood a single tall tree. I was amazed to witness a team of Japanese gardeners doing something I had never seen before. With the help of a bamboo ladder, one climbed to the highest branches and jumped around, shaking the dead leaves out of the tree. No branch was left unshaken. At the same time, other members of the team were pruning any dead wood from the ends and sweeping the fallen leaves into bags to be taken away. This was all going on around 7.15 am to prepare the pool area for the day and ensure that no leaves should fall into the pool. I wonder if they do this every day? They were wearing black canvas shoes with split-toes to divide the toes into two sections.

Around 7.30 Ian M appeared. He couldn't sleep either (as usual – he's a confirmed insomniac), so we chatted over the remains of breakfast until, at 8.00, I was overtaken by a major slump and had to go back to bed! I slept until 12.00 when I was called to prepare for the Bullet train journey to Osaka. We'd already had the pep talk about punctuality – being late is seen here as an insult on a par with multiple murder, and should be avoided at all costs. Promoter's rep, Katsu, arrived at 1.00, and band and crew were taken in a minibus to Tokyo station where we were shown to our reserved seats on the train. The carriages are spacious and clean, and fitted with wide aircraft seats which turn through 180 degrees so you can face the direction of travel, if you so choose. During the journey, stewardesses periodically pass through, offering drinks, food or ice-cream. There is also a restaurant car with large picture windows to give diners a better view of the scenery which, although for the most part consists of more of the same muddle of concrete blocks, occasionally offers a glimpse of tea terraces - like immaculately tended hedgerows striping along the hillsides - and rice paddies like fields of rich, vibrant, green feathers. I was told there was a slim chance of a view of Mount Fuji as we entered Osaka but, to my disappointment, it was not a clear enough day.

We arrived on-time-to-the-second at Osaka, and took cabs to the Grand Hotel where our room keys were already waiting. My room reminded me of the Mayflower in New York. I helped myself to a can of iced coffee from the minibar – they sell this stuff in vending machines in the streets here. It's good but, like everything else, terribly expensive – typically four or five hundred yen (around £3.50!). Relaxed for a while. Went out trying to find postcards and failed, which meant paying hotel prices for the ones on sale in the lobby.

In the evening we were taken out to dinner by Katsu to a traditional Japanese restaurant. We walked through the busy streets of blazing neon, teeming with people and hot and humid, despite the hour. The restaurant was situated in what Katsu called "the restaurant area" which reminded me of the covered market in Liverpool. Past alleyways of amusement arcades, karaoke bars, shops and restaurants, while Katsu tried to find the place – he's from Tokyo and doesn't know Osaka too well. He eventually waved us into a restaurant where we were ushered upstairs and obliged to remove our boots, which were placed in wooden lockers, before we sat down at a long, low, wooden table surrounded by a lower shelf on which to sit. The food here was an education – large bowls of chopped vegetables and thinly sliced raw beef were tossed into bowls of boiling oil in the centre of the table to deep-fry and be plucked out with chopsticks. I tried everything that arrived, but I had to decline the fish head which Katsu tucked into while telling us that the head is the best part of the fish.

At 10.00 I returned to the hotel where Shun from EMI was waiting to take me to Radio FM102 for a live interview on Massa Itoh's rock show. It went well. He seemed pleased to see me again – we had met in London earlier this year. Afterwards Shun and I returned to the hotel and had a beer in the bar. He's a nice chap, and somehow bears an uncanny resemblance to my father in law who isn't at all Japanese! The band seemed to have gone missing, so I went to bed and, amazingly, slept until the following afternoon!

Wednesday 13 July *Osaka, Club W'Ohol*

Woke thinking it was nine in the morning but was pleased to realise that it was 1.30, which means I'd slept over twelve hours. I felt much better for it, especially considering today was to be the first show. We left for Club W'Ohol at 2.00 and arrived to find our boys and the local crew working away getting everything working in time for soundcheck. The stage was 'compact and bijou', so it was all a bit of a squeeze. I was jammed against the drum kit, so I prepared myself for an evening of excruciating sound pressure levels.

Soundcheck took forever because we had hired quite a lot of equipment and were working with a Japanese monitor engineer, Tetsu, who turned out to cope very well with the unenviable task of rationalising our complex needs. By the time soundcheck was over it was six o'clock and the doors were open – the show was to start at 7.00.

There wasn't really a break in the proceedings from midday until after the show. Ten minutes before the show, I took a peek through a side curtain to see a scattering of men in shirts and ties staring towards the stage. Blimey. During the afternoon the management had attempted to set tables and chairs in front of the stage, and maybe we should have let 'em. We mounted the stage to polite applause and a little tentative cheer fluttered. When I got up there I was relieved to see quite a lot more people than my earlier glimpse had suggested (they must have been hiding) and at least a couple of girls among the chaps in ties. You could hear a pin drop during the songs which, during *Brave*, was quite a welcome change from the distractions of the wide-boys among the European and (especially) Scandinavian crowds. The Japanese seemed totally riveted to what we were doing. The first murmur of spontaneous applause happened as I approached centre stage to sing *Runaway*. Maybe they thought I had just arrived. They really like the rockers here in Japan and a much louder cheer went up after *Hard as Love*, by which time a few top shirt buttons had been loosened... Wild! I was having little mental blocks left, right and centre as a consequence of not having played for a couple of weeks but, on the whole, we all played well, despite an element of monitor mayhem. By the end of the show, the crowd were about as excited as dignity would allow them to express, and the boys in the band said things generally must have relaxed here since their last visit in '86.

It had been fun and it had been different. There's a lot about human behaviour here that I think is no bad thing – the importance of formal politeness helps the atmosphere, and is touching; the idea of honour, honesty and keeping ones word cuts out all the bullshit which, especially in the music business, comes as a breath of fresh air. On the other hand, though, there's something in all this that just doesn't add up… the restraint and formality acts as a barrier to expression of true feelings and turns living into something of an enigmatic game. The bullshit creeps back in through the back door and once again, truth evades. As the days went on I felt (again) that I had lost a couple of pages from the big instruction manual. Perhaps you have to spend a lifetime here to fathom these people. Perhaps the process of *trying* (as is so often the case) is what alienates us from them. Perhaps, perhaps… Perhaps I should get on with the diary…

After the show, the band sat down in the dressing room and ate a spot of dinner before heading back to the Grand Osaka Hotel. I later popped out with Alan, Mike, Phil and Nick in search of a beer, and ended up in a bar with **Casablanca** on the telly. Didn't stay long. Most of the bars and clubs have strict dress codes – if you don't have a collar, tie, jacket (and whatever else is imposed to keep out low-life like us) you don't get past security. Went to bed around 1.00, confidently having recovered from my jet lag. Woke at 4.00 and couldn't get back to sleep.

Thursday 14 July *Osaka – Tokyo*

Woke up for the twenty-fifth time at 11.00ish, showered, packed, and made my way downstairs to check out of the Grand Osaka. Left around 1.30 in the minibus, which took band and crew to Osaka Station for the bullet train ride back to Tokyo. Did a little shopping in the station concourse, marvelling at the strange foods and delicacies on offer – unidentifiable seafoods packaged like boxes of chocolate. All the presents were very dear, so I settled for a couple of handkerchiefs and a couple of decorative telephone payment cards, before being ushered up onto the platform by Katsu to board the train. Spent nearly all the journey in the restaurant car writing postcards to everyone I could think of while drinking beer and sightseeing from the large windows.

What will I remember about Japan? A bullet point or two...

- The refreshment girls on the bullet train, turning around to face us and bowing to the carriage before exiting.
- The mirror in the bathroom of the Osaka Grand, the centre of which, magically, didn't steam-up while I showered.
- The gardeners shaking the leaves out of the tree by the pool at the Roppongi Prince.
- The utter disregard to architectural beauty.
- The heat.
- It's so EXPENSIVE.
- That, try as I might, I never managed to have a conversation with anyone here that left me feeling that I'd had a conversation.

Wednesday 31 August *Home – Mexico City*

Got up around 8.00 with Sofie and Nial after having once again slept fitfully, thanks to my bad leg (I strained ligaments in my right knee during the show in Chur, Switzerland, three weeks ago) and perhaps due, in part, to the knowledge that I was to leave for Mexico this morning. I hadn't packed last night, so I showered and ferretted around gathering my things together for the two hours until the car arrived to take me to Heathrow at 10.15. It wasn't a pleasant departure – Nial became very upset at the sight of my suitcase leaving the house as he realised for the first time I was going away. Sue had been subdued all morning – I could tell she was depressed about it. I climbed into the back of the car feeling to blame for the misery of the people I love most - an almost permanent state of mind these days - and settled down for the 1 hour drive to the airport reading Tony Parker's **May the Lord in His Mercy be Kind to Belfast** – an impartial collection of interviews of a cross-section of Irish people from all sides of the complex political and diverse social spectrum, from the ordinary to the influential and radical. It's a depressing collection, offering insight into the history and the current state of the "troubles". My own problems quickly paled to nought as I read accounts from parents, brothers and sisters of the accidental or deliberate (all too often) innocent victims of Belfast's armed conflict.

Checked in and said hello to the chaps. Priv came off his motorbike yesterday and is sporting a surgical collar. He says he's okay, but very sore. He was nonetheless his usual amusing and entertaining self. I seemed to have turned up for this trip with (among other things) a shoebox full of tapes, sunglasses, headphones, keys, books, passport, money etc, which kept spilling its contents about the place. I really must invest in some hand luggage… Hung about for an hour, reading, and boarded the 747 which was to take us the first leg of our journey to Philadelphia. We were upstairs! This was the first time I had travelled on the upper deck of a 747. The novelty soon wore off of course, but it was nonetheless a new experience. Spent most of the flight reading and watching the in-flight programmes while Mike Hunter guffawed to himself in the seat behind me. He was listening to the comedy programme in his headphones – it's like having Harry Secombe on the crew.

When we got to Philadelphia we were put in a holding lounge to hang about for a couple of hours for the connecting flight to Mexico City. As I tap this into my laptop I'm watching silver US Air Boeings taxiing back and forth on the runways outside, and drinking a can of complimentary Wild Berry Seltzer which actually does taste initially like cherries and then delivers an aftertaste of Alka-Seltzer… Mmm. There's a massive oil-tanker moored on the river at the edge of the runway – I assume it's on the river, I can't actually tell; from here it looks like it's in a field.

We finally heard the call to go to the aeroplane which was almost empty – apart from the twelve of us. Considering there were so few passengers, the stewardesses seemed particularly uncaring and automatic. So much for US Air… There were thunderstorms raging in the area of Philadelphia, so the pilot avoided the weather by flying lower than usual – at least that's what he said (it doesn't seem to make much sense), so we were in turbulent cloud for most of the four-hour flight.

Mexico City was feeling the effects of the tail of a hurricane in the Gulf of Mexico and it was raining as we hit the runway with a jolt – uncommonly hard, but not my hardest landing. Mark and I once flew into L.A. on a 747 which encountered a low altitude air-pocket and hit the runway like a grand piano thrown out of a third floor window - BANG! - emptying many of the overhead lockers and dropping down the oxygen masks. People were screaming and praying. It then taxied to the Terminal with no trouble whatsoever – these 747's are built to bounce!

There was the usual Mexican welcoming committee of airport officials and promoters reps who ensured smooth passage through customs (it's dodgy… in a good way) and out into the waiting minibuses which were to take us to the Il Presidente hotel. We were met at the hotel by the staff who checked us in with customary Mexican warmth. I really like the Mexican people. They always seem to be smiling and, like the Brazilians, possess more of whatever it is that makes human beings human – a greater sense of caring, fun and willingness to express their emotions – the antithesis of the Japanese… or the English, for that matter.

By the time we had checked in it was 11.00 (6.00 in the morning in England), so we were all pretty tired. I had a beer in the bar with the promoter's people before going to bed around 12.00.

Thursday 1 September *Mexico City:* Day off

Bloody hell! September already! I managed to more-or-less sleep until around 6.40am, which wasn't a bad effort. I got up and showered before phoning home. Dizzy seemed better in her spirits today. She said it had rained in England since I left, and that everyone felt low all day yesterday. Today is Sofie's first day back at school and she had gone in this morning without any trouble. She had said to me she was looking forward to going back (something I can't recollect ever feeling). I spoke to Nial who was his usual pleasant and incoherent self. Dizzy said to call her on Saturday to let her know how the show went. Made my way downstairs for breakfast and ran into Jack who joined me. We chatted about the forthcoming album, and whether or not we would manage to record it in less time than **Brave**. I said I thought we might… time alone will tell. Came back upstairs to listen to the compilation tapes and kill time until Mexico City is up and running. It had been, of course, since 6.00, but I was waiting for the shops and the markets to open. Arranged a trip to a market with Ian and met him in the hotel café at 11.00. We took a cab to a couple of silver markets – I was on the lookout for a silver chain for Sue's old locket which I had brought along with me. The taxi driver was something of a tour guide. He pointed out monuments and explained the ins and outs of Mexico's extraordinary history in a heavily accented broken English, interspersed with unpronounceable and impossible-to-remember Mexican words (it once took me a whole day to remember 'Teotihuacan'), although I did manage to extricate "Zapata" from his enthusiastic account of the 1910 revolution.

I found a suitably unusual chain for Diz and we returned to the hotel, dropping in at the Hard Rock Café (just round the corner) for a snack, and chatting to the friendly staff. Returned to the hotel to do a telephone interview with Radioactive FM and bumped into Fernando Aceves - journalist and photographer - who invited me to the opening night of an exhibition of his rock n'roll photographs at a gallery across town tonight at 7.00. I said I would pop in to have a look, and returned to my hotel room for a mid-afternoon snooze – I'm still chipping away at the jet-lag.

Got up, showered, and tried to get hold of Nick to let him know I was going out but I couldn't find him – so I hailed a cab and we drove across town in a rainstorm. When we arrived at the address of the gallery the rain was so torrential that neither the driver nor myself could see out(!), so we drove up and down the street several times, squinting through the glass, before we found the Galleria Septembre (I think…) which was full of people and a hive of activity. As I entered, I wondered if Bono had followed me in – the place fell silent with a momentary gasp before a rush of flashlights popping and everyone in the place wanting my autograph and their picture taken with me. I wandered around perusing Fernando's pictures as best I could while being talked to by everyone at once. Mark K turned up and I said hello and exchanged mutual "What are you doing here?"s. I was invited to cut the tape declaring the exhibition open, so I made a little speech and did the honours. Chatted to everyone (really) for an hour or so before deciding to leave, so Fernando ordered me a cab. While I was waiting for it to arrive Raymundo appeared and told me he had been at the hotel: John A had gone to bed, the crew had gone to check out Saturday night's club venue and no one else was coming out and did I fancy some dinner? I did, so we went over to Zona Rosa and hit an excellent Italian before going over to La Diabla, the club we are to play on Saturday. It's one of those places which comprises a series of different rooms joined by a central entrance hall in an old building which has been refurbished and decorated with Gothic murals and the like. The stage is very small and it's not really a good club for a show, but it's a good club to have a party. I made a mental note to have a party on Saturday and not worry about putting on a show – it'll be alright.

Bumped into Nick, Tim and Cod, and had my ear royally bent by the club owner who is very excited about our decision to play. Had a couple of Coronas and returned to the hotel around 1.30, whereupon my lavatory overflowed all over the bathroom and into my hotel room. Nice. Put bath towels on the floor and went to bed.

Friday 2 September *Mexico City, Auditorio Nacional*

Went to sleep at 2.00 and woke up at 4.00, 4.30, 4.55, 5.20, 5.55, 6.20, and gave up trying at 6.45. Jet-lag. Showered and went downstairs for breakfast, immediately bumping into John who couldn't sleep either. We had breakfast together, chatted about the forthcoming twelve months, and then Priv arrived so we joined him. No sooner had we sat down than I noticed the distinctive and dishevelled form of David Hockney at a table across the room. Wow! I was surprised to see him make his way to the buffet table completely unnoticed by the multinational assembly of hotel guests. Fame is certainly a funny thing. Only death separates this man from the recognition awarded to Picasso and Warhol. I regretted not having the nerve to go across and shake his hand. I could have invited him to the show.

After breakfast I had arranged a lightning trip to the pyramids at Teotihuacan, mainly for the purpose of acquiring more bangles – I've been all over the city and it seems that the ones I already have are only available at the pyramids. It was raining hard and there was some debate as to whether we shouldn't go, but we eventually decided to do it anyway. Only Nick B and I seemed bothered, so we climbed aboard the minibus with Nuri, our promoters guide, and headed out of town. As we passed the corpse of a third dead dog on the freeway, Nick told me of his experiences backpacking around Mexico and Guatemala nine years ago, where it was common to see dead horses at the side of the road as you rattled along on a bus crammed with people, goats and turkeys.

At Teotihuacan it was still raining, so we conducted our bangle purchases from the open window of the bus, finding what we wanted almost immediately. The rain looked like it might stop and it seemed a shame to come here and not visit the Sun and Moon Pyramids, so we left the bus and walked along the little parade of shops where I bought a ring for Sofie and some earrings for Dizzy, before climbing the Pyramid of the Sun in the drizzle. As I puffed and panted my way upward towards the summit of this vast ancient monument, sporting a black rolled-up brolly (proper English gentleman), heart pounding like a boat-engine, I couldn't help questioning my sanity – tonight we play the National Auditorium, my right knee remains injured from Switzerland and I had forgotten my Ventolin, so if I was to drive myself to an asthma attack climbing in this high-altitude oxygen-lean place, well, there wouldn't be a fat lot anyone could do to help me. Nick and I arrived at the summit, short of breath but on the right side of physical crisis, to find a group of people in anoraks and Nike shoes cross-legged and eyes closed, communing, no doubt, with the ancient energies. I couldn't imagine a Sun god getting out of bed to commune across time and space with this lot. Personally, I have sometimes felt magic (or 'energies') which to me seemed to come from somewhere beyond 'normal' experience, but I have yet to feel anything here at the Sun Pyramid. We looked down from the summit in awe of the scale of this place, trying in vain to imagine it in its own time, and thanking my stars I wasn't here then – I suppose a white man with blue eyes would have been made a present to the gods pretty damn quick. Nick and I climbed back down to earth, putting on a brave face for Nuri who had waited below (girls aren't stupid), before returning to the bus, somewhat damp, for the return to Mexico City.

As we hit the outskirts of town, I remembered hearing about the boxing promoter Don King would today be at the Hard Rock Café to promote a forthcoming world title challenge to Mexico's (and the world's) No.1, Julio Cesar Chavez, who was also to be there. It was too good to miss so we stopped off for lunch, taking a peek through the door of the club to witness the events taking place. King was on the stage making a showbiz speech: "This boy is like a son to me!" etc, (yeah, right) flanked by heavy black guys in mirror shades and expensive suits to his left and, to his right, Julio Cesar Chavez, track-suited and with the countenance of a mild-mannered Latin American who wouldn't hurt a fly. Not so, evidently – he's never been beaten. We returned to our table to finish lunch, and half an hour later Chavez appeared in the café, still track-suited and glancing around the room, checking the place out. He seemed more approachable than Hockney, but I still didn't have the nerve.

Returned to the hotel and tried to sleep for an hour (to no avail). People kept arriving with baskets of fruit and the phone kept ringing, voices saying, "Hello Steve! Do you remember me? We met two years ago! Can you remember my name?" etc. I couldn't. I gave up around 5.00 and walked over to the National Auditorium across the road to see how the crew were getting along with the show. The day took a bit of a dive at this point. Some of the hired backline still hadn't turned up, the drums were missing a tom-tom, and the PA and monitors weren't yet working. My God. I reeled under the realisation that here, at my favourite gig in the world, we weren't going to get a soundcheck to speak of. Steve R said the amplifiers they had supplied him were, "basically, knackered" and that his stage sound was the worst of his career. We had brought a new monitor man, John, for this show who, although capable, had never worked with us before. Some of Mark's gear was wrong, half of Pete's bass rig had yet to arrive, Alan Parker was still focussing the lights and was running two-hours late, and Priv, bravely masking a face which nonetheless betrayed utter exasperation that simply said, "Don't ask" as I approached to say hello. And there were already a few thousand people queuing down the street.

I sat down in the catering area and tried to come to terms with the bitter disappointment of the situation. I have looked forward to this gig ever since the last time we played here, two years ago. It was one of my favourite shows, and I had hoped that we could maybe even beat it tonight. That possibility seemed extremely unlikely as I sat in the dressing room at 7.15 (30 minutes to doors), listening to Priv finally eq-ing the PA – something that normally would be done before we arrive at 4.00 in the afternoon. We finally managed a line-check before we were forced to leave the stage as the doors were opened and the 8000 strong audience filed in. It was already only thirty minutes to stage time. I prepared myself mentally for the show, determined to do my utmost to overcome the myriad problems and give these people the show they surely deserve. Moments before walking on stage we were told there was no intro tape. This threw me into further disarray as I stomped on to sing *Cover My Eyes*, unable to hear much from the centre-wedges.

The crowd erupted as we struck up, and I got that 'Bono' feeling again. Maybe they would carry us through this. Maybe Priv and Alan would defy the laws of physics and probability and make it sound and look great.

As it turns out, that's just what happened. But not before an additional setback – when I went to the T1 to play the opening movement of Brave it became clear that there was a fault, and at no time during the set did the bloody thing murmur a note! We even managed to get round *this* at the crucial moments with a combination of Mark's 'on the fly' reprogramming and me singing *Murder on the Street*, acapella, from the centre mic. During the second song (*Slainte*) I made the mistake of forgetting about my knee injury and threw myself down onto them with the resulting pain (which can only be compared to a cattle-prod in the knee-cap) setting back whatever healing may have taken place since Switzerland. At the time though, my legs were somewhere down the list of my worries. The whole experience was a bit of an Apollo 13, but the crowd saved us spiritually by generating a vibe only just short of mania. I began to suspect that Alan was well on top of the situation when the entire crowd let out a gasp at the dramatic lighting change for '*Tell me I'm mad...*'

When I came off stage to change for *Brave*, John A was in the wings to tell me that the sound out-front was great. Priv's a bloody genius.

My voice held out well for the set, which was up at around two and a half hours, and I still had a little headroom left during *The Space* which closed the show. We all came off stage dazed, confused and disappointed. I cheered up considerably when Priv and Alan appeared and announced that the sound and lights had been terrific, more or less throughout. The altitude of this city certainly seems to make a difference – I was completely exhausted and could barely stagger along the corridor to the shower. We returned to the hotel by minibus and I went to bed without reviewing the day's events in my head before passing out. I didn't have the energy to re-live the trauma or the thrills.

Saturday 3 September *Mexico City, La Diabla*

Slept until around 9.00 which was a major achievement, and woke up feeling like a traffic accident. My head was splitting and my body was aching. Surprisingly, my knee wasn't hurting as much as before – maybe the impact improved it. I staggered down to breakfast and was joined by Alan P, who looked like I felt. He'd been out abusing himself until the small hours so, unlike me, he deserved it. Periodically, people would come to the table to ask for autographs. I asked everyone if they had been to the first show two years ago – they all had. I was relieved to hear that, without exception, they all preferred last night's show! I still have trouble believing it, and I wonder what they might have experienced if everything had been working – maybe it wouldn't have made much difference. I would have been a lot happier, that's for sure. Oh well. There's always next time…

Chatted to John for a while. He was saying that if we have the album finished by Christmas there might still be an argument for coming back to South America in February to perform **Brave** in Brazil, Chile, Argentina and Venezuela.

At 1.00 we all met up in the lobby for a trip to the markets. We went first to Mercado Inserghente where I bought myself a silver chain with a little Mayan symbol of a girl in pigtails (she was to become my logo for future solo album **Ice Cream Genius**) and some more earrings for Sue. Outside, I bought a puppet on strings for Nial. The boys wanted to return to the hotel, so we dropped them off and Alan, Nick and I went on to the market at Ciudarella, chomping our way through a basket of fruit that I had brought down from my hotel room. At the second market I found a small silver bangle for Fi Fi and bought a tambourine to replace the one I had trashed last night, along with more leather laces for my boots.

We returned to the hotel via tonight's venue, La Diabla, to see how things were progressing. When we arrived, it was raining hard – this is the rainy season and it certainly does! I met our head of security, Soda, who I came to like and respect. He told me he had arranged a trip to the cinema for a private viewing of the E-max Rolling Stones movie after soundcheck. I told him I would like that very much but, after yesterday, I wasn't over optimistic that we would have time.

When the rain eased we drove back through flooded streets to the hotel. I decided to drop in to the Hard Rock for tea. Once again I was looked after by the staff, many of whom had come to last night's show as our guests. Xavier, the owner, came to my table and we chatted about life, England (his wife is from Surrey), Spain (I think he said he's from Barcelona) and Mexico, and the differences in the people. When I made to leave he said the meal was complimentary (I don't think I have paid here ever) and asked me if I would like a souvenir. I came away with a denim jacket for Dizzy and a leather waistcoat for me, before jumping into the waiting minibus which took me back to the hotel to leave for soundcheck.

As we expected, soundcheck was prolonged and noisy – things were humming and breaking down (I don't think I have ever heard Steve R's amps making more noise while idling), but at least we had time today to get things half-sorted. I returned to the hotel and got in the bath to try and soak some of last night's stiffness away.

We had decided to get changed at the hotel and go straight on stage. When we returned to the venue, the place was packed. There was a delay before the show as Ian refused to go on stage until he'd had a cup of coffee and no one could organise one, so I sat around strapped up like a footballer for another half hour while they tried to get it together. The show was fun. Security had to make a line through the people so that we could get to the stage – it was exactly like a world-title fight, pushing through the outstretched hands as people shouted encouragement and the security men linked arms to keep back the crowd. I got that 'Chavez feeling', without having to climb into a ring and get punched a lot. On stage, the sound was loud and out of control, but I enjoyed the excitement of it. I was taken back to the old days of the Europeans, when gigs like this were the norm and I could almost smell the sweat of the individual members of the audience. This kind of situation brings out a wilder side of me, which is reflected in the performance. It didn't really come home to me until long after the show that this was to be our last night with the crew before next year. Once again they had slugged and slummed their way through the day and made the best of a tough situation efficiently and with good humour. I will miss them, particularly Priv, who for me has become like that brother you had and loved but never quite got on with because he preferred the company of his mates.

After the show I went back upstairs to chat to Raymundo and Camillo from EMI, (two solid and amusing chaps) and sat at a table drinking Coronas, signing autographs and being spoilt until the club closed at 4.30. I got to bed around 5.00 knowing I had to be up at half seven and questioning the wisdom of not just packing and staying up.

Sunday 4 September *Mexico City – NYC*

Supernatural forces woke me at 7.30, so I phoned Nick to let him know I was up and about. I felt like death. Showering didn't seem to help. I packed like a zombie and staggered down to reception, hair still dripping, face white, eyes red (the very picture of a vampire with a drug problem) to find still more people wanting to have their photograph taken with me. Couldn't dissuade them.

Checked out, reeling once again at the price of telephone calls in Mexico (government taxes effectively double the hotel rate, which is already inflated), while a couple of girls and a boy called Aldo waited with cameras. Aldo gave me a little pot mug with my name on it, which he had made. I wasn't at my most talkative as I was passed around saying goodbye while Nick tried to get me out of the door into the waiting minibus. All the doormen wanted their picture taken with me as well. They might as well have passed a corpse around. I boarded the bus with a girl called Belina, whose job it was to get me to the airport and onto my flight to New York. I was checked in and installed for half an hour in the first class lounge, where I had the first coffee of the day and the blood began to drain out of my eyes and into my face. Belina effortlessly guided me through the various physical and administrative channels to the aircraft. I thanked her and she pointed me down the entry chute. My condition had improved immeasurably by this time – I only felt dreadful.

The flight to Newark was uneventful. It seems to me from recent experiences around the world that air stewardesses aren't nearly as pleasant as they were a couple of years ago. I wonder why this should be. I was reprimanded for not having the correct change to pay for a Bloody Mary. I only had a fifty-dollar bill (that's only thirty pounds), and she reacted as if it was some kind of ploy to get out of paying. Who cares. It seems I am treated like a necessary evil when I travel these days.

I got out of Newark without incident and took a yellow cab driven by a guy who was infinitely friendlier than the airline staff, and chatted affably to me on my journey into Manhattan. Today's discovery was Newark airport, which is closer to Manhattan and less congested than JFK or the horrible La Guardia. The journey into town is also more picturesque.

I arrived at the Paramount Hotel around 6.00, checked in ("Looks like all your troubles are over sir – all your expenses are covered," said the chap on reception. Thank you, Peter) and was shown to my room, which was small but interesting (we had a lot in common). I took a bath and relaxed, later going down to the restaurant for dinner and feeling very alone. There were no messages for me, so all I could do was kill time and wait for someone to get in touch. It was like being a spy.

After dinner I went out for a walk round the block. Once again I was contemplating the strangeness of fame – I had come from Mexico, adulation and complimentary everything, to a big city where I was a total unknown. I was thinking there was something to be said for anonymity when a voice said, "Am I mistaken or are you Steve Hogarth?" It was chap in a small party of German tourists. Two of them wanted my autograph. Ego duly restored, I wandered over to the big Sony TV screen in Time Square, trying to see round the back of it to get a clue as to how it works. All I discovered was cooling fans.

On my way back to the hotel I was pointed at and called a "White lesbian pimp motherfucker" by a black preacher guy standing on a box with an all black crowd around him. Nice to see the word of God being taken to the street. I returned to the Paramount and went to bed.

Monday 5 September *New York City:* **Tommy**

Woke around 9.00. Still no messages. Showered and went down to the restaurant on the second floor – all very casual. You can sit on the balcony overlooking reception. It was around 11.00 that I asked if they could still do me a breakfast. They could, no problem.

The Paramount seems to be well hip – something of an art hotel. It was designed in the Eighties by Starck (who also did the Royalton), and is sort of modernist art-deco. I tapped away into my laptop during breakfast, writing up the events of yesterday. The waitress kept the coffee coming and I drank industrial quantities until around 1.00 in the afternoon, when I decided to go out looking for a refill for my pen. This turned out to be something of a mammoth project – it's French and takes a different shape to all the popular American ones. I walked up the road to Macy's and had no luck at all. I did, however, take the opportunity to stock up on Z14 talc and underarm sticks (really interesting, eh?). I decided I'd have to go upmarket, and made my way across town to Fifth Avenue in search of Tiffany's. I couldn't find it, but eventually happened across Sacks, the other big department store. Every member of staff I asked gave me conflicting directions to the pen counter, so I wandered aimlessly around and round. Eventually I was successful; the chap on pens pointed out that if I cut a bit off the end of a Mont Blanc refill then it would fit! I popped upstairs to have a look at a white Issey Miyake shirt that had caught my eye in the window. They didn't have one in my size.

By now my bad knee was hurting from all the walking, so I took a cab back to the Paramount and relaxed in my room. Susan Weaving, the theatrical agent who represents Peter Rieger here, called to say she would be arriving at 6.00 to take me to Orsa for dinner before the show at St. James' Theatre round the corner. I went down to the hotel bar for a quick beer. The waitress said she was from Grand Rapids, Michigan – the only place in the USA where we're famous! She'd never heard of me. Susan arrived on the dot and waited downstairs as I scrambled around like a maniac, getting out of the shower and dressed. We walked to the restaurant where we joined Richard, Susan's husband, who is General Manager of Tommy for Frankfurt. He took a while to loosen up. He was to accompany me to the show (Susan wasn't coming) and then on afterwards, back to Orsa, for a chat with Des McAnuff (the director).

Dinner was excellent once again, and it was a relief to have some company after two days of solitude. I'm utterly hopeless at being alone. I like to be around friends, really. Richard walked me round to the theatre, and we sat in the third row during the performance. I enjoyed it much more than last time; the music was better played and better mixed, and the performers seemed to be in better form – you could tell Des, the director, was in the house. As for my impressions of the show – well, let's just say the translation to a musical had stripped a lot of the rock n'roll out of it. The music was still there, of course, but the performances from the actors - particularly the lead actor - were of the theatre, not of rock n'roll. There was no "rock n'roll danger" about Tommy, nor was there the sense of an alienated lost soul which Roger Daltrey portrayed so well in Ken Russell's mad movie. The Acid Queen had been cast as a black girl who was trying to reproduce Tina Turner's legendary portrayal. For me, this was a mistake. There's only one Tina T, and the role might have been updated brilliantly to a white girl playing it like Siouxsie Sioux. That would have given it some edge, and got away from it parodying the movie. I was quite certain that I could have intensified the lead role and introduced some real rock n'roll mania to the thing. After all, that's what The Who were all about!

Afterwards we returned to the restaurant ahead of Des, who arrived shortly afterwards. I took to him almost immediately – he seems confident and obsessive, but pleasant and not a bit showbiz; more or less what I was expecting of someone who could work with Pete Townshend. Unfortunately, and to my surprise (contrary to what I had been told), he hadn't the vaguest notion of me as a singer or a performer. He hasn't listened to or watched the audio and video material that had been sent to him. I got the impression his mind is immersed in other projects at the moment – he's working on a movie and another theatre production. This leaves me still unable to make a definite decision; in fact I haven't got a decision to make! I said cheerio to Des, and Richard walked me back to the Paramount. What a waste of time. Sounds like someone's been telling fibs to Peter Rieger while he sends his 'hard-earned' flying singers round the world on pointless missions. I should have been pissed off, but what the fuck, I'm in New York, and Rieger's picking up the tab!

I went to the downstairs bar and ordered a beer, but in the end I drank only a little of it and got bored. There's something a little desperate about sitting alone in a bar late at night (especially when the bar-girls look like porn stars as they do here at the Paramount). It had been a curious adventure. I had been shipped, all expenses paid, from Mexico City to New York to meet someone who I had been told was very excited at the prospect of working with me, to discover that he had no idea who I am, or what I do. Somewhere between Cologne, London and New York there has been a breakdown of communication; and, no doubt, I'm a pawn in a bigger game. Better off out of it (not a bad title for an album, that). Went to bed.

Tuesday 6 September *New York – Home*

Woke around 10.00. Susan's assistant called to say she would pick me up for lunch at 12.00. I showered, and then went downstairs to drink coffee and write this diary. John phoned from LA at 12.00 as I was leaving, to ask how the meeting had gone last night. I told him and he said he would see me in Brighton.

Susan was already waiting for me when I arrived in the lobby, and we walked down the road to a restaurant called Joe Allens. I ate omelette and, for what it was worth, outlined my feelings about the production, what I felt were its weaknesses, and what I thought I might be able to bring to it. It was all beginning to feel like some bizarre charade. Afterwards she had another meeting in the same restaurant, and she introduced me to two chaps called Robin and David who are something to do with the London **Tommy** – still in its embryonic stages at the moment.

I said bye-bye and walked over to Macy's again in search of a bag to replace my shoe-box which was showing signs of self-destruction. Bought a Samsonite thing and came back to pack. It took longer than I expected and, by the time I got down to the lobby, I was panicking. Jumped into a cab to JFK. There had been an accident on the freeway, and the traffic was jammed as we approached the airport. I arrived at check-in around 6.00 - which was cutting it a bit fine - but it turned out not to be a problem. Had a Haagen-Dazs and a Beck's, and boarded the 747 which was to take me home. The in-flight movie was Backbeat – the story of Stuart Sutcliffe, the fifth Beatle. Oddly enough, Des had been talking about it last night. I enjoyed it, particularly Don Was' soundtrack which captured the Beatles early spirit without playing a note of their actual music. By the time the movie was over there wasn't much point in trying to sleep as we were only an hour out of Heathrow.

We landed ahead of schedule at 6.30. The bad news soon followed – Heathrow didn't have a stand for us to pull up to, and there was some minor problem with the brakes which the captain had decided to have checked over by engineers before taxiing to the Terminal. We sat on the runway for over an hour. We, the passengers, were unable to stand up or summon cabin crew as we were technically still in the process of landing and the aircraft might move at any moment. It was terribly frustrating to be home and yet be unable to go home.

I finally emerged from the airport like a bear with a sore head around 8.00. The cab driver missed the turn off the M40 and went to Banbury as I snoozed in the back. Eventually got home at 9.15, having just missed Sofie. Said hello and went to bed. Slept 'til 12.00 and was woken up by Sofie and Nial to distribute presents. I can't remember feeling more tired.

1995

Friday 16 June *Home – Paris*

Couldn't sleep (again). Sue had arranged a wake-up call (the alarm clock is broken) for 6.00am. Got up at 7.55 and waited for the phone to ring.

Sue's mum and dad arrive today for a very rare visit to England. They land at 7.00, so Sue's driving to Heathrow at 6.30 while I get Sofie and Nial up and dressed. The driver of my car got lost and called me from Adderbury to ask for directions. I dressed the kids and finished packing for Paris and Utrecht. The car, a blue Jaguar, arrived at 7.45 and I put Sofie and Nial in the back seat. They sat there like a little prince and princess, grinning at their first experience of being chauffeur driven. I dropped them at Heloisa's (a dear Brazilian friend who had offered to drop them at school), and set off for Heathrow Terminal 4, keeping an eye on the oncoming traffic for Sue returning home. I think I saw her, but at 160mph it's hard to be sure.

Met up with Steve R and John A in the Terminal and popped to the Club lounge for a quick coffee before boarding the 10.00am flight to Paris, Orly. As I write this I'm sitting in the aeroplane, waiting for take-off, feeling the usual semi-nausea which tends to accompany the mornings after sleepless nights.

Today is a promotion day in Paris. I'm looking forward to being there – even for this! Spiritually I've always felt more at home in France than in England. We're staying at the Hotel California just off the Champs Elysees, where, the last time, I locked myself out of my room four times in one morning. On the third occasion, the security lock somehow engaged and they had to send a man up a ladder to climb in through the window...

Tomorrow we shall be reunited with the rest of the band for a fan club evening in Utrecht, Holland. We've been rehearsing for this the past few days, and my body is still hurting from the sudden return to several hours of singing. The way I sing, physically and emotionally, is very demanding, and when I haven't been singing for a while it takes a week or so before I stop feeling like I've been fired out of a cannon. Tomorrow should be fun – a long-awaited return to being in the same room as the people who care as much about the music as we do: the fans, bless 'em. It's been nine long months since the roar of the greasepaint and the smell of the crowd, and I suspect I'm in desperate need of being reminded why I do what I do. Lately, I have begun to wonder.

Saturday 17 June *Paris – Utrecht*

Last night, after a busy afternoon talking to the press, we were taken out to Café Marly, a restaurant that occupies part of the pyramid square in The Louvre. It was a nice evening. There was a good sky. I played the culinary philistine and ordered a cheeseburger, while gazing out on the timeless genius of the ornate buildings and watching Paris's young lovers, arm in arm, winding their way carelessly across the square. It was a little saddening to remember that blissful feeling of first being in love and to know that it inevitably fades to something more mundane.

We returned to the hotel around midnight, and only then did we realise that we had to be up at 7.30 to fly to Holland. At this moment I'm sitting in Charles de Gaulle airport, feeling slightly ill (drink) and they've just called the flight to Amsterdam.

Later –

Rijnus from the Web Holland met Steve and I at the airport and took us to a Motel just outside Utrecht. We were tired after the early start in Paris, so we killed a couple of hours at the hotel. I went to bed and slept for an hour, then got up around 1.00 and ran myself a hot deep bath. Luxury.

We left the hotel at 2.00 and Henk, a physical therapist and swimming instructor, drove us to the Tivoli theatre where we were greeted by several old chums and familiar faces. I chatted to René who runs the fan club, and helped myself to coffee and strawberries before going up on stage to check the monitors. It wasn't the crystalline sound that I have become used to back at the Racket Club (where I use a pair of Concert Sound wedges – £3000 a pair, with a sound 'to die for') but it wasn't at all bad, so I thanked Eric, the monitor engineer, and left the stage. The rest of the band were due to arrive from England around 4.00 which was when the doors were to be opened to the public, so it was touch-and-go as to whether the band could soundcheck together. In the event, Ian, Pete and Mark arrived at 3.45 so it was okay. Everyone seemed happy and well.

We returned to the hotel around 5.00 and I decided to have a swim. I could see the pool area from my window and it had been deserted all day; it's nice to have the pool to yourself. I called on Ian and gave him a bottle of Roederer Champagne for his birthday (16th) on my way down to the pool. I got changed in the women's changing rooms by mistake - it could have been controversial - but I was alone down there. Floated about in the pool for a while and then returned to my room to phone home. It was raining in England as usual (it was raining in Holland too). Sue said everyone's fine, so I said I would call tomorrow from the Wembley Hilton after soundcheck at the Mean Fiddler.

Back at the Tivoli, it had become a familiar routine: first we go on stage and answer questions from the audience. Someone decided to insult us with references to the new songs not being very good, etc. so I told him I didn't like his shirt. That was about the most memorable moment from question time. Someone else asked what inspired us to make this music. I tried to explain. Came off-stage for more, less public, interviews, and then got ready for the show.

The crowd were in fine form, singing many of the songs with such power that I kept stopping to listen to them. My on-stage sound was good, and I felt that I was singing better than ever – the rest has done my voice no end of good. No doubt when we return here to play the Ahoy in October I'll be as hoarse as a bat again from two months hard living and hard singing.

Every show I ever experienced in Utrecht has had the atmosphere of a birthday party, and this was no exception. What a way to earn a living! I don't take it for granted. I have experienced much in my working life. I have dug holes in the road with shovels and pneumatic drills. I have set up market stalls at 5.30 am and sold fruit and vegetables. I have worked in dirty factories in the industrial north of England. I have played rock n'roll in nightclubs on ocean liners and been attacked with broken glass by nut-jobs, and stitched up without anaesthetic by Swedish sailors. I have been a graphic artist for the British Ready-Mixed Concrete Association. I have made records in large country mansions and French castles. I have sat frozen in the open air of a helicopter platform, stood alone on remote mountain-top glaciers and narrowly escaped a mid-air crash in Iceland. Danced in the shanty streets of the suburbs of Rio. Sat waist-high in the Caribbean in Venezuela… and that's only the half of it. I have forgotten many precious moments and inexplicably remember rubbish; every word of certain Boney M songs, for example.

At this moment I'm a few days behind with this journal. I'm actually sitting in the gardens of the hotel Diane, Milan, enjoying breakfast in the morning sunshine, and trying to cast my mind back to Harlesden…

Sunday 18 June *Amsterdam – London*

It would seem I am writing this diary in airport lounges. I'm sitting at gate C1 in Amsterdam's Schipol airport. In a few moments I will board the BD104 flight to Heathrow and find my way to seat 4C. Tonight we have the UK fan-club evening at the Mean Fiddler in Harlesden – not one of London's beauty spots.

Later –

We arrived at The Mean Fiddler around lunchtime, feeling somewhat jaded. My first impression of the venue was a series of large posters along the outside wall sporting Paul Cox's photograph of me – gold trousers, half naked, holding up a pair of enormous paper wings at Battersea Power Station. A great photograph, but it does make me look like a self-important wanker.

Soundcheck was brief and painless, and the vocal sound needed no work at all. I complimented monitor man Grant (who bore a remarkable resemblance to Sting) on his sound, and set off to the Wembley Hilton where I was hoping to go to bed for much needed sleep. First I had to finish the interview with Rijnus from the Web, Holland, who had come over to England with us. We chatted in the bar while, on TV behind us, the All-Blacks were giving England a thrashing to remember in the Rugby World Cup semi-final.

When Rijnus was finished with me, I went upstairs and climbed into bed. I slept for an hour before Sue telephoned to organise the evening. She was to drive into town with her mum and dad who, despite my misgivings, had decided they wanted to come to the show. They've never seen me sing live in the twenty years I've known them. This is their only chance in the foreseeable future, so there was no putting them off. We decided Sue should bring the car to the Hilton and take a cab to the gig as I would already be there. I was picked up at the hotel by Tim Bricusse, our old friend and production manager, straight back from a tour with the Pretenders. Inside the venue I launched immediately into autographs and photographs for the assembled fans. It was busy inside the gig and hot. Soon it was time to go on stage and do our 'thing'.

We had decided to go onstage one at a time. First me. I sang *Cover my Eyes* from the piano, fronting out various bum notes along the way. Pete then joined me for a vocal and bass guitar rendition of an old B-side *The Bell in the Sea.* Next came Steve R for *Sugar Mice,* then Mark for *A Collection,* and finally Ian for *Beautiful.* The stage sound had changed utterly now that the place was full of bodies – very dry and defined, which was good for me although too lifeless for the rest of the band. Pete came off stage complaining about the sound but I can't remember him ever being happy after a show. The crowd were much more restrained than the Utrecht mob, although, as I looked out from the stage, every face expressed a kind of transfixed joy. Sometimes people party. Sometimes they quietly savour every moment.

After the show I chatted to our agent Ian Huffam, who seemed relaxed and happy with ticket sales for the forthcoming September tour – they went on sale two days ago and are already selling steadily. I managed to make my way out into the gig and grappled with the usual chaos of friends and fans. Met up with Sue's mum and dad and attempted to make conversation while having my photograph taken with people's girlfriends and signing yet more album covers.

There was a car outside to take us back to the Wembley Hilton. Sue and her parents made their way outside while I said a couple of last goodbyes. Sue later told me there were a couple of tall, pretty blonde girls outside who announced that they were jealous of her as they would both like to have my children. Oh gawd – just what the in-laws want to hear, I'm sure. Sigh. I finally made it outside and into the waiting car and we made our way home. Sue drove while I chatted to her mum and dad, between my heavy sighs of tiredness. Got to bed around 1.30am, feeling like parts of my mind and body were still lost in different parts of the world.

Monday 19 June *Studio – Home – Milan*

Tried to lie-in a little, but gave up at 9.00 when Nial went ballistic over not having had a chance to kiss Sofie goodbye before she went to school. She'll be back for lunch! He's a sensitive soul, bless him. I cuddled him until he calmed down and went back downstairs, so I went back to bed until around 11.00.

When I got up the house was empty – everyone had gone to the shops. There was a copy of our new album in the post. I had a listen to the CD which sounds great – noticeably better than the DAT master copy. I turned it up loud and was still listening, sat in my bathrobe, when Sue returned from the shops with her parents. Her Dad sat down next to me to listen. *King* was just starting. It was interesting to watch his reaction as the song veered from its sparse beginning to the screaming anarchy which happens later. At the end he looked visibly shaken!

It was a bright sunny day. We had lunch in the garden before I had to go to the studio for last chance rehearsals for the acoustic live radio show in Holland. Mark is unable to do the show, so I have to play the keyboard parts while singing. The parts aren't difficult in themselves, but to sing the songs at the same time gets a little tricky. Stuart, Steve and Pete were at the Racket Club and we ran through the set a few times, concentrating on *Beautiful* which I was having trouble with.

By the time I got home again it was 3.50 in the afternoon. I had a car arriving at 4.00 to take me to the airport and I hadn't packed. Running to stand still! I kissed Sofie and Nial and explained that I must go away for five days, before saying bye-bye to all and climbing into the waiting Jaguar. I arrived at Terminal 2 and met up with Ann and Ian for the flight to Milan. Bought socks in SockShop – my favourite socks (pink Paul Smiths) were all wet in a bag. There wasn't time to dry them after they were washed. I will dry them in Italy. There was a brief moment of panic when I realised I had left my sunglasses in SockShop. Ann says she'll phone them in the morning in case they have them.

In Milan we were met at the airport by our old friend Francesca Spada from EMI, who accompanied us to the Hotel Diana where we were greeted by Marco (our main man in Italy) and Michel, who was new to us. Also at the hotel was Marina Lenti with a posse of people from the Real to Read fan club.

I went upstairs to drop my bags before leaving for dinner and drinks in a créperie down the road. Marco seemed somewhat fazed by the size of the gathering – I think he had expected to have us to himself. It was late, so we didn't eat much. I had a couple of Caipirinha's (a Brazilian cocktail of Cachaça, a liqueur made from unrefined sugars and limes. Perfect on sunny days… and totally lethal!) and chatted to those present. It seems that *Beautiful* has been well received here by radio, unlike the UK where we continue to be the lepers of the media. Who knows, maybe we'll have a hit?! We returned to the hotel and said goodnight to Marco and Francesca. Tomorrow we start at 11.00.

Tuesday 20 June *Milan – Rome*

Didn't sleep terribly well. Woke up at 6.30 and couldn't really get back to sleep. Gave up around 8.30 and showered before going downstairs. Went out into the garden. I sat by a large pond next to a fountain, with the intention of having breakfast and writing my diary. Ann joined me shortly after I had made a start so, once again, I postponed the idea in favour of conversation.

I was wearing my shorts as it was a warm sunny morning. As the interviews progressed, I couldn't help noticing the mosquitos attempts to make a banquet of my legs. The interviews were relentless but, on the whole, quite imaginative. I seem to have finally exhausted the, "So, tell me… why did Fish leave the band?" questions, and lately I'm being asked about the music.

We had lunch out in the garden. I munched my way through a Caprese salad while theorising and philosophising to yet another journalist, who seemed to be making notes in the form of little pictures and flow diagrams.

After lunch, I gathered up my four pairs of pink socks (now nice and dry) from the windowsill and packed my bags. We had an afternoon of radio stations to tour before leaving for the airport and on to Rome. Late in the afternoon, as we drove through the outskirts of Milan heading for the airport, I was still at it, answering questions on the cellphone in the car. We said our goodbyes and hung around in the airport waiting for the delayed departure (this is completely usual) of the flight to Rome. By now I was feeling an accumulated tiredness of mind and body which had begun in Paris last Friday. I tried to sleep a little on the flight, but probably managed no more than fifteen minutes.

At Rome we were met by Frederico (a new acquaintance from EMI's Rome office) who accompanied us in a minibus to the Cavalieri Hilton (a familiar, much-visited hotel), which is on top of a hill overlooking Rome. We checked in, dropped our bags and returned to reception to leave for dinner with Frederico and Paulo, our product manager. The food was Italian at its best. I had a seafood salad of calamari and fresh anchovies in oil (absolutely scrumptious) with mozzarella and tomatoes. Paulo said the radio stations are playing *Beautiful*. It always feels a little peculiar when I hear we're getting airplay. I have become so accustomed to the apologetic and resigned shaking of heads which usually follows initial optimism by our radio promotion team in England. It would seem that, as far as the British media are concerned, Marillion are filed somewhere in the same drawer as Jethro Tull (dead and buried since the 70's) and we can expect to be treated much the same (dead and buried since 1985). This hurts me more than I can say. Anyway… at least it's not too bad in Italy.

We got back to the Hilton around 1.30, and I had a last beer at the bar with

Ian before going up to bed. We sat outside on the terrace, overlooking the pool, with Rome beyond and below. Beautiful. We sat and gazed in silence. I think we were both wishing we had someone to share it with. Went to bed and slept fitfully between scratching at yesterday's mosquito bites, which had assumed enormous proportions on my arms and legs. Ouch.

Wednesday 21 June *Rome – Zurich*

Arrived downstairs, a little late for the 10 o'clock start. Ian had already started the first interview. It took me a few minutes to get focused – I was still half asleep, and in need of more coffee. We sat out on the terrace for a while before moving inside, out of the heat. By this stage I was beginning to suffer from interview fatigue (or repeated explanation syndrome, or inevitable parrot fashion and switch-off syndrome), so I was consciously struggling to remain attentive and sincere.

At 1.00 there was a reception/lunch on the top floor of the hotel, where a selection of Rome's radio people were hearing Paulo make a speech about the new releases, blah blah etc. There was another band in the hotel called The Blessid Union of Souls, who are currently at No.1 in the American chart (so I'm told), and they were also guests of honour at this lunch-thing. We were announced to the radio people who were all sitting at round tables set for lunch. They looked as though they spend at least 60% of their annual income on their wardrobe – it's all food and clothes with the Italians; in England it's all beer and cynicism. There was a piano and mic set up, and I thought it might be nice to do a song with the Blessids', but in the heat of it we couldn't think of anything, so I got up and fumbled my way through McCartney's *Maybe I'm Amazed* and then later *The Hollow Man*. It seemed to go okay. After that we mingled a little and had some lunch from the buffet. I just had beer and ice-cream.

We had to leave at 3.30 for the national radio station where we were interviewed, having negotiated the complicated security doors – they seem prepared for an imminent visit by some sort of heavily-armed revolutionary movement, hell-bent on gaining control of the country's airwaves. After that we departed for the airport. We had half an hour to kill, so we stopped for an ice cream (the best known to man, topped with double cream = 4 million calories!!) and a quick 15-minute visit to St. Peter (just do it).

Back at the airport we said bye to Paulo, and he happened to have Marco on the phone from Milan so we said goodbye and thanks to him for the trip. I like Marco a lot. The flight to Zurich was delayed (of course). Ian, Ann and I hung around, drinking cappuccino and sitting on the peculiarly uncomfortable wire-work seats at the departure gate until the flight was called. When we boarded the plane we had the same cabin staff as the flight from London to Milan on Monday. Roberto, the steward, said it's very rare for this to happen so soon after, and on a different route. We told him a little about ourselves and he said he'd heard of the band. Nice chap.

At Zurich airport our old friend Gaby Weiss picked us up and took us to the Hotel Rössli - also a much visited and familiar hotel - where we shared a drink at the bar before we all retired. Ann was staying at a hotel round the corner. Gaby happened to have seen Fish recently in Zurich, and told me that he sends his regards.

Thursday 22 June *Zurich:* Day off

Got up, bleary-eyed, around 9.00 for a 10 o'clock start to the day's interviews. For some reason the Rössli's hot water system was suffering from its annual (so they tell us) malfunction, so the shower was bracing. I arrived in the breakfast room at 9.55 and tried to remember how to operate their curious coffee machines. You have to get a little plastic cartridge thing out of a sealed packet and then slam it into the machine with a little metal door, before it dribbles espresso into your cup. I have never seen them anywhere else. I remember watching Roger Taylor, drummer from Queen, grappling with it when I stayed here once before. "I'm going shopping – this is a good city to buy a toaster!" he said before leaving. Drummers tend to have their own window on the world. Ian rang down and said he was going to be a little late, owing to the time taken summoning up the courage to get into the shower.

Interviews lasted until around 6.15, with a 90-minute break for lunch at a Thai restaurant around the corner. I don't know why it should be but the Swiss journalists are, on the whole, my favourite in the world. I never know who they write for or what they say, because I don't speak the language; yet here in the breakfast room of the Rössli I have been asked the most intelligent and interesting questions. Pierre-Michel Meier and Nicky (I never knew his second name) are among the best of the lot.

By contrast there are radio interviews. We went to a radio station in the afternoon, where we were interviewed by a girl who seemed more excited by the arrival of her boyfriend in the building than in either of us. Fair enough. They've got you over a barrel and they know it. In the evening we had 40 minutes to freshen up before going out to dinner with the record company, so I got in the bath with Leo Tolstoy and splashed in the bubbles while Napoleon ransacked Smolensk.

Dinner with the record company lasted until around 12.30. Irwin Bach, the new MD (also known for being Tina Turner's other-half), came over and was friendly and pleasant, despite being obviously tired (he could have said the same about me). It was nice to see the Swiss company again, old friends Daniela, Minure (who Ian calls Mini Roll) and Peter. After six-plus years in the band I have now been with EMI longer than most of the staff worldwide. It's a funny feeling. I feel a bit like that dog listening to the gramophone on the old **His Master's Voice** logo. Woof! Announced to Gaby that I will do tomorrow morning's phoners in the bath and went to bed.

Friday 23 June *Zurich – Amsterdam*

Got up and decided that I wasn't in the mood for being interviewed in the bath. Had a shower and went downstairs for much-needed coffee. Gaby and Ann were already in reception. I was handed a phone and poured out my innermost thoughts and feelings into a piece of plastic, with someone I have never met at the receiving end (the word prostitute springs to mind, doesn't it? Or Samaritans). Then I went back upstairs to the breakfast room to talk to someone who'd just arrived. Blah blah OJ Simpson… blah blah Kurt Cobain… blah, etc… By the time I had finished we were already late for our flight to Amsterdam, so I grabbed my things and hurried to Gaby's car, lamenting not having found the time to buy finger cymbals at the music shop round the corner. Zurich's a good place for percussion as well as toasters.

"Hurry up and hang about" seems to be the catchphrase most relevant to international travel. Having checked in at Zurich airport and said goodbye to Gaby and Ann (she was returning to London), Ian and I made our way to the gate to be told there was a one-hour delay. Great! Today was to be the only day this week that I had a couple of hours off, during which, of course, I had been planning to sleep. We bought coffee with a 20 Deutsche Mark note I found in my top pocket and talked about 'life', forgetting about the time until our names were called over the P.A. We were told off by an airport official (who looked like one of those warders in **Prisoner Cellblock H**) and we hurried onto the plane, only to sit on the stand for another 30-minutes.

When we arrived at Schipol we waited at the baggage carousel for half an hour before the luggage came through. Jacquiline from EMI had been waiting for well over an hour, but was nonetheless relaxed and happy to see us. We made our way by minibus to the American Hotel (rapidly becoming something of a second home) when Jacquiline broke the news to me that there were two interviews scheduled for this afternoon. This would fill up the gap between arriving at the American and leaving for Arnheim at 5.15. I would have to find somewhere to sleep at the gig.

The one-hour journey to Arnheim was spent autographing CD sleeves. By the time we arrived at the Luxor Theatre I felt quite sick as a result of reading and writing for an hour, combined with general tiredness and the movement of the bus. Yeuchh! Soundcheck was lengthy and troublesome, and therefore nerve-wracking. Tonight's show is going out live on the radio. Mark isn't with us, so I'm covering the keyboard parts and I was depending on a run through of the set at soundcheck. The monitor engineer wasn't up to the job in hand and everything kept changing in between loud bangs and crackles. After an initial attempt at a soundcheck, it was decided that certain items of equipment must be replaced before we could continue, so we hung around for another hour and tried again. This time was better, and we managed to (more or less) sort things out before the doors were opened. Burt from EMI was to take us out to a Japanese restaurant for dinner. I declined, opting for an hour on the dressing room couch – it was my only hope. I dozed for a while, listening to the noises in the street down below and to the coming and going of theatre staff who, unfortunately, needed to pass through the dressing room to gain access to an office. Nonetheless, an hour of relative stillness can make all the difference and I felt better for it. Chatted to the Dutch fan club people on the stairs at the side of stage. I was getting tense vibes from the opening act, which I interpreted as some sort of resentment over their sound and soundcheck – or lack of it. It's the old story, I'm afraid. In all the shows I have played with this band there has never, to my knowledge, been an incident when we, or our crew, have deliberately sabotaged the opening act's chances of being judged fairly; but on occasions like these, when the stage crew are sub-standard and there are equipment problems, we will naturally attend to our own problems in the time available and the opening act will have to work with whatever is left. I remember only too well that it *feels* deliberate and unfair.

Stage time was 1.00 in the morning. The show was enthusiastically received by the crowd – better than we deserved under the circumstances. The equipment problems continued (due to the supplied stage crew not knowing their arse from a jack socket) and the keyboard player seemed to be malfunctioning somewhat, due to insufficient rehearsal, nerves, exhaustion, and having to sing at the same time. The crowd, transfixed and grinning with pleasure, still continued to stare up at me as though I had the whole thing under control. We really do get away with murder. Thank you, thank you, Arnheim.

After the show, Steve R and I were interviewed by a DJ on the balcony. This entailed walking us through the crowd like a pair of boxers, flanked by large security chaps who were there not to protect us (for we were in no danger whatsoever), but to make sure we arrived at the other end – we would probably have got chatting to someone otherwise).

Back in the dressing room it was like Paddington Station, so I decided not to shower, just to pack my things and get ready to leave. It was already 3.00 and we still had to drive back to Amsterdam. Arrived back at the American Hotel around 4.00 in the morning and got in the bath. Got to bed around 4.20. Phew.

Saturday 24 June *Amsterdam – Birmingham*

Got up at 10.30 and went downstairs to the restaurant café for a light breakfast and coffee. It was a lovely day outside – the sun was shining on the trams and canals and the people cycling and walking by. What a pity we couldn't have taken a late afternoon flight and spent Saturday here. Birmingham in the rain doesn't really pack much appeal compared to Amsterdam in the sunshine. I spent a day alone here in the sun after the Paradiso show last year. I want to do it again. Oh well. Chatted to Ian and Tim who had joined me for coffee, before going upstairs to pack and to leave for Schipol Airport. Maybe I should see if I can rent an apartment at Gate D3. Spent the flight to Birmingham writing this diary. The trouble with a journal like this is that its upkeep fills in the few spare holes in a frantic life, when I could really do with the time to relax. I suppose it keeps me out of trouble.

At Birmingham we were met at the Terminal by a limo which took us to the Hyatt Hotel (posh American mirror-glass high-rise, unfriendly receptionist, friendly cleaners). It wasn't raining after all, so I dropped my bags and went for a Saturday afternoon walk. I'd never really got my teeth into Birmingham, so I thought this was a good chance to suss out the shops. I was pleasantly surprised. During the course of the afternoon I found an optician who can put new lenses in my American sunglasses, a clothes shop full of great shirts and jackets (too dear at the moment, but nice to know about), a good little record store in the Piccadilly Arcade (reminiscent of London Piccadilly's Burlington Arcade) where I bought the current Radiohead, Elastica, and Björk CD's, and a flower stall where I bought a bunch of chrysanthemums and freesias – yeah.

Returned to the hotel and wrote in the diary again while sipping a Bacardi and Coke, and trying to imagine I was on a warm beach somewhere. At 6.00 in the evening I closed the curtains and went to bed, sleeping soundly for an hour until the phone rang. It was Tim Bricusse to let me know I was needed downstairs at 8.00. Got up, ordered a club sandwich from room service (£11.00!), showered, ate the sandwich, and then made my way down in the glass lift, which offers the nearest experience to jumping off a high building – without the sudden stop at the bottom.

We were driven the short journey to Exposure, a rock club festooned with posters of our forthcoming album. Oh dear. I suppose there was a time, a long time ago, when I might have been excited by all this. Lately I just feel like a car dealer in these situations. We were seated at a trestle table while people filed past getting CD sleeves, pictures, t-shirts and parts of their bodies signed. Quite a lot of them had previously spoken to me after shows and treated me more like an old chum than someone they were a fan of. It was a bit of a relief and defused much of the stupidity of the situation. People kept offering to buy me drinks. I had to keep explaining that I was getting drinks for nothing from the bar and that it's the thought that counts. Nonetheless, they bought me them anyway. Sweethearts. After we had signed all there was to sign, I hung around chatting to anyone who wanted to chat and we later moved on to another rock club, the name of which escapes me. One thing is for sure – we don't belong in these places. I can't really take this culture seriously. You might say I'm missing the point, that it's all just fun anyway – which is fair enough, but then it's not my idea of fun either. I'm sure the kids also know we don't belong here. Not belonging – it's that age old feeling. The thing about not fitting in is that it's OK if you can find an alternative sub-culture of people who 'don't fit in' in the same way, hence the phenomenon of the cult. But then not fitting in to a cult causes us the same worries as not fitting in to society as a whole… shut up Steve, you're wandering again.

I sat in the shadows, talking to Rory and Cathy who had been at the other place as well. I wasn't very good company, and eventually accepted their offer of a lift back to the Hyatt. Tim Bricusse, the consummate professional, materialised from the discrete distance where he had been keeping an eye on me, and accompanied us back. Staggered to bed wondering, once again, why I had stayed up so late.

Friday 30 June *Home – Nottingham*

It was one of the hottest days for several years. I had spent the latter part of the afternoon defrosting our old freezer on the lawn, and was still breaking the ice off it as Ian and Tim appeared through the garden gate at 7.30. They sat in the garden chatting to Dizzy and the children while I staggered into the house with the freezer, which will remain under the stairs until I can dispatch it to the Racket Club next week. Tonight we are to make another personal appearance at Rock City, Nottingham's famous rock club, which opened back in the Seventies just after I finished at college there. We said our goodbyes (fortunately I'll be back on Monday. Makes a change...) and drove the one-hour drive up to Nottingham, arriving around 8.30.

On the way I opened a couple of letters that had come through the office. One was an invitation to a garden party held next week at St.Giles College, Oxford. That might be fun. I had also received a letter from Darren in Luton who sounds like quite a character, writing to me about his life, his band and his family. A tragic story in many aspects, but written with great honesty and unique humour. I'll try and find ten minutes to write back.

The Royal Moathouse Hotel was already teeming with people out on the town for Friday night. A girl called Emma (I thought I'd better ask) came across reception and kissed me as I was checking in. Bloody hell – welcome to Nottingham! She didn't know who I was, she'd just decided to kiss someone. I dropped the bags in my room, and said hi to John and Aaron who were sitting in the restaurant. **Q** have given the album a four-star review. Not bad. **Brave** only got three – I was outraged. Nothing in the music business makes any sense to me. Returned to my room and set up my CD player and speakers. Listened to Jeff Buckley's **Grace** album – a gem.

We all met up in reception at 11.15 to go just around the corner to the club. Steve Rothery, Ian and I were representing the band. Pete is on holiday, and Mark is still recovering from a minor hospital operation. We sat upstairs behind a trestle table and signed posters and CD sleeves, just as we had last Saturday in Birmingham. It turned into a long evening. The Marlboro cigarettes sales team were working the club as well. Some of the boys in the band had bumped into them on the last tour in a hotel in Newcastle, and they invited us back to their hotel for a drink. I got sloshed and played the piano until it was light. I returned across Nottingham on foot, as I had so many times before at the crack of various dawns in '76 and '77, on my way from the Broadmarsh bus station to catch the 31 bus to Mapperley by the Market Square. The weather had turned much colder. I was going to regret not bringing a jacket with me on this trip.

Hit the bed running, hoping to God no one would disturb a crucial morning's sleep.

Saturday 1 July *Nottingham – Fflint*

I was woken by the grinding sounds of workmen drilling in an adjoining room (how do they KNOW?). This was around 10.00 – Ian later told me it had started at 7.00. I managed to ignore it and drift in and out of sleep, until I gave up around 11.45. Phoned Tim and Ian and asked if they fancied going out for a spot of lunch. We agreed to meet up at 12.30, and I took them for a walk up past my old college and to the Arboretum in the park, where we ordered cheeseburgers, chips and coffee, which we ate while overlooking the park. To my surprise, the Pink Floyd live album was being played over the P.A. system – this is a student pub, so I would have expected Elastica. We walked back through the park, stopping by the birdhouse at Ian's request – he has a long-standing affinity with birds, especially parrots. We returned to the hotel and checked out to drive to Fflint which is in North Wales, somewhere near Liverpool. And no, I'm not sure why we're going there either…

I slept for much of the journey. Tim got a bit lost during his attempts to take the route across country from Derby through Stoke-on-Trent. When I woke we were somewhere near Chester, 10-or-so-miles from Fflint – phew! A hinterland of power stations under construction. It has to be said that Fflint seemed somewhat grim, but as we followed directions to our hotel the road opened up into rolling countryside, and we eventually found The Green Lodge, a motel that consists of a quadrangle of buildings that reminded me of Rockfield Studios in Monmouth.

As we stumbled out of the minibus it became apparent that the hotel was host to a wedding party. I was immediately invited to kiss the bride for a photograph – that's two days in a row I've been kissed as I've got out of the bus. It's a dirty job, but someone's got to do it. The bride and groom invited us into their reception for a drink. I had a Bacardi and Coke and ordered up strawberries and cream, which I later ate outside in the courtyard while tapping away at the laptop on this journal.

It's Wimbledon week at the moment. I moved the TV in my room so that I could watch the end of an Agassi qualifier from the bath, and soaked my bones for a while. Heaven. At 8.15 we left to drive to another rock club – The Tivoli in nearby Buckley. We were ushered upstairs by the owner, Howard, who gave us a drink and told us he'd also advertised our appearance at Liverpool's Crazy House (which he also owns) later tonight. Fair enough. Ian and I went downstairs and watched the kids jumping around on the dance floor for a while, before making our way to the designated corner of the club to sign posters and CD sleeves for whoever was interested. There was quite a lot of them, and it took an hour or so before we were finished and set off again to Liverpool.

When we arrived at the Crazy House I was tempted to go out for a wander – we were only round the corner from Parr Street and the stomping ground of pubs and bars I know so well. We were all hungry so we sent out for tuna sandwiches, but at 11.30 on a Saturday night in Liverpool it's a tall order, and the runner came back with fishcakes and chips. Never mind.

We went downstairs and signed posters etc. Someone told me his wife fancies me and that he was prepared to make an exception in my case. I told him she wouldn't if she'd met me, she probably thinks I'm 6ft 2". At least he hadn't brought me her underwear. A couple of the local wide-boys were leering in the background and shouting for Fish. I have often wondered whether Fish has to put up with tossers shouting "Hogarth" at him. I hope not.

I went downstairs to have a look at the dance floor, and remembered seeing Dr. Phibes and the House of Wax Equations here back in '93. I wonder what happened to them? I didn't see anyone I knew. All these rock clubs are similar – everything is black inside. The boys wear ripped jeans, junkyard boots, and t-shirts proclaiming the advantages of death or grave-digging. The girls wear cheesecloth tie-dye, Morticia make-up and Doc Martens. On the whole they all look like vampires but, when you talk to 'em, they're complete sweeties. I'd have this lot any day in preference to the smart set. Someone said the new album had been favourably reviewed in the **NME**. Knock me down with half-a-feather. I'll believe it when I see it.

We made our way back to the hotel, arriving at around 2.00. Everyone had gone home, apart from the newly-weds who were still in the bar, still in their wedding clothes! Tim and Ian accepted their offer of a last drink, I made my excuses and went off to bed. I was desperate for some sleep.

Sunday 2 July *Fflint – South Shields*

Got up around 12.00, put Jeff Buckley on, showered, and then made my way to the breakfast room. Tim and Ian emerged at exactly the same time, and we walked across the rose-bordered courtyard into the main building. The French Grand Prix was just starting, so we watched the first few laps before we were called upstairs for Sunday lunch. We all had lamb and Yorkshire puds. By the time we got back down to the TV room, Michael Schumacher had the whole thing wrapped up. Packed and called home. No one was in, so I left a message.

We set off around 2.30 for the 4-hour journey to the North-East. John called to give us the chart position of the album – a disappointing 16. We drove up the M6 to Carlisle before taking the A-road east towards Newcastle, which was looking particularly grim – closed up on a late Sunday afternoon. I have never been to South Shields. We were staying in the Sea Hotel which, from the outside, looks like a fish 'n' chip shop. My room (114) was OK though – I even had a four-poster bed.

Ian and Tim were driving round the go-kart circuit in the amusement park across the road. We went for a walk through the arcades and past the helter-skelter to the beach, and I stared out across the slate-grey sea in the general direction of Sweden, thinking, "What, in God's name, am I doing here?" It definitely is a curious way to make a living.

Probably the best moment of the day was a TV programme about the Seven Wonders of the World, which I stumbled upon around 8.00pm. Unfortunately I had missed most of it, but managed to catch an examination of the archaeological arguments for and against the existence of the Hanging Gardens of Babylon. There was an account of the rediscovery of the temple of the goddess Artemis who had been worshipped for over seven thousand years by the Hittites, the forerunners of all Western culture, who were converted to Christianity by none other than St. Paul himself.

I was forced to abandon this fascinating programme in order to go to Victors, a Sunday night rock club in the town centre. Ian and I did the honours for the twenty-or-so people interested in having our signatures while we consumed free drinks and tried to make conversation over the deafening rock music blasting out around the room. Even the kids couldn't understand what we were doing here. Everyone was asking if we were coming to play the North-East when we tour. I had to confess that it seems unlikely – we already have the September tour dates confirmed, and the nearest will be Leeds or Glasgow.

The club doesn't have a late license for Sunday, so at 10.30 everyone was thrown out and we returned to the Sea Hotel. By now I was several sheets to the wind, and so when I noticed a table full of people sitting in a circle, like a religious discussion group, I waded straight in there and joined in. There was an Iranian called Emir who was planning a Channel 4 documentary about Geordie culture. I ended up giving some sort of speech (although I can't remember what I said) that took in everything from Nebuchadnezzar to Tears for Fears. They eventually all got up and left, and I found myself out in reception talking to two Sikhs, bearded and turbaned. One was from the Punjab, the other was born in Zurich. I asked him if he knew the Rössli Hotel, but he said he left there when he was still very small. They both agreed that I looked like a hippy from Goa and that I should go there and check it out. They said that South Shields is in the **Guinness Book of Records** for having a stretch of road with more Indian Restaurants per square foot than anywhere in Britain. That did it. Tim called a cab and we went out for an Indian. It turned out that the aforementioned road was less than half a mile from the hotel, and was indeed lined with more Indian Restaurants than Delhi High Street. I had chicken tikka masala (which was invented in England!). We walked back up the road to the hotel in a slight drizzle of rain. When we arrived back the night manager offered us a drink, but we weren't up to consuming any more. Went to bed feeling hazy and sad.

Friday 7 July *Home*

Got up with the children at 8.00 and got Sofie and Nial off to school. It wasn't a bad morning, so I thought I'd mow the lawn. Sue had a bit of a lie in and then spent the morning getting herself ready for the garden party this afternoon. It's always a pleasure to mooch about in the garden, monitoring the progress of the flowers and plants. This is going to be one of my last few days off before all hell breaks loose as we prepare for the forthcoming world tour, so I was enjoying the garden with a clear conscience.

At 12.00 I picked Nial up from play school (next door but one), and he disappeared upstairs to hinder Sue. He sticks to her like glue and it drives her crazy.

At 2.00 I had to call Lester Middleton, a journalist from from **The Mail on Sunday** supplement, to answer a load of questions and give him my views on sex. Desperate times call for desperate measures. Oh well – it'll publicise the new album. Ended up talking to Lester for the best part of 45-minutes, and probably ended up saying too much. My mum gets **The Mail on Sunday**, so I'm sure there'll be no lack of feedback from the article.

All of this had made us late for the garden party. I had been invited, out of the blue, by Angie, an old friend of a friend who I remember meeting briefly backstage at Oxford Apollo a couple of years ago. I have never been to a garden party, but have been singing about them for the past few years so I can justify this trip on the grounds of research. According to the invitation there was champagne and strawberries at 3.00. We arrived in Oxford at twenty-past and realised we had come out without any money, so we had to drive into the town and find a bank to be able to 'pay & display' the car parking fee. Oxford is notorious for speed cameras and punitive parking fines. We finally parked the car outside the Eagle and Child (famous for having been a regular meeting place for J.R.R. Tolkien and C.S. Lewis back in the Thirties), and crossed the road to St. Giles College. We entered through a large gate, which led us up through an alley and round past two builders to a dead end. A girl in a pink ostrich feather hat, carrying a teddy bear and accompanied by a chap in linen, made the mistake of assuming we knew where we were going and followed us up the same dead end, past the same two (suitably amused) builders.

We eventually gained entry into the garden of the smallish mansion house which is St. Giles House and said hello to Julia Simpson (who I had known from GWR radio) and hostess Angie, who set about plying us pleasantly with champagne and strawberries. She introduced us to the girl in the pink hat with the teddy bear – she was called Lise and she owns The English Teddy Bear Company. Returning with another drink, I caught the girls' mid-conversation and was asked to share any thoughts I might have on the subject at hand, which turned out to be menstruation. What a minefield. I said something about girls always taking their handbags to the toilet. Well, I *had* been drinking. Behind us on the lawn was a clown who was busy creating enormous tubular bubbles. He later took to balloon sculptures, and Lise presented me with a 'handbag' made of balloons, in memory of my earlier (half-witted) observations. They *had* sounded somewhat naive, but I thought it best to give that impression. She later also gave me the teddy as a present to little Nial. What a nice girl.

The music consisted of two young male musicians, one on trumpet, one on sax, who played along to various jazz and funk backing tracks and were very impressive players. I was introduced to them between sets. Although they were both very good players I thought the sax player, James, had it in him to be great.

His technique, intonation (pitching) and expression were faultless. He said he's been playing for five and a half years. Bloody hell, it sounded like fifteen years to me! Much to my surprise they both seemed to know all about Marillion, and were keen to know what we were currently working on. I invited them down to the Racket Club to meet the chaps later in the month. The champagne gave way to Pimms, and Angie, who works for Joy le Fevre (the PR company who were hosting the party), came over to chat. She said if ever a band needed sympathetic PR, it's us – we're the most misunderstood and underrated band in the world. I agreed. She said she's lost count of the people she has played our music to who, after initial scepticism, have really got into it. It's frustrating, but better than them thinking we're brilliant, only to hear us and be disappointed!

Monday 31 July *Home – Washington*

Slept well for the first time in quite a while – especially unusual as I leave for America today to start the **Afraid of Sunlight** tour. We will start in the clubs and small theatres of the American and Canadian North-East. This actually limits my pre-tour anxiety as we can warm up the show in low profile, adding creative ideas as we go. Hopefully, by the time we arrive back in England, the show should run like a well-oiled machine. Watch this space. I climbed out of bed around 8.15 and went downstairs, leaving Sue and the children to sleep. It's unusual for Nial to sleep past eight, but he's had a couple of late nights over the weekend.

I showered and wandered around, trying to gather together the various possessions I will take on the road for the coming 3 or 4 weeks. I intend to try and write some music while I'm out this time, so I will take a little battery operated four-track as well as my new Yamaha QY20 'pocket sized' sequencer. What with all that, and keeping up this diary, I'm not going to be the most sociable of creatures…

Where was I? Well, it wasn't long before the children arrived downstairs so I was temporarily hijacked into making breakfast, before popping down to the shop to buy a bottle of bleach. The last minute dash to wash my clothes had resulted in my blue shorts dying my yellow shirt and pink socks to dirty shades of yellow and pink respectively, so I wanted to try and bleach them back to the right colours before I left at midday. I returned from the village shop, Domestos in hand, to find Sue had risen and, of course, the children were upstairs 'helping' her get ready. Sofie and Nial, given the choice, will never be more than one room away from her, so I was left free to put my things in to soak and start packing. Sofie came downstairs dressed, so I took her with me to Banbury where I was doing a Marks & Sparks run for underwear.

We parked the car and she held my hand as we walked across the town, both conscious of my impending departure. She's such a lovely little girl. I shall always treasure her. We wandered in and out of the shops, bought flowers for Sue and sweets for Nial, went to the bank, and returned home. The children are having their hair cut this morning at 11.30, so I'll say goodbye to them and have half an hour to myself to finish packing before the car arrives to take me to the airport. We will all be spared the sight of my loading suitcases into the car. It usually makes everyone low. Well, I waved everyone off to the hairdressers and continued packing. Two minutes before the car arrived, I discovered all my socks and underwear for the trip still in a pile on the shower room floor. I thought I'd put them in the suitcase. Phew! Nearly went to America without socks and drawers!

At 11.45 I heard an engine running outside in the street and looked out to see not a taxi from Banbury, but a limo from London. EMI had laid on cars for the trip, so CP had sent my usual driver, Gary, to pick me up in a Merc. Nice. He was a bit early, so we sat in the garden drinking Coke and chatting about EMI. Once again, it was a beautiful morning – we're experiencing one of the warmest summers for years in England. I sat enjoying the garden and listening to the sprinkler watering the lawn as I stared at the house, trying to burn the moment into my memory so that I could recall it all (and remember who I am) when my feet start to leave the ground – they always seem to when I'm caught up in the unnatural chaos of touring. I locked the house and left, and sat in the front seat of the Merc to go to the Racket Club where we were to pick up Stuart Every, our sound engineer. He was waiting outside chatting to Aldo, our landlord at Lawn Farm, who shook my hand and wished us success. Aldo's living proof that you don't have to be a bastard to rent out property.

At the airport we met up with the boys to learn of the first fuck-up of the tour. The travel agent has booked Alan, Stuart and Roger onto yesterday's flight, so they might not get on the plane. They were sent to queue for a standby place while the rest of us checked in. Great. Later on, just moments before the 747 pulled away from the stand, I noticed Stuart board but no sign of Alan and Roger. Oh well… we always begin each tour with a fuck-up of some description. Stuart had managed to bag the last vacant seat on this huge aeroplane and, as luck would have it, he found himself up front in first class – wide seats, private bar, and a masseur doing the rounds. I sat back in economy with Tim, reading the last chapters of Tolstoy's **War and Peace** in between snoozing and watching the TV – they now have screens in the backs of the seats and you can select what you want to watch. I later wandered forward and had an ice cream and a couple of drinks from the bar with Stuart. We got talking to a girl called Jayne, who turned out to be the marketing manager of Virgin's Roof Gardens club, Kensington. She had just got married and was passing around the photographs. She invited me to drop by if I was in town to have a look.

Nothing much else of interest happened during the flight to New York, Newark, which passed quite quickly. It took a while to change Terminals at Newark, and we arrived to check-in for the 8.00 flight to Washington with only ten minutes to spare. They said not to worry, and that they would hold the flight for us. When we arrived at the gate I knew why – we were shown through a side door and down some stairs to the smallest commercial passenger aircraft I've ever seen. There were only three other passengers (apart from the seven of us) and the flight was full! I sat next to the wing where the noise from the propeller engines was deafening as we rattled our way down to Washington. At 9.15 we were back on the ground and catching a bus to the baggage carousels. Outside it was hot and humid, and everyone was working hard to pretend not to be exhausted and irritable as the bags were loaded into the taxis. I flopped into the back seat and it was a relief to sit quietly and enjoy the air conditioning.

Arriving at the Latham hotel in Georgetown, the air wrapped back around me like hot soup as I opened the cab door. The Latham is situated on a street which owes its appearance equally to the Wild West and Covent Garden. It's a classier hotel than I was expecting. That was the third pleasant surprise of the day (I was expecting a minicab from home to Heathrow. I was also expecting to have to drive from New York to Washington, and I was expecting the hotels on this tour to be basic).

I checked into room 909 and showered before meeting up with the boys downstairs in the bar, where we chatted to Jill from Las Vegas who was serving the drinks, before we wandered down the road to find somewhere to eat. By now it was well past four in the morning in England, so I was fading fast. We had a beer in a refrigerated bar called Nathan's and emerged, teeth chattering, into the comfort of the warm street. Ian and Mark were hungry and went off in search of somewhere to eat while Pete, Stuart and I returned to the hotel. Went to bed at 12.00 midnight and woke at 4.00, willing myself back into sleep until giving up at 6.30.

Tuesday 1 August *Washington:* Day off

Got up, showered, and took the elevator down to the breakfast room, clutching my faithful old Macintosh laptop so that I could write up this diary. The staff in the hotel restaurant were mostly Mexican and the waiters looked like a Mariachi band. I was reminded of the time in 1994 when Mark and I had flown straight from Tokyo (after our Japan dates) to Mexico City, and arrived at our hotel SO jet lagged we could barely stand up. Raymundo and Camillo from EMI Mexico had been there to greet us and were determined to take us out "just for one beer". We both explained that we were unable to function, let alone drink even one Corona, and we must go straight to bed. Somehow Mexican bonhomie won over physical possibility, and we ended up agreeing to go "to just one bar" before working our way around Camillo and Raymundo's favourite haunts (perhaps promises had been made to various bar owners). When I finally "hit the wall" around midnight and my head descended to the table we were sitting at (we'd probably been awake for 40-hours at this point), and just as my eyes were rolling upwards into unconsciousness, I was shocked rigid into terror as Mariachi trumpets suddenly blared towards us at point-blank range. Someone had arranged 'entertainment' at the table for us. The most vicious alarm clock known to man. To this day, Mariachi music induces a slight twitch, even though I enjoy it.

I spent my p.d's for the day on breakfast (eggs Benedict, hash browns, toast, OJ, coffee) which is a little excessive, but the orange juice alone was worth it. I make no secret of the fact that America isn't my number one favourite country on the planet, but I have never tasted orange juice like this anywhere else. Around 8.45, as I was finishing up, I was joined by Stewart and Mark. I gave Mark my seat at the table and went off in search of a hairdressers. I was told by the Iranian receptionist that they could do me at 11.00, so I returned to the hotel and to Tim's room, where I had a look through the stage clothes. It seems the 'expensive girl who went shopping' (I refuse to call her a stylist) hasn't bought Pete any shirts, the shorts and trousers she bought Ian are much too big, and everything else is generally wrong. Oh well. We've already paid her. She saw us coming.

Returned to the hairdressers and was 'done' by Jeff, who was born and raised here in DC. He said (with a grin) that the order of the day here is "a bob and a string of pearls", but I opted for just a trim. I was introduced to the staff – Alan from County Cork, Christine from Belfast, and Julia from El Salvador. Put the boys on the guest list for tomorrow night – the girls weren't interested. I wandered down the road in search of a music shop. I'm looking around for a reverb/delay pedal to put my voice through when I'm writing in hotel rooms. There isn't one in Georgetown, so I turned my attention to shower-gel and ankle-straps. No luck there either. Bought a couple of embroidered shirts in a hippy shop opposite the hotel, and returned to spend the rest of the afternoon reading. I have come to the last part of **War & Peace** where Tolstoy stops storytelling and starts theorising at length, refuting the accepted ideas of power, the course of history, political and social order as a product of the will of 'man'. He thinks it more-or-less all happens by chance (I tend to agree with him – look at rock n'roll!). It's the heaviest part of the book, and I'm not really in the mood to think about it. Will try again when I'm feeling more settled.

I had a dip in the pool and half an hour in the sun before going back up to room 909 to fiddle about with my recently acquired pocket sequencer. The next thing I knew it was 8.00 and I'd got earache, so I called Tim who told me the boys were meeting up in the bar. I showered and went downstairs where I said hello to our old chum, guitar tech and opening act, John Wesley Dearth - better known to us as Wes - who had arrived from his home in Tampa, Florida. He hasn't changed and seems currently happy with life and excited to be "doing it all again". We all walked round the corner to one of those rock n'roll diners, drank beer and ate hamburgers with chowder and cornbread like good all-American boys. There were lesbians holding hands in the corner, an office party along the wall, advertisements for fly-bait on TV, waitresses in white socks and Reeboks, and a sign on the wall read, "Put a piece of the South in your mouth". No one got shot.

Got back to the hotel around 12.00 and hung around in the street waiting for Priv, Alan, Roger, and Grant to arrive from England. I was tired so I gave up waiting and went to bed, falling asleep halfway through **Pulp Fiction** – which takes some doing, I can tell you.

Wednesday 2 August *Washington, The Bayou*

Woke at 4.00 once again and fought my way back to unconsciousness, not waking again until 8.10 – almost normal! Showered and went downstairs. Decided this morning to opt for the 'greasy spoon' over the road and sat surrounded by workmen in hard hats, while eating scrambled egg on toast with a plastic knife and fork, and tapping away at the laptop. I had to forego "Gods' orange juice", there were no tablecloths on the tables, and the seats were so hard they hurt my bum, but at $3.75 for breakfast it was a bargain. Yesterday cost $20. After breakfast I went off looking for a dry-cleaners in the hope of finding someone to take up the legs of my new jeans. Once again it's a scorcher of a day and very humid, reminiscent of Tokyo last year. I walked round the back of the hotel, over the canal lock where there was a large canal boat moored - some sort of a tourist thing - and beside it, two mules. I've only ever seen mules in movies. They were the size, shape and colour of thoroughbred horses, but with facial features that hinted of donkey – much larger and more beautiful than I had imagined and, of course, the very epitome of frontier America. I carried on walking down to the Potomac River, watching the aeroplanes landing. There was a girl out rowing, an image which took me back to the Eton Excelsior club that I almost joined back in 1987. I heard the wap-wap-wap of a Huey helicopter flying low over the river - a reminder of the political and darker military undercurrents: Vietnam, Watergate, Central America - associated with the Capitol. Whatever happened to Noriega? I never heard. Did they let him quietly out of the back door in return for keeping quiet about the 'old days'? It could never happen in England. They'd never even have arrested him in the first place. Why did Margaret Thatcher authorise the bombing of Tripoli? We were never told, were we? I pondered all this as I sat by the river, drinking cappuccino in the searing morning sunshine. On the return journey to the hotel I ran into Stuart on his way to the load-in at The Bayou, so I accompanied him down to the gig in order to say good morning to Priv, Alan, Roger, and Grant (who I hadn't seen since arriving in the USA). The Bayou is much as I remember it from previous tours – a rock n'roll club. I hung around for a while, writing out a set list for the boys and, as space was restricted, trying not to get in the way before I continued my search for a "repairs while you wait" laundry. I eventually found one and gave them my jeans, returning to the hotel to get my remaining stage clothes together. Spent half an hour removing labels from t-shirts and sewing up the holes I accidentally made.

Soundcheck was 4.30. I walked over to the venue with Tim. There were already a few fans outside the Bayou. When I got inside it became immediately apparent that I wouldn't be required for at least an hour, so I went back outside and chatted to the people in the line who seemed to have come from all over America. The soundcheck wore on until past 7.30. At 7.25 I remembered I hadn't been to collect my trousers, so one of the fans was dispatched and returned later in triumph, having arrived at the alterations place with only a minute to spare.

From my perspective the show went well. There were the usual monitor difficulties which always accompany the first few shows of a tour. Afterwards it was generally felt that the show was at too-low an energy level, with perhaps a little too much emphasis on the last two albums. I chatted to a few people after the show and signed autographs, before returning to the hotel to shower and check out.

Climbed aboard the tour bus at 4.30 and into my bunk, feeling utterly spent. I was to discover that Stuart had left his bum-bag at the Bayou containing his money, credit cards, address book and passport. He went back for it and it's nowhere to be found. Oh dear. Didn't sleep too well. It always takes a few days to get used to sleeping on tour buses.

Thursday 3 August *Philadelphia, The Theatre of Living Arts*

Arrived at the Comfort Inn in Penn's Landing, Philadelphia, around 10.00 and checked into a dayroom. Went downstairs and had a spot of breakfast from the buffet with Tim, our tour manager. I was feeling dog-tired and wounded after the first show (always a blow to the system) and the sleepless night, so I returned to the dayroom and tried to sleep for an hour. We were to be picked up at the hotel at 12.30 by Joe Estrada from the record label, who was taking us to lunch with someone from a radio station in Allentown, Pennsylvania. He took us down to a restaurant where we met up with Keith Moyer and his sister, Jane. Joe continued to bend my ear about trying to edit *Afraid of Sunlight* for radio. It's his favourite song. The food was good. I had salmon with a sort of orangey sauce while chatting to Keith. I remember him from before. He has a pet skunk. Apparently they're good pets to have, provided that the musk glands are removed at birth so they don't make the famed terrible smell. He says it's house-trained and you can take it for walks on a lead, down to the pub, etc. It would be an interesting sight down at the Rose and Crown in my village in England.

After lunch I was planning to go shopping again for shower-gel. My usual Halston Z14 is almost finished – I bought it in Köln earlier this year and, although it's murder to get hold of, I was confident of success somewhere in the department stores of Philly. Keith and Jane agreed to accompany me into town and point me in the right direction, a decision they probably came to regret as we ended up walking miles, visiting several stores - Wanamakers, JC Penney, Strawbridges - some of which stocked the fragrance, but none of which had the shower gel. This might seem like an awful lot of trouble to go to for shower gel, but I'm very particular about these little things, especially on tour when I feel the need to pamper myself a little to make amends for the damage I do to my body and soul every night. Rituals become very important. I can't explain exactly why, but it's something to do with the loneliness. Happiness is a pair of new Paul Smith pink socks after a shower with the right shower gel and the right talc. Anyway, no one had the shower gel or the talc, so Keith and Jane generously offered to drop me back at the hotel. I think I had worn them out. I invited them to the soundcheck and drove over with them.

The Theatre of Living Arts is situated in a good part of Philadelphia – South Street, a street all lit up with fairy lights and full of interesting and unusual shops. I had remembered the hat shop, 'Hats in the Belfry', opposite the TLA, where you can buy any kind of hat imaginable from a fireman to Napoleon. I never found the time to go inside. Nial loves hats. I once promised him a top hat, and I know he'd wear it, but I don't know where I would find one in his size (he's only four). Maybe I'll have a look when we get to New York.

Back at the TLA soundcheck was progressing slowly. Upstairs in the dressing room I discovered John Arnison, who had arrived from England, deep in conversation with the band. Apparently it's felt that last night's set was too long, too down (dynamically and spiritually), and they were discussing possible changes to the set. Well, that was to be expected – you can't really get a feel for things until you hit the road with them. It's a bit late to start changing things for tonight's show, but we decided to remove *The Hollow Man* and *Out of this World* tonight and see how it all feels. Returned to the hotel and went to bed for an hour - still tired - and was summoned to go to the show by Tim knocking on my door while I was still in the bath.

The show was very well received by the sit-down audience. I had trouble with my guitar, which didn't seem to be working whenever Wes handed it to me. Steve R was having a few problems also. Technical hell always accompanies the first few shows; you just have to grin, pretend all's well, and get through it without trashing anything (including yourself) or assaulting the crew. Afterwards I went out-front to sign a few things and chat to the kids who'd hung around. I remember from last time what a bunch of sweethearts they are in Philly. A black guy called Ron stunned me by lamenting the absence of *Market Square Heroes.* Marillion aren't known for being in touch with black culture, and over the course of a world tour I can count the number of black people in the audience on two hands, so it was amazing to meet such a die-hard fan in Ron. He invited the band to a club called Dobbs that was next door-but-one, so I dropped my bags on the bus and went and had a quick half with him. Thanks, Ron.

Out in the street I was approached by a guy who works at a centre for abused children. He told me that, according to his experience, **Brave** was absolutely "right on the money" in relation to the stories he's told every day. He said he had introduced the record to certain of his patients, who had found it to be helpful. He mentioned one particular girl with a history of serious problems who got completely into the album and is now (perhaps only co-incidentally, but y'never know) on the mend. I took an address from him so that I might drop her a line and wish her well. He said that would affect her very positively, so I'll send her a post card when I get a minute – maybe it'll be more fun if it comes from England. When I was writing **Brave** with the boys, it never really occurred to me that it could affect people to quite the extent it has. I've had a few letters from victims of abuse and, oddly enough (and to my relief), they have found the album uplifting.

Well, after our drink with Ron we returned to the hotel to shower, picked up our bags and climbed aboard the bus to sleep. Tomorrow, Boston.

Friday 4 August *Boston, Paradise Theatre*

The road from Philly to Boston should be world-famous. It's not as smooth as Sarajevo High Street. We all lay in our bunks in the dark, bouncing into the air as the driver negotiated pot-hole after ramp after pot-hole. I was reminded of my long journey bumping along the infamous Berlin corridor with a badly sprained ankle back in 1989, before the wall came down. I thought there wasn't a road in the Western World worse than that one. WRONG! Sleep was impossible, but I was still too tired to allay my curiosity and get up and have a look at what kind of a road could produce this effect on a tour bus.

Finally arrived in Boston at a Howard Johnson by the river at around 9.00am. Had breakfast with the boys and then went to bed for the day, rising around 4.30 to shower and go to soundcheck. When we arrived at The Paradise it was raining quite heavily. This is the first rain I've seen either side of the Atlantic, and the cluster of Bostonians already outside the gig blamed the bad weather on our English influence. Inside they weren't even into the drums yet, so I decided to wait on the bus and write my diary a little. Chatted to the people in the street for a while – someone had flown from L.A. to see the show and was flying back in the morning! Sat on the bus, talking to Alan Parker about the light-show in Europe and tapping away at my grey box until Tim came to let me know they were ready for me. There was a moment of panic when we thought we'd lost the ignition key for the bus. It also opens the loading bay doors, so Wes couldn't get at his stage clothes. He thought he'd have to go on in his dirty working clothes, and we all thought we wouldn't be able to go to Toronto! I made up a little tune about it, and was singing it into the mic during soundcheck when Priv announced that he had the bus key. Crisis over. Meet the next crisis. Stuart, still without passport, is unable to go to Canada. He's going to take the train to Newhaven tomorrow, have the weekend off, and wait 'til we arrive on Monday. Grant and Roger, without work permits, can't ride the bus with us or they'll be rumbled at the border, so we're having to fly them in and out. Oh well.

There wasn't time to return to the hotel between soundcheck and show, but I had anticipated that and I felt well rested after spending the day in bed. Had a listen to Wes's set; he's singing very well – his pitching's better than last tour in Europe... better than mine, I think (maybe I can pop something in his drink).

As for our set... well, what a crowd! The band played well, with the notable exception of the end of *Hard as Love* which sort of fell to bits after Steve got lost, Pete got confused and I gave up. All the equipment worked for the first time so far. We changed the set again to make it 'tougher' for these American Clubs, opening the set with *Incommunicado* and *Hooks in You.* It seemed to do the trick. I start the show at a higher energy level, which generally helps the intensity of my performance for the rest of the show. It gives the crowd a couple of oldies to begin with, so they're with us from the top of the set. The Boston crowd have always been great in the past, but tonight they were absolutely terrific, mouthing through all the words and, at the same time, totally engrossed in what the band and I were doing. I'd have bought them all a drink if I could have. I was really on form, feeling much more alive and adjusted to my surroundings than of late.

After the show I went back out into the club to sign stuff for the warm and enthusiastic Bostonians. At one point I was approached with a knowing wink by a kid who looked like Matt Johnson. He flashed the blade of a hunting knife at me and said, "I don't have anything to sign, but you can sign this if you like!" I declined.

We later returned to the hotel to shower, before climbing on the bus to sleep our way to Canada.

Monday 7 August *Newhaven, Toads*

Arrived at the Holiday Inn around 9.30, checked in, and made my way to the breakfast room for a spot of scrambled eggs and toast. My complimentary copy of **USA Today** carried the headline that the Croats have taken to arms once more and re-taken the Krajina region of former Yugoslavia from the Serbs – who had taken it from them at the beginning of this bloody ethnic war that has dragged on now for four years (despite the efforts (some might say impotent and half-hearted) of the United Nations). I was joined at breakfast by Steve Rothery, John (the bus driver), and Stuart (who had spent the weekend here in Newhaven (no passport)). He said it had rained for two days. The weather seemed to have recovered, it was once again sunny and sticky outside.

After breakfast I decided to postpone sleep until after soundcheck today, and go and enjoy Newhaven, perhaps do a little shopping. Plan A was to try and find a computer spares place where I might buy a new battery for this little grey box I'm typing on. I was directed to The Computer Center, a place on a map about half an hour's walk from the centre of Newhaven. I stopped on the way to try and buy a carrying case for my headphones (I keep breaking the plastic hangers when they're stuffed in my bag). Not to be. The man in the hi-fi shop suggested a shaving kit bag..? After having got a bit lost I found The Computer Center. No wonder I'd walked past it, it looked like a college building… it *was* a college building! Some bright spark had assumed I was a student and sent me here. To make matters worse, I was shown into a room full of computer systems and told that, yes, they do have a replacement battery for a Powerbook 100, but that they can't sell one to me because I'm not a student at Yale. Damn! For ten grand I could have probably enrolled for a term, but then it seems a little excessive for a battery…

I returned across town via the shops, looking for a certain jewellery shop where I had bought earrings for Dizzy last time. Unfortunately, the shop is no longer there. I returned to Toads Place (the gig) through one of the college's lawned quadrangles, reminded of those wonderful stop-frame sequences in **The Graduate**, Simon and Garfunkel floating around in my mind. Arrived back at the venue humming **Scarborough Fair**, and wondering if Dustin Hoffman has ever been to Jimmy Corrigans*. There were already a handful of people outside. Most of them said they'd been to the Boston show and that it was "aawwssmm" which seems to be the most common phrase here for something better-than-alright. Chatted to Priv, who complained affably about the band turning up during the day to eat the crew's lunch. It's a shame we can't work with him all the time – I miss the abuse.

Returned in the afternoon sunshine to the hotel, stopping off at a burger joint for junk-lunch and mooching around the tourist shops that sell the Yale t-shirts. Got back to my room to find a fax from Dream Theatre's manager to request passes for Mike, their drummer, for tonight's show. Called him and told him it was no problem.

Soundcheck wasn't pleasant. We've played Toad's three times now, and although we always bring the house down my sound at centre stage is always atrocious – it's something to do with the room.

After soundcheck there was an interview with a cable TV team which, unfortunately, went on almost until showtime, so it was all a bit of a dash to get back to the hotel and pick up my things. I could have really done with a couple of hours in bed at some point today, and consequently felt a little tired during the show. I don't think anyone in the crowd noticed – they were all too busy going nuclear! What a crowd. I've probably said this before, but sometimes I feel *we* should pay to see *them*.

After the show, I was complimented by the huge guy who was doing security. He reached down and patted me on the head as I staggered, dripping, into the dressing room. We later signed stuff for people who had come back to say hello. Most memorable was a conversation with Peter, a guy who looks a bit like Springsteen, and a hard-case at first glance. He told me he'd been in Somalia a couple of years ago and had a young girl die in his arms while he was trying to find a vein to save her life. Consequently he'd had a very bad year trying to come to terms with it, and our music had helped him through it. There's more to all this than selling records.

*Amusement arcade on the front at Scarborough.

Tuesday 8 August *New York, Tramps*

Woke up to the unmistakable sounds of Manhattan filtering into my bunk from 21st Street outside. Trucks thundering by, car horns, people shouting, and the city's peculiar ambience as its many sounds echo from the tall buildings. In Manhattan you can actually *hear* the heat on hot days. There's also the characteristic taste of metal in the air. You could drop me into this place blindfolded and I would know I was here.

Today's show was to be unusual in a number of respects. There are two bands playing this same venue today – Del Amitri are doing a live radio broadcast at 7.00pm, and we're on at 10.15. Our soundcheck will be at 12.00 midday, so the crew are already inside Tramps club setting up the show. I snoozed a while longer, but was eventually forced out of bed by pains in my stomach and an urgent need to visit the bathroom. Oh dear. I was overtaken by the suspicion that I was going down with something. I didn't feel quite right. Crossed the road and entered the club. Even the glitziest of nightclubs feel somewhat shabby in the cold light of morning (like many of the relationships they spawn), and Tramps ain't glitzy at all. I kept my head down so as not to attract the crew's attention - I always feel partly to blame for the difficult gigs - as I crossed the dance floor in urgent need of the toilet. I won't go into too much detail, other than to say it would appear my insides had turned to liquid. Returned from the toilet feeling relieved but in no less pain. Maybe it was something I ate.

I decided to go to Macy's and check out their supplies of Halston Z14, so I hailed a cab and drove uptown in the hot sunshine of a high summer's morning in New York City, bumping over the holes in the road that the city can't afford to fix, through the sea of faces of every nation on the sidewalks, the advertisement hoardings, the 'bargain' electronics shops, the delis and department stores. When we got to Macy's I got out of the cab, realising I hadn't made a note of where I'd come from (I know I mentioned 21st Street earlier, but I have since found that out!) Oops. Well, I made a beeline for the correct part of the shop, but to no avail. They don't have talc or shower gel either. Came back out and hailed a cab. The cab driver was called Obi and she was from Nigeria. What a brave, brave girl to drive a cab in this town. She'd never heard of Tramps, so I pointed back down 6th Avenue and said, "That way". We had to go back up 5th because of the one way system and, eventually, after no small amount of trouble, I recognised a poster on a wall and decided we must be close. I paid the cab and walked around the corner where I found Tramps, just where I'd left it, on 21st & 6th. Some people live and learn. Some people only live and live.

Soundcheck surprised us all by sounding a lot better than it looked. As we were running through *Hard as Love,* Del Amitri's crew were loading in. They stopped to listen and nodded approvingly. My stomach was feeling progressively worse as the day went on. We left the venue and took cabs to the Howard Johnson on 8th & 51st. Again, I decided to go walkabout and try and locate a battery for my laptop. I made the mistake of spending most of the afternoon walking around Manhattan and gradually wore myself out. When I got back to the hotel I felt extraordinarily weak and, again, in desperate need of the toilet. My digestive system was still turning all incoming solids into outgoing liquids. I necked half a bottle of Pepto-Bismol – a fluorescent pink American potion that settles the stomach (whilst dying the insides black, including the tongue as I had discovered a few years back in Canada – I thought I'd caught the Black Death!) and went to bed for the rest of the day, foregoing dinner with the record company.

At 8.30 I was summoned from a deep sleep by Tim, who was making the alarm call for departure in 45-minutes. I climbed out of bed and I knew immediately that I was in trouble. My head was pounding, my body was aching, and my brain was demanding that I go nowhere other than back to bed. I staggered into the bathroom in order to commune with nature once again, before downing Nurofen, Pepto-Bismol and showering in an attempt to get myself into the mental shape required to spend two hours in front of a New York audience.

Back at the venue the place was packed with an enthusiastic crowd. Downstairs in the dressing room I discovered some chicken pieces, which I ate in order to give my body something to liquidize during the show, and drank a couple of beers in order to give myself the will to do what must be done. David Stopps, who used to manage Marillion in the early days, popped his head in the dressing room to say hello. He was with another chap who manages Suzanne Vega. Also, Dwayne Welch had come over to see us. He's the son of The Shadows bass player Bruce, the former business partner of John Arnison, and the man who pestered me to join Marillion. I wasn't really in the mood for meeting and greeting. It was almost a relief to get on stage and get on with it. The sound was not great - a cross between a riveting shop in a Clyde shipyard and the Battle of Borodino - but the crowd were in phenomenal spirits and singing along with every word. I was carried along by the energy of the people who more than compensated for my physical and acoustical woes. During the final encore I threw myself into the crowd and, in so doing, panicked Stuart into making a run across the stage to help me. I didn't need any help of course, our audiences are total sweethearts but he wasn't to know. In the dash to get to me he knocked an ice bucket into the mains distribution transformer, which duly went bang and all the backline went off, leaving Ian drumming on his own. We had almost finished the set so it wasn't as big a disaster as it might have been earlier. I shouted goodnight to the crowd who had taken it all in good spirits and were cheering as we left the stage. What a finish!

After the show I said hello to Tony and Susie Smith and met a few people from the Hit & Run office in New York, before returning to the hotel to sleep. I climbed into bed wondering how I'd managed to get up in the first place, let alone perform for two hours.

Wednesday 9 August *New Jersey, Club Bene*

Woke up feeling decidedly better. It was around mid-day and the long sleep had helped – I felt much stronger. I went downstairs and asked a porter where I can get coffee. "Across the street," he said with characteristic New York don't-give-a-damn. I found a deli over the road and brought a coffee back to my room, where I phoned home to see how Sue, Sofie and Nial are getting on. They're all still in Yorkshire with my mum and dad. Everyone's fine and they all went to the seaside yesterday. It's still sunny and warm in England.

I had to be out of my room, so I packed and dumped my bags in Tim's room. Got a message from John saying we were to meet up with Dwayne for lunch at the Parker Meridian. After parting company with John back in '89, Dwayne returned to record company work. He got a job with BMG Music in the Far East, living and working in Hong Kong for the last five years. I remember bumping into him on a 747 a couple of years ago as we returned from Brazil to Heathrow.

He has recently been transferred to New York, hence his presence at the show. He said he'd really enjoyed it, and chatted about old times with the boys while I tried to look interested and tried not to look envious. Unfortunately I'm having to live with the fact that the band was commercially more successful before I got involved, and it's sometimes frustrating to sit in a circle of people reminiscing about parties in posh hotels, hiring the entire upper decks of 747's, helicoptering into the backstage areas of large open air gigs etc, while I remain painfully aware that we're currently staying round the corner in the Howard Johnson. In many ways it's probably worse for the rest of the band, who have had further to fall than me. Oh well. I sipped orange tea and declined lunch, still feeling somewhat peculiar at the idea of food.

Dwayne had to leave for a meeting, so we wished him well and returned to our dodgy hotel to meet up with the bus for the short drive to New Jersey, arriving around 4.00 in the afternoon at Club Bene, Sayerville. There was an open air pool at the venue and we were told to feel free to use it, so while the soundcheck was in the initial stages I took my bathrobe and set up camp poolside, stretched out on the diving board, catching a few rays and floating around in the afternoon sunshine.

I soundchecked still wet and wrapped in my robe, and then chatted to the kids outside already waiting at the door for tonight's show. During a conversation I had with one of the girls at the Philadelphia show, I had mentioned my quest to find a top hat for Nial, and here she was again, with the very thing! She said she knew where she could get one and that she thought I probably wouldn't have time, so she was making me a present of it. What a sweetie! Later on the same afternoon, I learned from the bus driver that yet another present had been handed to him for me. It turned out to be two flasks of Z14 talc from Keith and Jane, the guys I'd walked all over Philadelphia with, trying to find some. It's a hard life being a singer, eh?

The show went well. Technical problems seem to be fewer now. From the stage I thanked Robyn for the top hat and Jane for the talc – it must have sounded like a peculiar acknowledgement.

After the show, three Federal officers boarded the bus and announced a drug raid, lining up Priv, Grant, Stuart and Alan - legs spread and hands up - along the bus. A tense and terrified silence followed as they contemplated spending the rest of the night in jail, before the officers announced that they were big fans of the band and that it was all a joke. Pete had asked them to stage a raid for a laugh. It was some time before the colour returned to the faces of the crew. Unfortunately I wasn't there to witness it, I was still in the club signing stuff and talking to people.

The trip to Cleveland turned out to be a 12-hour one. We drove from New Jersey back to New York JFK to drop Priv at the airport. He is returning to Europe to do two shows with Mike and the Mechanics in Germany so, for the next three shows, we have Mike Scarfe -an English sound engineer who, I'm told, was Priv's original mentor - mixing out-front sound.

Thursday 10 August *Cleveland:* Day off

Woke around 10.00 and climbed out of my bunk, wandering forward to talk to bus driver John and find out where we were. I was expecting to be in Cleveland by now, as I was supposed to be doing phone interviews this morning. It turned out that John had got somewhat lost during the night in the process of detouring to JFK, and we were still in Pennsylvania. He wasn't expecting to cross the state line to Ohio for another hour, so it would be 2.00 in the afternoon before we were to arrive in Cleveland. There goes another day-off!

I checked into room 502 at the Stouffer Hotel and showered before Tim arrived to start me off on my interviews to Quebec City.

I spent the rest of the afternoon snoozing and relaxing, and later went down to the 'flats' area - Cleveland's riverside, bordered by nightclubs, cafés and restaurants - to have dinner in an Italian restaurant – calamari followed by sole. Very nice. Returned to the hotel and went to bed early, ordering breakfast in bed where I was determined to stay until at least 12.00 midday.

Friday 11 August *Cleveland, Odeon*

Had breakfast and lazed around for a while before going out for a mooch round the shopping arcade next door. Didn't buy anything. Outside it was another gorgeous day, so I wandered back down to the flats again and spent the afternoon sitting out by the river, drinking Belgian cherry beer (which tastes a little like cider) and had a late lunch of seafood, before crossing the street to the Odeon – tonight's venue. Inside, new sound-man, Mike, was soundchecking the band and trying to get to grips with the daunting task of mixing us for the first time without any rehearsal. It was obvious I wouldn't be required for a while, so I returned to the river to drink coffee and watch the pleasure-craft making their way down to Lake Erie. I found myself humming *Camp Granada* to myself – "*Guys are swimming... guys are sailing*". Recreation is to American culture what gardening is to British culture. They take it very seriously.

Sunday 13 August *Columbus, Newport Music Hall*

The weather just keeps getting hotter. We arrived in Columbus late morning, and I decided against checking into dayrooms in the middle-of-nowhere in favour of staying on the bus and hanging around at the gig. The bus parked at the rear of the Newport Music Hall, and quite a few of us tumbled out into the hottest day so far (and I mean HOT) in search of a café. We found Café Insomnia as it turned out, my favourite café of the tour. I ordered a café mocha with coconut and cinnamon, and sat down with Pete, Mike, Grant and Alan. Ella Fitzgerald was playing in the background as we sipped coffee and slowly woke up. As it turned out, I was to spend most of the day in the Insomnia: the coffees and the fruit teas were great, and the atmosphere perfect for doing a little catching up with the diary. I had nowhere else to go except the bus, and outside was so incredibly hot and humid that one was better off inside. During the day I got talking to Matthew (who makes the best iced-coffee on the planet) and I invited him to the show. From then coffees were on the house, so I had even less reason to leave. I bought a t-shirt that simply says, 'Café Insomnia, Columbus, Ohio.' Around 3.00 in the afternoon I wandered into the gig and gave Grant a hand eq-ing the monitors. It was time well spent – I ended up with the best stage-sound I have had so far. It's funny how some halls sound good for singers while some, which sound good for the band (Toads in Newhaven is a good example) sound awful at centre stage. In my experience, the room has more influence on a stage sound than any amount of monitor equipment. I was enjoying the sound and having the place to myself, so much that I sang and played for longer than I should have in the afternoon, and wore myself out a little. I was singing Stevie Wonder's *Living for the City* when I noticed an old black fella had wandered in off the street through the open back door, and was listening and nodding in approval. He said, "Wow man! You got SOUL!" Praise indeed. I did a little work on Pete and Mark's vocal sounds too which made a difference, especially to Pete whose pitching during *Easter* later was spot-on.

During the soundcheck I mentioned to Wes that I'd always fancied one of those pink, paisley-patterned Fender Telecasters. He agreed it was the kind of guitar that would suit me down to the ground and, moreover, that he knew where he could get me one for 500 dollars. His local music store in Tampa, Florida, had one in the window. Fabulous! He offered to sort it out, so I gave him a credit card and he said he could arrange for me to have my hands on it before I leave America. Whoopee!

The show was to be the hottest of the tour, in all senses. There is no air conditioning in the hall, so the stage temperature was 100 degrees plus. During *The Great Escape* I felt that movement of everything which always follows oxygen starvation and precedes fainting, but I took a few deep breaths and recovered enough to finish the song, sitting with my head between my legs during the guitar solo and giggling for no particular reason.

After the show I sat outside in the street, somewhat exhausted, chatting and signing my name for the fans as usual, when a man with a vaguely familiar face asked if he could have his photograph taken with me. His girlfriend took the picture while he asked me who the astronaut was in the publicity photograph we'd done at Battersea Power Station. I said it was meant to be Buzz Aldrin. He said, "I'm Rick. My dad is Neil Armstrong and I want to tell you that some of the songs on your new album could be the story of my dad's life – the fame thing. That's just how it was for him." Needless to say, I'm still recovering from the encounter. I would have come to America for this conversation alone. I gave him my address and he promised to send me a copy of our photograph together, and maybe a signed photo from his dad. I boarded the bus with my head spinning, well and truly star-struck!

We had a new bus arrive today to replace the one we started with, which was itself a substitute. There was some problem or other… anyway the new one is bigger, swisher and, crucially, has slightly wider beds and a smoother suspension. Each bus has its own driver, so we must get to know a new face about the 'house'. It was a shame to lose our previous driver, John. I had grown to like him.

We returned to the 'hotel nowhere' to shower up, and Dan and Dana Sherman (Web, USA) went out at 2.00 in the morning and procured the best chicken burgers I have ever tasted. Ate, got fat, went to bed full of regret and dreamt of walking on the moon...

Monday 14 August *Grand Rapids, The Orbit Room*

For some reason - probably the process of adjustment to the new bus - I didn't sleep terribly well, and when new bus driver Dave roused us at 8.30 to say we were at the hotel in Grand Rapids I had only just got to sleep. I directed all my attentions to trying to check into the hotel, find my room, and go back to bed without waking up – a frequently practiced art when touring. Unfortunately the reception staff at the Holiday Inn were brain-dead and, after waiting half an hour in reception, Steve Rothery and I were given a room to share. We trudged along the corridor, like zombies with luggage, to discover the room was already occupied. Steve went back down in the lift while I lay face-down into the corridor carpet, causing some consternation among passing guests who, I think, assumed I was the victim of some kind of attack. We eventually occupied an empty twin-room and went to bed.

I slept until around 12.00 and then got up and wandered over to the gig, which was round the back of the hotel. At reception I bumped into Judy from IRS records, who accompanied me over to the Orbit Room. It's the same venue as we've played before – it used to be called Club Eastbrook. When we got over there I learned that Wes had lost his guitar! It was last seen leaning up against the wall of the Newport Music Theatre in Columbus, but it wasn't in the truck this morning. It's a beautiful and rare Takamine Santa Fé and it's not insured. He called Columbus, but they don't have it. It's almost certainly been stolen. Tonight he will use one of Steve's. What a terrible shame. Wes has worked really hard on this tour and had to swallow an entire bakery of humble pie looking after our guitars. Asking Wes to look after my red Strat is comparable to asking Frans Klammer to look after Eddie the Eagle's skis. I'm more than a little aware of the irony Wes must feel every time he passes a guitar to me, and now he's lost his own instrument. Not fair. But then, what is? I didn't have the heart to remind him about the pink Telecaster, so I mentioned it to Tim and left Wes to his work while Judy accompanied me across the street to Fridays burger place for a spot of breakfast. We chatted for some time, and I called the hotel to invite the boys over for lunch before we had to drive into town for a live radio performance on acoustic guitars.

It went okay. We hadn't rehearsed so there were a couple of interesting chords in there, and it was much too early in the day for me to hit any high notes, but these things are all about spirit and a sense of occasion in doing something different, so everyone seemed happy.

Pete, Steve and I met up with Ian and Mark at a record store to sign sleeves for the fifty-or-so people gathered there, before returning to the Orbit Room for soundcheck. Priv had returned from his lightning trip to Europe and was in good spirits despite being exhausted from the journey, so Mike was to mix tonight's show. This is one of those rooms that completely changes from cavernous echoes at soundcheck to 'studio dead' when the audience are in. Tonight was no exception. We hadn't any side-fills and the stage sound was very isolated. I returned to the hotel and floated around in the pool and poolside jacuzzi for half an hour before returning to the show. We were taken in the back way through a launderette, and I was reminded of **The Man from Uncle** (Napoleon Solo and Illya Kuryakin used to enter the secret nerve centre through a curtained lift at the rear of a dry-cleaners).

The show was a disappointment for me on a number of levels. The audience was somewhat smaller than I remembered last time, my sound was dry and lifeless and, worst of all, my voice had finally started to succumb to the rigours of the schedule and was hoarse and patchy. I had lost falsetto completely and there were areas of my normal range that just weren't there to be had. I could tell that while Mike was doing his best out-front, he wasn't sufficiently familiar with the set to do a comparable job to Priv who tonight was simply a spectator. I cancelled the first encore and removed *The Uninvited Guest* from the second encore. I physically couldn't have sung it.

After the show there was a meet-and-greet on the balcony. Said hello to Arris Hampers, the DJ responsible for our fame here, who lamented the fact that we didn't have a day off in Grand Rapids to socialise. Everyone said the show was great and that I was singing well! I seem to get away with murder.

Thursday 17 August *Montreal, Le Spectrum*

I felt the bus stop in the darkness and wondered once more where we were. Drifted back into sleep and was woken by Tim saying I could check into the hotel. Decided not to bother and stayed on the bus, remembering that the Spectrum is in the centre of everything and not knowing where the hotel might be. I remained in my bunk for an hour or so and then entered the venue. It was around 11.00am, but there were already a handful of kids waiting outside the venue. A Venezuelan girl pleaded with me to come back to Caracas – if only these decisions were that simple. It's strange when people ask you why you don't do things that you passionately would like to do. It's difficult to come up with any answers.

The crew were busy assembling the backline on the stage. Le Spectrum is a large club well-suited to live music, well maintained and staffed by professionals. Everyone was pleasant and helpful, and I was shown downstairs to the production office to use the phone. There's some problem or other with paying for the new guitar, so I had to get on the phone myself and sort it out. They'll have it freighted to the hotel in Poughkeepsie for the last show of the tour. I helped myself to coffee, made myself a tuna roll, and went back up on stage to talk to Mark about the set. I would like to recite the French *Surf Babe* speech before *Beautiful* tonight, so I asked him to recreate the flutes which accompany it. I was planning to ask some of the kids from the line outside to write it down for me. We are, of course, in the French speaking part of Canada now, and I know they'll appreciate my making the effort. I've been having trouble hearing the keyboard line that I play in *Easter* lately so I spent some time reprogramming that.

I took a walk along the Rue Ste. Catherine and mooched about in and out of the second hand shops looking at guitars, CD players and old watches. Even *I* am not naive enough to buy a second-hand CD player from a shop on the other side of the world from me.

I returned to Le Spectrum, stopping outside once again to be photographed and to scribble autographs. I'm sure I've signed more record sleeves than we've officially sold. There must be only a handful of **Season's End** sleeves on Earth without my scrawl on them. I spent the rest of the day hanging around in the hall, listening to Priv eq-ing the PA, and shuffling around to the music. Soundcheck took a while, but it was all sounding pretty good from where I was standing. I had to be careful with my voice, which is sounding a little cleaner today, although my throat is now hurting.

After soundcheck I walked back a couple of blocks with Steve R to the Intercontinental Hotel. When I got up to my room Mark had beaten me to it. We were supposed to be sharing a twin room but they had given us a double. Much as I love Mad Jack I wasn't going to sleep with him, so I walked back to the Spectrum and got on the bus to snooze for half an hour, muttering to myself about having been inconvenienced. It sounds petty, doesn't it? But, at this stage in the day, any energy I expend has to be deducted from available energy for the show.

I returned to the bus which was parked at the front of Le Spectrum. By now there were a lot of people making their way into the show and I was immediately recognised, but I managed to board the bus without being detained. I slept for half an hour and then made my way back round to the rear of the building to the dressing room. I was feeling less than ready for the show, so I decided to have a shower to wake myself up. The band hadn't arrived back from the Intercontinental so I had the dressing room to myself. I dried off and helped myself to a beer from the tray of iced beers in the corner before starting the search for my stage trousers – a nightly ritual. We haven't got a wardrobe person with us in America, so there's always an element of uncertainty when it comes to gathering together clothes for the show.

By now the band had returned, so chaos reigned in the dressing room while the five of us tried to locate clothes and prepare ourselves for the forthcoming show. When we finally made it onto the stage it became immediately apparent that this was to be a special evening. There was a great atmosphere in the crowd which the whole band was feeding off, spiralling up during the show to something really electric. By the end of the set the response was deafening, and similar to some of the rare French shows from the past. We gave our usual two encores and returned upstairs to the dressing room, listening to the entire building pulsating to crowd noise. We returned to the stage once more to play *Made Again.* I thanked the crowd for the best show of the tour so far and said goodnight. Ten minutes later, with the house lights on and the stage equipment partially dismantled, there was no let-up in the crowd noise, so we felt obliged to do something else. The keyboards were already down and the monitors no longer connected, so Steve played acoustic guitar and I sang *Hide your Love Away,* a John Lennon song. As we finished and the hall once more erupted, I was moved to climb into the crowd. I lay down on the uplifted hands (something I have never done) and felt myself floating as I was passed around on a moving carpet of arms. It's a great feeling – a combination of trust, respect and of strength in numbers of like-minded people. When I arrived back at the stage I waved goodbye once more and we returned again to the dressing room. And still they cheered, and still the floor boomed below us. It was impractical by now to do more, so Steve and I went back down to take a bow and wave one last goodbye. Only now did the hall begin to empty. Five encores! That's a first. I finally got changed and showered in the dressing room. Outside there were still people waiting at the bus when I arrived in the street, over an hour after leaving the stage. One of the young women said she works with young kids with psychological problems and that she found **Brave** to be an inspired piece of work. That's the second time in three weeks.

Saturday 19 August *Poughkeepsie, The Chance*

By 3.00 I had probably got off to sleep. By 4.30 I was in that valuable deep sleep that not even the rumbling and rocking of the bus can interrupt. Tim Bricusse, however, was determined, and I was shaken awake to be told that this was the American border and we must all go to the passport office to show our documents. He gave me mine (tour managers never allow me to carry my own passport, it wouldn't last a week) and I passed Alan, returning from the office. He said he'd been asked to spell the word banana by the passport official. As I entered the office, Ian was coming the other way. He muttered, "Xylophone…" to himself as he passed by. By now I was in the blackest of moods having been disturbed from deep sleep and about to have my intelligence insulted by some border official. I decided I would spell imbecile, irrespective of whatever word I was asked to spell, and irrespective of the bureaucratic consequences. I approached the uniformed official and slapped my passport down, assuming a confrontational-yet-bored pose against the counter. She glanced through the passport and waved me on. No 'orangutan', no 'Leicester Square', no 'success', 'yacht', not even a 'mouse'. I returned to the bus and said, disappointedly, that I hadn't been asked to spell anything. Alan and Ian laughed – they hadn't been asked either, it was just a wind up. Bastards.

I returned to bed and woke up at 12.00 in Poughkeepsie. Entered the Sheraton Hotel after the long drive south from Quebec and, to my relief, set eyes on a guitar-sized cardboard box behind reception. I checked in and they handed me the box, which I opened at the bar while ordering coffee and toast. The bar girl was already in conversation with bus driver Dave. They were talking about "four hots and a cot", a phrase only understood by prison-inmates. "Keep your voice down!" she was saying, embarrassed in case anyone from the management might hear. The phrase refers to hot meals and a bed. It would seem that when people get out of jail here they get jobs in hotels, or drive buses for rock n'roll bands…

My new guitar looked awfully basic at first glance, but I'm reliably informed by Wes and Steve R that Fender Tele's are just that. I gave it to Wes to take to the gig and then went upstairs to check into my room. The view from the window was a wide panorama of a woodland valley, dominated by two bridges; a suspension bridge and an old viaduct that span the Hudson River. The viaduct is quite a sight and, at first glance, appears to be of timber construction. I was later to discover that it is in fact made of iron which was supplied by the British Navy at the end of the last century. There wasn't enough iron in the USA in those days to build such a project. The bridge had caught fire several years ago (which explains it's black and brown colour) and is now disused.

I decided to go out shopping and took a cab to The Galleria, an out of town shopping mall. Like so many American towns and cities, there are very few shops in the centre of town. I wandered around the mall - a characterless balconied Arndale Centre of a place - and bought mini Etch-a-Sketch toys for Nial and Sofie and a handbag for my mother. By now I was hungry, and I had heard a rumour from the receptionist at the hotel that there was a good little steak restaurant overlooking the river called The River Station. I hailed a cab which took me there from the mall. It was, once again, a beautiful day and there were lots of guys in boats enjoying the river and the sunshine. I sat out on the terrace watching people zooming about on wave-riders (like motorbikes on water) and was reminded of my thrills and spills on the ocean at Virginia Beach a few years ago (I have a scar below my lower lip). I ordered steak from the friendly waitress and relaxed in the sun, reading the menu which gave me a potted history of the establishment and the surrounding area (that's how I found out about the bridge and the Navy). The River Station started out as a riverside hostelry to accommodate and entertain the river traders. I imagined some sort of Wild West saloon on the river. When the steak arrived it was as big as a pair of shoes and I couldn't manage to consume more than half of it. I gave it my best shot, drank a beer and pondered, once again, that I couldn't really grumble if I dropped down dead tomorrow. I returned on foot back up the hill to the hotel, stopping to sign something for a young couple who shouted, "Hey, Steve! We hope you're having a nice afternoon!"

When I got back to the hotel I was late for soundcheck, so I dropped my shopping in my room and made my way to The Chance, where I was detained in the car park in order to sign a Dodge van. It belongs to one of our serious US fans, and is black with various Marillion imagery, illustrations and logos meticulously and accurately air brushed into the paintwork. Art on wheels. Inside the gig the band was already jamming, so I made my way on stage and joined in. For once, I didn't get my wrists slapped for being late. Tonight is to be the last show of the American leg of the tour, and everyone seemed relaxed and looking forward to the evening ahead. The Chance is positively tiny and I can't really move much on stage without crashing into someone or something else. The audience are almost up my nose here, but we've been a few times before and there's always a terrific atmosphere.

The show was to be a long one. I like to carry on singing until I drop when I know I'm going to get a break of several days afterwards. I can't remember how many encores we played; we just kept going! We were more or less doing requests!

After the show we returned to the hotel and partied in one of the ballrooms. I remember Mark doing the trick where you pull the tablecloth out from under everything. I winced and turned my back to the ensuing sounds of shattering glass and crockery.

Can't remember going to bed, but I must have because I woke up in bed the following morning. I found a hotel exit sign on the hall carpet outside my room. I would have bet twenty quid it was something to do with Jack or Priv.

Tuesday 19 September *Cambridge – Wolverhampton Civic*

Didn't sleep at all well. I got through the night in 20-minute naps, unable to fall into deep sleep. I gave up trying at 8.30, so decided I would get up and go back into Cambridge and continue the search for new trousers. I took a cab into town through rush-hour traffic and returned to a shop with Paul Smith stuff in the window. No luck. They didn't have anything that looked good once tried on. I ordered a cab back to the hotel, packed and checked out.

Had a spot of breakfast with Paul, and then left for Wolverhampton in the hire car. There was just the two of us. Ian had gone overnight on Sunday with the crew. Mark had gone home and was coming up on the train. I tried to sleep during the journey but couldn't. We arrived at the Britannia Hotel in Wolverhampton and set about the protracted process of checking-in. I wanted a non-smoking room and that's what seemed to cause all the trouble. I decided to leave them to it, so I left my bags in reception and walked down to the Civic Hall in order to retrieve a pair of my old boots. My new shoes were still killing me. It was a rare pleasure to get backstage and lace myself into footwear that didn't hurt.

I walked back to the hotel through the streets of Wolverhampton which seem to comprise mostly of building societies, banks, and fish n'chip shops. Mark never made it to soundcheck, having forgotten to get off the train and ending up in Liverpool or somewhere. It didn't help. At least he got to Wolverhampton for the gig, which wasn't terrific.

Wednesday 20 September *Wolverhampton-Manchester Apollo*

Woke at 11.00 to the ringing telephone. It was Paul telling me I have an interview with **The Times**, and could I come to his room when I'm awake and call them. I couldn't get the shower to work, so I ran a bath and cleaned my teeth, trying to wake up and become articulate enough for a chat with a "proper" newspaper. The phone rang again while I was soaking in the bath. I returned to the bedroom, naked and dripping, to discover it was Paul again trying to hurry me up. "If you look through the window, you'll be able to see me," he said. Sure enough, there he was, at the window opposite my room, grinning at my wet nakedness. "You should close your curtains, y'know," he said. I got dry and dressed and hurried over to Paul's room where he called the journalist in question, Nicola Venning. She was writing a column in the business section about people who work from home and rely on computer technology for their work. Angie Moxham, my newfound PR friend, had connected me to her. Like everyone else, she thought Marillion are some kind of Scottish heavy metal band. I explained the truth to her, and invited her to the London show next week. The interview went well, and she said she was more than happy with what we'd done – a lot of talk about my Macintosh Powerbook 100. Apple ought to give me a freebie after all that (they didn't).

I checked out of the Britannia and we left Wolverhampton for Manchester. It didn't take long. After America all these British dates feel like they're next door to each other. Checked into Sachas hotel (which looks like a nightclub from the outside), and had a spot of brunch in the hotel restaurant with Ian. I'm currently nursing an injury somewhere in my upper back, which is causing a lot of pain in my left arm. I felt something happen during the Forum show in London, and it's been hurting like hell ever since. The hotel in Manchester had a health centre, so I asked if there was any chance of a massage. They hadn't got a masseur but they booked me in at The Britannia Hotel down the road for 4.00pm. It was only 3.00, so I had a session on the sun bed first.

The band left for soundcheck at 3.45, so I got Paul to drop me off. The massage was a bargain at only a fiver – I remember being charged over a hundred pounds for the one I had in Paris on the last tour. Anyway, the massage helped to ease the pain a little but not as much as I'd hoped.

Paul returned to pick me up at 4.30 and drove me down to the Apollo, where there were a few fans gathered at the stage door. I could already hear the band soundchecking so I didn't stop to chat. Soundcheck went well – Mark Kelly had joined us today! The Apollo has a round-fronted stage which sweeps forward in front of the PA system, so if I'm in the middle up at the edge, I can hear the out-front sound and watch the band without leaving the stage. I did this during

Easter and basked in the phenomenal sound Priv had put together – he just keeps getting better. I haven't heard a vocal sound as good as this since I saw Peter Gabriel back in '87 at The Bercy in Paris. I was singing well, much better than yesterday in Wolverhampton.

We returned to the hotel where I spent an hour enjoying **Das Boot**, a re-run of the excellent German drama based on a U-boat crew hunting the Atlantic convoys during the Second World War. It's beautifully shot, like a Bergman movie, and brilliantly directed and performed. I feel claustrophobic watching it. I can smell the oil and the sweat, and the tension between men crammed together in a small, enclosed metal machine. Essential viewing.

We returned to the Apollo for the show which was, I think, the best so far. The sound was terrific, as I knew it would be, and we had no technical problems. My voice was feeling powerful and controllable, and once again Geoff Hooper's Concert Sound monitors were dreamlike. The team we have with us on this tour are probably the best I've worked with in their respective fields. You can't really go wrong with people like this around you. After the show my spirits were high. I spent almost half an hour in the shower, enjoying the slow burning return from exhaustion and sweat to reality and freshness. I went back down to the stage to watch the crew clearing the last few pieces of equipment. Priv invited me next door to join the crew in an after-show drink. While I was outside signing stuff for the after-show hangers, I learned from Paul that his wife Annie was not well and that he was to return to Liverpool, so I told him I would improvise my way back to the hotel after I'd had a drink with the chaps (i.e ask the crew bus driver for a lift!).

The crew were in high spirits, especially after the lows of last night. I sat enjoying the wind-ups and listening to the banter between Priv and Alan, and between Brian and our dear cook, Helen, and the Universe according to Cod (our merchandiser and East-London loudmouth), all in fine form like pirates after a successful raid. I had a couple of bottles of Newcastle Brown (after the handful of Becks I'd consumed during the gig), and was saved from sickness by the landlady who denied my demands for a Snowball to finish it off. I was surrounded by the local crew of Manchester's finest: huge, tattooed, shaven-headed, hobnail booted hard-cases. I can't resist ordering Snowballs when I'm in such company, it always elicits an amusing four-lettered response. Fell out of the pub feeling somewhat vague and onto the crew bus where I ate a sandwich – the contents of which remained peculiar but undiscovered. To my relief I managed to get to sleep at the hotel without discovering later what was in the sandwich. What a great day!

Thursday 21 September *Leeds, Town and Country Club*

Woke feeling remarkably un-hungover. However, on getting out of bed, I realised that the pain in my arm was worse than ever – a sort of cramp in my upper left arm, which seems to be coming from my left shoulder blade. I decided to cancel my hotel in Leeds and go overnight to Glasgow with the crew, so I called Paul on his mobile to let him know. He was already back from Liverpool and downstairs settling up the hotel bill. I asked him how his wife was feeling. He said it's food poisoning, so all self-induced. He's all heart. It was still half an hour before checkout time, so I went down to the health centre for another half-hour on the sun bed. When I checked out there were no telephone charges on my extras. My phone *had* been behaving strangely. Whoopee.

We drove the M62 across the Pennines and past the huge reservoir, reduced to a small lake by this summer's drought – the Yorkshire Water Authority are already planning water rations. There is, of course, no 'greenhouse effect', just a lot of hysterical hippy talk.

We arrived at The Holiday Inn in Leeds, and I dropped my bags behind reception for Paul to bring to the show. I hung onto my laptop so that I could catch up on the diary. I found a shoe repair shop, bought dubbin and laces for my boots, and had some of the lace holes repaired before wandering off in search of a certain cafe I'd discovered last time. I think I'm a creature of habit. I'm always on the lookout for new, pleasant and interesting things, but I remain loyal to my past discoveries too. It took a while to find it, but I eventually settled down with a huge cappuccino and a sandwich and began tapping away at the keys of this machine to record yesterday's events. I spent all afternoon in there and eventually wandered off in the general direction of the T & C, stopping to ask for directions on the way.

Soundcheck was uneventful – that's how I like them; our 'events' are usually technical problems. Today is Amy's birthday (Amy is the new cook), so I wished her a happy birthday as she served me up with a tuna steak with carrots and courgettes. After soundcheck I climbed aboard the bus and slept for an hour before returning back through the front entrance, failing to recognise my sisters, Gill and Sue, who were having trouble getting in. I had got their names wrong – I had forgotten about them being married! I'd also forgot to leave passes for my old school chum, John Leedale, who must have had the time of his life persuading security to let him in. Oh well! Never mind.

The show went really well, despite the fact that I was still on the loo when the intro music was already playing. I only just made it. The crowd lived up to my memories of them from the **Brave** tour, going fairly berserk from the moment we started until the end. Afterwards I decided I would go and chat to my guests before I showered, so as not to keep them waiting. I returned to the hall barefoot, wearing my bathrobe inside out, and said hello to Mum and Dad and sisters. They seemed a little tired so I didn't stop long, and returned upstairs to shower under the gig's excellent Aqualisa showers (it's the little things).

I packed and went down to the crew bus, where I had a long chat with Geoff who told me all about Concert Sound, the PA company he's part of along with his immaculate cousin, Adrian. He told me how it had all started in the Seventies with WEM columns and how they had bought the first ever Martin system and the first Midas desk; how they had gone on to help the designers perfect the components, and on through various systems and bands, until today. He's almost evangelical in his passion for the ultimate PA. It's always a treat to listen to the history of a labour of love, especially when you can appreciate the end result to the extent that I do. We all went upstairs to sing happy birthday to Amy, and share strawberry cream cake and champagne. I didn't drink mine, the stuff gives me a headache. I walked up to the front of the bus to get undressed. Tim, Alan and Brian were at the front upstairs, gazing out at the road which was weaving its way up between the wild hills of North Yorkshire. I said goodnight and slept fitfully, unable to cope with the size of the pillow – obviously designed for real men with broad shoulders…

Friday 22 September *Glasgow:* Day off

I have a window in the wall of my bunk. They don't usually have them, so it was something of a luxury to slide back the little curtain and squint out at the morning light. I could see flagpoles, with the logo of Hilton hotels fluttering on the flags above in the Glasgow morning breeze. I slid out of bed, onto the floor, and began the process of gathering together my clothes, jewellery, boots, socks and bags from the places I couldn't remember leaving them the night before. I staggered through the rotating door, into the reception hall of the Hilton and checked into room 1216. Wes was also in reception, and invited me to join him for a spot of breakfast. Before returning to the Hilton's fake American diner to dine with a real American I dropped my bags in my room, wincing under the worsening pain of my left arm. I booked myself in at the basement health centre for another massage at 12.45. The staff here are all very helpful and friendly, and we were served cappuccinos by a smiley waitress while Wes worked his way through a sandwich as big as a bungalow. We were joined by Stuart, and we sat chatting about Key West, Hong Kong, Japanese sunglasses, transvestites, JFK, Marilyn Monroe, Jack Ruby, John Peel, Ann Boleyn, and Winston Churchill until it was time for my massage. I lay face-down on a couch with my face in a hole, staring at a pedal-bin while Shiena rubbed aromatic oils into the parts most beers cannot reach. She knew little about contemporary music and I know nothing of aromatherapy or massage, but we managed to chat effortlessly for the 1hr 20 minutes it took her to get from one end of my body to the other.

I returned to my room, covered in a film of sandalwood and peppermint oils (and with a red ring round my face like I'd had my head stuck against a toilet seat), and gathered my dirty washing together. Today is my only chance to get my clothes laundered and I'm out of clean clothes. I took a cab into town and found a cleaners on Sauchiehall Street who could have my stuff ready for tomorrow. Wandered along Glasgow's most famous street, and eventually found my way down onto Buchanan Street (where the good shops are), and then onto Princes Square. There is a new shopping centre on three storeys, featuring myriad designer shops and cafés – beautifully designed and built from wood and imaginative art-deco wrought ironwork. I set up my laptop in the October

Café and spent the afternoon writing this diary while drinking coffee and fruit tea.

At 5.30 my laptop battery was flat, so I returned along Buchanan Street, stopping to try on a Paul Smith jacket in Frasers. I wasn't sure about it and, well, you have to be sure. Back at the Hilton I decided I'd have a go on the solarium in the basement, so I killed half an hour under the tubes before showering and ringing home to see how my important people are doing. Sofie answered the phone. She seems to have adopted a very businesslike telephone manner lately. "Hello daddy… Yes, I'm very well, thank you. How are you? Would you like to speak to mummy? Bye bye. I love you, daddy." Nial's more of a heavy breather. He says hello and then thinks a lot about what he should say next. This can take several minutes and, unfortunately, costs a lot of money when using long-distance from posh hotels, so the pleasure of hearing him struggling to form sentences is tainted by a growing sense of unease over bankruptcy. Dizzy sounds OK but tired. She says she misses me. Sigh.

I had a shower and went down to the hotel bar. I was planning to check out King Tut's Wah Wah Hut - a nearby music club - but, in the end, I settled down with Priv, Stuart, Helen, Amy, Pete, Mark and Simon Lake (our lovely truck driver – currently sporting a swashbuckling moustache and beard that the laughing cavalier would be proud of). Never managed to move until bedtime.

Sunday 24 September *Glasgow – Nottingham Royal Centre*

It's a long drive from Glasgow down to Nottingham, so I met up with Paul at 10.00, feeling more than a little beaten up. The pain in my arm continues, so I sat fidgeting about for the first hour of the journey, trying to get comfortable and find a place to put my left arm so that it didn't hurt. An hour later I decided to move to the back seat and lie down. I slept for much of the journey, and we were heading south on the M1 by the time I regained consciousness.

We were in Nottingham by 2.00, which was pretty good going. Checked into the Post House hotel, still feeling a little odd. I decided I would go for a walk. Nottingham becomes a ghost town on a Sunday. I realised this as I walked along the empty and closed streets, and I eventually decided I might as well just go to the venue and have a cup of coffee in catering. Helen, in her blue rubber-gloves, was busy pulling the skin off a partially cooked chicken while Cod, the merchandiser, was making after-show sandwiches for the crew. He isn't paid to do this – it's something he does by way of a thank you for travelling on the crew bus. Strictly speaking he isn't part of the crew as the merchandise is a separate business concern. Traditionally though he's part of the family, and I suppose this is his way of being spiritually part of the crew.

By soundcheck I was feeling downright ill, so I left the venue early and returned to the hotel around 5.30 and went to bed. When I woke at 7.00 I ran a bath and soaked for a while. Baths are good things for singers – the hot water helps ease the muscles a little, whilst the steam from the water opens up the nasal tubes and takes the edge off any hoarseness. Most of this is psychosomatic I daresay, but where performance is concerned, 80% of it is down to state of mind anyway. I climbed out of the bath feeling a little better and met Paul in the lobby for the short walk to the Royal Centre.

I got off to a nervous start, stretching and scratching my way through *Incommunicado* and *Hooks in You*, but as the set continued my voice seemed to open up and settle down a little, and my terror of the descent into complete hoarseness subsided.

After the show I quickly showered, then made my way to the guest room to say hello to my mum and dad and sisters. Sister Gill had brought her little girls, Amy and Holly, to the show, and everyone seemed to have enjoyed it. I had dedicated *No One Can* to my little nieces and Holly, who doesn't usually say much, was moved to tears. Bless her. I said goodnight to everyone, and then returned to the Post House for a nightcap in the bar with Cathy and Rory from Birmingham, before going up to bed.

Monday 25 September *Nottingham – Cardiff, St David's Hall*

Woke at 10.00 and decided to take a walk through the city centre. I had been here at college for a couple of years, so I'm always a little nostalgic when I'm in Nottingham. I walked down the hill and across the old Market Square, and then up towards the Broadmarsh Centre, trying to find the Paul Smith shop. This diary is beginning to sound like one long advert for Mr. Smith but, I guess, it's how I divert myself in my spare moments. Paul Smith started out here in Nottingham and still has a little shop tucked away up a side street. I was trying to replace a pair of pink socks I wear on stage as they'd come back from the laundry a filthy shade of grey. They didn't have any pink socks, so I bought a pair of maroon and orange instead (oh well, there goes another twelve quid), along with a pair of dark blue velvet trousers. I returned to the hotel to pack and check out with Paul and Pete, before the long drive to Cardiff.

We made pretty good time and arrived at the Hyatt around 3.15. I haven't stayed here before – it's new, and the staff were all friendly and helpful. It was only a short walk to St. David's Hall, so I made my way over there for soundcheck at 4.00. The Green Room backstage reminded me of the abusive and peculiar letter I received when we came here on the Brave tour. I wondered if I'd get another one today but, fortunately, it wasn't to be. Maybe they've lost interest… or gone completely mad and can't write letters anymore. Whoever it was, from their writing, looked like they were heading for self-destruction.

I ate a spot of late lunch – the girls had done chicken satay and tempura vegetables today. I declined the banoffee pie.

I called a quick meeting with Alan and Priv to review the general progress of the show. They both say the set works well and recommend no changes – other than sorting out the end of *Gazpacho* which "sounds like a mess". After much umming and ahhing we decided to shorten it, so we ran through various options at the soundcheck until Priv was happy. The show's sold-out here in Cardiff. St. David's Hall is another one of those places where I know, from experience, that the audience noise doesn't really travel too well to the stage. You're usually under the impression that you're not going down as well as you are. I remember once at Manchester Apollo, after the main set, we weren't going to bother with an encore as the crowd seemed distinctly lethargic. John arrived backstage at that moment, raving about the level of excitement in the crowd. At first we didn't believe him, but it was later confirmed by Priv. I have come to know the venues that don't carry the crowd noise to the stage and I always watch the audience a little more carefully at these shows to see how they're responding.

Tuesday 26 September *London:* Day off

Slept late and arrived down in the lobby of the Hyatt in time for a quick cup of coffee before departure at 12.00 with Paul and Pete for London. It rained hard all the way from Cardiff to Kensington, making it almost impossible to see the M4 motorway through the windscreen, so, although I'm not normally a nervous passenger, I heaved a sigh of relief as we pulled into the car park of the Kensington Hilton at around 4.30. I don't like the Ken Hilton much – it's old and shabby, and they have a habit of checking other people into your room while you're out (back in '89, we were shooting the promo vid for *The Uninvited Guest* somewhere in Notting Hill. I was booked into the Ken Hilton for two nights and, after staying there overnight, I was on set from around 7.30am, falling back through the door around 2.00am the following morning. When I got upstairs and opened my room door, there was someone else sleeping in my bed. I had been checked out! My toilet bag and several shirts left in the room had been discarded and lost. I had to return to reception and try and persuade the night-porter to give me another room so that I could sleep – not what you want after a 19-hour day at work).

Anyway, here I was again! The budget, unfortunately, wouldn't stretch to the lovely Halcyon down the road. Shame. I dropped my bags in room 3036, and decided to have a wander around Kensington Market before the shops closed. I took a cab through the rainy elegant streets of Holland Park and got stuck in traffic on Kensington High Street. When I got out of the cab, the meter was showing £6.40. "Just call it a fiver, mate," said the cabdriver, proving that there's still a sense of fairness to be found in this city. I made my way through the narrow bohemian aisles of Kensington Market, past the stalls of t-shirts, jewellery and second-hand clothes.

PS – I must have got distracted after that. There's no further mention of the day, or the show!

Kensington Market has long since ceased to exist; a shame, it was an Aladdin's cave of second-hand clothes and an arty, antiquey treasure-trove of a place. I always used to love wandering round there.

Saturday 30 September *Luxembourg, Dudelange Sports Hall*

As I write this, I'm sitting at the front of the tour bus alongside Robbie, our bus driver, who arrived yesterday in Rotterdam from England. We're on our way to Luxembourg, and at the moment I'm looking out through the front screen as the road winds through the green wooded hills of Southern Belgium. It's not a bad day, sun shining through broken cloud.

My shoulder still hurts. Yesterday's massage seemed to help, although the muscle tissue is now bruised as a consequence of the vicious manipulation of the thumbs of Jos, the masseur. Ouch. I'm more or less living on beer and Ibuprofen at the moment.

We eventually arrived at the gig in Luxembourg. I thought I had been here before, but I haven't. It's a little sports hall. There was an interview for TV so I freshened up and put a proper shirt on.

Sunday 1 October *Hamburg, Grosse Freiheit*

I'm sitting at the ship-shaped bar in the restaurant of the Hotel Hafen in Hamburg. It's 11.10am and, unfortunately, there are no rooms available to us until this afternoon. Never mind. I'm drinking coffee in industrial quantities and watching the river. The Hafen overlooks the Elbe and the docks of Hamburg. There are huge dry-docks here, large enough to service ocean-going ships and, from my bar stool, I can see the bow of one large freighter stretching away into the distance. Last time I was here I had a memorably bad gig, where voice problems and a strange vibe in the crowd combined together and I allowed myself to get rattled. I remember sitting on my bed in tears after the show, hoarse and dispirited, ashamed at having lost my temper with the crowd. I also remember the honey and pineapple diet I started here at the Hafen - a recommendation by Geoff, the monitor engineer - in an attempt to repair my damaged voice. So far on this tour, vocal problems have been minimal (touch wood), and I'm determined to make amends tonight for last time.

Well, I gave up waiting for a room to become available and decided I would take a walk down to the gig and have breakfast in catering. I wandered along the Reperbahn, past endless sex shops, live sex show theatres and shops that sell hi-fi goods, cameras, knives and guns… what a place… and eventually found my way to the Grosse Freiheit, our gig for tonight (which I was later to learn is next door to the old Star Club, where the Beatles cut their teeth). The crew bus was parked outside the stage door but, unfortunately, Simon hadn't yet arrived with the truck.

Out in the street were a great many people just standing around. Opposite the club there is a Polish church, which was full to overflowing with Sunday churchgoers. The people in the street were selling things. I never found out what was for sale because they advertise their wares on little strips of paper that are fastened to the lamp posts, but there was a man in a Mercedes who was selling Polish magazines which were all laid out on the rear parcel shelf.

When Simon arrived with the truck he couldn't find a way into the street – they are narrow and lined with parked cars. He eventually negotiated his way slowly up the Grosse Freiheit as the street people looked on curiously. I lay down in the road in front of the huge truck, like a suicide demonstrator. No one realised I was chums with the driver, so it was a bit of a spectacle. The side road with the backstage door was even narrower, so Simon had to reverse the huge trailer into the street while everyone looked on. For a moment it seemed impossible – until the gates of the church were opened so that he could put the front of the truck into the churchyard, which gave him the few extra inches to make it possible. I installed myself in the catering area, and helped Helen and Amy set up their things so that I could make myself some toast and coffee. They were listening to INXS on their cassette machine as I sipped my coffee, contemplating, once again, what would induce a man to leave Helena Christiansen for Paula Yates. Once the truck was unpacked, Simon arrived in catering and announced he was going to pop down the road to get his nipples pierced and get another tattoo! We chatted for a while about body piercing, and I came out of the conversation with my mind somewhat broadened. He showed me a catalogue of components from a company based in Brighton. It included labia rings, penis and anal inserts, and a kind of can that is designed to house the scrotum (with optional accessories, including a screw press which applies pressure to said organs. It included the cautionary note, 'Please take care. This device is designed for sophisticated enjoyment, but can be dangerous'). Just when you think you've been around and seen everything, you find out you're an old prude. I wished Simon luck and returned to the Hafen Hotel around 3.00. They had a room ready at last, so I checked in and watched half the German Grand Prix, falling asleep halfway through. It's a good job I wasn't driving.

Rondor had left me a package in reception: a pen and a letter from new addition Chris Bell (husband of my old chum Sylvia Bell, who runs Virgin in Hamburg). They were both coming to the soundcheck and would see me later. Sure enough they did. I had lost contact with Sylvia some years ago. She was the first person to let me hear the **Hats** album by The Blue Nile. That was in Hamburg back in '91. I remember sitting in her car by the river Elbe, listening to *The Downtown Lights* for the first time. I still see the silver river and the big ships sailing majestically (and somehow sadly) out to sea whenever I hear the song. We chatted for a while, and she invited me to lunch tomorrow on my day off. Paul had a word with her and asked if she might find a masseur and acupuncturist to give me another going-over tomorrow. She said she'd call in the morning and let us know.

Soundcheck was uneventful. We returned to the Hafen and, as I'd been asleep for most of the afternoon, I had a beer in the bar with Paul.

The gig went well. The atmosphere in the crowd was much better than last time and I was enjoying myself. During the first encore I found myself singing *A Walk on the Wild Side*. Everyone joined in with the "doo doo doop's". If a city were to have an anthem then this must surely be Hamburg's. Returned to the hotel wondering if I'd done enough to repair the faith that many might have lost from last time. We had actually only sold half as many tickets. People tend to vote with their feet.

Monday 2 October *Hamburg:* Day off

Got up around 12.00, showered, and went downstairs. Paul had called to say that Sylvia would arrive at 12.30 to buy me lunch and then take me to a clinic that specialises in massage and acupuncture. I checked out of my room, and had a coffee with Steve and Ian in the bar, before leaving with Sylvia. She took me to a restaurant which seemed vaguely familiar. She told me that this place used to be Onkel Po, the club that Europeans played when I came to Hamburg for the first time. She was here too, in her capacity as CBS product manager for the band. We were both a lot younger in those days. Onkel Po, by the way, gets a mention in the opening line of the Tom Robinson/Peter Gabriel song *Atmospherics.* I ate steak and salad while we caught up on one another's life stories, before she took me round the corner to the clinic. The doctors spoke little English, so Sylvia hung around to explain to them what my problem was and then left us to it. First of all I was stripped off. Then the masseur, Sammy Gori, wrapped me up in what looked like very large tea bags. This is called a mour bath, and the bags contain some kind of hot mud or volcanic soil or somesuch. I was wrapped up like Tutankhamen in the bags and in blankets, and left alone to sweat, unable to move, for half an hour. I drifted in and out of sleep in the white room, getting hotter and hotter. The whole experience seemed more and more like a dream as consciousness came and went. I could hear voices speaking German down the corridor, like some surreal thriller movie. Sammy returned and removed the blankets, washing off the mour deposits and feeling at my muscles while muttering, "Ah… sehr gut… mmm… gut." He then left the room and returned with what looked like a ballpoint pen. This was in fact some form of electric shock generator (a bit like those things they have for lighting gas cookers) which, he explained, was 'magnetotherapy!' He pressed it against the soles of my feet while flicking the trigger. It felt like a staple gun. He worked his way up the backs of my legs, my back and into my neck, before turning me over and doing the front of me. After that it was massage time. He thoroughly worked at my neck and shoulders while giving me a brief resumé of his client list. I only recognised Jil Sander, the fashion designer, among the German glitterati of stars and royalty he proudly mentioned. After the massage I was already feeling a bit better. He said I could now dress from the waist down, and he took me along the corridor to the acupuncturist (whose name I can't remember). He inserted fine needles along the length of my arm from my shoulder down to my inner wrist, along with a couple in my left leg and ankle. There was a large diagram of acupuncture points on the wall next to me. I couldn't help noticing one mid-way between the scrotum and the anus – fortunately I was wearing my trousers, so I was spared. The acupuncturist returned every ten minutes to adjust the needles sticking out of me. I felt like a bull in a bullring. What a way to spend the afternoon! I emerged at around 5.00 feeling considerably better. It really works. I wasn't hurting for the first time in over two weeks.

Sylvia picked me up and took me across the road to the Virgin office where I was introduced to her assistant (Ullie) and given coffee while she finished her phone-calls for the day. We went back down to the river for a beer, and I watched the big ships sailing by as *The Downtown Lights* hummed around in my head. By now it was 7.00pm, and time for our bus to leave for Paris. I thanked Sylvia for all her help, and vowed to keep in touch before boarding the bus. Paul cracked open a bottle of red, and we all assisted him in drinking it while watching **Absolutely Fabulous** on TV in the back lounge of the bus. After that we loaded a video, a movie called **Single White Female**: American, derivative plot - halfway between **Fatal Attraction**, **Basic Instinct** and **The Mary Tyler-Moore Show**. Got bored. Went to bed. Woke up outside the Libertel, Terminus Nord, opposite the Gare du Nord in Paris. Yeah!

Wednesday 4 October *Paris, Le Zenith*

Dizzy and I enjoyed our first lie-in together since either of us can remember. Once you have children, forget it.

We got up around 12.30, and set out to have breakfast in Montmartre. Ordered a cab and waited in reception. All the newspapers were reporting that OJ Simpson was found NOT guilty yesterday. Maybe he isn't. Who knows? No one seems to believe it. A cab arrived, and we discovered we were only a short walk from Montmartre anyway. We climbed out in front of Sacré Cœur and walked round the corner to the square where the artists paint (La Place du Tertre). We sat outside a café, drinking coffee, while trying to adjust to being able to have an uninterrupted conversation. I ate croque monsieur as we tried to decide where we should live next. We have both missed our last place in Englefield Green, and often wonder whether we might be happier there. We find village life too isolated, especially in the winter, and have often contemplated moving into Oxford. We came to the usual conclusion – give it a year and see how we're doing… and what's possible.

We took a walk around the square and were hounded by the street artists who prey quite shamelessly on the tourists. They don't take no for an answer, and we were presented with matching paper silhouettes of ourselves which took 45 seconds to create and for which, after haggling, I was charged 50 francs (well over a fiver). We got out of there and stopped at another café by the steps for another coffee. It was three o'clock, so I had to be getting back to the hotel. Dizzy decided she'd rather see the Impressionist collection in the Musée d'Orsay than hang around at a Marillion soundcheck all afternoon, so we walked back to the hotel and I said I'd see her later. I told her not to talk to any other strange men. She later told me she was followed all the way to the river by some rich-looking geezer in a suit. I'm told that French men prefer English women to their own.

The band took the bus to Le Zenith and I wandered around the black backstage area of my favourite gig, soaking up the old ghosts, and immediately certain that tonight would be a bit special. I wasn't wrong. Steve R had arranged for Barbara Lezmy (who sang and talked on *Cannibal Surf Babe)* to come along with a view to her joining us on-stage during the show. During the soundcheck we worked out what she might do. We decided she should talk over the flutes before *Beautiful,* and return later to get involved in *Surf Babe.* I had imagined she could come on, scantily-clad, and scream a little. She had other ideas, preferring to throw me to the ground and straddle me while singing into my face. Fair enough. We ran through it several times at soundcheck while the crew stared on aghast at her shapely form that was covered only in a leopard-skin body stocking. Thank you, Barbara.

There were a few interviews to do at soundcheck. I was told by the first radio station that, from their perspective, there had been no promotion whatsoever by EMI for our new album.

Friday 17 November *Home – Leipzig, Haus Auensee*

Rose at 7.30 to shower and be ready for the car at 8.15. I had more or less packed my things last night, anticipating the early start, and added the last few precautionary pullovers. Central Europe in November is going to be cold. Sofie appeared at 7.45. "I wanted to see you before you go," she said. Nial arrived soon after, looking tousled and clutching Rabbit, his night-time companion. I showered while they watched TV. I couldn't have been blessed with lovelier children. Sue appeared in the kitchen at 8.00 and answered the phone while I was still in the shower room. It was my driver. He was already in the village, outside the pub, and needed directions to the house. He said no one in the village seemed to know where I live. He must have been asking the few people that don't!

At 8.15 I said goodbye (this time it's only for a few days) and climbed into the back of the Mercedes. I forget the driver's name, but he was a nice chap. He chatted affably and non-intrusively during the trip to Heathrow – obviously a pro. We arrived in plenty of time at Terminal 2 and I made my way to the check-in desk, where tour-manager Paul Lewis and the rest of the band were already assembled. We checked in and went through passport control and security to the departure area. I bought a new recording Walkman at Duty Free – my other one's had it. Before I had to go to the gate I spent the remaining 15 minutes trying on Oakley sunglasses at the shades shop. I came within a whisker of buying some E Wireframes, balancing the desire to be fashionable and the unwillingness to be a fashion-victim. I left my favourite sun specs on a restaurant table in La Rochelle in the summer. In the end I passed on the whole idea. It seems daft to buy sunglasses in November, I'll have lost them by Christmas. The Lufthansa flight to Leipzig was uneventful, apart from the stewardesses and the food, both of which seemed a cut-above my recent recollections of BA. We're only travelling economy today.

At Leipzig we took cabs from the airport into the town, passing through flat countryside along tree-lined roads, slightly reminiscent of the journey from the airport to Gdansk in northern Poland. It seems that on the journey between the airport and Leipzig, we passed by all the cranes in the world; there were construction sites in every direction I looked during the twenty-minute drive to the Astoria Hotel.

The lobby bore the old familiar Eastern bloc smell of something halfway between damp cabbage and sewage. Strange. I checked in, wondering if every place to the east of Berlin bore a hint of this aroma, and how might that be? We only had time to have a quick shufti of our hotel rooms before leaving for soundcheck. My room was more than adequate, but the decor was most definitely typical of Eastern bloc luxury. A bit like a high-rise flat in a suburb of London in the Sixties – apart from the slightly gothic brass door-handles. I decided to unpack only my toothbrush and take everything else to the show, so that I could leave my suitcase with the crew tonight and not have to worry about dragging it on and off the trains to Poland tomorrow – a momentous decision, as it turned out. We took cabs to the Haus Auensee, a big hall next to a lake. It's always strange and pleasant to fly so far and to catch sight of Simon Lake's big silver truck as if it's beamed around the world, Star Trek fashion, and, on this occasion, to see Tim Bricusse emerge from a side door, beckoning to us in welcome. There were already a handful of young men and women stamping about in the cold outside the front entrance of the venue. They waved to us cheerfully as we skirted the building and entered around the back, accompanied - once again - by that sewagey/cabbagey smell.

Inside, everyone was busily preparing for soundcheck. I shook hands with Alan Parker, who seemed mutually pleased to see me. Tim and Alan have just returned from America where they were doing the Pretenders acoustic tour. I told him I'd seen it on the TV, and that it looked and sounded great. I had Chrissie Hynde down as a serious songwriting talent, but I'd never thought of her as a great singer. I do now. I wandered backstage to drop my suitcase. The smell of sewage was much worse backstage for some reason (God knows where it was coming from) so I didn't hang around back there. Went out front to say good afternoon to Priv. The hall was done out like a disco: black rubber flooring and neon lights everywhere. Priv seemed happy enough. Said hello to Jeff Hooper, who also seemed relaxed and happy. It was nice to see them all again.

I thought I'd go outside and talk to the kids out in the cold. There were four boys and three girls. I invited them in for a drink at the little bar at the rear of the building. They seemed like a good bunch, so I gave them aftershow passes so that we could have a drink afterwards. I left them in the bar while I went off to soundcheck.

For these last few shows we are using guitar tech Phil Joiner, so I went through my cues with him, telling him when I will need the pink Telecaster. We had worked together on the **Brave** tour so he remembered much of it. Everything sounded fine. Jeff's capacity to reconstruct exactly the same monitor sound, seemingly from memory, with a different system, after several weeks off, in another part of the world, leaves me awestruck. After soundcheck we all sat down in an adjoining room to eat. The food wasn't bad, considering it was supplied locally. During the wait to showtime it became apparent that we weren't generating too much excitement in the area. Ticket sales were low, and we were going to be lucky to have 500 people in. Oh well. We would give it our best.

As it turned out the numbers were small, but those present listened carefully and the band played well. Sometimes in these situations there's a greater element of control achieved in the absence of adrenaline, which makes the songs tighter. I missed the enthusiasm of a bigger crowd, but even though I wasn't singing at my best I enjoyed playing the songs tonight.

After the show I showered and returned to the bar with the people I'd invited in earlier. I got pleasantly drunk and, after a while, Tim called by to tell me he'd put my suitcase on the crew bus. My guests all sat round me, hanging on my every word as though I was some kind of a guru. They must have been drunk too, otherwise they'd have noticed I was slurring and talking rubbish. Talked rubbish until around 1.00 in the morning, in between trying on other peoples sweaters (I tend to swap chairs and clothes when I'm sloshed), before getting a cab back to the hotel with Ian.

Saturday 18 November *Leipzig – Kunowice – Poznan*

Woke up, and called Paul at 11.00 to check what time we were leaving today. He said 12.30 and recommended the room service breakfast. I took his advice and called to see if I was too late. "No problem!" they said, and sure enough there was a chap knocking on my door as soon as I'd showered. I couldn't let him in, though. Someone had locked me in as I slept! I hunted around for my room key, shouting, "Just commen" in my best German accent. Paul was right, breakfast was most enjoyable. A pleasant surprise, considering I'm in the east of Germany.

I packed, arrived downstairs at 12.15 and checked out. The smell of sewagey cabbage seemed to have departed from the hotel reception area this morning – or perhaps I'd got used to it. To my delight it had just started snowing outside - big feathery flakes - as I made my way across the road to Leipzig railway station in search of coffee and a place to push the buttons of my pocket sequencer. I entered the station amid temporary chilling visions of wartime Germany (nothing much will have changed to the fabric of the building since then) and found a baker's shop inside the station, with a coffee bar inside. I sipped coffee and arranged cellos on my headphones until 1.00, when I had arranged to meet up with the chaps on platform 4.

When I got to the platform, the train was already there – but no Paul Lewis and no Marillion. According to the announcement board the train was leaving in three minutes, to a destination I couldn't pronounce and had never heard of. I seemed to recall a departure time of 1.20, so I didn't know whether to assume I'd got the departure time wrong (in which case I was about to miss the train that everyone else was already on), or that I'd got it right (in which case the worst thing I could do would be to climb alone onto the wrong train, going God-knows where). Sod's law says I would do the wrong thing, but as the last minute ticked away I spied Paul at the far end of the train and jumped aboard.

It was a very nice train. We were travelling first-class in a clean, spacious and empty compartment as I spent the first few minutes chatting to Paul, who said he had been in the process of taking his bags back off the train as he saw me on the platform. The rest of the boys seemed unconcerned (but mildly amused) that I'd almost missed it. Twenty years of touring teaches you to look after number one, and if anyone else has a crisis, well, enjoy it – it spices up the day, and it will all get sorted out eventually. Little did I know, as we sped through the East German countryside, that I was later to spice up the day once again.

I continued programming my sequencer with my headphones on, oblivious to all around me, until we changed trains for the first time in a place called something like 'Cats piss'. We found a café on the platform and ordered up currywurst, fries and beer, which we took with us and ate in our new train – the connecting train to Frankfurt Oder, where we must change again for the train across the border into Poland. As we sat munching and quaffing in the train, Paul was taken over by a moment of clairvoyance: "You didn't put your passport in that suitcase that you sent overnight with the crew, did you?" he said.

I felt the colour drain away from my cheeks as I realised that I indeed had.

"...and your credit cards?" he said. I winced and nodded. Oh well! We'll just have to worry about it when we get to the border.

When we arrived at Frankfurt (no, the other one) we had a 40-minute wait for the connection, so we left the station. We found a café over the road where I had a coffee and played Pete what I'd been up to in the headphones. He seemed impressed, but I don't know whether by the arrangement or the machine. We returned to the chilly platform to await the 5.00 train to Poznan. Frankfurt Oder is right next to the Polish border. Paul and I decided to make a plan of action with regard to my absent passport and the necessary excuses and theatre. "Don't worry Paul! I'm good at acting," I said as we climbed aboard.

After that, everything got a bit tricky.

Before we had managed to sit down, we were stuck in the corridor as uniformed passport officers checked all passports.

"Pass-Porta! Pass Porta!" they shouted.

"Hello, good afternoon..." I said in my best Oxford English. "Now, allow me to explain, I am a singer in a rock n'roll band (I mimed guitar playing as I said this) called Marillion. We played a show last night in Leipzig, and I have placed my suitcase on a bus with the road crew. This bus has travelled overnight to Poznan, and is already now in Poznan. The band is travelling today by train – this train. Unfortunately, I have put my passport in my suitcase so it is also already in Poznan. Silly, I know. Unfortunately, my credit cards are also in the suitcase. Perhaps when we arrive in Poznan there will be a TV crew there who can verify that I am who I say I am…"

"Pass-Porta! Pass Porta!" they continued to shout.

Oh dear. No one speaks a word of English.

I eventually shortened my explanation to, "No Passporta".

"No Passporta?!?"

"No Passporta."

This message seemed to get through, because I found the machine guns were no longer casually slung over their shoulders. They were now pointing at *me* as I was escorted along the train corridor and locked into a compartment along with a young soldier, my guard, also carrying a machine gun.

The train was stopped at Kunowice (pronounced Ku-no-vich-a), the home of the border police, and I was taken off the train in the company of about twelve uniformed officers. Paul only had time to give me his cellphone and some additional money before I was gone. I watched the train containing my alibi, my band and lifeline to the outside world pull away from the platform and disappear into a massive, barren and suddenly very alien land. It was 5pm, and in Poland it's already dark at 5pm in November and bloody cold. Oh dear. I thought, "Well, here comes an entry for the diary!"

I was marched across the railway lines and into a chilly rail-side building block, up a flight of stairs, and told, via sign language, to sit on a wooden-slatted bench in a reception room. The room was bare and linoleum-floored with one radiator (which was enough to prevent the air from freezing, but not enough to keep it warm). There was a wrought iron fence and locked gate to prevent me leaving. There was one of those old coffee tables with the screw-in legs, on which was a large ashtray containing thirty or so cigarette butts. This was the only item of furniture, apart from the bench I was seated on. A noticeboard on the wall carried what might have been public safety notices on it, but everything was in Polish so I wasn't sure. Another sign on the wall said 'Graniczna Placowca Kontrolna Strazy Granicznej w KUNOWICACH' (I wrote it down). Two young soldiers were posted to watch over me.

So picture the scene: before leaving Leipzig, Paul had advised us that there was a distinct possibility that we would be met off the train in Poznan by the national Polish television channel, who would film us arriving for the news the following day. I had decided to dress up, just in case. I was wearing my new Kevlar boots (dark-grey with an orange zip which ran from the toe upwards); above these, a pair bottle-green velvet trousers, a white shirt, many silver bangles jangling at my wrists, beads hung around my neck, and it was all topped off by a Jean Paul Gaultier jacket – double breasted military style of fine black felt, and a dark red velvet strip which extended down the front beneath the fine gold and black buttons. In short, I looked like a rock star – and something halfway between Napoleon and Adam Ant. Locked in a barren cell, next to a railway line on the Polish border, I must have looked like a space alien. In 1995 in Poland, a pair of genuine Levi jeans was haute couture and would stop traffic. Unsurprisingly, soldiers faces would periodically peer in through the little window in the door to have a look at the human Christmas tree in the cell.

After half an hour or so, a man with a Lech Walesa moustache entered the room and began to question me in extremely broken English:

"Who… you… are?"

I told him that I was the singer with a band called Marillion. This caused an immediate flurry.

"Marillion?!?!"

He seemed to know of the band, and began a heated exchange of words with the officer who had pulled me off the train. I was asked if I had any proof of identification – credit cards or anything. I had absolutely nothing. My credit cards were also in Poznan, in my suitcase. I didn't even have a photograph of myself with the band. I had only my little Yamaha drum machine, a pair of headphones and a toilet bag. I was asked where the band will be staying in Poznan but I didn't know that either, so there was really very little the border police could do to help me. Paul's mobile phone turned out to be useless as it was passcode protected and he'd forgot to tell me the code. I told Lech that if they called my wife at home in England she could tell them the name of my hotel in Poznan. Lech explained slowly that the telephones in the office could not dial international numbers, only Polish ones

So that was that. I decided all I could do was sit it out, and trust in Paul to get me out of there. The train wasn't to arrive in Poznan until 7.30, so the earliest he could do anything (now that he didn't have his mobile phone!) would be in another three hours.

The soldiers and the passport officials kept coming and going, asking me for my autograph: "It's for my daughter, Andrea," said Lech Walesa. As for the two young soldiers posted to keep an eye on me, the guard seemed to change about once an hour. They too asked me, via sign language and broken English, for my autograph – "To Sebastian, please", or "To Piotr".

Every so often there was the noise of footsteps trudging up the stairs, and more uniformed officials would arrive to rattle the metal gate next to me so that they could be let into the office block behind. They would disappear, and a murmur of conversation would ensue from the back room: "Murmur murmur, Marillion, murmur murmur, vocalista," followed by heads being craned around the doorway to discretely have a look at the famous zoo animal.

I settled down to arranging a musical idea on the QY20 pocket sequencer. I was trying to re-work an old pre-Marillion song called *Victoria Station,* about a girl on a train. It will now forever be *Kunovicha Station* in my mind.

After a couple of hours, around 7.30pm, the attitude of the officials seemed to thaw and become friendlier. Sebastian, a young border guard who I recognised from the train, was interested in the sequencer and asked to hear my song. I gave him the headphones, and he grinned in awe at the rich arrangement of sounds coming, improbably, from the little box. He told me, slowly and painstakingly, that they had spoken to "the big boss" and "everything will be OK!", that there was another train at 22.00 hours (still another three hours), and that I should be able to go to Poznan. It wasn't much of a relief really – Paul hadn't called, and I couldn't get his mobile to work. If I ever got to Poznan, I didn't know where to go when I arrived. I still felt totally cut off from the English-speaking world – and from the free world. The cold was beginning to seep into my knees, and my backside had fallen victim to the wooden slats. I got up and paced around a little, but it didn't seem to help.

At 9.00 a plump, bespectacled official ran into the room and excitedly beckoned me inside to a warm office where the phone was off the hook. I picked it up to hear Paul Lewis, who sounded even more pleased to hear my voice than I was to hear his. He apologised for the delay in contacting me, they had been trying to find out where I was being held. He said that the good news was that I hadn't been deported back to Germany – there would have been very little he could have done from inside Poland to help, and I couldn't have got out of Germany either. Paul said the border guards had agreed to accept a fax of my passport details and that this would arrive shortly. I would be free to leave on the next train. The one thing he'd managed to do in the panic on the train was give me my ticket to Poznan, so at least I had a ticket! The bad news was that the next train wasn't until 11.00 – another two hours! He said I would arrive in Poznan at 2.00 in the morning, where I would be met at the station by the promoter's rep. Both Paul and the border guards impressed upon me that the "late train" has a reputation for robberies, and that under no circumstances should I go to sleep, or play with my expensive gadgets, and that I must keep my luggage close to me and NOT on the luggage racks! I thanked Paul for his efforts and returned to my bench feeling, for the first time in four hours, that I had returned to the known world... but I wasn't home and dry yet...

Lech Walesa reappeared with a fax. Sure enough, there was a scan of the information page of my passport. Where the photograph of me should be there was a black square. "Is this you?" said Lech, pointing at the black square with a smile.

"Yes!" I said. That seemed good enough for him and off he went, grinning.

The official in the specs invited me into an empty room with a TV. This seemed to be where the soldiers (who had now departed) hang out when off duty. The James Bond movie **Thunderball** was on TV – but dubbed into Polish, so I couldn't really follow what little plot there might be. I returned to my headphones and cuddled up to the room's only radiator while explosions, car chases, shower and bedroom scenes accompanied my efforts to write a bassline for *Kunovice Station.* At 10.00 my sequencer batteries gave out, so I returned to an hour of staring at the clock. A pointless exercise – it was stuck at 8.45, and probably had been for many years. James Bond had waved goodbye and sailed off into the sunset with a beautiful submissive young woman on a peerless Carribbean sea, as usual. Clinging to the radiator here in the guardroom, I pondered what he would have done in my situation, and decided he'd have been out of the train window and up onto the roof for a scrap instead of meekly clinging to a radiator to stave off frostbite. Miss Poland would have shown up by now with a whip – or tea and biscuits. Everyone had asked for my autograph but no one had offered me so much as a glass of water in six hours. I thought of Brian Keenan and John McCarthy, and consoled myself that at least no one with a moustache had made any amorous advances or given me a kicking. Apart from the first half hour I had been treated as well as could be expected. I was, after all, an illegal alien.

As 11.00pm slowly approached, I became increasingly nervous that they might forget about me and I would miss the train. The thought of sleeping at Kunovice was not an enchanting one. I asked to go to the toilet so that the two remaining officials (Specs and his colleague) would be reminded of me and so I could freshen up a little.

At 11.00 I was told that the train was not until 11.30! They had mistranslated the time. I settled back down to my radiator rubbing for one last, long half hour.

At 11.20 a civilian girl appeared in my room. She was dressed up for a Saturday night out. I don't know where she might have come from, but they weren't happy about her papers and officials began questioning her. She must have wondered who the hell the pop-star in the Gaultier jacket trying to have sex with the radiator was. They were still questioning her when I was escorted away at 11.30. I went with Specs, back down the concrete stairs, out of the block into the bitter cold Polish November midnight, over the railway lines, and up onto the public platform. John Le Carre would have been proud of me.

The train was already approaching the platform. A uniformed guard climbed down and Specs had a long chat with him. He must have told him to be nice to me, because he escorted me onto the train and was most courteous and pleasant, showing me to an empty compartment (which was blissfully warm) and wishing me good luck, shaking my hand and smiling, almost apologetically.

I settled down, revelling in the comfort of an upholstered train seat and the blissful <u>warmth</u>.

My worst fears about being mugged never materialised. I was joined by a chap carrying a four-foot wide satellite dish(!) who seemed civilised enough and uninterested in me. I ignored all the advice and drifted in and out of sleep until, three hours later, we arrived at Poznan. Paul and two promoter's assistants greeted me on the platform. They seemed very relieved to see me. I was hugged and bundled into a car and taken to the Novotel (I <u>knew</u> it was the Novotel!) where I shared a beer with Paul before going to bed. Bloody hell!

Sunday 19 November *Poznan Arena*

Got up around 11.00 and made my way downstairs in search of coffee. I sat at the bar while it was prepared and, while I was waiting, John and Paul appeared. I sat with them as John ordered breakfast and discussed his meeting in London yesterday with the PR girls, Angie and Jools. Returned to my room with not enough time to get ready for the first interviews of the day at 12.00. We were interviewed by local TV and various radio stations in the hotel lobby before being bundled into a minibus that took us through the stark and shabby streets of Poznan to the venue: the Arena, the same spaceship-shaped dome that we played last time. A few fans were hanging round at the stage door for autographs and were very excited to see us. We seem to be pop stars here.

Chatted to the crew about my interesting day yesterday and ate a spot of lunch in the catering room while giggly girls stared and waved through the glass. Soundcheck went well – I wandered around the hall while singing and, at one point, went out into the foyer where the t-shirt stall was being erected. I helped myself to a couple of shirts - the psychedelic **Brave** ones - while still singing *Incommunicado*... you could never have done this in the days before they invented radio-mics.

It was to be an early show (7.30), so there wasn't much time to hang around between soundcheck and showtime. The vibe at the show was like a football match – a terrific level of excitement and a sense of occasion. Since listening to the live tapes (we're currently working on the mix of a live album for release next Spring) I'm a little more conscious of tempo during the show, so I was trying to hold the pace back a little; Steve R has a tendency to begin *Easter* either too slow or too fast, depending on whether or not he's rattled. Ian tends to play faster at the big gigs. Some of the songs, particularly the old Fish lyrics, are damn near impossible to sing any faster – they're so wordy (try, *"I'm a Marquee veteran, a multi-media bona fide celebrity,"* as fast as you can say it). The show went down a storm and two encores seemed paltry, but we have two more shows to go so I was being careful not to wear my voice out. After the show we were mobbed outside as we tried to sign album sleeves and tickets for everyone who'd waited; there must have been sixty or seventy of them. We returned to the hotel and sat at the bar with John and Paul. I was shattered - I usually am - so I had a quick beer and went to bed.

Monday 20 November *Warszawa Coloseum*

We took the train from Poznan to Waszawa. I spent much of the journey in the restaurant car with my friends, the laptop and the sequencer (sad...). I ordered a spot of breakfast (omelette with bacon) which was very good. The coffee, on the other hand, seemed to have been made with some kind of mud that had been dredged from the bottom of the Ganges. When we arrived at Warszawa we were met at the station by Kinga Siennecka, our colleague and friend from the record label, who co-ordinated my last two promotion trips to Poland.

A minibus took us to the hotel. We were already late for the interviews scheduled in the hotel bar. I checked into my room, dropped my bags, and returned downstairs and straight into my first interview. I was seated opposite a slightly grubby tabloid journalist who had come to ask me about women. All the usual stuff – something to titillate the readers, but nothing too personal.

That's a relief. In England they'd want me to draw diagrams. The rest of the band were busy with other journalists; I could hear Mark K going through a brief history of the line-up of the band. I decided I'd rather be talking about women.

I had a second interview with two girls from a radio station before being hurried through the door into a waiting minibus to soundcheck. The drive took about half an hour, during which I heard the new Beatles single, *Free as a Bird*, on the radio. It sounds like ELO to me; Beatles imitating Jeff Lynne imitating Beatles. Maybe he produced it. When we arrived at the gig, it turned out to be a big circus tent in the middle of an otherwise empty and very cold field. We found our way inside and were shown to the dressing rooms which, like every other part of the gig, were mobile units. Apparently the chap who owns and manages this venue, the Coloseum, occasionally packs it all into trucks and takes it on the road as a travelling disco. He must need quite a few trucks, it's easily capable of housing 2000 people. Upstairs, to the right of stage, was a little bar and kitchen where we were to be given dinner. I suspect the manager handpicks his staff – all female and extremely beautiful. I tucked into barbecue chicken and breadcrumb-coated mushrooms, served by a sultry young woman with her nose in the air. Her general demeanour was sending out the message, "I suppose you expect me to be impressed... but I'm gorgeous... and I'm not. Enjoy your meal. It's better than anything anyone in Warszawa has eaten in the last fifty years... and don't even dream about getting to know me." I didn't.

I moved to a place a bit closer to the radiator as it was still quite chilly. The crew boys said that the space heaters had been going now for a couple of hours – when they loaded in this morning it was like an ice station. I got the impression that it had been something of a spiritual triumph to put the show in here at all. As usual, when the band arrived everything was in place, up and running as if by magic although the crew had that, 'You can't imagine what we've been through to make this happen' look about them. Soundcheck went without a hitch, apart from a brief moment when one of the cigarette company's promotional girls decided to adjust the top of her stockings in full view of band and crew, resulting in a simultaneous outbreak of bum notes, missed cues, and flight cases being dropped.

Once again we were too far from the centre of town to return to the hotel before the show, so we kicked our heels and mooched about the place until the doors opened, and then barricaded ourselves into the backstage Portakabins.

The show turned out to be my favourite of this last part of the tour. I was singing really well, the crowd were terrific, and the sound was very good at centre stage. During the final encore I climbed the PA stack at stage right and stood on top, literally in the roof, to realise that I was pressed against one of the tubular aluminium supporting beams which ran down to the floor in the crowd. It was an opportunity too handy too ignore. I looked down behind me at Mark K who had already read my thoughts and nodded as if to say, "Yeah... I'd do it!"... I slung my arms and legs around the pole and slid down into the sea of hands which ensnared my legs as I landed. I couldn't get free to sing the last verse of

Garden Party so I sort of sang it upside down, managing to return to the stage for the final chords and to say goodnight. I returned to the 'dressing rooms', covered in black grease and grime from the tent pole, to discover we were to go straight from the show to a party in our honour at a nearby club – and there are no showers. I had a makeshift wash care of Paul Lewis, who poured bottles of mineral water and shower gel over me, before changing into my party frock.

The 'party' turned out to be a low-key thing in a little nightclub. It was another one of those slightly 'industrial' clubs with lots of stainless steel and black rubber flooring. It took a couple of hours before they got the disco to function in any other area of the sonic spectrum than the treble-end. The bass amps had fused. When I pointed this out to the people I was talking to, no one seemed to know what I was on about. It's a fascinating lesson in how little most people care about sound. I have been so obsessed with it for so long that I am actively irritated by bad sound (and bad music) at any level of volume, and often can be seen inexplicably wincing in pain as I eat breakfast in some public place where they're playing crap background music. Anyway, in the end they got it going and we all hung around for quite a while. I don't think the place was open to the public, just invited guests, so my every move was being observed. It's a good feeling if you like a bit of attention but, after ten minutes of it, even an egomaniac like me has had enough.

We eventually rattled back to the hotel in our minibus. It was late and the hotel bar was closed, so we all went to bed taking care not to get into the wrong lift. All the lifts in this hotel go to different places. You can easily end up in the Twilight Zone…

Tuesday 21 November *Warszawa – Cracow, Korona*

We left the hotel at 11.00 (I think) and were driven in the ever-present minibus to Warszawa central station, opposite the gargantuan Palace of Culture ("Stalin's Gift") where we had played last year. We had a few minutes to spare so I went to buy batteries for my sequencer. Paul gave me that "Please don't wander off and get into any trouble and miss the train" look. I suppose he has good reason to worry. I do seem to be incident prone. I got back to the platform in plenty of time and we all hung around, chatting and stamping our feet, in the bitterly cold air of this sunny Polish November morning. We signed the occasional autograph as we waited. "Are you Marillion?"

"No, I'm freezing"

"I think you are Marillion"

"Oh, go on then."

"It's not for me, I don't like you, it's for my cousin…" etc.

The train arrived (on time) and we boarded. I settled down in a compartment with Paul, along with a distinguished looking middle-aged woman. As Paul and I chatted away I discerned from her eyes that, although she appeared to be reading the newspaper (which was printed, of course, in Polish), she was following our conversation. I got the feeling that not only did she speak very good English, but that she was possessed of a certain sensitivity and humour. When Paul and I later shared a joke together I noticed her smiling discretely to herself. I introduced myself and Paul, and said I had suspected she spoke English. Her name was Olga Stoklosa. It transpired that she is a theatre director from Warzsawa, currently working on a production in Cracow – hence the journey. Her husband is a composer. We discussed yesterday's general election, during which the people had ousted their president and long-standing hero, Lech Walesa, in favour of Aleksander Kwasniewski, the ex-communist. She explained that Walesa, although probably the founder of the resistance movement which was to indirectly bring about the collapse of the Russian-controlled Eastern bloc, had become something of an embarrassment as President. She said that his coarse working-class accent and simple-minded thinking were not appropriate to a position which must command respect internationally. I don't know that I agree. Give me a visionary with a pure and incorruptible heart any day in preference to a cynical opportunist who knows how to hold a knife and fork. She said that the young people had turned against Walesa (not "hip" enough etc). Oh well. Let's hope they know what they're doing. History owes Poland and its people quite a few favours. I have seen this country transformed in the last few years. It would be heartbreaking to see a backward slide into dictatorship and decay.

Paul kept coming and going, nervously checking everything was OK with the rest of the band.

I chatted to Olga for much of the journey from Warzsawa to Cracow as we sped through seemingly limitless snow-covered countryside.

As we got further south and nearer to Cracow, the surroundings became hilly and, consequently, much more beautiful. I had been looking forward to Cracow. I was there in the summer. It's a very old and Gothic town, like every Frankenstein movie you ever saw – Peter Cushing is everywhere, emerging from the old wooden doorways into the cobbled streets (I can easily imagine myself in a big shirt, screaming, "LIVE!!" in some attic laboratory full of high-voltage equipment, as my coach and horses rattles nervously in the courtyard below). The people are friendly and we're quite well-known here, so we don't pay for drinks very often. I couldn't wait to see the domes, spires and rooftops of the old town covered in snow. When we arrived I said farewell to Olga, who invited me to her house if ever I should find myself alone in Warzsawa. "We have a Bösendorfer piano which I'm sure you would love to play," she said, "and you could dine with my family and talk about music with my husband." That would be something. I thanked her. I'll take her up on the offer if I should ever have the chance; you never know.

We climbed down from the train and made our way out of the station into the snow-covered street where a mini-bus was already waiting, care of Eva, the promoter's assistant. It was great to be back so soon. Unfortunately the hotel wasn't in the centre of town, which was a shame because I would have been off for a walk across the town square (the Rynek) and a mooch round the market. There wouldn't have been time anyway. We had to regroup immediately in the hotel lobby for TV and radio interviews. I was dog-tired and bluffed my way through them. No time. No time.

We left for soundcheck straight after the interviews, driving back into town to the venue, the Korona – a 1000-ish capacity hall where, if I'm not mistaken, gymnastics displays are the usual form of entertainment. Our dressing rooms were in the basement of the building, in the changing rooms. Outside in the corridors there were old posters and photographs of Olympic gymnastic heroes and heroines: muscular young men holding impossible positions on the rings and, pinned to a notice board, images of pre-pubescent girls frolicking on the beach. This latter picture probably represented the local team's annual holiday, perhaps a luxury extended by the coach in return for a childhood dedicated to obsessive training. I found something slightly disturbing about the holiday photograph. All the girls seemed to be adopting curiously flirtatious poses for the camera. I've heard rumours about the power that coaches in the Eastern Bloc had over their athletes. At one time here, to be an accomplished athlete was one of the few ways to elevate yourself to a better life. Maybe you would put up with anything to remain part of the elite… maybe I'm reading too much into a holiday snap… it's just a feeling.

We were shown into a gymnasium where two small tables were set for dinner. We ate noodle soup next to the wall bars and had curious salad with sweet crispy things in it, before going upstairs to soundcheck. Tonight is to be the last show of the **Afraid of Sunlight** tour, so I was keen to throw a few extra songs into the set. We rehearsed *Out of this World,* but decided it wasn't going to measure up without spending more time on it. We went for the easier options – a couple of Beatle songs and the old standby's, *Sugar Mice, The Space* and, to my relief, *Alone Again in the Lap of Luxury.*

After soundcheck I was tired out and, for the first time today, there was the prospect of an hour with nothing to do. So I arranged with Paul and Tim to borrow Tim's bunk on the crew bus so that I could sleep. I was spirited out of the hall, into the street, out of sight of the people waiting to come in. Everything was frozen solid. There was a half-inch of ice covering everything in the darkness. I jumped gratefully onto the warm crew bus where my eyes fell immediately upon an immaculate wooden sledge. One of the bus drivers had bought it for his children. It had a curved wooden frame, metal runners, and was big enough for two. "Wow! It's fantastic!" I said.

"Do you want me to see if I can get you one?" said Tim, always willing to help.

I thanked him and said I would love one to take home for Sofie and Nial. The bus driver said I could have this one and he would arrange to buy another for himself. I checked he was absolutely sure as I didn't want to appear to be pulling rank. He said he wanted something slightly smaller anyway, so I accepted his offer and arranged to pay Tim for it. It would make a lovely souvenir of Cracow and a fantastic present for my small people. I climbed into Tim's bunk and lay there for some time, listening to the noises filtering in from outside, the footsteps of passing strangers and the murmur of happy anticipation (one of the best sounds I can imagine), as well as the recognisable shouts of the crew. I love to lie in the darkness and listen to the rich cocktail of the noises of the outside world until I drift into dreamlike thoughts – that not knowing whether or not I'm asleep.

At 7.30 I roused myself and was taken back into the building by Paul, stopping briefly to sign an autograph for a girl who had obviously waited outside the bus for quite some time and was almost frozen solid. Upon entering the hall, we realised that I would have to cross the hall and then the stage in full view of the audience. I tried to keep my head down, but I was quickly spotted and a cheer went up for me, which I acknowledged with an embarrassed wave. At this point in an evening I'm still the "off-stage" Steve h, so I react nervously to the kind of adulation that, in thirty minutes time, I will take completely in my stride.

Well, the show turned out to be great fun. The crowd were totally into it, and the atmosphere was such that the military-looking security men between the stage and crash barriers gradually relaxed and adopted a low profile, apart from pulling out the occasional fainters in the front row. At the end of the set we got into three or four encores, and I sang 'til I couldn't sing anymore. It didn't matter. I wouldn't have to sing live again until next spring.

After the show we returned to the worst hotel bar in the world. It reminded me of one of those nightclubs on ships with the obligatory dreadful cabaret band. I was in one once. Well, I sat at the bar for a while and chatted to our promoter, Oleg (I think!), who said that perhaps with the next album we might do some shows in Russia. I would love to see St. Petersburg and Moscow. The two Piotrs from RMF FM called in, despite it being late, and one of them gave me a book: a souvenir of Cracow, the city photographed from the air and the interiors of the many churches. Something to flip through and remember when I'm back in England. I can't begin to imagine receiving such generosity from any DJ working in the UK (apart from, perhaps, the lovely Bob Harris). I hung around a while longer at the bar, but was eventually driven away by the drab atmosphere.

Wednesday 22 November *Cracow – Warszawa – Frankfurt – Heathrow – Home*

Woke at 11.00, and made my way down to the lobby in several layers of warm clothing in order to be insulated against the icy air. I had arranged yesterday to meet up with the boys at 11.30 to go into Cracow centre and do a little shopping. I wasn't surprised to find myself alone in hotel reception as 11.30 came and went. I will never understand how anyone would pass up the chance to explore a town as beautiful and unique as this in preference to an extra hour in bed. I changed up some złotys and ordered a cab into town.

As I was leaving, Mark appeared so we left together and a taxi took us to the main square, the Rynek. I had been here with Pete in the summer. We had stayed in the centre of town at the Grand Hotel, so I know my way around. I took Mark to the market, and we wandered up and down the stalls looking for potential Christmas presents. I bought some amber and silver earrings for Sue (amber is found in large quantities on the Baltic coastline, so there is a tradition of using it in jewellery in all the Baltic States). I also bought some postcards from a little stationery stall. I wondered how the man serving could justify sitting freezing there all day in the cause of earning such a small amount. He didn't look particularly poor.

It wasn't long before the cold worked its way into our bones, so we abandoned shopping in favour of finding a spot of breakfast somewhere. Mark fancied toast and eggs, so I took him to the breakfast room/café at the Grand Hotel where the waitresses had been so helpful and amusing last time. I was looking for one particular woman whose name I can't remember (Irina?) who was most kind to us whenever we arrived late for breakfast last time. She would tease us and say breakfast is finished with a certain playful, matronly humour common among mature Polish women. When Mark and I arrived at the café, still beating out the cold from our hands and feet, there she was! She was pleased to see we had returned, and I kissed her cheek as we sat down for omelette with bacon, toast and coffee. I scribbled a few postcards as we ate. We returned to the streets of the old town, feeling much warmer and refreshed, and I took Jack over the square to the St. Mary's Basilica – the beautiful old church in the corner, which is not to be missed. There's an amazing wooden sculpture of Christ inside. There's also a man who pops out of one of the upper windows to blow a trumpet every hour – a human cuckoo clock! What a way to make a living…

We returned to the hotel to pack and prepare for the long journey home – first by train to Warzsawa and then by plane, via Frankfurt (the), to Heathrow. On the long train journey back to Warszawa we were approached by a man wearing a suit and carrying a briefcase. He told us he was the owner of a computer software company in Gdansk and a big fan of contemporary music for many years. He had specially made the journey from the North to South of Poland to see us play in Cracow. He was over the moon at having bumped into us and insisted on buying us lunch in the restaurant car. I wasn't hungry myself, but joined him to talk about his life and his business. He invited us to his home to talk further about (and listen to) music if ever we should come to Gdansk. He also promotes shows and has been responsible for bringing quite a few known international artists to Poland.

At Warszawa station we were met by Kinga and Eva, who took us to the airport and waited to ensure we had no problems at check-in. We thanked them both and said bye-bye, hopefully until next time. I wandered round the Duty Free and bought vodka before climbing aboard the jet to Frankfurt. There was one nervous moment when we spied a SWAT team – about twelve of the hardest looking cases I've ever seen, complete with sub-machine guns, donning black balaclavas as they ran along an opposite corridor. Well, a hijacking would have made the trip complete! But we boarded the plane without incident, so maybe they were just on some training exercise…

1996 APRIL

Sunday 21

1996

Sunday 21 April *Home – Hilversum – Utrecht*

Woke at 6.50, but dozed determinedly until 7.30 when I decided I couldn't leave it any longer. Went downstairs and made myself a list of what not to forget, showered, and cleaned my teeth. Sofie appeared and wished me good morning. Today is Sunday, so she disappeared into the lounge to watch the TV while I carried on putting my things into little piles, en route to the suitcase and Europe.

I was expecting a car to Heathrow at 8.30. I made Sue a cup of tea. The suitcases are jammed into a noisy cupboard in our bedroom, so I knew I would wake her in the process of retrieving one. As I made my way upstairs, there was a knock on the front door. It was my driver, come to pick me up at 8.00. I had got it wrong again! I now have a tradition of not packing until the car arrives. I went upstairs and chatted to Sue for a few minutes to tell her I will miss her while I'm away, and noisily dislodged my Delsey from its hiding place. Finished packing and said my goodbyes and drove to Heathrow via Bicester, where we picked up Stuart, our engineer.

The morning was truly the first day of spring – a wide open, sunny, warm morning at last. The winter has made us wait until now.

At Heathrow I bumped into Dan and Dana Sherman, our American fan club presidents, flown in from Chicago for the European shows. They presented me with a red rose from Min, an English fan whose marriage they had attended yesterday in Cambridge.

And so the madness begins again.

I checked in and gave my passport back to Paul. After Poland I'm nervous about trusting myself with it. That was mistake number 2. When I got to the gate they wanted to see it, so I was detained until Paul arrived from the Duty Free.

I sat at the front of the Boeing 737 inbetween Ian and Mark for the short flight to Amsterdam Schipol, relaxing in anticipation of the days ahead. We were met at the airport by two chaps from the record company, Dureco.

"Hello," said one, "I'm Hype."

"Do you do promotion?" I quipped.

"No. I'm the product manager."

Perhaps the joke was wearing a bit thin. I didn't pursue it. It turned out he was called Hybe not Hype, so no wonder he didn't even pretend to be amused. Not that it was funny anyway...

We were driven in a minibus (which looked like a Stealth bomber) to Hilversum – my second surprise of the day. I thought we were going to Utrecht to check into the Hotel and freshen up. Not possible.

At Hilversum we arrived outside a radio station, where there were a small group of fans waiting with album covers and magic markers. When I say album covers, I mean CD wallets; vinyl is now very much a medium of the past. I entered the radio station, marvelling at the fact that the fans always seem to know where we are – until I discovered that today's show includes a small invited audience of 90 or so people. The studio area was set out like a little nightclub, complete with stage and bar. I immediately warmed to the situation.

The staff seemed to know their gig, and we soundchecked without any trouble. There was a row of Martin wedges along the front of the stage, which effortlessly provided us with a good monitor sound. We all went downstairs and sat in the sunshine of a perfect spring afternoon, waiting the two hours before we were on air. I chatted to René, Peter and Rijnus from the Dutch fan club about my solo album plans, wondering if I was, once again, opening my big mouth too soon.

When we returned to the studio it was full of people, a great many of whom I recognized. I chatted and signed bits of paper, CD inserts, arms and legs, and posed for photographs with the various fans before doing a short interview with the programme DJ – and then we were on stage. I started with a piano and vocal version of *Cover my Eyes,* before introducing Pete for a bass guitar and vocal rendition of *The Bell in the Sea. Beautiful* followed with the whole band, and then *Easter, Sugar Mice* and *Made Again.* All were received with enthusiastic applause by our little audience.

Afterwards I was given a birthday present by Inge and Natasha, regular contributors to the Dutch fan club magazine. It was a pair of jangly vibe balls, blue with little Chinese peace signs on them. I thanked them and we headed off to a restaurant to have dinner with the record company people and with Yvonne and Yvette from Rondor (my publishers) in Amsterdam.

I was interviewed during dinner for some magazine or other, and escaped for a little walk in the warm evening air when nobody was looking. I found a couple of great furniture shops at the end of the street containing a lovely old coffee table, a fantastic sofa, and a few light-fittings to die for. I have a weakness for lights. Fortunately the shops were closed, or I'd have been in debt by now.

I returned to the meal. Half the band were pleasantly sloshed, but I remained sober for the next radio interview at 10.00 pm, where we were to play a short live set with acoustic guitars and vocals. This was a much more intimate affair in a small radio control room. I was monitoring on headphones and no one else, including the DJ, had a clue what was going on. What I was hearing sounded good though. I'm singing well at the moment and there's a relaxed feeling in the band, a little bit like when I first joined. The three-month break has done us all good, I think.

We finally emerged from the radio station around 11.30 and were driven to Utrecht to check into the Hotel Smits. Called home and said goodnight to Dizzy, before climbing into a much-needed bath and then going to bed, waking at various times of the night wondering where I was.

Monday 22 April *Utrecht*

Woke up at 8.40 (only 7.40 in England) and couldn't get back to sleep. So much for the lie-in! Got up and showered and called home to say hello to Sofie and Nial before they went off to school.

I made my way to the breakfast room where breakfast was being cleared away, and managed to grab a pot of coffee and some bread and cheese before it was removed. Retired to the adjoining bar and spent an hour-or-so writing this diary before I was accosted by a couple of boys from Switzerland who had made the journey to Holland to see us, and who were staying in the hotel. I talked to them for quite some time about the state of things in general, peoples goals and ambitions, the shape of the planet and the folly of measuring success in terms of growth. I showed Francois (who played a bit of piano) how to play the chords to *The Hollow Man.*

Returned to my room and called my mum – it's her birthday today. She sounded fine. Bumped into Paul L, who was on his way out to have coffee in the sunshine of another excellent day. We found a café by a canal where Mark K and Manu (Mark's girlfriend) were already sitting.

I was soon driven back indoors by hay fever. For some reason, the week of my mother's birthday is a bad pollen week for me and, every year, no matter where I happen to be, I have a couple of days of sore eyes and sneezing. I called home again. Things are pretty difficult at the moment between Sue and me; my enforced absences make everything worse. I put down the phone feeling terrible and went back to bed to try to sleep. Gave up around 3.00 in the afternoon and went back out for a walk. Found a bank and changed up a few guilders before making my way back to the Muziekcentrum to prepare for soundcheck.

All things considered, soundcheck ran fairly smoothly – this is the first show since last November. New monitor man, Andy, seems to be on top of his gig. I returned to the hotel around 7.00 and slept for another hour before returning to the show.

The place was packed and, as we mounted the stage, the 2000-crowd put up a roar which sounded like a stadium gig. We had the odd memory lapse here and there but, on the whole, we played well and I felt I was singing as well as ever. Each song was rapturously received and the atmosphere during the show really defies description. As they say, you had to be there.

Afterwards I stayed up far too late, talking to the Dutch fan club and drinking with the Rondor mob. Fell into bed exhausted in the middle of the night.

Tuesday 23 April *Köln, E-Werk*

Woken by the telephone at 7.45. It was Paul to say we will leave at 8.30 to take cabs to Schipol. I don't know what it is about this airport, but I always seem to feel like a corpse whenever I'm here. This morning was a good case in point. We checked in and went through passport control (twice) and X-ray machines (twice). Security's tight this morning. Walked about 10 miles to Gate B4 where the café was closed and the vending machines were out of order. Just like England. We were to fly to Dusseldorf in a light aeroplane, but Dusseldorf airport had burned down a couple of days ago, so we were diverted to Dortmund where we were to hire cars to drive to Köln.

The turboprop rattled its way down onto the tarmac at Dortmund. The stewardess happened to be sitting immediately opposite me, and looked extremely nervous as we landed, heaving a discrete sigh of relief once we were down. Maybe she knew something that we didn't. When the stewardesses look nervous, that's the time to worry!

For some reason Customs seemed nervous too, and detained several people to ask questions and open bags. I was asked where I had come from. It seemed an odd question – everyone had been on the same plane.

I snoozed as we drove for an hour down the motorway to Köln, and then checked into the Ascot Hotel. Closed the curtains and went to bed until Paul called at 3.30 to leave for soundcheck.

The E-Werk, as its name implies, was once a power plant of some kind and is situated on the edge of the city in an industrial area. The Germans have done a typically first-rate job of converting the building into a nightclub. Perfectly designed for rock n'roll. I looked around the place, quietly lamenting the fact that no one in England would ever spend this kind of money on (and attention to) a rock club. Contemporary music is now one of Britain's top five exports, and yet the industry receives nothing in the way of financial support or even a cursory nod of respect from the politicians or establishment. The Exchequer receives millions upon *millions* from live and recorded pop and rock music in the UK. Why haven't we got a national rock radio station? Why hasn't each major town and city subsidised a purpose-built club where up-and-coming bands can play? Why doesn't each major town and city provide rehearsal facilities for bands to hone their talent? They do in Germany. The British Arts Council annually pumps millions into opera which earns the country nothing and, for the most part, employs and exploits the work of non-British talent. Why not build the country a few venues like the E-Werk? Oh well. Might as well ask 'em to cancel a missile project for all the good it would do.

Rant over. Back to the gig. I made my way downstairs and had a spot of dinner with John and Pete. We hadn't brought caterers with us, so the food was supplied locally and cooked by a German chef (who shattered the myth about German cooking by serving up a first-rate mushroom soup, with a not-at-all-bad second course to follow).

Soundcheck went without a hitch. I was still tired from last night's scarcity of sleep, so I returned to the Ascot and went back to bed for another hour under the big chandelier in room 104.

The gig was sold-out at around 2700. As I was about to go on stage, bending down to fasten my boots, I was given a friendly slap on the backside by our promoter, Peter Rieger. I have come to like Peter over the years. He has a streak of insanity about him, to which the people around him sometimes fall victim. He seems to do himself more damage than anyone else, though. I know the feeling.

Unfortunately, tonight was to be blighted by technical problems. They centred around the guitar radio-systems which, combined with Steve's current curse of breaking guitar strings in the solos, more or less put paid to the last song of the set, *100 Nights.* This took the wind out of our sails at the most crucial point in the show, and I was pretty upset about it. I was reminded of the Toronto show on the **Afraid of Sunlight** tour which went west for the same reasons. Some people live and learn. Fortunately for us, the crowd was not easily discouraged and gave us a warm welcome back to the stage for two encores which were to save the day. Thank you Köln, you were terrific. Last time I played here, a few years back, I experienced several supernatural phenomena: I was thrown inexplicably to the floor several times during the show, and during *100 Nights* (oddly enough) a butterfly fluttered down from the ceiling and landed on my shoulder. It's the only time I have ever seen a butterfly in a nightclub. To my relief, there were no such strange happenings tonight.

After the show, I signed a few things in the hall and we returned to The Ascot, where I phoned home to wish Sue goodnight.

We had arranged to have a drink with the record company chaps, but I was worn out and it hadn't been a good phone call home, so I went to bed.

Wednesday 24 April *Köln – Paris, La Cigale*

Woken by Paul at some unholy hour of the morning for yet *another* early departure. The cumulative physical excesses of the shows, combined with not enough sleep and a state of increasing domestic unhappiness and mental exhaustion left me in not-the-best of spirits as I staggered down the single flight of stairs from the first floor to reception. I thanked the staff and paid my extras like an automaton, emerging into the street and ducking the oncoming cyclists in the cycling lane, which always catches me out every time I leave the Ascot. I sat in the back of the car and told everyone I would probably be quieter than usual today.

At Köln airport John and Paul got rid of the hire cars and checked us in for the short flight to Paris, which I can't remember at all. We arrived at CdG in a different Terminal to the usual 60's **Thunderbirds** affair I'm used to. This one's newer and a little reminiscent of the beautiful and modern (I know it's normally a contradiction in terms) airport at Barcelona. We walked the short distance to the train terminal, where Paul bought tickets for Paris Gare du Nord. The hotel is right across the street from La Gare du Nord, so the train is quicker and easier than taking a cab through Paris's famously congested roads.

As we emerged from the station it began to rain, despite being quite a sunny day. It almost felt as though my state of mind had brought the rain on, like it was my own cloud.

We checked into the Libertel and I made my way upstairs into the maze of corridors, where room numbers seem to bear no relation to their position. Finding your room is made even trickier by the wallpaper in the corridors, which challenges the perspective and makes you feel like you're trapped inside a crystal or a set of encyclopedias (go and have a look). I eventually found my room and called home. No answer. I left a message on the machine and hung up. My urge to wander up to Montmartre and have lunch on the hill was outweighed by an inability to summon the will to move, so I lay on the bed in limbo until 3.30, when Paul called. I told him I would rather walk the half-mile to La Cigale than go by car, so he arranged cabs for the rest of the band and said he would accompany me on foot.

At around 3.45 Paul and I wended our way through the streets of Paris in the approximate direction of the gig. The rain had given way to occasional sunshine as we walked along Montmartre's back streets. We eventually intersected the Boulevard Rochouarte, and I recognized the wide avenue – memories came flooding back of the Manor Mobile parked outside La Cigale back in '94, when Dave Meegan recorded the **Brave** shows. Outside the venue there were already a clutch of fans waiting, and I was politely mobbed, with that combination of affection and restraint that seems to come as second nature to the French. I signed sleeves and tickets and posed for snapshots while Paul patiently looked on, before entering the theatre. It was good to be back here. It's always a private achievement to return to the place where you've had a great gig in the past and feel the ghosts and echoes going off in your mind as you look around. There's also the additional boost of knowing that a Marillion crowd awaits. Our audience are so faithful that there's a good chance of repeating the experience again tonight. The atmosphere will probably live up to my best expectations.

I made my way backstage and up three flights of steep wooden stairs to the catering area, where a French boy and girl were in the somewhat uncertain throes of cooking us dinner. This was supposed to be ready for us at 5.00, although I think 5.00 came and went before they got around to turning the oven on. Minute steak and rice eventually happened.

On stage things were sounding loud but controlled. I remember this from last time. Andy (new boy on monitors) was still working well. After last night's fiasco with the guitars I was relieved to hear the systems working OK. Things had been hired.

1997 FEBRUARY

Tuesday 11

1 9 9 7

Sunday 9 February (h Band) *London, The Garage*

Sue was still feeling dreadful, so it looks as if she's going to miss seeing any of my solo shows. If she's better in the week then maybe we can meet up at one of the European shows. I packed my things and arranged a cab to take me to the station at 1.30 – I was leaving early in the hope of going shopping for stage clothes. The cab arrived a little late at 1.15. I kissed bye-bye to Sofie and Nial at the front door. Sue was still in bed.

We just made it to the station in time to buy a ticket and jump aboard the train, which was already at the platform. The journey to London was uneventful. There were no cabs at Marylebone, so I walked along the West Way towards Baker Street before hailing a cab to Covent Garden. I headed for Neal Street, where I thought the shops were most likely to be open. Paul Smith was closed, which was a pity. There was a great embroidered jacket in the window. I eventually found a pair of black trousers and a black t-shirt in Agnes B, along with some green velvet trousers over the road in Jones – always a good bet for something wacky.

By now it was 4.30, so I took the tube to Highbury & Islington and made my way across the road to The Garage, which was deserted. I rang the bell in the doorway next to a couple of pictures of myself labeled "Steve Hogarth of Marillion". Numerous instructions to both the promoter and the venue NOT to bill me in this way had made no difference. Never mind, spilled milk. They'll always do what they've gotta do to sell tickets. Someone let me in and I had a sniff around the club, which seemed OK. Priv was ensconced in a sort of DJ console thing and said anything that keeps the punters out is just fine by him. Richard B was already on stage, and he came down and introduced me to his wife, Suzanne, who was sitting in the shadows. We didn't talk for long but she struck me as a really nice person. It's a shame I didn't have Sue with me, I think they would have got on. Stewart was busy searching for the power supply for the drum-sample pads which seems to have gone missing since the Oswestry gig; otherwise, he seems fine. Nick B was busy doing tour managery things – writing things on bits of A4 paper and talking into a mobile phone while shaking his head and wearing his, "I don't believe it!...Why doesn't anyone listen?!... I thought we'd already sorted this out... I'm surrounded by idiots..." expression. The dressing room was small and smelly, so I decided to avoid it if I possibly could. I went on stage and checked everything was OK with the Kurzweil. It was. I diddled about checking this and that while the musicians arrived one at a time; first Dave Gregory, then Clem Burke, then Aziz Ibrahim. Chucho Merchan had called to say he was running a little late as he was trying to sort out the problems with his crashed car. I said hello to Angie Moxham who had come down to soundcheck, and then I got photographed eating a filled roll in the smelly dressing room for Jill Douglas, who wanted some casual photographs.

The band were on stage playing by the time Chucho appeared at around 6.30. Everything seemed OK – my monitors were sounding good, apart from an intermittent hum which was coming from the house system.

The bus had arrived behind the venue so I transferred my stuff onto it. It's a Len Wright tour bus and I recognised it from the decor inside as the crew bus from the **Afraid of Sunlight** tour. I bagged a bunk "in the middle in the middle" which is where I like to sleep on tour busses. I lay down and had half an hour with my eyes closed until Nick returned with John A to say hello before the show. I called Sue with Nick's mobile and she wished me luck before I got changed for the show. I also met Chucho's wife, Anne-Marie, briefly – I had seen her before back in 1990 in Rio. I remember her walking into the hotel with Annie Lennox; they were both wearing identical leather sandals which they'd bought in one of the leather markets, and I remember thinking I'd like a pair of those myself. I didn't mention it, although I probably will if I get to know her better – maybe she's still got 'em in the back of a cupboard somewhere.

I don't really remember too much about the gig; I think we got most of it right. I didn't think about who was in the audience, although I guessed there would be quite a few record company people and, much more fearsome, the rest of the boys from Marillion! Afterwards I found out that Ian, Pete, Mark and Steve were there – Ian was typically first backstage to say hello and that he enjoyed the show. Thanks, Ian. Priv seemed happy with it, so by now I was feeling like it must have been a good gig (I have to be told).

I didn't hang around too long in the dressing room. When I went out front I only managed a couple of paces into the room before I was nobbled by the faithful, so I couldn't really mingle. Mark came over and said he thought it was great, particularly *King* which he said he'd never really liked up until tonight! When there was almost no one left in the club, Steve R came over and said hello and said he'd enjoyed the show. I tore myself away from the remaining fans and returned to the tour bus, which was a bustle of musicians trying to work out where to sleep and where to put their things. We eventually got semi-organised. I was sleeping with Clem above me, Aziz below me, and Richard across the aisle. I handed out Glo-Stars – little luminous stickers of planets and space rockets which we stuck to our bunk ceilings for enhanced cosmic experience in the night!

I had brought too many bags on this tour – lots of little ones: toilet bag, laptop, suit bag, hold-all, and numerous Agnes B carriers. Chaos. I'm bound to lose at least one of them. I bundled them all into an empty bunk below Richard, and went to the back lounge to see what was going on. Overcome by tiredness I made excuses, said goodnight and entombed myself in my bunk.

Monday 10 February (h Band) *Paris, Le Divan du Monde*

Woke up for the umpteenth time to realise that the bus was stationary and so we are probably in Paris. Pulled back my little curtain to have a squint through my bunk porthole. DayGlo awnings assaulted my delicate eyes, proclaiming 'SEX... HOMO... LESBIENNES... HETERO... 400F.' We were in the heart of La Pigalle, the red light district, about 100-metres from Le Moulin Rouge. I decided I would sleep a little more and take advantage of the chance (rare these days) of a lie-in. I'd had too much to drink after the London show and my head wasn't ready for the day.

By 11.00, the sounds of people creeping about (which are somehow always louder than natural movement) roused me into action. I realised my teeth were in desperate need of a brushing and staggered into the bus toilet to sort myself out. Nick had left a map to the hotel on the table, and I was deciding which way up to hold it when Clem emerged from the bunk deck, grinning affably, with one of those masks that block out the light pulled up above his hair-line. He seemed reminiscent of one of those early pioneers of flying machines... or a Sixties speed record holder. Clem's my hero at the moment. He lost his father in December and I've heard they were very close. Nonetheless, here he is, giving it all he's got without a word of complaint about the compromises that come with a tight budget. We're all having to slum it a little to make ends meet. All the boys in my band have been there, done it, enjoyed it, seen through it, and have a perspective on the whole game which has left them enthusiastic yet, like me, tinged with a certain realism and a necessary pragmatism. We all know what it's like to be adored, and we've all been ripped off too – me probably least of all.

I made my way over to the hotel Blanche Fontaine to shower and call home, before setting out with Dave Gregory in search of French brunch. We wandered about La Pigalle trying to find somewhere to eat. Dave fancied an omelette, so it was a while before we spotted said item on the menu of a small but beautifully formed brasserie, the name of which escapes me. There was only one customer in the place – a mature lady who was seated next to a little dog which appeared to be her life's companion, and to which she was feeding forkfuls of her lunch. Dave and I struggled with our pidgin French to communicate our desire for omelette to the waitress (and, I suspect, owner of the establishment). She seemed amused by our efforts (in a motherly sort of way), and condescended to translate the menu into English. Everybody says the French (and particularly the Parisians) don't like the English. I have never found this to be the case, apart from the cab drivers who are, by and large, ignorant, crooked and hate everybody.

We returned to the bus around 4.00 and I later walked alone to the venue, Le Divan du Monde. I was temporarily waylaid by Samantha, who stopped me in the street to expound on the delights of her sex club. "Only four hundred francs. You can 'avve a free drinks and watch zer sex show - woman and woman - woman and man - there are girls - you don't have to go wizzerr girl… but perhaps you would like to 'avve zer Special Moment…"

I thanked her for her time, but explained that I must work and continued down the street where I encountered Nick B, who had watched all this from a distance – to considerable amusement. We wandered round the corner, where a group of five or six people were shivering in the drizzle. Nick showed me the way into the building before returning to the Hotel for the rest of the band. I hung around in the street talking to the fans, most memorably a girl called Noox who had brought a considerable collection of photographs and album booklets which I was asked to dedicate to half of France: "…This one to Eric please… this one to Hervé… this one to Sandrine… to Louis… to Noox – that's me…"

My curiosity soon got the better of me, and I hurried inside the club for a look at the interior. The club was small and balconied, with a tiny PA system that Priv was wrestling with in the hope of creating a sound worth hearing. He seemed resigned, but made a show of optimism for my benefit. I found the backstage area and made a couple of cups of coffee, which I took outside for the kids to share out. Back inside the club there was much concern expressed by the management with regard to noise levels – new legislation in Paris etc. Over the years I have learned to totally ignore any such concerns. A rock drummer hitting a kit has a natural acoustic level which exceeds 100db in any room other than a padded cell – and that's before anyone strikes up a note of music. So as far as noise restrictions are concerned, it's best to agree, sympathise, and then forget about it. Ironically, the sound onstage was really well balanced, thanks to the house monitor man who seemed to know his onions. Priv might have concluded that his best option was to leave the PA off for the show and come and sit up there with us.

Soundcheck went well and I had a long chat with John A about the way everything was progressing. Situation normal: no good news. Ticket sales for tonight's show are inexplicably small at around 200 – I daresay I'll never find out why. It's spilled milk already. The promoter, Gerard Drouot, was unavailable for comment – on holiday on St Bart, his Caribbean retreat. He had sent me a bottle of Dom Ruinart, the champagne whose cellars we had visited together when we were last in Rheims. It looks expensive. If I were a cynic(!) I might calculate that it was a toss-up between the champagne and advertising the gig, but that would be unkind.

We returned to the hotel to pick up our bags and trudged back to the bus in the rain. "I bet you didn't have David Bowie doing this," I quipped over my shoulder to Nick as I staggered along the Pigalle with my heavy bag and the water dripping off my nose and eyebrows. Nonetheless, I was looking forward to the show. Another chance to listen to Aziz Ibrahim and Richard Barbieri weaving their magic carpet of atmospheres which form the introduction to my album and cloak the songs with echoes of other cultures. Also another chance to play to a Paris crowd, no matter how small.

The vibe in the room was to prove to be out of all proportion to the size of the crowd and it was, once again, a rare evening. We were called back for three encores. We had prepared a maximum of two, so I went out alone with the intention of fumbling through half remembered piano/voice versions of *Easter* and *The Hollow Man.* I amazed myself by playing *Easter* almost correctly, and then cried my way through *The Hollow Man* as the irony of its sentiment broke over me anew. I always blub in Paris - like rock n'roll's' equivalent of Paul Gascoigne. Thank you all the same, Paris.

Afterwards I was interviewed, keeping my old friend Sally waiting. It was a shame we couldn't have grabbed more than a minute. I was hustled away, last as usual, to a restaurant across town to have dinner with Jean Marc from the record label. I ordered all the wrong things and didn't really feel like eating them. There was some confusion over the bus which was supposed to meet up with us after dinner but had failed to show. We eventually had to move next door to allow the restaurant staff to go home to bed. It was kind of fun. All Aziz's fault for confusing the arrangements. Nick made a show of annoyance, but I don't think anyone really minded much. The bus finally arrived at around 3.00 and we clambered on. I wasted no time getting to bed – I was suddenly tired, and looking forward to the day off in Amsterdam…

Tuesday 11 February (h Band) *Amsterdam:* Day off

Woke as the bus cut its engine. Opened my porthole curtain, and I could tell by the light that it was 9.00 or so in the morning. As far as I could tell, we were in some kind of a parking spot in the country – a hill and a line of trees… perhaps the only hill in the Netherlands. I drifted back into sleep after contemplating the luminous spaceships I had stuck on the ceiling of my bunk. When I awoke again we were moving along a river that was unmistakably Dutch – lined with houseboats and crisscrossed by those bridges that lift up to let the taller boats pass underneath. We passed the Amstel Hotel, and I realised we were in Amsterdam following the Amstel River, very close to the Leidesplein and the good old American Hotel. I debunked and made my way to the front of the bus, where Priv and Stewart were enjoying the sunshine of a fantastic morning and planning a day doing the museums. John (bus driver) parked the bus outside the American and I gingerly opened the door of the back lounge, hoping to avoid the cars and cyclists whizzing by from every conceivable direction. I made my way to room 416 where the Pretenders were playing on the radio (*Back on the Chaingang*), and had a much-needed shower before calling home. Sue's feeling a little better at last, although she doesn't think she'll be up to a trip to Köln tomorrow.

I strolled out along the Leidesplein in the sunshine to enjoy a light lunch in my favourite little café on the top floor of Metz department store, overlooking the city. Heaven. I had a club sandwich and lazily fell back in love with Amsterdam's beauty before I returned to the American and went to bed for the afternoon. At 4.30 John rang to talk about the financial pros and cons of filming tomorrow's show at the Milky Way. We decided to do it and worry about the money afterwards. Neils van Iperen and Bert will shoot the show. Whoopee! After that, I couldn't get back to sleep so I got up and decided to go shopping. I spent a couple of hours wandering around without seeing anything I would want to wear – I was hoping to find something for tomorrow night's show. In the end, after hours of walking, I found an Agnes B and bought a black t-shirt just as they were closing.

I returned to the American and sat down in the bar with an Irish coffee (oddly enough, something of a speciality in the Netherlands. Try asking for a Snowball or Advocaat and they stare blankly back), nonchalantly scanning the walls which are festooned with all the celebs who've stayed here over the years: everyone from Clapton to Crowded House and Estefan to Springsteen. When I was here in December shooting the video for *You Dinosaur Thing*, the bar-manager Cor (as in "blimey" – his words) took my photograph, so I was wondering if I'd made it onto the wall, perhaps tucked away in some corner behind the jukebox or something. Just as I stopped looking and returned my attentions to my drink, there I was, right in front of myself. They'd hung me in just about the most prominent position in the bar , just above Nina Hagen and next door but two to Eric C. Fame at last! (I wonder if they'll take me down after I've gone...)

PS They didn't – I was up there last time I looked in 2013.

Yvonne from Rondor appeared in the bar. She was there to meet some Australian boy-band who were arriving. We chatted for a while and were joined by Aziz, who had an orange juice. He's a muslim and his religion forbids alcohol. It's just as well – he seems to be on a planet of his own as it is...

Around 8.00 I went upstairs and phoned around to gather support for an excursion out to dinner but no-one was in, so I dined alone in one of the many Indonesian restaurants found here. I returned to the American around 11.00 to discover a promotion schedule pushed under my door for tomorrow, starting at

11.00 am through 'til 2.00. I was still tired. When Niels Van Iperen (photographer who took the ICG "Ice Cream" shots and directed the *You Dinosaur Thing* video) called my room at 11.30 to say he was downstairs in the bar, I was already asleep and unable to contemplate getting up again. Sorry Niels, you're dealing with a lightweight.

Wednesday 12 February (h Band) *Amsterdam, Melkweg*

The phone rang at 10.30, rocketing me from dreams to reality – the opposite direction of travel to most people, I suppose. I usually dream about mundane things, like going to the shop or putting a plug on, and then wake up to the prospect of being a rock star... sometimes I just want to go back to sleep. It was Nick B with my alarm call: 30 minutes to the first interview...

At 11.00 there was a knock at my door and I opened it to a six-foot blonde beauty with an ear-to-ear grin. She's Diane, the record company 'get-the-artist-to-the-interview' girl. She seemed interested to see my room so I gave her a quick tour and we left to go to another hotel room where the first interviewer was waiting to begin. As we walked along the corridor Chucho was coming the other way, so we stopped and I introduced him. He said he'd spent yesterday looking at the Van Goghs and "vibing in theess byoodifool ceedee... I LOVE Amsterdam, man!" He was followed closely by Dave G, who I also introduced. By now we must have been causing some commotion in the corridor because Richard B appeared from the door next to us to say good morning. He was trouser-less and grinning, not quite prepared for an introduction to Diane. Richard's something of a prince of darkness, so it was particularly amusing to see him, in his shorts, shaking hands. I said I would see them all later, and spent the rest of the morning and early afternoon giving three interviews. As I was getting into the lift to go for my last interview, a couple of fit, young, sun-bronzed boys joined me – I guessed they must be part of the Australian boy band. I suddenly felt like I was in a scene from **Home and Away**. One of them shook my hand and said, "Hi! Will you be interviewing us this afternoon?"

"No... I don't think there's much chance of that... Cheerio!" I said.

The last interviewer said that he thought James Redfield must have written **The Celestine Prophecy** after hearing *I Will Walk on Water*, as my song pre-dates the book. Hmm...

Once I was clear of the interviews, I decided to go and have a look at the Milky Way. Nick B walked me round the corner. I know it sounds pathetic but, as tour manager, his job is to look after "the artist", which means stopping "the artist" getting lost, locked out of his own gig, mobbed, assaulted etc... In my case, and in this instance, none of the above are likely to happen, but he's a pro and it's the thought that counts... and anyway I enjoy Nick's company. If I was a millionaire I would happily employ Nick, Stewart and Priv, just to have around for laughs. Inside the venue everything was looking good – the stage is a good size. Stewart had unfortunately fallen out of the truck and dropped one of my monitors, injuring his knee (thankfully not seriously) and the monitor still sounds okay... I chatted to the fan club chaps who really do a great job here in Holland and were no doubt responsible for the ticket sales tonight, which are up at around 850 – more or less a sell-out. I was feeling distinctly dodgy by now, tired and fluey, so I thought I'd return to the bus for forty winks. Outside it was coming on to rain and I ran into Inge, Ciska and Natasja from the fan club. I invited them onto the bus so we could chat in the dry. They all seem to be keeping well. Inge and Ciska qualify as my 'oldest' Dutch fans, having both been at my first gig here with the Europeans. Incredibly, Inge tells me we played here exactly thirteen years ago to this day in 1984. Amazing – I've never been here at this venue since. The girls went off into the rain to grab a coffee, so I jumped into my bunk to relax and rest for a while. I love the solitude of tour buses. I dozed and dreamed until Nick appeared to tell me everything was ready for soundcheck.

Soundcheck with this band consists of setting levels of the drum machine so that Clem's happy to play to it, and the Roland SPD 8 drum sample pads which have the tablas and African drums for the end of *The Deep Water*. My vocal sound has been consistently good and audible, thanks to the decision to bring my own "Concert Sound" monitors from the Racket Club, along with a rack of graphics. Thank you Stewart. Shows like these, which have been a complete pleasure for me to do, could just as easily have been a total nightmare if I couldn't hear myself. I'm having Chucho's bass in my wedges also as his backline levels are really quiet compared to Pete T, who I can always hear clearly on all but the biggest stages. No trouble hearing Clem however, who remains a child of the post-punk movement in spirit and attitude. Dave G seems uneasy live, surprisingly lacking the balls-out confidence that one would expect from a man of his raw talent and pedigree. If I'd had a little longer I could have coaxed some arrogance out of him, I'm sure... but he's a perfectionist, and his imperfections plague him as much as they excite me. Aziz, on the other hand, has balls to spare in all departments and with good reason. He's like no guitar player I've heard, and is possessed of a consummate knowledge of Indian, Arabic and Chinese scales along with a Ronson/Page ability to turn on the attitude, and a terrific sense of funk rhythm. If you think it sounds good on paper, you should hear it happen! As for Richard, he just does his spooky thing on stage right – controls his own levels and gets on with it. I've got some serious talent assembled here, with a couple of geniuses amongst them. Lucky me. If you're reading this and you missed our shows, I'm here to tell you that you missed something rare and unique... and probably never to be repeated...

Well, soundcheck went off without a hitch, although Clem seemed a little uptight about something. I said hello to Niels and Bert who were down to film the show. Niels always seems laid-back. He was grinning away with his row of new teeth – he smashed his originals when he blacked out and fell over while making love in the shower after a particularly raucous night out...

We were shown to the caff where we were to be given dinner. It took an age for mine to come – something to do with Stewart eating what I'd ordered. John A appeared with John Knowles from Castle, so I said hello before running back round the corner for a quiet drink at the American.

Showtime was delayed by 15 minutes or so as the opening act had finished a little late, but that was just as well since I had a little trouble getting back into the building.

The show went by in a haze. Richard and Aziz were on stage before I had noticed they'd left the dressing room. The audience were great, although there was a little talking during the quiet moments, which is a little distracting for me. I learnt long ago not to get rattled by this sort of thing - especially as it's probably an expression of excitement rather than boredom - and it was to be by far the biggest crowd of the 'tour'. The encores were well received, particularly *The Last Thing* which has been going down really well live. We encored again with *You Dinosaur Thing* for the benefit of the recording because Clem had broken a kick drum skin or something during the set. After Paris I was ready to go out and do a couple of impromptu things on my own for a third encore, but the audience had decided the show was over and were filing out of the gig. I went back upstairs and showered. Clem had cheered up, but Chucho was disappointed with his gig. He says he gets spooked by the filming. When I got out of the shower, Niels was in the dressing room with the camera still running. Great! I dried off and we went back to the American for a drink with the record company: John, Hybe and Dianne. Hybe said he loved the gig and wants us back for more. We'll see. The American bar was closing, so we walked across the Leidesplein in a rainstorm and down Lijnbaansgracht, and we found a little bar where Richard and I drank too many Hawaiian Punches. We had my favourite couple of hours of the tour here, everyone mellowing out in the afterglow of a good show, before tramping back to the bus for the ride to Köln. The boys were watching **Pulp Fiction** in the back lounge. I joined them for a while, but I had overdone the Hawaiian Punch and was forced into the chemical toilet to do penance for my sins. Not one of life's better experiences. I'll spare you the odious details…

Thursday 13 February (h Band) *Köln, Luxor*

Woke up outside the Holiday Inn Crowne Plaza on a grey rainy day. It was going to be a long slow climb back up to a reasonable state of mind and health. Fortunately we had time on our hands, so I staggered to the back lounge. Chucho and I watched **Pulp Fiction** all over again.

By the time it had finished I was able to contemplate leaving the bus and braving the rain to take a shower in hotel room 222. It's a nice hotel. I bumped into Clem who had been down and done the sauna and the pool. Shame I wasn't in a fit state to do the same. I showered, and was later joined downstairs by Richard, Aziz and Clem for club sandwiches in the bar. Richard seems to have warmed to me; we're getting on like old friends.

By now I was really close to functioning properly, which was just as well because we were leaving to go to the Luxor for soundcheck. We tumbled into taxis and were there in a couple of minutes. There were quite a few people hanging around in the front of the club, waiting to interview me. We soundchecked first – trouble free once again. However, 13 was to live up to its reputation when a large truck smashed into our truck in the street outside, rendering it useless for the journey home and jamming the roller shutter closed. Fortunately the equipment was inside the club, but the t-shirts were still in the back of the truck so there was some doubt over whether we would be able to sell them at the gig. Oh well! More administrative headaches for Nick B and more financial complications, which will eventually work their way back to yours truly. In the end we had to hire a truck and driver in Germany to take our equipment home to the Racket Club.

The bus was still down the road at the Holiday Inn, so there was much hanging about in the dodgy dressing room backstage at the Luxor. One of the interviewers accidentally caught the heel of my shoe which promptly fell off, so I hung around in my socks waiting for Priv's glue to dry.

The show went really well. I think it was probably my favourite of the lot. Everyone in the band seemed happy and relaxed, even Dave Greggs! *Better Dreams* went particularly well tonight and felt quite magical. *Living for the City* was stupidly fast (and consequently a bit of an embarrassment), but no one seemed to mind. I did my third encore tonight, playing *Easter* and *The Hollow Man* as I did in Paris, and inexplicably blubbing through *Easter.* No one I spoke to afterwards mentioned it though, so maybe they couldn't tell...

After the show I went out front to chat to the people still in the building and to sign my name here and there. As luck would have it there's a good bar called The Blue Shell almost next door to the Luxor. I had been there before with Kai Fleschmann from EMI; in fact it was here that I first heard a band called No Man, which might well have been the beginning of the process of fate which lead me to Richard Barbieri. We all relaxed there for a couple of hours. The record company girl came along to buy the drinks, but it seemed that every time my hand was empty someone would buy me another Kölsch beer. Chucho and the boys wired into the tequila, but I declined; I didn't want another conversation with the chemical toilet tonight. I must have been doing okay though because I remember dancing on my own in the middle of the bar to a remix of *Isobel* by Björk, probably my favourite of her songs. It's rare for me to dance.

Around 2.30 we returned to the bus via a take-away kebab place, and we all sat in the back lounge watching **Reservoir Dogs** and munching junk. I didn't get to see too much – I went to bed. I woke up to half-sleep as the bus drove onto the ferry at the channel, the sounds of the car deck, diesel engines revving, men shouting, and the thunder echo of the metal cave surrounding us all. I drifted back to sleep amid uneasy memories of The Herald of Free Enterprise and the Estonia. If I'm to meet my maker tonight, then a watery grave in a tour bus bunk would be a natural and fitting way for me to go. I woke up again to the same flurry of action outside, and guessed that the bow-doors had held and we must be at Dover. Unease crept over me again as I remembered overhearing someone say that Chucho had taped his grass to the roof of the bus and that he would have to get rid of it before Dover because the customs men have overhead cameras. I wondered if it was still there – the last thing we needed was to get busted. I lay there waiting to be told to get up by some frosty uniformed official: Rockn'roll band, returning from Amsterdam via Cologne, including Colombian, American and Asian personnel… Blimey. If I was a customs man I'd have taken the bus apart! They waved us straight through.

I drifted back into sleep for the last couple of hours, before I'd have to do the "thanks and goodbyes" which I so hate.

Friday 2 May *Cambridge Corn Exchange*

Glorious weather accompanied the journey to Cambridge. It was a little too warm for sitting in a car for 3 hours in congested motorway traffic, but I drifted in and out of sleep in the sunshine as Tim's mobile phone bleeped, demanding his attention. I remember passing the Civil Aviation museum and being treated to a glance of a shimmering VC10 in BOAC colours, bringing back an explosion of 60's imagery in my head: Georgie Best and Simon Dee, watching the wrestling on a Saturday afternoon with my Gran…

The sun was shining down as we arrived at the University Arms Hotel. It overlooks an open space of parkland populated by students; young scruffy boys in deck shoes and girls exuding their own summer beauty. I wasn't staying at the hotel, so while Steve R checked in I popped over the road to Oddbins; I was on a mission. One bottle of Pimms and a bottle of lemonade. This is the way to start a tour!

Tim drove me round the corner to the Corn Exchange which, thanks to Cambridge's virtually impossible one-way system, evaded us as usual. There were already a scattering of fans looking for an autograph or just a hello outside the stage door. I entered the building to catch my first sight of this tour's production (This Strange Engine). The backdrop looks great. Also, Shelley's erected the lighting poles in just the way I had imagined, curving out organically from a cluster at the base. The projection screens need attention though; at the moment they look like a couple of morning-after bed sheets.

I made my way upstairs to catering and was introduced to our new cooking girls, Mary (Glasgow) and Denise (Dublin). "Who wants a Pimms then, girls?" I announced, "Point me at the ice!" I mixed a few Pimms with a couple of strawberries floating in the ice and toasted the forthcoming tour, before going down to the stage to see how Mark K was getting on. Stewart E has fixed the midi cricket bat – it's down to me now to learn how to play the thing. Jeff Hoooper had woven his Welsh magic and my monitors were sounding great. If only rehearsals sounded like this!

Soundcheck took a while as it's the first proper show. I ate a spot of dinner -

a little chicken and veg - and then returned to the bus for a pre-show snooze in my bunk. Bliss. At 8.00 I reappeared into the warm evening air of an early summer in Cambridge to see Ian Mosley padding up the street on his own. Neither of us knew how to gain entry backstage, so we had no choice but to walk round the front and go in with the crowd. Someone came up to me and shook my hand, saying "I've waited for years in the hope of doing this!" It's a great feeling to quietly mean this much to people.

The show went well. Unavoidably, certain uncertainties crept in here and there but, all things considered, it wasn't a bad "first night".

Later, we all returned to the hotel where the Dutch record label had flown in a load of Dutch retailers, so I was introduced to them. Some wanted to talk, some didn't. I chatted until I felt it wouldn't be rude to cross the room and relax. The proceedings were punctuated by a student scrap in the bar. They were having some kind of a college ball in the next room. By now it was 1.00 in the morning and they were all as drunk as it's possible to get without passing out. The boys were doing the pisshead macho-in-front-of-the-girls thing, and the next thing we knew there were six of them kicking the life out of someone who was curled up on the floor. Tim and Jack went over to try to break it up while I heroically drifted over to the opposite end of the room. I've never seen the point in intervening with or moderating the behaviour of drunks. They don't deserve help and they certainly won't thank you for it. Been there, got the stitches. Leave 'em to it. They'll all be best of mates in the morning.

At around 2.00 the bus arrived to take me to Cardiff. I sat upstairs for 20 minutes and had a beer with the crew before turning in. It's great to drift off into sleep knowing that you're on the road to another adventure. St. David's Hall beckons.

Saturday 3 May *Cardiff St. David's Hall*

I decided to lie-in long after the crew had departed the bus to start the load-in. I eventually surfaced at about 11.30. Next to the bus was a loading bay for Marks & Sparks. I ran out of underwear last night after the show and had been walking around without any on, so I asked directions and found my way out of the maze of loading bays behind St. David's Centre. The next thing I knew I was on the first floor of M&S, which was packed with Saturday shoppers (not a "first-thing-in-the-morning" experience I would recommend). I queued up with a fistful of underpants-on-hangers, feeling shell-shocked and semiconscious. The customers chatted to the checkout ladies, telling them what they'd been up to and generally socialising in a timeless Welsh fashion while the queue waited, oblivious of the concept of impatience – apart from yours truly, muttering, sighing and shifting from one foot to the other, bursting to pay and get out of the place.

I returned to the St. David's Hall and found my way backstage to a dressing room where, at last, I was able to shower and clean my teeth. Unfortunately I had forgotten about towels, and emerged from the shower dripping wet and unable to make myself heard as I craned my head round the door, starkers, shouting for help. There are beds in the dressing rooms at St. David's Hall, thoughtfully included to accommodate and refresh tired performers (I have this image of Dame Kiri Te Kanawa, spark-out with her hair in curlers, napping peacefully). I dried myself on the pink candlewick bedspread and hung it up to dry. As I did so, I noticed a rugby ball surreally balanced on the ledge of the tall building opposite. Wales.

I went down to catering and had a spot of light breakfast and a gallon of coffee, while chatting to the crew and watching the Saturday football feature on TV, before wandering into the hall to listen to Priv eq-ing the PA. It occurred to me that the front lighting towers needed to be curtained black, so I asked Shelley if there were any spare drapes around. He said there were and that it would be done. I decided to go out for a wander round Cardiff. I soon found a music shop and bought a saxophone strap for my cricket bat. You can imagine the conversation I had with the shop manager. I signed an autograph for one of the customers while trying to explain why I needed to hang a cricket bat around my neck. On the return journey to the venue I passed a shop called The World Trading Company, which was full of Balinese and Indian Arts and Crafts. I browsed through the room, filled with Buddhas and other woodcarvings, textiles and icons. I found two enormous masks hanging on the wall – Balinese or African, I think; perfect for the lighting towers, and in harmony with the tribal/mythical elements in the production. They're each about six feet tall. I bought them both for less than a hundred pounds and staggered back to the venue through throngs of Saturday shoppers, with one of the shop assistants tagging along behind with the second mask.

Monday 16 June *Brasilia – Goiania, Jao Sportscenter*

Managed to sleep til 9.00ish. It had been a late night and, all things considered, I didn't feel too bad. Today is Fathers' Day back in England, and Sue, Sofie and Nial had placed presents in my suitcase for the occasion. I opened them as soon as I got up. Sofie has bought me a yo-yo which lights up when it spins. It's a fabulous thing. I had one of these when I was seventeen... it takes me back. Nial's present turned out to be a Sherbert fountain. Sherbert is a sweet, white powdery substance which fizzes on the tongue. There's also a hollow liquorice stick, which comes out of the top of the packet like a firework, which you're supposed to suck the sherbet through. "I'll have it later", I decided and made my way down to breakfast playing with my glo-yo as I walked along the dark corridors of the hotel. Thank you Sofie. Thank you Nial. Thank you Dizzy! I called home before I left for breakfast but the answering machine was on, so they must all have been out somewhere.

I arrived in the breakfast room and joined Ian and Pete at a table. I had a spot of scrambled egg and a small bucket of coffee while passing the yo-yo round.

There had been talk of including *Incommunicado* in the set, so I spent the rest of breakfast writing out the words, most of which I had forgotten. Took the lift back up to 1214 and packed my bags, before checking out of the hotel at 11.00 ($78.00!!) for the bus journey to Goiania. On our way out of the city, I pondered, once again, upon Brasilia. Almost every building here has been a grand architectural attempt at creating a work of art. This makes it quite a unique city if you're turned on by modern architecture. Unfortunately, there's something of the feel of a building site about the whole place and, having torn up the natural flora and fauna to build it, Brasilia, for me, is like a moon-base; no expense spared, but it just doesn't seem to belong where it is. You can keep the buildings. I liked the bus stops best – yellow and curvy, like something out of **The Flintstones**. I chatted to Alfredo, the promoter's rep, during the long journey to Goiania. The Brazilian countryside undulates here with patches of forest and hillside. The trees are a mixture of deciduous and palms. We pass through occasional small settlements of concrete roadside buildings with attendant roadside vendors selling strings of unripened oranges.

The journey took around three and a half hours. We climbed down from the bus and into Castro's Park Hotel, Goiania; the usual high-rise modern building with a large open reception area flanked by vigilant men in suits (a common sight in the developing world), probably armed to ensure the safety of the well-heeled guests. There was a Sunday buffet lunch in full swing for $18, so we dropped our bags in our rooms and came back down to eat. Mine was cold, but okay. By now I was ready to sleep so I went upstairs and closed the curtains. I couldn't find a way to turn off the TV, so I ended up crawling around under the desk, pulling all the wires out of the wall socket until it reluctantly died. Brazilian TV is, in my limited experience, dreadful.

I slept until 5.30 when I was woken by the phone and someone enthusiastically saying, "Is that Hoggert?" It was a university student hustling me for an interview. Anyone can decide they're a journalist (as easily as anyone can decide they're a musician) and there's no way of knowing to whom you should give or deny your time. Back in 1990, I remember having breakfast in our hotel in Rio when someone plonked himself down next to me and asked if I'd mind being interviewed. Tour manager, Paul, quickly crossed the room to get rid of him, but I said I didn't mind and we chatted as I ate my muesli. Then another chap magically appeared with a camera and they took a picture of me standing on the balcony with Copacobana curving away below and behind me. Next morning, the interview and the picture were on the front of the national newspaper **Journal do Brasil**. So y'never know. I agreed to meet him downstairs at 5.45.

When Tim called to let me know soundcheck time, he suggested we use pseudonyms from hereon in. I agreed, remembering my last time in Brazil when the phone rang every ten minutes, day and night. He asked me who I wanted to be. I thought Ronaldo would do – he's currently Brazil's most famous footballer. So I became Mr. S Ronaldo. Tim told me there have been a few "interesting" developments at the venue. The opening act are a very well-known Brazilian rock band who had all their gear on stage before our crew had arrived. We had to soundcheck without moving their equipment. Well, whatever – it's Brazil.

After my "interview" at 6.00-ish, we took a minibus down to the venue; an open sided bus garage of a place, with the worst slap-bang-around-a-cave-reverb of any venue I've played, been to, or can imagine. Every sound we made at soundcheck came back several times at one-second intervals. Oh wow. We stumbled around in amongst the other band's gear, banging our shins and falling over leads, trying to convey what we needed from our new monitor man, Steve May (on a hiding to nothing!). Every word we uttered bounced around the building like rubber, producing a sound like jellyfish having a heated argument underwater. The good news, however, was that the crowd numbers were up to 2,200, which will look good in a hall this size.

We returned to the hotel and I decided against going back to bed - I'm having trouble with my voice and I daren't risk it closing up - so I sat in the restaurant area with Tim and Ian and had a beer, before going upstairs for a bath. We returned to the venue at 10.15 – showtime has been moved from 9.30 to 11.30 to 11.45. Monica, from the promoter's office, seems to have repaired my trousers, although they don't look as though there's much life left in them (Jean-Paul Gaultier silk blue and silver stripes. Wonderful, until they get wet, then there's no "give" in the material so it simply rips open. At the moment the gusset is an unforgiving "chastity belt" of gaffer-tape). Shame. The crowd looks good... I wonder how they'll cope with the sound of the band? I wonder how *we* will? Not as well, I suspect...

As it turned out, we seemed to go down very well. We all kept everything under control, despite the appalling slap and reverb. My voice was in a bad way, but I came through most of it without embarrassing myself. After the show I was exhausted and somewhat depressed – a combination, I think, of jet-lag, lack of sleep and two, two-hour shows in less than 24 hours. I showered, despite the suspect appearance of the shower fittings – live electric wires dangling out of the shower head... totally illegal in England, of course. I needn't have worried, it was quite safe. Switched off and stone cold. We returned to the hotel and I staggered straight upstairs to bed after wishing Ian Mosley a happy birthday.

Tuesday 17 June *Brazil, Porto Alegre Gigantinho*

I'm in a heel bar in Porto Alegre. They're putting new heels on my black shoes while I wait. It's a little different from a heel bar in England. I'm surrounded by leather products, many hanging from the ceiling. There are hand-made saddles, bags, second-hand boots, disembodied high heels, old footballs, straps, buckles, stirrups, leather water-bottles, tins and bottles of leather preservers, polishes and glues – all packed into this concrete shop, open to the busy, dirty street outside. This morning I came out in search of tambourines. My favourite little tambourine was nicked by someone in the front row of the Goiania show last night. It fell off the mic stand and, if something falls into the audience here, forget it! No one in Porto Alegre seems to understand the word tambourine. After much confusion and searching I have found a white plastic contraption. It's a Remo 'Whistle Tambourine' which, as the name suggests, is a tambourine incorporating a whistle into the plastic rim; essential kit here in Brazil, although I don't think they'll catch on in Europe.

I did my washing this morning. Room 1209 looks like a laundry or, more accurately, a gypsy encampment, strewn with socks and underwear drying in the sun at the window. I spent the rest of the morning waiting for a TV crew who never turned up, before coming out shopping and then on to here to fix my shoes. It's been quite a while since they took my shoes away and I'm beginning to doubt the wisdom of rendering myself barefoot in a developing country on the other side of the world. I'm wondering if my shoes might already have been sold out of the back door and it's an odd feeling to be in the middle of a city without shoes – strangely powerless and dependent.

As I wrote the previous line my shoes arrived, not only heeled but polished and looking like new! I paid, and carefully checked my change, remembering the time I was charged the equivalent of £35.00 for a shoe shine that I was nagged into accepting in Mexico City.

I emerged back into the dusty street and wound my way back to the hotel to spend the rest of the afternoon killing time, watching TV until soundcheck at 4.00. The venue today is much better (acoustically) than last nights 'bus garage'. It's a theatre with about a thousand seats. It became apparent once I started the soundcheck that I don't have much of a voice today. I don't really understand why I'm having so much trouble with it since we arrived in Brazil. Maybe it's tiredness or something to do with the climate. Maybe I have got a throat infection… I never had this much trouble with my voice before, and there doesn't seem to be a reason.

I spent the ninety minutes after soundcheck back at the hotel, sewing up my stage trousers which had torn again in Goiania. Sue rang while I was sewing, and we had a chat while I stitched away at the silk. As I said, the trouble with silk trousers is that when they get wet they stick to you, and when you move suddenly, they tear. All you budding pop stars, please take note!

By lobby call I still hadn't finished, so I told Tim to take the boys and come back for me.

The show was both strange and memorable. By stage time the theatre was only half-full, and I had the feeling of playing in somebody's front-room at home. My voice was the worst I can ever remember it being for a show. I squeaked and squawked my way through the songs, expecting my voice to quit completely by the end of each song. Somehow though, the audience got into it and I felt an affection for them which lifted me and helped me through it. They were all close enough to me that I could see their faces, and I could see how special it was for some of them. We finished with *Garden Party* and, during Mark's long solo, I made a run through the theatre, up along the aisles, shaking hands with the crowd who pushed toward me to be part of it. Oddly enough then, this was the most enjoyable show so far, despite being as hoarse as a bat. An important lesson.

I showered after the show, under another of Brazil's horror film deathtrap devices, trying not to touch any metal components in the process. If the water is hot then the fittings are usually 'live', i.e. connected to the mains electricity and uninsulated.

After the show we were taken to a nightclub full of Porto Alegre's rich and beautiful, where we were given free beer and sushi. The place had a distinctly German feel about it; apparently this area of Brazil is full of Germans and Poles who have been campaigning for autonomy, in much the same fashion as the Quebecers in Canada. The whole place was luxurious and decadent, and smacked a little too much of Bavarian elitism for my comfort. You were either beautiful and "in", rich and "in", or plain and curiously absent. Looking round, I think *we* were the least glamorous people in the place. It was really strange to be in something like a Munich nightclub, full of blondes and with a car-park outside full of Porsches and Mercs, having been surrounded by the poverty of Brazil for the last few days. I was reminded of similar clubs in the European Eastern Bloc. Oases of wealth. Maybe such places are characteristic of developing economies. Maybe I should get out more.

We had our photograph taken with the owner, a slick young entrepreneur who looked like a model – obviously used to using the 'glamour' set to his advantage. Still, we *were* drinking his drink and eating his food. I endured it for an hour or so, but in the end I had to get out of there. I'd started to feel like a pawn in someone else's game. I guess we all are.

Saturday 18 June *Porto Alegre:* Day off

I woke up in the dark several times. My room has shutters and, as I had taken off my watch last night, I guessed from the noises outside that the morning must be progressing towards midday. I went back to sleep and was roused by the telephone. It was Tim, reminding me of telephone interviews at 4.00 this afternoon. It was 12.45, so I thought I should get up. I hauled up the shutter to a cloudless blue sky and a hot sun, realising for the first time that the window slides open all the way to allow an all-too-easy jump from the 12th floor to the ground. I leaned out, watching my spit fall, and wondering if death would be instantaneous. I decided it might well take a few seconds to die after the massive, shattering impact. A chilling thought.

I could have actually sat on the bed and sunbathed, but I felt I should go and walk down to the river-front before we leave Porto Alegre. I telephoned our local flower shop in England to arrange some flowers for Dizzy before rinsing out my underwear and socks and placing them on the windowsill to dry. I'm wearing shorts for the first time since I arrived here…

And here I am sitting at the docks by the water, looking out at the river and an island densely covered with tropical trees. The waterfront is an uninviting place. I don't think they expect tourists here. It's a working waterfront lined with warehouses. The boats here are only small – freighters and tugs. Perhaps the big ships unload further downriver.

There's a cool breeze coming off the water, which is therapeutic for my slight headache. I'm constantly aware of my lost voice. Last night was the worst I can remember it being for a show, so I'm keeping to myself and trying to rest. Today and tomorrow are days off. There's a TV show tomorrow, but they only need two songs (and the TV here has a habit of last-minute cancellation anyway), so I have sixty hours before my next concert. That should be enough to sort me out.

Military men keep ambling by. I think they're port security people. There was a man posted at the underpass when I came through here. I got the impression that access is restricted to prevent burglary, but I think he probably decided that an Englishman in pink shorts with a writing pad was a safe bet.

While I have been writing, the peace was disturbed only by an Indian-looking girl who sat down further along the dock and unpacked some paintbrushes, preparing to paint a picture of the river. There are two white herons sitting on the roof of the warehouse to my right. They arrived flying with their necks bent, so I assume they're herons and not storks. They sit in the sun with their shoulders hunched like vultures and their long, thin beaks pointing up at the sky. Two buses full of five-year-old schoolchildren have pulled up amid sounds of chaotic excitement, and the fumes of diesel exhaust are overtaking me. I will walk back into town and see if I can find a decent café for some breakfast.

I couldn't.

I walked back through the dirty town, the streets almost impassable from the density of people thronging the pavements and roads. I returned to the hotel and my room, where I ordered up a hot sandwich and some coffee on room service. I tried to call home but couldn't get through, so sent a fax instead. By 4.00 the interviews had cancelled or postponed, so I went downstairs and ordered a beer while I wrote some more of this diary. Promoter's rep, Alfredo (who I have come to like) came by to say the Argentinian interview was ready to happen and, if it suited me, I could do it from the hotel telephone at the bar. They would call me in five minutes. We had to leave for the airport at 6.15, by which time (1 hour later!) they still hadn't called. Alfredo came by to say the interview is now totally cancelled, so I packed and checked out.

As we arrived at the airport in the minibus, Alfredo's mobile phone rang. It was the Argentinian radio station, ready to do the interview live on air! While everyone checked in to the flight to Sao Paulo, I stood outside in the street trying to have a sensible conversation with an Argentinian DJ, whose main objective seemed to be to get an introduction from me for his radio station, and for the song *Kayleigh* "…the song is very special for us here in Buenos Aires…" Not for the first time, I wondered why I don't just tell them to fuck off.

We flew down to Sao Paulo, and got into another minibus which took us to the Imperial Hall Hotel on the Rua da Consolacao in the Jardins area of Sao

Paulo – a well-to-do area, full of expensive shops and bars. We checked in, and then band and crew went up the street to a groovy bar where we had a beer or two. There was a little stage with a band playing, so we got up and had a knock for 15 minutes. Great fun, and the owner paid for the beers. Came back to the hotel around 1.00 and crashed out.

Sunday 19 June 19 *Sao Paulo, Olympia*

I won't say much about today. In theory it was a day off. In practice, however…

We spent much of the day at a radio station, and then a TV station. We were doing a TV show called Live which is a national broadcast and, apparently, very popular. Typical of daytime TV everywhere, I suppose. The audience had been bussed in from what appeared to be several schools. The average age of the assembled 200 (or so) teenagers was 15, all in frantic Brazilian mood and completely surrounding the band. The soundcheck had been painless; the technicians knew their stuff and the equipment (Electrovoice) is good. The sound in the room was so clear that I asked them to take the monitor wedge away. Immediately before we went on, there was a bizarre live advert for sanitary towels which was something of a first. A girl in a grass skirt was placed next to a little stall of the product, singing a little song and doing a Hawaiian dance. I'm ashamed to say I made up my own translation of the words.

Well, I sang reasonably well, and the children went, "Whoopee!!"

Back into the minibus. It took ages to get back to the centre of Sao Paulo in heavy traffic, and when we finally returned to the hotel I got out and left my sunglasses in the minibus! They're Armani's. As I write this I'm still trying to get them back (note: I never did).

In the evening I phoned home. Between stony silences and choked-back tears, Dizzy told me she'd had enough and that our marriage was over. I felt the big stone fall in my stomach. There wasn't much I could do about it from a hotel room in Sao Paulo and she wasn't in a mood for discussing it. Things have been pretty erratic between us for a while now. I totally blame myself. I have asked more of her than any woman could reasonably bear.

I decided the most constructive thing I could do would be to get roaring drunk and try not to think about it. I failed on both fronts and went to bed at midnight.

The following day I called home to see where we stood. She said she was sorry about last night, and that she couldn't help it. I was, in fact, still married. Still, I have to reflect that as long as I continue living this life - as they say - the writing is on the wall.

Wednesday 22 June *Sao Paulo – Buenos Aires, Teatro Opera*

8.00am! Right now I'm sitting in the executive lounge in Sao Paolo, feeling like I ought to be in hospital. Last night's show in Sao Paulo was one of the best we've had. Consequently, I burned up every last ounce of energy and then staggered through a couple of hours of autographs and photographs, after yet another "electrically interesting" cold shower. We played here five years ago in 1992, and after the show I climbed into the backstage shower to discover that the shower-hose is a metal goose-neck which, for some reason, was LIVE. Instead of fixing it, it had been completely covered along it's length with insulating tape! Once in the shower, when I touched the plastic of the tape on the hose, I could actually feel a tingle as the voltage beneath fizzed through to me. When we were later asked to sign the Olympia's artistes guestbook, there was a column marked "comments". I wrote "FIX THE FUCKING SHOWER! SOMEONE'S GOING TO DIE!"

Well that was in 1992, and as I climbed into the shower last night I was shocked (in every sense) to discover that IT'S STILL THE SAME!! I think that tells you all you need to know about Brazilian venue manager's respect for artists i.e, at a level somewhere below farm animals.

We got back to the hotel at 3.00 am and my alarm call roused me two-hours later at 5.30am. Who said musicians sleep late? Had a row with the night staff when checking out. They tried to charge me 35US dollars to have ONE white shirt laundered. Gave him 10 and told him to lump it. I slumped on the back seat of the minibus and tried to sleep as we bumped over the pot-holed roads to the airport. It wouldn't be quite so bad, but for the knowledge that I have a show to do tonight and my voice is bound to suffer as a consequence of being so tired. I just tried (and failed) in the protracted process of making a telephone call to England. When I finally found a way through (BT and reverse the charges), the answering machine was on and the operator wouldn't let me leave a message.

The exhaustion comes in waves, alternating with indigestion and euphoria... See you in Buenos Aires.

I slept a little on the flight and then had a spot of breakfast before we landed. The road from the airport into town seemed strangely Swedish, reminding me of the bus ride from Stockholm airport into town. We eventually arrived at the Intercontinental Hotel, Buenos Aires, and I checked in and found my way to room 1205. The only sensible thing to do was to go straight to bed, so I went downstairs and ordered too many coffees before returning to my room to lie in the dark, staring at the ceiling, for the rest of the afternoon. I finally fell into a deep sleep around 4.30 and was immediately woken again by the ringing telephone. When I picked up the receiver there was nobody there, so I was denied even the satisfaction of verbally abusing them. That did it. I never got back to sleep and when I got up at 5.00 to go to soundcheck, I was still exhausted and could barely stand. The venue is a big theatre like Hammersmith Odeon, and we soundchecked in the darkness while the sound bounced back at us from the auditorium. My sound wasn't too bad, although I wondered what would happen to the ambience tonight when the room is full of people. We were fed steak and mashed potatoes down in a corridor beneath the theatre. The steak was first-rate and deserves a mention. Thank you Cynthia.

We returned to the Intercontinental, but I didn't dare sleep for fear that my voice would close down for the show. Instead, I watched the second half of a football match where Brazil beat Paraguay 2-0. I called home to wish Dizzy sweet dreams and set off for the show.

For some reason the promoter had decided that we should enter the building via several lifts and locked-doors from the adjoining building. At one point we seemed to wander through someone's apartment, and I was expecting us all to get arrested for breaking and entering. The backstage area of the Teatro Opera in Buenos Aires smells distinctly of cat's pee, and it was in this questionable ambience that I quickly got dressed for the show.

The show itself was a little sedate to start with – I have come to expect that in all-seated venues. The audience were responsive and interested, but not downright enthusiastic until we played *Kayleigh* and *Lavender* – what I surmise they had come to see. I was still singing well-below the benchmark I had set in Europe, and the majority of the crowd were invisible in darkness. In South America the concert tickets are very expensive, the most expensive seats being, of course, near to and on the front row. This is unfortunate for the band, because all the serious fans end up at the back of the hall, or in the balconies, and are not allowed to move forward, while all the rich kids (who are probably only here to check each other out) are seated at the front where I can see them. For the majority of the show I could see little else, so I felt my (already knackered) spirits being constantly sapped. One particular slime-ball in the front row actually made a point of looking singularly bored and unimpressed for the entire show. Why on earth do such people leave home? Why don't they hire a movie, or read a book, or go to a brothel, or whatever it is (if anything) that would satisfy their idea of having a good time. It's not as though they can't afford it. *Incommunicado* was the penultimate number in the set, after which I was to decide whether to finish with *King* or *The Space.* I could see no point in either so I simply said, "Goodnight". The applause was suddenly rapturous, but then they were applauding another old song. I could happily have called it a day right there. We had planned *This Strange Engine* for encore 1, but we abandoned it in favour of *Garden Party* which, predictably, went down very well. Not really my crowd, this lot. We had no desire to return to Cat's Piss Cottage to get changed, so we returned to the Interconti to shower up before going out (I still can't believe I didn't go straight to bed) to The Hard Rock Café, who had sponsored the show and invited us over for dinner. There was a small stage there with some backline, so we jammed a couple of songs. I sang *Abraham, Martin and John* and then the band played *Kayleigh.* We weren't great (understatement), but then we didn't have to be. We all returned to the Intercontinental around 3.00 and I fell into bed, thanking my stars for the forthcoming two days off!

Thursday 23 June *Santiago, Chile:* Day off

The approach to Santiago airport consists of a sudden drop down from above the Andes, on to what appeared to be a plateau. We remained in cloud almost until touchdown. God knows how they landed the aeroplane. Top marks to the pilot for making it feel so straightforward. We emerged from the airport to heavy grey skies into which black mountains rose, their peaks obscured. Until one month ago, it hadn't rained here for six years. A month ago it began raining hard, day and night, until today. There has been widespread flooding, and many buildings and bridges have been destroyed. We drove by bus along country roads until we approached Santiago. First impressions were of a gold-rush town. Shabby, single-storey wild west buildings lined the main road, exuding a 'frontier' vibe; I was half expecting to see Clint Eastwood, poncho-clad and hat pulled down against the weather, riding into town towards us.

Strange anomalies surprised us as we arrived at the edge of Santiago: a large shop proudly displaying the sign Ferreteria O'Higgins, and later, my favourite – La Casa Del Gasfitter. After what seemed like an age, we eventually arrived at the Intercontinental Hotel Santiago and checked in. Everyone here is friendly, and clearly excited to have an international rock n'roll band in the hotel, so maybe it doesn't happen very often. We were invited into the bar for complimentary cocktails and I sat with our guitar tech, Guy, drawing pictures of cartoon cat's trampolining so I could fax them to Sofie and Nial. There was a TV interview at 10.00, so I killed time exploring the hotel until then. We drove to the TV station, and Mark and I did a very brief spot with some chat person before leaving to go to a bar called Pub-licity, where I had grilled salmon for dinner and said hi to various members of the British Embassy staff who were there for whatever reason! They all seemed pretty eccentric to me…

We returned to the hotel bar around midnight and I joined the crew for a drink. I felt so tired and ill by now that I donated my beer and went to bed.

Woke up around 10.00 to the sound of construction work: banging, clattering and the relentless grind of hammer-drilling on some not-too-distant wall/floor. I felt quite ill and drifted in and out of sleep until around 2.00. We had a press conference at 3.15, so I showered and managed to rebuild a shell of myself in time for the onslaught…

Question 1: "Do you consider yourself to be progressive or regressive?"

Off to a good start…

After the press conference ended, I went back upstairs for a phone interview in Tim's room – before changing to another room, further away from the construction work. In the evening the band went out to a couple of bars. I was constantly recognised, signed autographs, and had my photograph taken. We returned to the hotel bar and I joined a table with a B.A. aircrew of 4 stewards and 2 stewardesses. They were all from the north of England, and their accents made a refreshing change to hear. The boys were all gay and great value to be around… "We're not supposed to drink, y'know, when we're flying… not supposed to, but we do… we were coming into Santiago over the mountains, the pilot was being sick into a bowl, the hydraulics were leaking, and the cabin crew were all pissed!…"

I said it's okay, I'm not a nervous flyer.

"Bloody hell! I am!" said one of the stewardesses…

They're leaving Chile tomorrow so they'll miss the show, but they'll be in Rio next Saturday so they're all coming to that one instead.

I didn't stay up too late. I still felt ropey and tired. We arranged to meet up at 12.30 tomorrow to go into town for some lunch with Francesco, our local promoter.

Tuesday 28 June *Sao Paulo – Rio de Janeiro, Metropolitan*

Woke at 9.30, and spent the next hour showering and packing for check-out at 10.30. My phone bill wasn't the horror I was expecting, only $66.00. We climbed into the minibus for the short ride to Sao Paulo City Airport where, after a short wait, we boarded the shuttle to Rio de Janeiro. Climbing down the stairs from the 737 aircraft, it was immediately apparent that the air is warmer here in Rio, despite low cloud and showery rain. There is still much magic in the place – the very topography of it with its dumpling and coconut-cake hills, seems strangely mystical. The ever-present minibus (which seems to arrive, as if by magic, everywhere we go) took us to the Rio Palace Hotel. And here I am. For the second time in my life I'm enjoying the heavenly sensory wash of the air in my room, scented with fruit, flowers and the sea, as I listen to the waves crashing in on Copacabana, which sweeps before me in a floodlit arc (it's now 8.00pm), along with the bustle of night-traffic and people out walking along the wavy-patterned pavement promenade. Even now, in "mid-winter", the air is warm and heady. In the summer I heard the boom of drums in the distance pumping out samba, but tonight only the waves and the traffic.

As we drove back from soundcheck at the Metropolitan, we came along the coast road and watched massive waves crash violently up against one another in a cauldron of white foam. Even the sea here is somehow massively alive, like the people and the city. I've never been anywhere that can touch this place for natural spectacle or visceral life-affirming energy. Rio is a reward I can't remember earning.

Seated in the bar downstairs this afternoon, I had many flashbacks: Roger Taylor (Queen's drummer) leaning against the bar, Roland Orzabal and Kurt Smith, Dave Stewart and Chucho (now my friend) Merchan. Annie Lennox, pale and straw-hatted, returning from some excursion or other to buy sandals with Chucho's wife Anne-Marie.

I sipped a beer (foregoing the complimentary Caipirinhas) and gazed around, pondering with Pete T how many ghosts had passed through this lobby along with ours. You name 'em, they've probably been here. The old Rio Palace is looking slightly shabby at the moment – the carpets have started to smell a little dusty. There are plans for an imminent refurbishment of the hotel, so if I should ever return then perhaps I'll hardly recognise the place. I suppose I was lucky to get in here now.

Well, I should talk about tonight's venue – it's quite something. It's called the Metropolitan, and it's housed within a shopping mall. It's a huge club with a capacity of around 7000. The stage is massive, and the place exudes a "money no object" feeling. All the technology is state-of-the-art – there must have been fifteen grand's worth of TC eq for the stage monitors alone. The stage sound was clear and defined, and Jeff Hooper (who's mixing out-front sound for us on this tour) said the out-front technology was similarly fine. Alan Parker had had a bit of a day re-rigging the lights for the TV cameras. O Globo TV are shooting the show – there are manned and automatic cameras zooming about. But it's the backstage area that takes the cake... adjoining the dressing room are two jacuzzis! I arrived at tonight's gig to find Pete bubbling away.

Between soundcheck and show, we returned to the hotel and I called home before taking a stroll with tour manager Tim along Copacabana (which feels noticeably safer than in 1990, when I was constantly pestered for money by laughing street kids tapping at my pockets). We wandered along the promenade past café stalls hung with coconuts and stared out at the floodlit beach: the palms, the waves, and the passing characters - joggers, lovers, old friends chatting the night away - every race of people and every perspective. We walked back in the middle of the road where market stalls sell football shirts, leather goods, jewellery ("Your name on a grain of rice!") wood carvings, biquinis and sarongs. We didn't stop to buy anything.

For me the show turned out to be a strange one. The band sounded a little self-conscious of the cameras and recording equipment (32-track digital!), I felt I was over-singing a little and, two songs before the end of the set, my voice cracked and deserted me once again. We played *TSE* for a first encore, which killed the atmosphere somewhat – very few people in Brazil have heard the album. We redeemed ourselves with *Incommunicado* for encore 2, but I left the stage shaking my head in recognition of the fact that my voice was still far from right. I cheered up a lot after both Alan and Jeff came back to say it had looked and sounded great. I cheered up some more when Tim showed me one hot jacuzzi, full of bubble bath ready and waiting for me. I undressed, climbed in, and luxuriated, beer in hand, bubbling away my aches and pains alone. What a way to earn a living.

Back to Rio Palace at three in the morning. I leant against the balcony, watching the sea and the still-busy promenade, pondering the tragedy of being alone in the one place on Earth that God made for the sole purpose of shared awe and romance.

We had to be up at 7.45, so I tucked myself up and was in a deep sleep at 5.00am when I was stirred by a knock on my door. Unbelievable. The world conspires to stop me sleeping! I didn't have the strength to get up. I called security and asked them to please investigate. I guess I'll never know who it was or why.

Saturday 16 August *The Sky – Laguna CA + reminiscences of Gstaad, Switzerland*

As I write, I'm sitting in my seat next to Sofie on a 747 bound for Los Angeles. We're three-hours into the journey from Heathrow, so I'm going to review the last couple of days.

At 5.00am on Saturday morning, I left home for a show with the SAS band in Gstaad, Switzerland. We were to fly from London City Airport at 9.20. Unfortunately, the return journey was to be to Heathrow, as all Heathrow-Zurich outbound flights were full. This presented a logic puzzle. After much deliberation and inquiry, I decided that the best plan was to drive to Heathrow, park in the long-term car park, catch the bus to a Terminal, take the tube into London, change at Holborn to Stratford, *then* catch a bus (423) to London City Airport! It was a laborious plan but, in the event, although it took three and a quarter hours, it worked out as a straightforward journey. I arrived at 8.20 and gave my passport to Streaky the tour manager (who had gained his name either from bacon or running naked onto sports events – both equally likely…), who was checking everyone in. The SAS band is a big band: rhythm section, keyboards, two guitars, sax, trumpet and SEVEN singers. It's the brainchild of keyboard player/M.D. Spike Edney, and consists of a session band of accomplished players along with an array of "star" singers. I must have made it – I'm in the company of Tony Hadley of Spandau Ballet, Paul Young of Mike and the Mechanics, and two of my heroes – the incomparable Roy Wood (The Move, ELO, Wizzard), and the extraordinary Roger Chapman (Family). We also have two girls, Suzie and Zoe, who do an Abba tribute complete with costumes and choreography. I've already done three shows with this lot and they're a lot of fun. Each singer does three songs with the band, then we do a couple all together at the end. I got into it after meeting Spike (who was Queen's live keyboardist – along with Freddie, obviously) while he was playing for the legendary Peter Green (Fleetwood Mac) at a festival in Madrid. He called me the following week and asked if I fancied doing it. To share a stage and get to know Roy and Roger was more than enough inducement. I wasn't disappointed – everyone in the outfit is affable although the singers are particularly eccentric in their own little way. Roy's completely gorgeous and goes out of his way to be pleasant to me. Roger's a little more choosy who he gives time to, but he's been more than gracious. He has the loudest and most distinctive voice in rock (or perhaps, anywhere!), yet when he talks he's soft-spoken… I also suspect he's a little deaf. Tony Hadley is pleasant yet, somehow, constantly distracted. I'll never forget him holding the door open for me in the café at rehearsal studio Nomis many years ago, when I was rehearsing with the Europeans. At that time, Spandau Ballet were major pop stars and enjoying a string of high-charting hit singles and albums. Big Tone (as he's affectionately known) was everywhere - on radio and TV - and yet he held a door open in a café for unknown little old me as I tried to negotiate the doorway with a tray of sandwiches and coffee. He doesn't remember it, of course. But I do.

It's funny that most people in the entourage tend to talk but not to listen.

Either that or I'm on a different wavelength and they don't follow what I'm saying. Roy's the exception, he's quick to enjoy whatever company he's in. Paul Young's a total scream: uninhibited, drunk after breakfast and a born comedian. It's down to him to provide the vibe amongst the unit, and he does it effortlessly. We sat around in the café at the airport until our flight was called at 9.20. The plane was small and cramped, but I managed to find a spare seat in front of Tony. It was one of those short take-off things and accelerated into the air like a Ferrari (unlike our current 747 to L.A. which ambled down the runway, seemingly at 55mph, and then magically rose into the air defying gravity like a carpet… I love Jumbo Jets). All the way to Zurich I could hear Spike's distinctive guffaw at the back of the plane – he really enjoys himself on these outings.

At Zurich airport we boarded a stuffy coach for the long journey to Gstaad. I tried to sleep during the coach ride, still tired from my 4.30 wake up, but to no avail really. Some of the views of the Swiss countryside were truly awe-inspiring as we drove through the mountains which are heavily wooded with pines: snowy mountain tops above the tree line and rich, green pastures below.

At last we arrived at the Golf Hotel des Hauts, Gstaad - one of many 'cuckoo-clock' buildings dotted amongst the hillsides - and I checked into room 35, calling home to say hi to Sue, who couldn't believe I'd only just arrived. The band went straight to soundcheck, while the singers were told to be ready at 5.00. I hung around in my room taking in the view from the balcony, still unable to sleep. At 5.00 we made the short journey down to the airstrip where the festival was to be held. This is the airstrip that Burton, Taylor and recently, Gstaad's most famous face, Roger Moore, drop their Lear Jets and helicopters en route to their luxury homes in the town. The view from the stage was across a flat valley-floor of green, rising up to vertical slopes of pines and the snow-peaked rock faces high above. "Not quite Shepherd's Bush Empire!" quipped Keith Airey, our guitarist.

Soundcheck was okay. For once, I had brought a camera with me, so I was snapping away. Roy had the (already traditional) problems with his guitar-amplifier humming, so I tried to capture the concerned head-scratching on film. He ran through *See My Baby Jive,* which was a new addition. Great! I was hoping Roger would repeat his performance of *Burlesque* (he did it a fortnight ago at our gig in England – magic), but apparently the song isn't so well-known here in Europe. Shame.

After soundcheck we hung around while they fed us big sausages and fries. I declined and drank coffee instead, and then we went for a walk around the festival site. This is a biker festival, so there were quite a few stalls selling Harley accessories: t-shirts, leathers etc. I nearly bought a belt with a 'Knucklehead' engine logo on the buckle, but I rarely wear belts so there's no point really.

We returned to the hotel and hung around in the bar for quite a few hours, listening to the piano player and watching Paul getting funnier and funnier with each successive beer. I managed to fit in half an hour's sleep before showtime, when I noticed it had started to rain. What a shame. Unfortunately the show was sparsely attended, but the band played with great spirit and this was my favourite of the SAS shows so far. I sang *Abraham, Martin and John* better than I have sung it to date, so I was in celebratory mood for the rest of the evening. After the show we were fed backstage, before returning to the hotel where we took over the bar, taking turns at the piano for a sing-song. I got to bed around 5.30 and slept 'til 9.45, when I was roused by the phone. Went downstairs and had coffee with Spike, Kyle (his wife) and Keith, before boarding the bus back to the airport. On the journey back to Zurich I chatted with Paul Young, who appeared remarkably unscathed this morning and quite lucid. Amazing*. We arrived at the airport and I wandered off to do some shopping. Zurich airport Duty Free isn't up to much though, so I didn't buy anything. I just wandered around aimlessly, checking out the army knives and Toblerones. Popped to the bureau de change to change my money into US dollars for next week's trip to California, and made my way to the gate where I ran into Laurie Wiseman (guitarist) and Andy (trumpet player). I carried Laurie's pedal board onto the plane and sat next to Andy during the flight. We didn't chat much, though – we were both a little jaded from last night. At Heathrow I said bye-bye to the musicians, and to Zoe, Suzie, Roger, Paul and Roy, who gave me a hug. Hugged by Roy Wood – fucking fantastic! What a sweetheart. I think we'll do some more shows together in December when I return from the Marillion tour. A Christmas gig with this lot would be a blast! I caught the bus back to the long-term car-park, and made the long drive home where everyone was busy packing. Sue seemed somewhat exasperated by all of it after a weekend with two over-excited children. Sofie and Nial are vibrating with excitement at the prospect of a holiday in California and time with their twin cousins. We're going to spend a week with Sue's sister's family who recently emigrated from South Africa to Bakersfield, three hours north of L.A. Next weekend we'll drive down to Laguna in Orange County for a couple of days by the sea before the first Marillion gig in San Juan Capistrano which is only down the road.

Well, the flight to L.A. was unremarkable – the children were so well-behaved that, by the end of the flight, complete strangers were actually approaching us and commenting on it. They make Sue and I very proud, bless 'em. The in-flight movie was **Volcano**, some nonsense about, you guessed it, a volcano which erupts beneath the tar-pits just outside L.A. That bit's real, they dug up mammoths and all manner of prehistoric creatures which were preserved by the tar. I went to the museum there with Jack, the first time we played L.A with the Marillos. When we landed at Los Angeles I began wondering if it was a movie after all, or the lunchtime news bulletin. L.A. airport was in a state of chaos. The queue for immigration was 300 yards long, and it took us one and a half hours to clear passport control. But no, a volcano hadn't erupted. Apparently "it's always like this on Mondays in August". Welcome to America…

*Paul's partying was, sadly, to catch up with him. He died from heart-failure on 15 July 2000. I wouldn't be surprised if he died laughing, and I hope so.

Sunday 24 August *Holiday Inn, Laguna Hills, Room 411 – San Juan Capistrano, The Coach House*

There was a bump in the night, which woke me from a light sleep. I got out of bed to investigate and immediately trod upon Nial in the darkness. He'd fallen out of bed without waking. I lifted him back onto the bed he's sharing with Sofie, and I returned to the bed that I'm sharing with Sue. Not long after that, he woke up with a nightmare so I gave him a drink of water. I think I was asleep once more when he shrieked and woke up again with another bad dream. "A naughty man is chasing me!" he said. I climbed into bed with him and gave him a cuddle until he was properly calm and asleep. By 9.00 everyone was up and about except me. I felt duty-bound to try and have a lie-in today - it's the first show tonight - so Sue took the children down to breakfast and on to the pool, leaving me alone. I couldn't sleep, so I read for a while. Too tired to get up… too awake to sleep. At 10.30 I gave up, got up, showered and wrote this before making my way downstairs. Maybe a swim will wake me up…

When I arrived poolside, Sofie and Nial were swimming and Sue was just drying off. I sat with me legs dangling in the water, hoping to see Nial repeat yesterday's feat. He swam a breadth of the pool for the first time, but he wasn't in the mood today. I was out of phase with everyone as usual, and they were ready to return to the room to shower and pack, just as I was settling down by the pool. I hung around in the baking sun and read another chapter of **Crime and Punishment** by Dostoevski, before swimming a couple of lengths in order to cool down.

Around 1.00 we took the bags downstairs and checked out. I can't say I would recommend two days at the Holiday Inn, Laguna Hills – confusion reigns. We ordered chicken nuggets for the children, which they tucked into while I strapped the cases onto the roof of Tina's space wagon-thing, and then drove down the freeway a couple of exits to San Juan Capistrano. There were already one or two fans outside the entrance to The Coach House. No one commented on my peculiar mode of arrival (as if interrupted from a camping holiday), they simply said "Hi Steve! Nice to see you back here after so long!"

We made our way inside. It took me a minute to recognise anyone on stage. Simon had had a haircut. Stewart and Alan were under the stairs grappling with a transformer. I soon noticed the familiar figure of John Wesley, our Florida guitar tech and opening act. He's his usual affable self, and hasn't aged a day since the last time I saw him in '95. Alan appeared to say hello, and Nial latched onto him and assumed the role of assistant lighting designer for the rest of the afternoon. Ian M arrived with Jean (who's from Hollywood, down the road) and her sister Jo, and Jo's husband Peter. Peter is an optician to the stars and eye surgeon, and Jo is a clinical psychologist here in L.A. It was Peter who supplied me with replacement Armani sunspecs after I lost my own in Brazil recently, so I am indebted to him. As for clinical psychology, well, I guess she's got her hands full in L.A… the whole place is a mad-house.

Bit by bit the soundcheck evolved, beset by the customary "first gig" hums and glitches. It took an age, and when the doors were opened at 6.30 we still weren't ready. I said bye-bye to Sue, Sofi, Nial, Tina and the twins (who were all going back to the Sunset Marquis Hotel), and spent the next couple of hours sitting on the roof of the venue watching the sun go down and the people entering the club. There were also interviews with a Mexican University radio station and the US fan club kids, who are filming tonight's show.

Our expectations of tonight's performance weren't high. We have a new monitor man (Gary), new keyboard tech (Erik), house P.A., and Stewart Every is trying his hand at out-front sound for the first time. Notwithstanding all of this, and the fact that the band haven't played in a couple of weeks, I really enjoyed the show! The crowd were fantastic, despite being forced to sit at tables, and the band played well, apart from a dodgy moment during *Estonia* when I was plagued by the throat-frog. My sound was, on the whole, quite manageable and, after the show, I met most of the audience at a signing session by the door and everyone seemed to be over the moon with the gig.

The trip back to L.A. was further than I expected, and seemed interminable along Uncle Sam's potholed freeways in a minibus with sponges for suspension. I got off to a bad start at the Sunset Marquis Hotel by not being able to make my room-key open the door. I had to return to reception for a replacement. This must seem like no big problem to you, dear reader, but at 2.00am and after a show I tend to be exhausted, physically and mentally, and all the straws are last straws. I have lost count of the number of times I have traversed elevators and half-mile long hotel corridors, dragging suitcases and carrying bags, coat-hangers, bottles, laptops and God-knows-what in the middle of the night, completely knackered, to get to a room which wouldn't open. At times like this you'd almost prefer to lie down and sleep in the corridor than go back to reception.

When I eventually found my way into the right room (and the right bed) in the darkness, I lay there feeling so tired. I privately wondered if I was up to this life any more. I think last night's kiddy-nightmare-hell hadn't helped…

Tuesday 26 August *L.A. – San Francisco, Fillmore West*

Woke up feeling tired, but determined to enjoy breakfast by the pool before our departure from the Sunset Marquis at 10.00am. I was unable to shower last night so I crept into the bathroom and did so. When I emerged, Sue was already up and in the bathroom of the adjoining room. Sofie and Nial were up and about, and Tina knocked on the door to say that Rocco and the girls were all up, so I went down to the courtyard and the waiters pushed together a few tables so we could all have breakfast together. It was all a bit of a rush of course, but we checked out only a few minutes late. I made sure at reception that Tina wouldn't be charged too much after we'd gone. Tina and Sue were both tearful upon our departure. Sisterly love and living on separate continents. They say they'll try and visit us before Christmas. The trip to the airport took an hour or so in the spongy mini bus. I took a couple of pictures of everyone standing about at the Terminal – I'm trying to keep some record of this tour in pictures also.

The flight up to San Francisco was scenic. We flew along the coastline, which remained permanently visible below the cloudless sky. The sea gave way to a white line of beach adjoining a flat plain, suddenly rises up into mountains. I was too tired to enjoy the view for long and slept a little.

At S.F. airport we boarded a minibus (band, Tim, Jean, Sue, Sofie and Nial) to downtown San Francisco and the Triton Hotel, which is lovely and arty and brilliantly situated in the middle of everything. Sofi and Nial had been given a separate room, but seemed happy and unfazed by this first-time experience. We took a walk up through Chinatown looking at the shops – Oriental artefacts, large and small, expensive and cheap. Nial bought a little mandarin hat (he likes hats) and Sofie bought some beaded slippers. Sue saw much of interest, but seems not to want anything. She's not a particularly material creature. I had to go to soundcheck so I left them browsing and returned to the hotel where we were due to assemble at 4.00. On my way back to the hotel, I spotted a little lamp in the window of one of the shops. It was to be a monumental moment as I ambled in to enquire about the price. I met the owner, Jacob. He's a Lebanese Jew who's in the process of "selling off his grandfather's estate" – and the lamp was $1200. Yup, monumental. "Thank you," I said, turning to go. Jacob's a born salesman though, as I was to discover. He asked me how much I thought it was worth. "Make me an offer!" he said. Out of the air I plucked a figure $500, and we struck a deal at $550 for cash. It WAS a very nice lamp. It said Gallé on it. If it was genuine then it would indeed have been worth over a grand, but that wasn't the point. I simply thought it was a beautiful thing. He asked if I was a musician and I said yes. One thing led to another – he likes Pink Floyd and the Doors, so I figured we'd be right up his street. I told him I would leave two tickets on the door for him at the Fillmore tonight. He wrapped the lamp for me and I took it to soundcheck. It was of deep red-orange glass, with a bulb in the base as well as the main bulb beneath the glass shade. I took it from the bubble-wrap and plugged it in. Unfortunately the bulb in the base had blown. Shame. I'll have to pop back in the morning and see if I can find a replacement bulb. I wrapped it back up again.

The Fillmore's a great gig with a greater history. It's a 1500 capacity hall with two lines of beautiful chandeliers hanging along its length. There's a narrow balcony along the side of the auditorium with tables and chairs – perfect for Sofie and Nial, who can watch us from a balcony-seat overlooking the edge of stage-right, with access to our adjacent dressing room. Soundcheck went well, and betrayed few of the problems awaiting us at the show to follow.

I returned to the hotel, and a fan outside the Fillmore handed me a box of chocolate-covered strawberries. I went to bed for half an hour to sleep; I already felt like I'd done a gig. It had been a long day.

Well, we didn't get off to a good start. The show was delayed by a technical problem with the bass-pedals. When we eventually got on stage, my guitar wasn't plugged in at the amp so I spent most of *Lap of Luxury* getting it sorted out. With each new song a new technical malfunction arose. I had problems with the mic and the monitors, which ruined *Estonia*. The bass guitar went down for most of *Easter* and, although I tried to remain cool, eventually it got the better of me and my nerves and temper began to fray. Throughout all this, the crowd were amazing – incredibly supportive and enthusiastic from beginning to end, and stomping for a third encore long after we'd called it a day and were back in the dressing room, trying to make sense of what had gone wrong technically. I decided that alcohol was the best course of action and poured a tequila and orange. Diz was on the JD and Cokes. We wobbled back to the hotel and put S&N to bed. Once again, they had both been really well-behaved all night. Nial had dozed off during the show, but Sofie, bless her, had watched every minute.

Wednesday 27 August *San Francisco:* Day off

Didn't get up 'til 10.30 or so. I was a bit surprised that Sofi or Nial didn't come knocking on our door. I popped across the corridor to check they were both alright. Sure enough, there they were sitting side-by-side on the bed, watching TV. "Good morning, daddy. Did you have a good night?" said Sophie. What a sweetie. She has never changed.

We got ready and then went out, walking through Chinatown and climbing onto the streetcar which took us down to the bay. Fisherman's Wharf on Pier 31 was a mile or so along the waterfront, so we waited for a cab. While we waited, two boys on taxi bikes (or passenger-tricycles) pulled up and offered us a ride. I climbed in one with Nial, Sue and Sofi climbed aboard the other. We got there, and we were all eager to have some breakfast, so we settled on a café and I ate clam chowder. This is the only city in the world to eat chowder (PS – and Boston!). It was delicious (I have found in the past it is also a great hangover cure). We spent the rest of our free time on the pier, wandering around the many shops. We bought exotic sea-shells and found a carousel. At the end of the pier I photographed Sue in front of Alcatraz across the bay. From here you can see the Golden Gate Bridge as well as the infamous prison island, and the opposite side of the bay where seals played in the fast current of the bay channel. I'm told the water is as cold as the North Sea, even in the summer.

At 3 o'clock we took a cab back to the hotel to pack, and at 3.45 we took a car to the airport. Sue and the children return to England today. I helped everyone check-in, and gave the children hugs and kisses. They promised to be good and look after mummy until I come home. I said bye-bye to Sue; she will fly to Washington in two weeks to see me again for a few days, so at least we won't be parted too long.

I returned to the hotel with no idea of what was about to unfold. It was almost 6.00, so I returned to Jacob's shop in the hope of getting a spare bulb for my new lamp. When I arrived there, he greeted me like a friend and was most excited that I had returned. He had gone to last nights show with his wife. He was grateful that I had gone to the trouble of leaving him complimentary tickets at the door, but he was downright blown away with the show. He said he loved the band, and had no idea yesterday that we were so brilliant. He seemed most charmed by me as a performer and human being, and determined to become a lifelong friend. He insisted I sit down at the back of the shop and instructed the shop boy - a Mexican called Arthur - to go out for a case of beer and a pizza. He said he had something he wanted to show me, and he went upstairs to search around for a Persian rug with gold woven into it. He couldn't find it, and returned downstairs, still enthusing about the show and my generosity. He bears a striking resemblance to Robert De Niro in **Goodfellas**, both physically and in terms of his delivery of an endless tirade of words. After 10 minutes my head was swimming. Arthur returned with Coronas and pizza, and was sent upstairs to fetch three rugs, which he unfolded at my feet. One of them was particularly beautiful – a tree of life, hanging with pomegranates, all woven in silk against gold. He says it's worth a fortune. I say it's beautiful but I can't afford it (and I don't need it). He says he wants to KNOW that it's in my house and, although it's worth "much, much more", I can have it for $6000. By this time I'm laughing, but he won't take no for an answer. He asks me if there's anything else in the shop that I like the look of. There's a Tiffany lamp in the corner. It's lovely, but it's repro I think. In a cabinet there are two art deco vases that catch my eye. "I'm going to package them and send them to your wife as a present!" he said, clapping his hands and instructing Arthur to pack them up for delivery. Somehow this wizard enchants me, shames me, and literally juggernauts me into buying the rug. He says it will bring me luck. He wants to give me whatever will make me happy. He throws the keys to his Mercedes on the table: "It's yours for the night! Take it for a drive! Enjoy yourself! See the city!!" I say thanks, but I don't need to borrow his car. He drags me over the road to meet the people who run the kosher Lebanese restaurant over the road. He wants all his friends to meet me. Eventually he insists I go out on the town with him. I shudder to imagine where he would drag me off to! I decline as I must be up early in the morning, so he drives me back to the Triton Hotel, playing The Doors at ear-bleeding volume in his Mercedes from the CD player in the boot. I get back to my room and sit on the bed wondering how I have so easily been parted from 4000 quid! I only wanted a light bulb.

I call Tim Bricusse, the tour manager, to my room, telling the whole story, asking his advice. He asks to see the rug, so I unpack it and show him. He says all the wrong things: "It IS very beautiful! ...Well, now and again in this life you have to forget about the money..." etc. I tell Tim he is not supposed to be saying this! He's supposed to be telling me I'm insane and I've been conned! We go and get Alan Parker. He also thinks it's lovely. I get Tim to change my air ticket and hotel reservation. I'd better stay another day and sort all this out.

I lay awake all night - half of me thinking I have been conned out of a lot of money, the other half hoping I haven't - dismayed that someone for whom I had done a favour could use me so brazenly to his advantage when I was so obviously prepared to trust him. He is either rich, generous and a little crazy, or he's a total bastard. I had invested £4000 in finding out. I know all this sounds naive, but you'd have had to have been there…

Thursday 28 August *San Francisco:* Day off

At 8am I called Jacob at home. I get his answering machine. I call the shop. No answer. At 9 o'clock I call the shop again and Sion, his partner ("Put your money into TWA and Homestead gold") tells me that the Tiffany lamp and vases have already been couriered. "They've gone already!?" I almost scream. "Yup, picked 'em up this morning!" I flop back down on the bed and enter a half-sleep. At 9.10 the phone rings and it's Jacob. I tell him I've been up all night worrying. "What are you worried about?!" he says. I try to explain that I've spent more money, much more money, than I can afford, on something I don't really need. If you read this next bit in a Robert de Niro **Goodfellas** accent, you'll be close – "Don't think about the money!" he says. He seems to think $6000 is nothing. "Don't worry about the money! I want you to have a nice relaxing time and feel good, and now you're getting all worried. Don't worry! Come down to my store in two hours, I'll be there by then and we'll work it out. Don't WORRY!" and he hangs up. There's nothing I can do so I try and sleep for two hours. I get up at 10.30, shower, and then pack up the carpet and walk down to the shop…

PS. As I compile this diary in 2013, I can't remember what happened next. I must have blocked it out. What I DO know is that the rug is rolled up in a cupboard in my house. I have moved house a few times since 1997, and got divorced (not *because of* the rug but it probably didn't help). To this day, I never lived in a house for which the rug had much use (there was never a wall-space where I could hang it and I can't put it on the floor and *walk* on it!), and yet I have never had it valued nor have I attempted to sell it. It IS a very beautiful rug. I'm sure it has a value, but probably nowhere near what Jacob charged me. The fact is, I can't face the confirmation that I was conned by someone to whom I had first extended generosity, and the consequential blow to my fundamental belief in the goodness of humanity. Maybe it IS worth $6000. Maybe it's worth $20,000. One day, I'll bite the bullet and find out…

Thursday 4 September *Toronto, The Guverment*

Woke at eight, unable to properly sleep and annoyed with myself. I need to sleep late if I can. Willed myself back to sleep until 11.00, when I got up and wandered out and down to Yonge Street, looking for a place to get my roots done. I have an interview today with Much Music (the Canadian MTV) here in Toronto. I stumbled upon a hairdresser called Hair by Sofia, a rundown looking salon, but what the hell, it's only roots. Sofia is in her 50s I'd guess, half-Russian and half-Iranian, and, I can tell immediately, a sweetheart. She does my roots and I blow-dry myself while she talks to another customer. I head back to the Primrose Hotel, dropping in at a pharmacy to buy vitamin B which I *imagine* will make me sing better.

When I arrive back at the Hotel, Tim rings to say Pete T has been mugged last night! He was set upon and beaten up by someone who then took his wallet. He's at the hospital, being x-rayed to check if anything is broken. Everyone I meet tells me that NO ONE EVER GOT MUGGED IN TORONTO – it's one of the safest cities on earth. Well, Pete T managed it! We are invited to lunch today by our new (watch this space) record company, so we meet up in the lobby at 2 o'clock with Mia, who seems okay but not terribly clued-up and not overly interested. She takes us to the Bambu Café on Queen Street and her colleague (whose name I forget) turns up an hour late. Didn't particularly like him either. By this time the Much Music TV interview is cancelled (surprise!). Shame. I was looking forward to mentioning Pete's mugging. Maybe that's why it's cancelled – not "happy TV" and the label can't risk damaging their relationship with Much Music any more than Much Music wants to piss the mayor off by publicising a mugging in the "safest city on earth!").

The band went straight to the soundcheck while Tim and I returned to the hotel to pick up Pete who was back from the hospital. His face is swollen on both sides, and his eyes are both black and bruised. He's obviously in great pain, but he insists on coming to the soundcheck although we suggest he should stay at the hotel until the show. He says he'd feel better if he soundchecked. What a man!

At the soundcheck it becomes apparent that we're not really wanted here. There is some Film Festival opening in the next room tonight, and they want us on stage at 7:30pm to get us out of the way before the real action happens. The room we are playing sounds dreadful and my voice ain't great (whoopee!). We return to the hotel to pick up our things for the show. I pack everything away, including my new lamp (back into its bubble-wrap and carrier bags), and by the time I'm finished we have to go back to the gig.

When we get back, there's hardly anyone there – maybe 70 people. It filled up during the show, but the total attendance was still pitiful. During *Afraid of Sunlight* my voice just about stopped working, leaving me to cough and speak my way through the rest of the show. Tonight was being filmed for an Internet transmission – that will have to be canned for a kick-off. I managed to curb my temper and despair, despite feeling at an all-time low. Pete - black-eyes hidden behind sunglasses - played tenaciously throughout the set, although at times there was an uncertainty in his playing which betrayed how much pain he was in. He shamed me into good behaviour, despite all the problems. My guitar levels were odd again tonight, and the vocal sound came and went in my monitors. I came offstage feeling wretched, really feeling like packing it all in.

I went back to the hotel to shower and I had to do an interview to explain why the TV people can't broadcast the show. Decided to do it in bed and Mark K got in too. By this time my mind had already left Toronto; fortunately my body only had to stay there for another hour.

Sunday 14 September *Washington DC, The Whitehouse*

Clambered out of my bunk and went up to the front of the bus to discover a bright, sunny day. Kent, our bus driver, was trying to find a place to turn the bus around so that he can drop me at the Wyndham Bristol Hotel on the edge of Georgetown. I was still half asleep as I made my way to reception to pick up a key, before going up in the elevator to the third floor. Sue was already out of bed when I entered the room. She flew into Washington last night so that we could have a couple of days together. Spent most of the day sleeping and lazing around. At 4.00pm I had to be at the Holiday Inn, Alexandria - where the boys are staying - for a live Internet interview. Mark, Steve and I huddled around a computer for 90 minutes, frantically attempting to answer questions which came up on the screen from participating fans in cyberspace. It was a new experience and quite good fun. Occasionally abusive questions or statements came up on the screen like "Marillion suck!" (probably Lloyd Cole again...), but nothing that couldn't be shrugged off on a Beavis and Butthead level. I promised Sue I would return at 6.00 and I was late as usual.

Before I left I phoned Dave Keane (not real name – I'm being careful...), a Secret Service security agent whose card (yes, they have business cards!) Ian Mosley had passed onto me after meeting him after a show somewhere. He's promised a guided tour of the White House to anyone in the band who's interested. No-one's sure if he's "for real" – I couldn't imagine MI6 handing out business cards ("George Smiley, Spy"). Well, I called him and he said there are no guided-tours on Sundays or Mondays, but he would see if he could arrange something special for us tonight and would call me, so I gave him my number at the Wyndham. I took the Metro from Alexandria back to Foggy Bottom station, and walked back around the corner to our Hotel. Sue was getting dressed. She had been sleeping off the jet-lag when she was woken by a phone call and a loud voice saying, "This is Dave from the Secret Service", which just about scared her out of her skin! We're to meet him outside the White House at 8.45. I explained everything and she relaxed considerably, having realised we hadn't, after all, stumbled into a national-security-threatening conspiracy. We decided to go and eat first, wandering along the main street (I'm not great with names) of Georgetown in the warm evening air, looking at the beautiful antiques and *objets d'art* in the shops. We settled on a Vietnamese restaurant with a garden at the rear - all lit up with fairy lights - and the food was terrific. Sue had char-grilled shrimps and I had cinnamon and orange beef.

After dinner, we took a cab along Pennsylvania Avenue to the White House, where Dave was already waiting for us with his wife and a couple of chums. He wore the expression of someone who had difficult news to break. "You're never going to believe this," he said, "...but he's workin' late! He's in the Oval Office right now. No-one's allowed in the West Wing if he's in there." "Wow! I didn't realise he was even in town!" Dave said he could take us next door to the government offices and show us the Vice-President's office and, sure enough, we found ourselves sitting behind Al Gore's desk! We were introduced to the duty guard, James, who had no objection to all this and even posed for a photograph with Sue.

It's a tradition for Vice-Presidents to sign the desk drawer, and it was pulled out to reveal the autographs of a dozen or more. I could pick out Lyndon B.Johnson, Richard M. Nixon, and Harry F. Truman at a glance. I think Bobby Kennedy was in there too! The desktop was clear, apart from a big white telephone which James suggested we didn't pick up. "You'll have half the Secret Service in here in a minute!" he said. By now I was already too awe-struck to contemplate touching anything, let alone picking up the phone. The security men were so friendly and relaxed, it was almost surreal to think we were in the inner sanctum of American government. Dave's radio occasionally crackled into life – he's constantly updated as to the whereabouts of Bill, Hillary and Chelsea Clinton (codenamed "Eagle", "Evergreen" and "Energy" respectively). Dave explained that his job is to patrol the roof of the East Wing, where the First Family live, and to travel and patrol the roof of wherever they happen to be. He's just got back from Martha's Vineyards - an island up in New England - where the Clintons were holidaying. Dave's wife complains about his constant and prolonged absences; Sue could relate.

I had a live radio interview at 10.30 which I had to do from the hotel telephone, so time was running out. However, at around 9.50, Dave's radio crackled, "The Eagle is moving" (I'm not kidding!), and Bill Clinton was off to the East Wing and to bed. We all hurried downstairs across the way, and Sue and I found ourselves in the West Wing of the White House. Dave led us through a couple of security checks and through a few stately (but not "over-the-top" luxurious) rooms and corridors, to the Oval Office where we stood in the open doorway, gazing at The President's Desk – the heart of the USA!! The room is so famous that there's little point in me describing it. Bill had personalised it with his own little mementos placed here and there, photographs of the family, etc. A book that Hilary had written was proudly displayed on a shelf. His footprints were still clearly visible in the huge, blue, circular rug which carpets the Oval Office. There's a circle of stars in the plasterwork of the ceiling at the apex of the room. Dave pointed out that they're not five-pointed stars, but six. This was an error made at some point in history, and Roosevelt planned to have them replaced with the more American five-pointed stars during his term of office. Apparently however, when he got the quote for the work, it was so expensive that he spent the money on something else instead. No President since has been able to justify changing them either, so they have become an unexpected anomaly of the decor of the Oval Office. I asked the security guard if I might take a couple of photographs. He said it isn't allowed, but that he wouldn't tell anyone if I didn't (so keep it to yourself…).

From the Oval Office we walked down to the press reception office, where I had my photograph taken behind that famous lectern: the one you saw every day during the Gulf War. From there we walked through the Rose Garden to the East Wing, and out into the street. The President has his own cinema here, and

Richard Nixon even had a two lane ten-pin bowling alley put in! What a beautiful place the garden must be on an early summer afternoon, or in midwinter, decorated for Christmas. I wonder if the occupants of this house can ever get into a state of mind to enjoy it? I suppose the retired Presidents who return later can, perhaps, sit quietly for a moment and reminisce in the sweet rose-scented air. Such reminiscences are probably plagued by demons and regrets. Can you be great *and* happy?

Dave and his wife returned us to our hotel where I arrived just in time for my 'phone interview to Philadelphia –

"How are you, Steve?"

"Fine, I was just in the Oval Office!"

"Tell me about your new album…"

Why don't media people listen?!

Friday 3 October *Munich*

Got up around 8.30, and helped Sue to get Sofie and Nial ready for school. At 9.00 I walked them round the corner and down the lane to school. Nial ricked his neck on Wednesday, and had a couple of days off school. I took him to my masseur when I went for my customary mid-tour session, and he seems much better now. Sofie got upset at the school gate. She doesn't want me to go away again, and she cried quite a lot as we said goodbye. I know she'll be okay, but it's difficult for both of us. Nial wasn't too bothered – he walked on towards the playground as she sobbed into my arms. I didn't want him hanging around getting upset as well.

I returned home and showered, before packing my things for the forthcoming last leg (and I'm on mine) of the tour. At 11.00 a car took me to Aylesbury to pick up Steve R, and then on to Terminal 1 for the 1.30 flight to Munich. Sue seemed to be okay when I left home, so I was spared that upset at least. It's hard enough as it is. I don't really want to go away again. I've had enough.

Once you get to the airport and get caught up in the hustle and bustle of travel, you don't feel so low, you just get on with it. Thankfully it's only a two-hour flight to Munich – a pleasant change from the 11-hour long hauls. I spent the flight relaxing and reading and grappling with aeroplane food and drinks. The food on British Airways was noticeably better than the stuff they placed before us on American Airlines.

In Munich the weather was sunny but crisp. We took cabs to the Munich Park Hilton and arrived around 6.00, and I checked into room 830. I have stayed here many times. I remember being here with the Europeans: Spandau Ballet were in the swimming pool… the terror of discovering that the sauna was mixed and full of naked German blokes with bushy moustaches and bulbous stomachs, German ladies with floppy breasts and legs akimbo. I was young at the time, and more easily embarrassed than now. It was also here that, downstairs in the nightclub (it's now a Chinese Restaurant), Joe Cocker advised me to "Never drink anything you can't see through..." He was drinking something I couldn't see through at the time. I left my scarf in the nightclub and, when I went back searching for it the following morning, he was still sitting at the bar. He'd been there all night!

Here again in 1997, there's no Spandau Ballet (although I've been known to play the occasional gig with Big Tone) and there's no Joe Cocker. The hotel appears to be full of old men from America, all wearing matching blazers and shouting unselfconsciously across the lobby as only the Americans (and possibly Australians) can.

We're in Munich during the Oktoberfest and Chrissy Uerlings, who represents our promoter, Peter Rieger, has arrived at the Hilton to take us there at 7.00. Peter's reserved a table in one of the beer tents. It wasn't what I was expecting... I was expecting a large canvas marquee in a park, but in actual fact the whole festival is like a big fairground, complete with side-shows and brightly-lit rides and stalls. Flanking the fair are huge stripy circus-like tents with security men at the entrances. Once inside, there are seemingly endless rows of trestle-tables packed with people amid the noisy chaos of a party in full-swing. There's a stage in the centre with a band playing oom-pah disco music and everyone's having a ball, singing along to the dreadful music. When I was younger this would have been my idea of a nightmare. Tonight I see it for what it is. Despite having been somewhat hijacked by the tourist industry, the Oktoberfest is, at heart, a simple celebration of relief and thanks for a harvest gathered-in when, traditionally, the working people could relax and take a break from their labours before the rigours of the winter. The atmosphere here tonight retains that spirit of simple and good-natured drunken celebration. I was "into it" even before Chrissy handed me the biggest glass of beer I'd ever held so, after consuming an excellent plate of roast pork and another beer, I was having a great time. Some of the revellers bring their own musical instruments and drunkenly play along with the band from wherever they happen to be sitting. A man in a Santa-Claus hat at the next table - definitely sloshed - had brought a trumpet and, between beers, played along without once missing a note. He must be a brilliant musician when he's sober. An older chap at the end of our table had brought a melodica, which he tootled on to himself in between affable grins. People were constantly milling around, tottering along as only drunks can, while buxom waitresses carried fistfuls of steins, empty or brimming, en route to the tables. Believe me, these girls are strong; a handful of steins weighs about the same as an anvil, and these must be carried the length of these enormous halls. I know I would be struggling to do it.

I chatted to Chrissy about Peter's traumatic experiences with **Tommy** the musical. From the outset he'd wanted me to play the lead, and he flew me to NY a couple of times before his intentions were hijacked by the politics and agenda of the production company. In my opinion, Peter was shafted royally as a consequence of his inexperience in the Byzantine calculations of American showbiz. Is that vague enough so I don't get sued? The big production musical is a lot further away from rock n'roll than we all thought. A musical *about* rock n'roll is still a musical. Any connection with rock n'roll is tenuous. To this day I'm still surprised that Townshend got into bed with it. I guess he just looked after the "art" of it and left the politics to someone else. I'm thankful I never got involved – it would have driven me nuts. It damn nearly finished Peter Rieger; he lost millions of marks and ended up with a triple heart-bypass. That deaf, dumb and blind kid SURE plays a MEAN pinball.

By 11.00 I too was drunk. We returned to the Hilton by cab and I staggered around my room for a while before going to bed. Luckily the room wasn't spinning – one more beer would have done it…

Tuesday 7 October *Bonn, Biskuithalle*

I lay in my bunk long after I felt the bus park outside the Biskuithalle. The bustle of the crew getting up and out and the clanking of the truck being unloaded all washed over me as I drifted in and out of sleep. I eventually got up at 1.30 and made my way into the familiar backstage area. We've played here four or five times now. Alan Parker was coming the other way, singing, "A life on the ocean wave." He said, "Good morning! Are you only just up? You lucky bastard!"

I helped myself to the first coffee of the day and wandered into the hall to see how the crew were doing. The Biskuithalle is a comparatively easy gig for the crew; the equipment rolls out of the truck and onto the stage. When I arrived, most of the back line was already set up. My guitar amp blew a fuse yesterday, so I was anxious to see if it would work today. It seemed to be okay. I returned to catering for another coffee, and Jane made me a cheese and ham toastie for breakfast. Wes wandered through catering and told me that there's a music shop across the road. I went there with Erik in search of a repair man, and we were in luck – a repair boffin was in residence, and could look at my amp around 4 o'clock. I returned to the gig and carried the amp back myself. Meanwhile Oliver, our promoter's rep, had arranged for my stage trousers (torn to bits again) to go to a seamstress for more repairs. I seem to be dogged by amps and trousers on this tour. When I returned to the venue the band had arrived, so I said hello and had a chinwag before returning across the road to discuss my ailing amplifier with the repair Docktor. It all turned out to be a waste of time – he said he couldn't fix it, but he's arranged a replacement component (which he doesn't have) to go to the hotel in Bielefeld in two days time. Oh well. I had to take the amp back in the car, as it had suddenly started to rain really hard.

Soundcheck involved borrowing Duncan's amp again. Duncan is the guitarist/bv-ist from our opening act Picture House, a good-time pop group from Dublin. Naturally they are a friendly bunch of chaps. Nothing seems to faze them and they've been going down really well with our fans during the shows. I've been using their amplifier since Luxembourg. I'm going to try and get my combo fixed just one last time, then it's going in a skip. After soundcheck I chatted with a bunch of Dutch and German fan club people who were hanging at the stage door – Rob Crossland (Marillion's most dedicated and well-travelled fan) needed a photo pass. I arranged for everyone to get in okay before climbing on the bus for my pre-show nap. I lay in my bunk, listening to the bass-bumps from Picture House coming through the walls of the building to the car park outside, and drifting in and out of sleep.

When I emerged at 8.35, John A was in the dressing room. He said there's news so I arranged a 10-minute briefing after the show. And what a show it was! I suppose it must have been the lighting and the crowd size (around 1800) making the temperature on stage almost sauna-like. By the third song I was ringing wet. Heat makes everything much more tiring and, physically, the show was the most demanding since the high-altitude Mexico City gig. It took me (and the crowd) a while to get going. I lost it for a while after I discovered the multicores on the front of the stage hadn't been taped down. One slip (or trip) and I'm off the front of the stage and head-first onto concrete. I do occasionally fall from stages; so far I have been lucky. Further irritation ensued during *Estonia* when the crew remedied the situation, tearing off strips of gaffer tape - a sound identical to pants splitting - during the quiet, spiritual verses of the song. I had to reach down and throw the roll of tape into the crowd to stop it. I hope nobody caught it in the face. I'm experienced enough now to know that getting annoyed is the worst thing I can do during a show. It doesn't stop me getting annoyed though, unfortunately. I then get annoyed for GETTING annoyed! Anyway, the show progressed and the crowd began to come to life – and me with them, of course. It was a steep upward spiral, and I can't remember quite where it came from. Maybe the sweat did it. By the end of the show the crowd were amazing, and somehow more affectionate than I can ever remember a German audience being. I was losing myself in them; not a good idea because then I forget the words. Verse two of *Slainte* (known affectionately to the band as 'Slange") went missing almost completely. Am I losing my mind or is the world getting better? I'm sure the food is better in America than two years ago. Both in Munich and Bonn I noticed some strange spiritual awakening in the crowd – a most "un-German" tenderness (strong enough, at last, to be beautiful? It ultimately boils down to strength). I don't think I imagined this change.

After the last encore we stood together as a band at the front of the stage, to enjoy the noise and, in our unspoken, ungestured way, to salute the crowd here in Bonn-Cologne. We never do this, but tonight it felt like a natural thing to do. Thank you Bonn.

I returned to the dressing room to grab a robe. I was almost on my knees with exhaustion, but I returned to the edge of stage to watch the last of the people filing out of the back of the hall and trying to save the last, lost drops of magic from this evening in this room.

At midnight it was Angie's birthday. Champagne was popped and we toasted her health and thanked her for her many efforts on our behalf, which have gone unrewarded for so long. I had my 10-minute meeting with John. He reckons we're only 18 months away from recouping our considerable debt to EMI, and then we'll start receiving royalty cheques. I'll believe it when I see it. It's never happened to me before. Our current record label, Castle, has ceased to exist in all but name. It seems we now have a legal case in favour of getting out of the contract. Watch this space. I drank beer and tried to chat with the assembled throng backstage, but I was still too buzzy to really make conversation. Eventually I emerged outside to sign a few things and have my photograph taken with yet more strangers, before climbing onto the bus with a sigh of wonder and relief! I suppose I must have had a drink with the crew, but it's all a blur. I probably read a little in my bunk before sleeping. I'm currently on **A Prayer for Owen Meany** by John Irving.

Monday 20 October *Nice, Theatre de Verdure*

When I rolled out of my bunk at 9.30, we were still on the motorway travelling towards Nice. I made my way down to the back lounge, made a coffee, and was soon joined by a bleary-eyed Pete T. We watched from the windows as the bus swung along the sea-front, where almost everyone seems to be over sixty-five years old. Bald heads bobbed around in the sea – people already having a swim at 9.45 in the morning. After a slight delay around the one-way system, the bus pulled up outside the familiar stripy tent on the Promenade d'Anglais. I dragged my bags along the street to the Meridien Hotel next door and up the escalators to reception, where I was informed that Mrs. Hogarth is in room 538. True to form, it was the furthest room from the elevator and I arrived tired and irritable at the door, although I managed not to be grumpy. Poor Sue said she'd been up most of the night with a streaming head cold. I found her some pills in my toilet bag. I'm a walking pharmacy when I'm on tour.

I was dog-tired after Toulouse, but it's important that I spend time with my family. So we both took Ibuprofen, and we all went out for breakfast on the seafront, stopping at reception to send a fax to Peter, Jo and Jean. Ian's girlfriend (Jean) has a twin sister (Jo) who's married to Peter, an eye-surgeon from L.A. Jo and Peter travelled to Toulouse from California to see our show yesterday. For some reason, despite having passes for our show and backstage, security wouldn't let them in. They stood outside in the street until after the show had finished!! We all feel responsible for this – they came from California! It's spilled milk now of course, but I sent a fax to say sorry on behalf of the band. I still can't believe it!

Anyway. Back to breakfast in Nice. Sofie, Sue and Nial had English breakfast while I had a ham and cheese crépe. At 12.00 Sue had arranged to meet Ann-Sofie Prevot, friend and photographer. We decided I should go to bed while Sue and the children went out with Ann-Sofie and Jacquiline (journalist and writer of a book about Marillion). I went upstairs and slept until 3.00 when Sue returned. We walked over to the venue in a rainstorm, and drank coffee backstage until soundcheck. I filled in the time sewing a button on my waistcoat and finding a place to dry my socks and underwear. It's all glamour.

I had agreed to a record shop appearance at FNAC, Nice, which was scheduled for after soundcheck. We soundchecked to the accompaniment of torrential rain outside and on the roof of the tent. It sounded like being under a waterfall, or singing through a noisy old analogue effects pedal. Soundcheck progressed well, despite the waterfall above and the massive natural reverb of the tent, until people started streaming into the building. It was all news to me, but apparently the FNAC music shop appearance had been moved to the gig where we were to answer the fans questions and sign autographs. This was supposed to happen after soundcheck, but someone had decided to get everybody out of the downpour outside. All reasonable decisions of course, when viewed one-at-a-time, but it would have been a good idea to okay all this with the band first.

I was like a bear with a sore head for the impromptu signing session. I don't like such surprises. I looked like shit and, after an hour on stage, I badly needed a coffee. I was hoarse and still tired, and Jacquiline who had "organised" all this was busily arranging copies of her book ("**Marillion - the Fish era**") to be bought by the kids and signed by the band. I got the feeling she'd hijacked the whole thing for her own personal gain. I fumed my way through the signing session before returning to the hotel to have an hour with Sue, Sofie and Nial before the show.

Sue had a bath while I played with the children. Sofie lent me her metallic blue nail varnish and I painted my toes. They're quite entertaining sticking out from my Doc Marten sandals. I painted Nial's toenails too, but he wasn't really sure that boys should have painted nails so I removed it again.

At 9.00 we went down to the bar, where Sue had a quick JD & Coke before Tim B walked us across the road. At the gig the audience were in top form and party mood – it's always a great atmosphere here in Nice. There were around 1400 people singing and stomping their way through the songs. We really couldn't go wrong. It all went slightly pear-shaped on the last verse of *Warm Wet Circles*, when the guitar, bass, and keyboard power supplies fused simultaneously, leaving me singing to drums only. Oddly enough it worked, and turned the end of the song into a rap. Luckily the PA had stayed on, so Steve and Pete picked up acoustic guitars and we played *Hide your Love Away* by the Beatles, *Substitute* by The Who and *Sugar Mice* while our crew were sorting out the power supply. It all turned out to be a happy accident, the crowd loved it and the rest of the show was one long ovation. Sue and Nial were standing stage right watching from the wings. Sofie was out-front with Stewart and Alan, but appeared at the side of stage a little later. I ran off from time to time to give them sweaty hugs in the dark. The best moment of the show happened when little Nial walked across to centre stage with a towel to dry my face, which was dripping as usual. He received deafening applause and I thanked him with a kiss, taking care not to bash him with the guitar around my neck. He ran back to Wes on stage left, looking as though he'd had more than enough fame for comfort! It's a good feeling to have my family around for the odd show here and there. Sofie and Nial are very well-behaved and fun to be around. They get on really well with the crew as well. Sue's a great calming influence. Everyone's always pleased to see her and she has an instinct for keeping a low profile when we're busy.

Well, after the show I ran away pretty quickly. I'd already mingled enough for one day during the surprise meet-and-greet and I wanted to be on my own with my family, at least for an hour, so we did a "runner" (this is the term for coming off stage and straight out of the building). We all scooted out of the back of the big tent and across the street on the Promenade d'Anglais to the Meridien. Nial pointed out that I'd forgotten my sandals, as we walked back. For a five-year-old he doesn't miss much.

By now it was well after midnight. The kids had done well to stay up so late, especially little Nial. He's growing up fast now. We got them straight into bed and he fell asleep in an instant. Sofie took enough time to say goodnight and tell me she really enjoyed the show before drifting out of consciousness with her arm around my painted feet. She'll probably go back to school and tell her teacher, "It was at the age of 39 that my father took to painting his toenails." Sue and I hugged for a while. She was exhausted after a night of no sleep and still suffering with a head cold, so I showered and changed and said goodnight. They will stay here tomorrow and return to Toulouse by train, and then to England by plane on Wednesday, while I shall board the bus and sleep my way to Lyon for tomorrow's show.

Wes gave me a hand with my luggage. Back at the bus there were still a handful of fans waiting for signatures. I love and respect our fans, they're total sweethearts and without them we'd have to get "proper" jobs. But just occasionally, when I'm tired, or late, or in crisis (which is usual), I would appreciate being left alone.

As we drove along the coast road next to the black sea, I thought of Sue, in bed alone with her cold, and hoped she'd have a few good days until next week when I'll be home for good, and we can try, once again, to fill the space that opens up between us.

Saturday 25 October *Strasbourg*

By some feat of genius, Nick Belshaw had booked us into Le Petit Regent Hotel in Satrasbourg. Not cheap, but lovely.

Had an indulgent (but necessary) long lie-in, not stirring into life until around 12.30. I opened the curtains to a cold sunny morning and a view out over the Lill River which can have little competition on Earth. I'm looking out above the rushing water everywhere. To the left is a lock, through which boats occasionally pass. The river meanders through the town in front of me. Two bridges are visible, the first reminiscent of the Bridge of Sighs in Venice. Indeed, the view from my window of the river, flanked with 16th century buildings, is an easy match for Venice, and in a much better state of repair. Swans bob around effortlessly on the river. It's an immaculate view to overlook while eating breakfast, which is exactly what I did next. Took a photograph of my breakfast tray in front of the open window. Showered and called Dizzy and the kids in Yorkshire.

to be continued...

7.04.92. Bloomington Indiana

Overtaken by this great sadness
The lonelyness of the moment
Five minutes like a year
The product of an endless dislocating movement
Nothing I can put my finger on
Nothing really real
Waiting till we talk again
Heal me with your silence
Heal me with your listening
I know your silence understands
Mop my brow with your understanding eyes
While I fumble and try to ~~explain~~ find ~~the~~ words
To explain
What you already know.
There There There
What does that say to you

Black Blue Sky Bird Peace Love You Me White

Darkness Light God Understanding Trust Fear
Faith Magic Jumbo Jets America Heaven Hell
Silence Mrs Robinson Paul Elaine The Sea
Tears Me Dog Walk Run
While you watch Silence

ALSO AVAILABLE FROM **MIWK PUBLISHING**

JAUNT

AN UNOFFICIAL GUIDE TO THE TOMORROW PEOPLE

by Andy Davidson

Shape-changing robots, military masterminds, ITV technicians – it's a deadly universe out there, but the Tomorrow People are here to help.

The Tomorrow People are man's next step up the evolutionary ladder: Homo superior. From their secret base deep below the streets of London, they offer hope of a better future for the human race as members of the all-powerful Galactic Federation.

Jaunt follows **The Tomorrow People** from its origins in the creative melting-pot of 1970s children's television to a worldwide hit. It revisits them in the 1990s for some light-hearted **Avengers**-style action and returns a decade later for a series of bold, challenging audio plays.

Homo superior has been with us for forty years, and **Jaunt** chronicles the phenomenon that is again preparing to return to our screens in a big-budget US adaptation.

Jaunt includes exclusive interviews with series creator Roger Price, producer Ruth Boswell and the Tomorrow People themselves – Nicholas Young, Peter Vaughan Clarke, Elizabeth Adare, Mike Holoway and Misako Koba.

With an introduction from Roger Price, **Jaunt** also features the complete script of the unmade ninth series adventure *Mystery Moon*.

ISBN 978-1-908630-23-0

ALSO AVAILABLE FROM **MIWK PUBLISHING**

THE QUEST FOR PEDLER

THE LIFE AND IDEAS OF DR KIT PEDLER

by Michael Seely

For many people, Kit Pedler is best remembered as the man who created the Cybermen for **Doctor Who**, a real life scientist who was brought in to act as an advisor and bring some science to the fiction. The Cybermen were his ultimate scientific horror: where the very nature of a man was altered by himself, by his own genius for survival, creating a monster. Pedler was that rare animal, a scientist with an imagination. He liked to think 'What if...?'

With two doctorates to his name, and as Head of Anatomy at the Institute of Ophthalmology investigating the nature of the retina, Dr. Kit Pedler began to share the suspicions being voiced in the 1960s towards the role of the scientist in society, who saw research as an end to itself and left the moral dilemmas to the politicians in a world where the people were conditioned to accept an intolerable environment.

Together with his friend and writing partner Gerry Davis, he created the hugely successful and controversial BBC1 drama series **Doomwatch**, which captured this fear and frightened the adults as much as the Cybermen scared the children.

Resigning from the Institute, Pedler turned his back on the world he had spent his adult life working in, and spent the rest of it campaigning for a real Doomwatch, to stop the unnecessary and cruel animal experiments in the laboratory (which he himself had seen in his earlier academic days), experiment in what we would now call eco-friendly housing, alternative technology and began to change his own relationship to the world. With contributions from his family, friends, colleagues and critics, this book tells the story behind a fascinating, charismatic, complicated, and demanding human being; a natural teacher who didn't just want to pontificate about the problems facing the world in a television or radio studio, but actually do something practical about them.

ISBN 978-1-908630-12-4

ALSO AVAILABLE FROM **MIWK PUBLISHING**

HOODED MAN

Volume One: Robin of Loxley

by Andrew Orton

'In the days of the Lion spawned of the Devil's Brood, the Hooded Man shall come to the forest. There he will meet Herne the Hunter, Lord of the Trees, and be his son and do his bidding. The Powers of Light and Darkness shall be strong within him. And the guilty shall tremble.'

With its distinctive mixture of history and mythology, **Robin of Sherwood** was an innovative treatment of the Robin Hood legend. Broadcast on ITV between 1984 and 1986, the series has been a major influence on later versions of the Robin Hood story.

Now for the first time, a guide to the series in two volumes, from its beginnings in fifteenth century ballads of Robin Hood to its modern tale of a band of guerrillas striking from their forest hideout.

Hooded Man Volume One takes a fresh look at each episode starring Michael Praed. It explores the production of the first two series and the legends, literature and history that influenced them. On the way you'll find new trivia, goofs, quotes and translations, a comprehensive atlas of filming locations and the full story of the creation of the series.

Hooded Man is an essential guide for every true fan of the series, detailing everything you might have missed along the way... because nothing is ever forgotten..

ISBN 978-1-908630-05-6

ALSO AVAILABLE FROM **MIWK PUBLISHING**

THE LIFE & SCANDALOUS TIMES OF

by Richard Marson

For more than a decade, John Nathan-Turner, or 'JN-T' as he was often known, was in charge of every major artistic and practical decision affecting the world's longest-running science fiction programme, Doctor Who. Richard Marson brings his dramatic, farcical, sometimes scandalous and often moving story to life with the benefit of his own inside knowledge and the fruits of over 100 revealing interviews with key friends and colleagues, those John loved and those from whom he became estranged. The author has also had access to all of Nathan-Turner's surviving archive of paperwork and photos, many of which appear here for the very first time.

"Extraordinary. A great piece of work. I read it in two days' flat, I couldn't stop. I've never seen a biographer enter the story like that, it was brilliant and invigorating. It really is a major piece of Doctor Who history and the history of an entire industry. An entire age, really. In the end, I think the book is clear - we have to forgive JN-T. That ending - he didn't deserve that. And I think by writing about it, you have made something elegant and even beautiful out of such a wretched mess. And I think that's very kind of you indeed. This book says a lot about JN-T but it says a lot about your good and kind heart too."

Russell T.Davies (Writer/Producer)

ISBN 978-1-908630-13-1

publishing